W9-AHL-336

Encyclopedia of

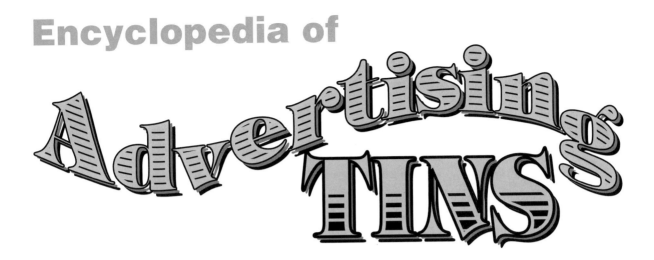

Advertising TINS

Identification
& Values

Vol. II

David Zimmerman

COLLECTOR BOOKS

A Division of Schroeder Publishing Co., Inc.

The current values in this book should be used only as a guide. They are not intended to set prices, which vary from one section of the country to another. Auction prices as well as dealer prices vary greatly and are affected by condition as well as demand. Neither the author nor the publisher assumes responsibility for any losses that might be incurred as a result of consulting this guide.

Searching for a Publisher?

We are always looking for knowledgeable people considered to be experts within their fields. If you feel that there is a real need for a book on your collectible subject and have a large comprehensive collection, contact Collector Books.

David Zimmerman
6834 Newtonsville Road
Pleasant Plain, Ohio 45162

Most of the photographs in this book were taken by Kent Schellhause.

Cover design by Terri Stalions and book design by Kent Henry.

Collector Books
P.O. Box 3009
Paducah, KY 42002-3009

Copyright © 1999 by David Zimmerman

All rights reserved. No part of this book may be reproduced, stored in any retrieval system, or transmitted in any form, or by any means including but not limited to electronic, mechanical, photocopy, recording, or otherwise, without the written consent of the author and publisher.

Contents

Dedication 4
About the Author 4
Learning About Tins
    Value 5
    Condition 5
    Age 5
    Tin Manufacturers — American 6
    Tin Manufacturers — Canadian 8
    Pricing 8
    Associations 9
    Care and Cleaning 10
The Warehouse Finds 11
Automotive 13
Contraceptive 17
Cosmetic & Hygienic 22
Cleaners, Polishes & Waxes 37
Dental 40
Medicinal 44
Needles (Phonographic) 111
Shoe Polishes 118
Samples
    Cocoa 122
    Coffee 123
    Food 125
    Talcum Powder 127
    Tea 133
Shaving 134
Spices 137
Sweets
    Candy & Mints 167
    Cough Drops, Lozenges, Pastillies & Throches 169
    Gum 172
Typewriter & Adding Machine Ribbons 174
Veterinarian 192
Watch Parts 194
Zinc Oxide – Adhesive and Surgical Plaster 195
Miscellaneous
    Fishing 198
    Incense 199
    Ink Pads 200
    Powder 201
    Saffron 203
Index 215

Dedication

This book is dedicated to the children who were tragically killed or permanently injured while innocently attending a prayer group at Heath High School in Paducah, Kentucky. There needs to come a time in one's life when you start to realize what is really important. Then, one should step back and be still and reflect on life's values.

Special thanks to Medra Kleinman, James Voss, Don Wallingford, Harvey Leventhal, Christian Daniels, Lee Jasmine, Mark McNee, David DeLongchamp, Todd Elder, Mike Hirschberg, Phylis Wryn, Marilyn Scribner, and to a network of people in 38 states who have made this publication possible.

And to B. Moscan, from Ontario, Canada, who spent a great deal of time researching the Canadian tin manufacturers and provided the information on the Canadian tin manufacturers.

Special thanks to John Syorka and Mark French for supplying the spice tin photography.

About the Author

David Zimmerman and his family live in a small farming town just a few miles northeast of Cincinnati, Ohio. He has collected advertising tins such as coffee, peanut butter, cocoa, tea, and other various food products since 1978. In 1985, with the encouragement of his wife, he started specializing in smalls and samples. They are displayed all around their 1861 farm home. "I won't collect anything I can't display. I doesn't make sense to me to buy collectibles and store them in the basement or attic."

His collection of tins represented in this guide are displayed in styrofoam and pressed into a standard blank printers type drawer which acts as a frame and is hung on the walls. Each drawer houses from 75 to 130 tins, easily dusted and appreciated by most guests.

Country Home magazine sent their editor and photographer to the Zimmermans' to publish an article which appeared in September 1996.

Learning About Tins

Value

The value of a certain tin is dependent on four important factors. First; availability, you know, supply and demand. How often is it seen and how many are known to exist today? The second factor is condition. Third is age, and finally desirability of the packaging (art work), and not necessarily in this order.

Condition

It is very important whether you're buying or selling that you consider the overall condition of the tin. If you're buying the tin to complete a certain collection then you would have a tendency to sacrifice quality. If you're buying it as an investment, then you should not be satisfied with anything less than an 8. An 8 is no rust, fading, dents, very minor wear, and minor scratches. Hardly anyone will be interested in a dented, chipped, faded, rusty tin, but I have seen quite a few around. Buy collector grade and you'll always be proud to show off your collection. Hopefully, after reading this book you will be smart enough to pass on those less desirable tins. The price just for this advise, is worth many copies of this book.

Age

It's not the author's intent to try to explain the history of tin lithography. However, there are many books on the subject. It is my intent to inform you of the earliest of American and Canadian factories in order for you to be fairly accurate in dating the tin cans. Manufacturers of American and Canadian tins usually printed their names along the hinge, under the lid, or the bottom seam in small obscure lettering, or embossed it on the bottom, providing there is no printing on the bottom. In 1869, Daniel, Joe, and Guy Somers started one of the first U.S. tin printing businesses called Somers Brothers in Brooklyn. In 1879, they started printing on tin under a new method (lithographic). Somers Brothers stayed in business until 1901 when they amalgamated into the American Can Company and became plant 11-A, and remained open until 1917. In 1901, 123 tin manufacturers amalgamated into the American Can Company. Many of these factories were very small, but valuable for their patents. I will not attempt to list all the factories and manufacturers here, but will mention the ones pertinent to this book.

Tin Manufacturers — American

2-A	Campbell Company	Waltham, Massachusetts	1880s to 1901
2-A		Boston, Massachusetts	1901 to 1957
4-A	Slepper Company	Boston, Massachusetts	? to 1901
6-A	Whitestone	Long Island, New York	? to 1901
7-A	Dial Company	Brooklyn, New York	? to 1901
8-A	Ilsley	Brooklyn, New York	1865 to 1920
9-A	Jos LeComte	Brooklyn, New York	1901 to 1902
10-A	Mersereau	Brooklyn, New York.	1880s to 1901
11-A	Somers	Brooklyn, New York	1862 to 1920
12-A	Wm. Vogel	Brooklyn, New York	1870s to 1901
	American Stopper	Brooklyn, New York.	? to 1906
12-A	American Stopper	Brooklyn, New York	1906 to 1920
14-A	Ginna	New York City	1874 to 1902
22-A	U.S. Can Company	Buffalo, New York	? to 1902
25-A	Art Metal	New Brunswick, New Jersey	? to 1901
27-A	Phoenix Metal	New Brunswick, New Jersey	1901 to 1901
28-A	C.P. Pole	Philadelphia, Pennsylvania	1901 to 1902
30-A	Taite	Philadelphia, Pennsylvania	? to 1902
43-A	Miller	Baltimore, Maryland	1889 to 1953
50-A	Hasker & Marcuse	Richmond, Virginia	1891 to 1951
51-A	Conklin Mfg.	Atlanta, Georgia	1901 to 1950
53-A	Breckinridge	Toledo, Ohio	1901 to 1901
54-A	Albet Fischer	Hamilton, Ohio	1901 to 1931
62-A	Clark Co.	Detroit, Michigan	? to 1901
69-A	Frank Diesel	Chicago, Illinois	1893 to 1926
70-A	Illinois Can	Chicago, Illinois	? to 1958
73-A	Norton Bros.	Maywood (Chicago)	1885 to 1903
82-A	Horne/Danz	St. Paul, Minnesota	1901 to 1906
89-A	Columbia Can	St. Louis, Missouri	1905 to 1936
	American Can		1936 to 1944
104-A	George R. Weed	Brooklyn, New York.	1901 to 1901
	Shonk Charles	Maywood (Chicago)	1906 to 1973
	Southern Can	Baltimore, Maryland	1901 to 1914

Hints on identifying age based on tin construction, lithography, and color

- ➼ Seamless tins first appeared in the 1850s.
- ➼ First tins usually produced from one piece of metal – 1890s.
- ➼ Vacuum packing patent – 1896.
- ➼ Embossing (raised printing) common from 1895 to 1900.
- ➼ One-color lithography – patent 1876.
- ➼ Stencil labels pre-1875 in the U.S.
- ➼ Multicolor lithography 1890s, usually a color plus black.
- ➼ Britians hand-painted tin 1830s and coated them with Morie Metallique and then subjected to high heat. The heat caused a crazing condition.
- ➼ 1800s U.S. patented printing on tin.
- ➼ 1930 four-color process first used, two colors at a time.
- ➼ 1906 Food and Drug eliminated claims of cures and remedies.
- ➼ Notice the price change compared to the amount of product per package over the years.
- ➼ Addresses change when companies got larger or smaller.

Chicago Stamping	Chicago, Illinois	? to ?
TINDECO	Baltimore, Maryland	1900 to 1944

CANCO was used to refer to the American Can Co. 1912

Other Companies

Acme Can	Philadelphia	1880s to 1936
(became Crown Can)	1936 to ?	
American Box	Auburn, New York	
Art Metal Co.	New Brunswick, New Jersey	? to 1901
Berry Can Co.	Lancaster, Pennsylvania	
Buckeye Stamping	Columbus, Ohio	
Clark Can Co.	Detroit, Michigan	? to 1901
Colonial Can	Boston, Massachusetts	
*Continental Can		1904 to now
J.L. Clark Co.	Rockford, Illinois	1904 to 1987
became Clarcor, 1897 to now		
Collas R.G.		
Decorated Metal	Brooklyn, New York	
Ellisco	Philadelphia, Pennsylvania	? to 1901
General Can	Chicago, Illinois	
Wm. A. Gill & Co.	Columbus, Ohio	1885 to 1901
Hekin Can Co.	Cincinnati, Ohio	1901 to now
H.L. Hudson	Brooklyn, New York	1887 to 1902
Liberty Can Co.	Lancaster, Pennsylvania	1919 to 1955
(bought by J.L. Clark Co.)		
Missouri Can	St. Louis, Missouri	
Myers Mfg.	Camden, New Jersey	
Pacific Sheet Metal	Los Angeles, California	? to 1901
Parrish & Bingham	Cleveland, Ohio	
Passaic Metalware	Passaic, New Jersey	
Republic Metalware	Boston, Massachusetts	
Southern Can	Baltimore, Maryland	1901 to 1914
Taite-Wesser Can	Philadelphia, Pennsylvania	1901 to 1914
(became Clark Can, 1914 to ?)		
Towle F.S.	N.Y.	
U.S. Can Co.	Cincinnati, Ohio	1903 to 1927
Wilkes-Barre Can	Wilkes Barre, Virginia	

*Continental Can started in Chicago by Norton 1904.

Other Unknown Companies that Produced Small Tin Cans

B — Code on Klutch Tooth Powder
F.G. & Co. — Ex-Lax free sample
XXXX — Postum Cereal sample
MP — Analax Laxative
MPC — Regs Aspirin small size

Norton Bros. started in Toledo, Ohio, in 1868, moved to Chicago in 1871. Ed Norton who originally headed up the American Can Co. left in 1904 to start his own tin manufacturing company known as Continental Can.

Usually the numbers after the (A) tell the date that the tin was produced. Such as 11-A 03 means made in 1903.

The Food and Drug Act of 1906 prohibiting the word "cure" to be used supposedly eliminating false advertising, which is another way to be able to help date the tin.

In 1943 the postal delivery zone system was introduced. This was a two-digit number between the city and state. July 1, 1963, the Zone Improvement Plan went into effect. This is what we know as ZIP codes today.

Tin Manufacturers — Canadian

Thomas Davidson & Co. (1869 – 1927)

Originally known as the Dominion Stamping Co. from 1869 to 1890. Originally located on 187 Delisle St., in Montreal. No manufacturers name on tins in this era. Thomas Davidson and Company, used 1890 – 1894.

Thomas Davidson Mfg. Co. Ltd., used 1894 – 1927. Originated in Montreal, they opened an office in Toronto by 1891. Had offices all over Canada, U.S., and world.

In 1927, Thomas Davidson Mfg. Co., McClary Tin Manufacturing of London, Ontario, Sheet Metal Products (Brantford), and Happy Thought Foundry Co. (Brantford) all merged and became General Steel Wares. Today known as G.S.W.

MacDonald Mfg. Co. Ltd. (1884 – 1943)

Original name Victoria Tin Works, used 1882 – 1896. Located at 231 King St. E., Toronto, 1884 – 1886. MacDonald Mfg. Co. 1896 – 1901, located at King and Simcoe St. 1896 – 1905. MacDonald Mfg. Co. Ltd. 1901 – 1943 located at 143 – 145 Spadina, 1905 – 1943. Kemp Mfg. Co. bought MacDonald in 1911 but continued to use MacDonald name. Sometime before 1927, Kemp changed its name to Sheet Metal Products or SMP. (SMP was one of the companies that merged with T. Davidson Mfg. Co. in 1927. Both MacDonald and Davidson were with SMP.) When SMP took over Kemp, the MacDonald name pretty well disappeared on tins. In 1944 the Continental Can Co. bought the MacDonald subsidiary from SMP and completely stopped using the MacDonald name.

Other Manufacturing Companies

Acme Litho. Co.	Montreal	
A.R. Whittall Can Co. Ltd	Montreal	
General Steel Wares or G.S.W.		1927 to present
Happy Thought Foundry	Brantford	? to 1927
McClary Mfg. Co.	London	? to 1927
Kempt Mfg.		
Sheet Metal Products		? to 1927
Victoria Tin Works	Toronto	1882 to 1896
Dominion Stamping Works	Montreal	1869 to 1890

American tin manufacturers got a head start on the Canadian companies. That's why the Canadians used the tins from the United States. This went on until the 1890s. Up to this point, the Canadians stenciled names on their tins. These stencils were usually one color and did not display the manufacturers name.

During the 1890s, the multicolored litho appeared in Canada and so did the tin manufacturers name.

Pricing

The best places for purchasing tins, for both availability and prices, are flea markets, garage sales, estate auctions, other collectors selling off their duplicates (or getting out of the collecting frame of mind), and specialized antique shows featuring such items as china, glass bottles, paper, and jewelry.

Prices in this guide do not reflect phone calls, gas, ads, hotel, food, or time. These prices do reflect the most current prices of tins available for sale today, and may vary as much as 20%. These variations are caused due to a double value system. By this, I mean, the tin itself has a value, but because of it showing a black person or a specific animal or something collectible other than just the tin, a collector of that particular category may be willing to pay much more. Another example is the shaving razor tins. To a razor collector it would be worth many times more if it had a razor inside. Still another example might be location. If a person is from St. Louis he may only collect tins from St. Louis, thus he may be willing to pay more for a St. Louis medicinal tin than one similar, but made in Chicago. Be patient, there are still good deals around. Don't say, "I'll never see that one again," because you will, and usually for less.

The people who will appreciate this guide are those who have purchased these little tins for next to nothing, and who have seen them appreciate steadily in value, and who have never seen this many different tins in one place before. Those who won't appreciate this guide are the many dealers who paid more than they should have, and who are now trying to recoup their investment. You know who you are.

I have been at an extravaganza (antique/flea show) where a tin was selling for $45 and several booths away the same exact tin in the exact same condition was selling for $9. So how can a person put a price on a tin that would be uniformly consistent around the country? Five years ago, I was at an auction with my then 12-year old son. There was a Scotts Blood Tablets tin in mint condition, full with the wrapper. There were three people bidding on it along with me. Lucky me, I bought it for the prize-winning price of $180. Wow! What a deal, I thought. I had never seen one in this good of condition before. We walked out the proud owners, smiling all the way home. Nine months later I was at the advertising show in Indianapolis, one of the three shows a year (March, June, and September) and saw the same exact tin in the same exact condition for $45. The problem was that my same 12-year old son was with me. Guess what he said? As recently as February 1994 I met a man who just started collecting the year before, who showed me photos of his collection. There were several dozen pictures featuring about 400 small and sample tins. Not bad for collecting for almost a year.

Since I specialize in smalls and samples, I have now developed a sixth sense about pricing, and many of my constituents around the country will occasionally call me to price one, and ask about its rarity.

Many tins have appreciated in value faster than most lower priced collectibles such as coins. So put away an extra $40 per month and invest in some local history. You'll be amazed at what they will be worth in just a few years.

Samples

So why, you ask, are the samples more valuable than the regular size package.

As printers of tins became more common, the manufacturers of various products started to package samples in tins, as a way to market their products. These samples were made in somewhat limited quantity, in relationship to the regular size product and were generally thought of as throw-away items. These companies would run ads in trade journals, newspapers, national magazines, and any other media to attract consumers to try their product. The consumer would send in a coupon with his name and address and the company then would send out their samples. These samples were not given out, as a rule, in grocery or drug stores, and should not be confused with small packaging sold over the counter. Usually one can detect a sample by the elimination of the price tag, or the words "trial size" or "free."

The reason you can find early decorative advertising tin cans today is that when they were emptied of their original contents, they were so pretty and useful in storing other products, they weren't thrown out.

One reason you don't see as many of these tins around was the "tin recall" during the war years, and various crafts using tin cans in the finished product such as lamps. Then there are the collectors of the '60s who hoarded away a lot of the really great tins, to be uncovered by collectors like you and me, at estate, garage, and auction sales.

If you would like to find a very large amount of advertising tins and other ad memorabilia under one roof at one location, I suggest you visit the Advertising Show held in Indianapolis, Indiana, three times a year (March, June, and September) at the Indiana State Fairgrounds. Take lots of cash, because they don't take VISA or American Express.

Associations

These associations exist to further your knowledge in collecting advertising and advertising tin cans.

Tins and Signs — newsletter started in 1971
Box 440101, Aurora, CO 80044

Antique Advertising Association — newsletter started in 1991
P.O. Box 1121, Morton Grove, IL 60053, (847) 446-0904

Tin Fax — newsletter started in 1993
899 Powers Ferry, #K-10, Marietta, GA 30067

Ribbon Tin News — newsletter on typewriter ribbon tins, 1993
28 The Green, Watertown, CT 06795, (860) 945-3456

Care and Cleaning

Before you start to clean any tin, you will need to determine what type of tin or printing paint or ink you are working with. They are as follows.

Transfer Prints — where the design (art work) has been applied to a very thin transparency which is then pressed onto the surface of the tin prior to shaping it into a container. This technique will usually have a tendency to chip more easily than to fade or scratch.

Paper Labels — much harder to clean. You should secure all loose edges with glue on the end of a toothpick and allow to dry thoroughly before attempting to clean.

Lithographed Inks — have a tendency to fade and discolor faster than coming off while rubbing. These will water mark easily.

Pre-Lithographed — where the paint is applied directly to the tin, usually by hand. Usually seen in golds, blues, and crimson. If the colors have oxidized, either by heat or direct sunlight, the color will have a tendency to rub off easily. An example of this is the Train tin, illustrated in Volume 1, page 201. Not only was the coloring done by hand, but the rounded corners were reinforced with additional metal and the hinge lid was the earliest design. No one really knows what was inside, but one could guess.

Cleaning — is an art and should be considered dangerous to the tin, because every time you clean and/or wax it you take off a little of the color. Now that I have discouraged you, you can begin to carefully consider cleaning. I have ruined more tins than I would like to admit. Be sure to test an unexposed part, the rim under the lid for example. I have also never been successful at removing paint specs or scotch tape, so I don't buy those even if they're one of a kind. Every time I use a diluted mild detergent, it usually seems to fade the tin and I'm disappointed. I have found, over the years however, that using a non-abrasive wax on a damp soft cloth rubbed lightly over the coloring not only cleans it, but provides a protective coating. Waxing should be done as frequently as you handle your tins. Always check the cloth for color loss and stop if the color appears on the cloth.

If you keep the tins in an enclosed case and never pick them up, then you won't have to wax them often. If you are inclined to handle them, then you'll need to wax more often. Colors (paint or ink) over an embossed or raised surface are more susceptible to pitting.

To remove rust you should first try a pencil eraser by lightly rubbing. Some experts recommend using a wet silicon paper (emory paper). Never try to remove rust on the painted surface. Tape off the painted area with a tape that won't permanently stick to the paint/ink. Treat as mentioned.

Never submerge the tin in water or let it drip dry. Water or wetness in the seams starts corrosion (rust). I use a blow dryer on medium heat, held at arms length until thoroughly dry. Rust can be removed with diluted oxalic acid which is available at most drug stores. It attacks the iron and not the paint saith the experts, but not me.

Dents can usually be spooned out with the use of a wooden spatula. Creases will never be spooned out perfectly.

Never...

→ Use a clear lacquer
→ Try to remove scotch tape
→ Saturate a paper label with water
→ Use shellac, lacquer thinner, or alcohol
→ Immerse tins in water

→ Store tins in hot or damp areas
→ Display in direct sunlight
→ Put a price sticker on the painted surface
→ Wrap in newspaper

* Represents a warehouse find. Many of them are overpriced today, but remember when they are gone they will be valuable.
+ Represents tins borrowed from collectors used for photography and not owned by author.
Sizing in this book is depth, width, and length.

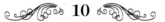

The Warehouse Finds

"A neighbor of mine has been making his business for years hunting and acquiring warehouse finds. Usually, when he uncovers a large quantity of tins, he calls me with all the fascinating details. Sometimes I am fortunate to be invited to go with him."

— David Zimmerman

The following are answers to the most commonly asked questions regarding warehouse finds.

❶ **What is a warehouse find?**

There are several types. Old factory or business stock is probably the most common. To understand this type of find, you need to understand a little bit about how businesses used to operate. If you were making a product 100 years ago, and decided to change your packaging (perhaps from a tin container to a cardboard one), you did one of two things. You either sold all the old stock, and then sold the new, or you put the old stock in storage when the new was ready to sell. This was kind of an insurance policy, so that if the new packaging didn't work out, you would still have some of your old reliable stock available. Oftentimes, this meant large quantities of items were put in storage and were never used again. Old stock of this type is a major source of warehouse finds. In fact, every year we find businesses still in operation that have some of this forgotten stock still in storage.

Another big source of warehouse finds are businesses that were thriving at one time, but were eventually forced out of business. There are many reasons this happened. Sometimes the owner died, and no one carried on. Sometimes, they just went bankrupt, and the building was boarded up. Occasionally, one of these places turned up with a bunch of old inventory still there. A good example of this is the old Valmor plant in Chicago. Several years back, there were thousands of Sweet Georgia Brown and Lucky Brown tins found that were just left there amidst all sorts of other items (bottles, labels, you name it).

Another less common, but very interesting, source of warehouse finds is wholesale groceries. They used to be large businesses that serviced "Mom and Pop" grocery stores. Surprisingly, to a lot of people, a fair number of these places have survived. In fact, there's usually one near almost every big city. Look in your phone book under wholesale grocers and you might be surprised. Almost all that remain, have been around for a long time. Occasionally, they will have a storage area or an attic where they kept non-perishable items that didn't sell too well. Sometimes large quantities of old tins and all sorts of old store stock have been found there.

Ironically, the least common type of warehouse find is the one people think of first. That is the old country store. There are still a fair number of these places around, but there are two problems with finding anything there. First, most of them never had large quantities of any particular product to begin with, and secondly, almost all of these places have had at least 400 or 500 other people who have already asked if they have any old stuff lying around! Honestly, most of these places were picked clean over 20 years ago! Drug stores are a different story. Many have been around for a long time, and occasionally we still find one that has the remains of an earlier business in the attic or basement.

❷ How is the value of an item affected when it comes from a warehouse find?

This depends on several factors. First of all, how interesting is the item? Second of all, how old is it? And third, how many were found? Here are two examples: The Lucky Brown tin that was referred to is a very interesting item. It is very colorful, and pictures a fair-skinned African-American lady. It is from the 1930 – 40s and was found in large (around 2,000), but not huge quantities. Because it is a very interesting tin in excellent condition, it retails for $8 – 12. It would go for more than that if it were a little older. Two thousand of a nice tin like this is really not all that many. They will all be distributed to dealers, collectors, and decorators in as little as five years. At that point in time, the price will go up because it is a desirable tin, and because most people who will have paid $8 – 10 for it, will not likely sell it for under $15. Another example is the smaller size Cloverine tins pictured in this book. They are not very exciting looking (black and white, no picture), are from the 1960s, and were found in huge quantities (maybe as many as 100,000). This is a real dog. Someone who doesn't have one in his or her collection shouldn't pay over a dollar for it. It's not interesting, it's not very old, and there was a huge quantity found.

Whether or not it's interesting is probably the most important, and can be determined by most people just by examining a tin. The age can also be deduced with a little experience. However, the quantity found is often a well-guarded secret by the finder, and may never be known. Consequently, it is probably never wise to spend more than about $15 – 20 on a tin from a warehouse find unless it is extremely old and interesting, and you know for sure that it was found in quantities of less than 1,000. Caveat — unfortunately, and in spite of what some dealers will tell you, no one except the finder usually knows how many there are in existence.

You probably figured out by now that there is an opportunity to make money with finds such as this because the source is selling them to retailers for half or less of what the retailer is selling them for. If you can find the source (the finder), you can get some real bargains!

❸ How do I know if a tin or other item has come from a warehouse find?

It's really pretty simple. If it is in unused, near mint condition (which usually means it was never filled), you can pretty well bet it came from one of the warehouse situations described above. The only other tins that surface in this kind of condition are the rare item that sat unused in a house. Ironically, some of the most expensive tins today came from warehouse finds that happened years ago. Tins that were very interesting and old at that time, and found in quantities of less than 1,000 were dispersed to collectors/dealers long ago. It seems to me that they used to go for around 25 cents in the late '60s at Washington Court House Flea Market. Hey, you old-timers! Remember what I'm talking about? These have appreciated very substantially in value, as they can't be found anymore.

The latest find has been the Pinex Laxative tins in two different sizes found in the original 1915 wooden crates. Thousands of these have just recently been found.

❹ So, where do I buy warehouse finds?

Keep your eye on trade papers where they are advertised regularly, particularly in the *Antique Trader*. Buyer beware though. Make sure an advertiser has a money back guarantee and is willing to put in writing the approximate age of the item.

Armour's sample, Motorists' & Mechanics' Soap Paste, ⅝ x 1¾", Am. Can 70-A, $35.00.

Carborundum sample, Valve Grinding Compound, ¼ x 1⅛", $15.00.

Clover Brand sample, Automobile Nickel Paste, ⅜ x 1¼", $12.00.

Comet, Auto Fuses, ⅜ x 1¼ x 1¾", $15.00.

Dixon's sample, Axle Grease, ¾ x 2¼", $25.00.

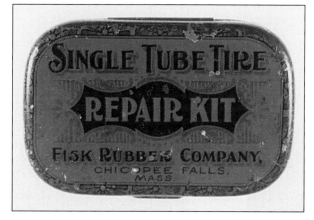

Fisk Rubber Company, Single Tube Tire Repair Kit, ½ x 1¾ x 2¾", Mersereau, Brooklyn, $65.00.

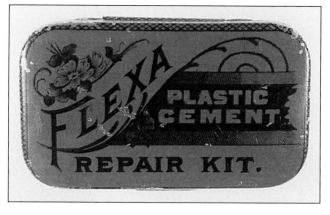

Flexa, Plastic Cement Repair Kit, ½ x 1½ x 2½", Art Metal, N.Y., $55.00.

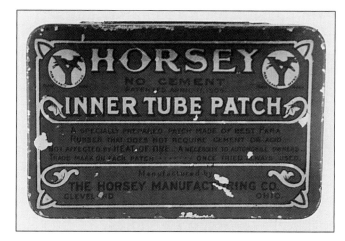

Horsey, Inner Tube Patch, 1 x 2½ x 3⅞", $55.00.

Johnson's, Prepared Wax, ⅞ x 2⅜", Am. Can Co. 70-A, $75.00.

Jefferson, Auto Fuses, 20 AMP, ¼ x 1¼ x 1¾", $20.00.

Killark, Auto Fuses, ¼ x 1¼ x 1¾",
$12.00.

Mir a cle, Motor Gas, $1.00, ¾ x 1¾ x 3¼", Buckeye Stamping, $75.00.

New Brunswick, Tire Repair Kit, ½ x 2 x 3⅛",
$80.00.

Norwesco sample, Grinding Compound, ¼ x 1⅛", Am. Can Co. 70-A,
$30.00.

Perfection, Tire Repair Kit, ½ x 4 x
2½", Chicago Stamping, $70.00.

Thorsen "Indiana," Tire Repair Tool, ½ x 1½ x 2½", Frank Diesel, $70.00.

Quick Seal, Tire Repair Kit, 1 x 3⅜", Mersereau, $50.00.

Van Cleef Bros., Valve Grinding Compound, ¾ x 2½", $18.00.

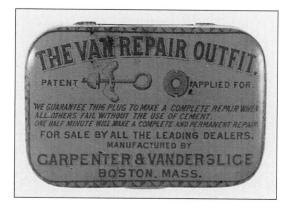

Vanderslice, Tire Repair Outfit, ½ x 1⅜ x 2", Frank Diesel, $45.00.

ZIP sample, Grinding Compound, ⅝ x 1¾", $18.00.

Contraceptives

Arrows, Condoms, ¼ x 1¼ x 1¾", Cont. Can Co., $75.00.

Cadets, Three, Condoms, $.35, ⅜ x 1⅝ x 2⅛", $75.00.

Blue-Ribbon De-Luxe, Condoms, ¼ x 1¾ x 2¼", Am. Can Co. 10-A, $180.00.

Derbies Rolled, Condoms, ¼ x 1⅝ x 2⅛", $70.00.

Blue Ribbon, Condoms, $.50, ¼ x 1⅝ x 2⅛", Am. Can Co. 50-A, $275.00.

Derbies Three, Condoms, ¼ x 1¼ x 2", $75.00.

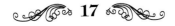

Duble-Tip, Condoms, ¼ x 1⅝ x 2⅛", $200.00.

Merry Widows, Steam Cured Condoms, ⅝ x 1⅝", $30.00.

Goldbeaters, Condoms, ⅝ x 1⅝", $50.00.

Merry Widows, Condoms, $1.00, ⅝ x 1⅝", $30.00.

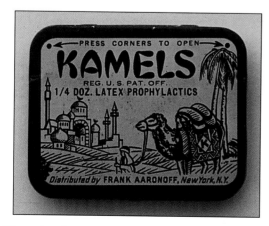

Kamels, Condoms, ¼ x 1⅝ x 2⅛", $65.00+.

Nutex, Condoms, ⅝ x 1⅝", Acme Can, $210.00+.

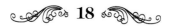

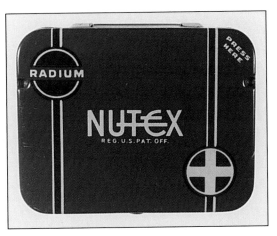

Nutex Radium, Condoms, ¼ x 1⅝ x 2⅛", CANCO, $70.00.

Owls (Improved), Condoms, ¼ x 1¾ x 2⅝", Am. Can Co. 50-A, $65.00.

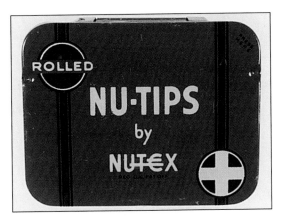

Nutex Rolled Nu-Tips, Condoms, ¼ x 1⅝ x 2⅛", CANCO, $70.00.

Peacocks, Air Tested Condoms, ¼ x 1⅝ x 2⅛", Am. Can Co. 50-A, $70.00.

Orissa, Condoms, ¼ x 1¾ x 2⅝", Am. Can 50-A, $190.00.

Perfection, Condoms, ¼ x 1½ x 2⅛", $55.00.

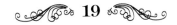

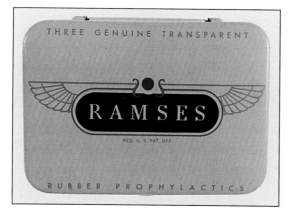

Ramses, Condoms, ¼ x 1¾ x 2⅝", $70.00.

Royal-Tex, Condoms, ¼ x 1½ x 2", $85.00.

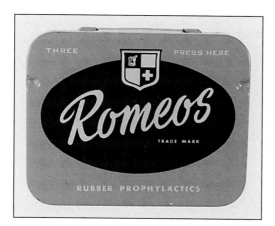

Romeos, Condoms, ¼ x 1½ x 1¾", $90.00+.

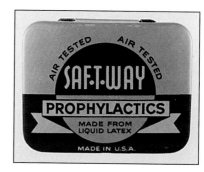

Saf-t-way, Condoms, ¼ x 1⅝ x 2⅛", Am. Can Co. 50-A, $70.00.

Shadows, Condom, ¼ x 1⅝ x 2⅛", $35.00.

Romeos, Condoms, ¼ x 1⅝ x 2⅛", $80.00.

Sheik, Condoms, $.50, ¼ x 1 ⅝ x 2⅛", $45.00.

Sheik, Condoms, $.50, ¼ x 1⅝ x 2⅛", $55.00.

Smithies, Condoms, ¼ x 1⅝ x 2⅛", $65.00.

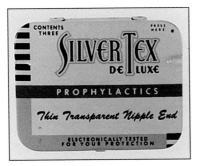

Silver Tex De Luxe, Condoms, ¼ x 1⅝ x 2⅛", $60.00.

Tally-Ho, Condoms, ¼ x 1⅝ x 2", Am. Can 50-A, $200.00.

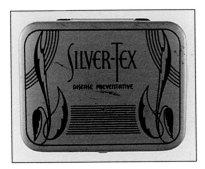

Silver-Tex, Condoms, ¼ x 1⅝ x 2⅛", $50.00.

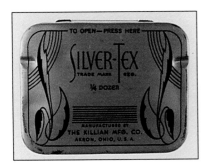

Silver-Tex, Condoms, ¼ dozen, ¼ x 1⅝ x 2⅛", $50.00.

Trojans Improved, Condoms, $.50, ¼ x 1⅝ x 2⅛", $55.00.

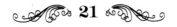

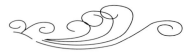

Allen's Royal, Face Powder, 3 x 3 x 1¼", $55.00.

Armand sample, Cold Cream Powder, ¼ x 1½", $15.00.

Armand sample, Bouquet Complexion Powder, ¼ x 1¾", $15.00.

Armand sample, Wind Blown Rose, ¼ x 1¼", $18.00.

Armand sample, Bouquet Complexion Powder, ¼ x 1⅝", $25.00.

Armand Symphonie sample, Face Powder, ⅜ x 1½", $15.00.

Bourjois sample, Face Powder, ⅛ x 1½", $20.00.

Gardenia Richard Hudnut sample, Face Powder, ¼ x 1½ x 1½", $18.00.

Colgate Florient sample, Face Powder, ¼ x 1⅝", $18.00.

Gould, Barbara, sample, Face Powder, ¼ x 1⅝", $15.00.

Dr. Charles, Face Powder, $.50, 1¼ x 2¾", American Stopper, $45.00.

La-May, Face Powder, ½ x 2½", $18.00.

La Jaynees, Complexion Powder, ¼ x 1½", $6.00.

Melorose sample, Powder, ¼ x ⅞", $15.00.

Max Factor's, Face Powder, ¼ x 1⅝", $8.00.

Miner's, Theatrical Blending Powder, ⅞ x 2⅜", $12.00.

Melba Bouquet, Face Powder, ⅝ x 1⅜ x 1⅜", $15.00.

Miner's sample, Theatrical Face Powder, ½ x 1⅜", $25.00.

Nadine, Flesh Face Powder, ⅜ x 1¼ x 1¾", $12.00.

Parisian Beauty sample, Face Powder, ⅛ x 1½", $25.00.

Palmer sample, Gardenglo Face Powder, ¼ x 1⅝", $18.00.

Tangee sample, Face Powder, ¼ x 1⅝", $12.00.

Palmer's sample, Skin Success Ointment, ¼ x ⅞", $25.00.

Woodbury's, Facial Powder, ½ x 2⅛", $55.00.

Glazo sample, Cuticle Massage, ⅜ x ⅞", $40.00.

Melba sample, Cuticle Salve, ¼ x 1⅛", $10.00.

Miraglo, Nail Bleach, ⅜ x ¾", $8.00.

Nail White, Polish, ¼ x ¾", $5.00.

Max Factor, Moist Rouge, ½ x 1", $15.00.

Miner's, Natural Blush Rouge, ¾ x 2¾", $10.00.

Mrs. Jessie Roulston, Harmless Color, ⅝ x 1¾", $25.00.

Princess Pat, Lip Rouge, ¼ x 1⅛", $10.00.

Armand sample, Vanishing Cream, ¼ x 1⅝", $15.00.

CPC Trailing Arbutus, Cold Cream, ⅝ x 1½", $45.00.

Azeada, Skin Whitener, ¾ x 1⅞", $20.00.

Djer-Kiss sample, Cream, ⅜ x 1⅝", $12.00.

Belcano sample, Skin Firm Cream, ¼ x ⅞", $15.00.

Doctor & Nurse, Baby Cream, ⅜ x 1½", $18.00.

El Estado sample, Cleansing Creme, ¼ x 1½", $18.00.

Hygienic Cutigiene sample, Toilet Cream, ¼ x ⅞", $35.00.

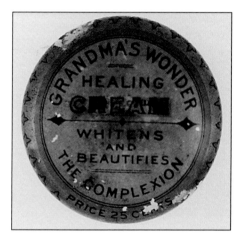

Grandma's Wonder, Healing Cream, $.25, 1¼ x 2", $25.00.

Ingram's Elite, Cold Cream, ¾ x 2⅝", $20.00.

Hydrosal sample, Skin Ointment, ¼ x 1⅛", $10.00.

Ingram's sample, Milkweed Cream, ¼ x 1⅛", $45.00.

Jergens Marie Antoinette, Cold Cream, 1 x 2", American Stopper, $40.00.

Miner's, Cold Cream, ⅞ x 2⅜", $12.00.

LaValliere, Sub Rosa Cream, ⅞ x 1⅜", $15.00.

Otto, Cold Cream, ¾ x 1¾", $12.00.

Mavis, Cold Cream Vivaudou, ¾ x 1", $10.00.

Ovelmo, Skin Balm Cream, 1 x 2⅜", Am. Can Co. 70-A, $15.00.

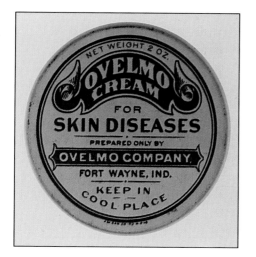

Ovelmo sample, Skin Balm Cream, ¼ x 1⅛", Am. Can Co. 70-A, $15.00.

Ro-Zol, Complexion Clarifier, $.25, ¾ x 1¾", $15.00.

Paramount sample, Cleansing Cream, ⅜ x 1½", $12.00.

Snow White, Bleaching Cream, ¾ x 2¾", $22.00.

Pompeian, Day Cream, ⅜ x 1⅜", $5.00.

Superior, Cold Cream, ¾ x 1½", $20.00.

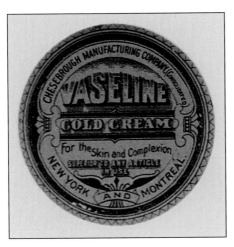

Vaseline sample, Cold Cream, ½ x 1½", $18.00.

Madam Walker's sample, Tan-Off, ⅜ x 1⅞", $30.00.

Victoria, Complexion Cream, ¾ x 2", American Stopper, $20.00.

White's Specific, sample Face Cream, ¼ x 1⅛", $12.00.

Vivaudou, Astringent Cream, ½ x 1⅛", $120.00.

White's Specific, Face Cream, ½ x 2", $15.00.

Aubry Sisters, Beautifier, ¼ x 1¼", $22.00.

Cashmere Bouquet, Cleansing Pads, ½ x 2¼", $8.00.

Deere, Eye Brows\Lashes, ¼ x 1⅛ x 3", $12.00.

Blair's N.B.O., Deodorant Cream, ⅝ x 2¼", $8.00.

Bo-Kay sample, Perfume, ¼ x 1", 18.00.

Goldman's, Mary T., Shampoo, 1 x 2⅜", 70.00.

Hess', C.D., Clown White, ⅞ x 2½", Am. Can 72-A, $15.00.

Johnson & Johnson, Beauty Spots, ¼ x 1⅝", $40.00.

Hush, Deodorant Cream, ¼ x 1⅛", $10.00.

Maybell, Lash-Brow-ing, $.50, ½ x 2⅛", $12.00.

Hush, Sno Deodorant, ⅜ x 2⅛", $12.00.

Mum, Deodorant, ⅜ x 1⅝", $4.00.

Murphy's sample, Oil Soap, ⅞ x 2⅛", $25.00.

Princess Pat, For Lips and Cheeks, ¼ x 1¼", $15.00.

Nyal, Dandruff Shampoo, 1 x 2¼ x 3⅛", $35.00.

Sapo sample, Hand Soap, ¾ x 1¾", Liberty Can, $50.00.

Palmer's sample, Skin Success Ointment, ¼ x ⅞", $25.00.

Stein's, Black Wax, ⅝ x 1½", $12.00.

Bickmore XYZ sample, Skin Ointment, ¼ x 1⅛", $30.00.

Golden Brown sample, Ointment, ¼ x ⅞", $18.00.

Chanty sample, Lavender Solid Brillantine, ⅜ x 1¼", $6.00.

Koskott sample, Hair Cream, ¼ x 1⅛", $12.00.

Ford's sample, Hair Pomade, ⅜ x 1¼", $15.00.

Parker's sample, Hair Dressing, ¼ x 1⅛", $35.00.

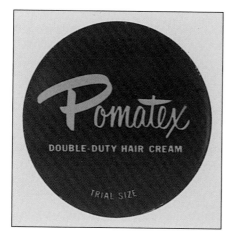

Pomatex sample, Hair Cream, ⅜ x 1½", $6.00.

Renner's Rose Jelly, Hair and Skin Salve, ⅝ x 2", $28.00.

Prof. Dyke's, Hair and Beard Elixer, $.25, ½ x 1½ x 2½", $60.00+.

Madam C.J. Walker's, Wonderful Hair Grower, ¾ x 2½", Am. Can Co. 70-A, $50.00.

Renner's Rose Jelly, Hair and Skin Salve, ⅝ x 1⅞", $30.00.

Wylon sample, Pressing Oil, ½ x 1¾", $18.00.

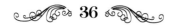

Cleaners,
Polishes & Waxes

Betterwear sample, Lavender Wax Polish, ½ x 1¼", $18.00.

Chemico sample, Bath & House Cleaner, ¾ x 2", $25.00.

Betterwear sample, Wax Polish, ⅜ x 1¼", $25.00.

Feasel's Noxal sample, Metal Polish, ⅜ x 1⅜", $30.00.

Burnishine sample, Nickel and Chromium Polish, ⅝ x 1½", $15.00.

Gre-Solvent sample, Hand Cleaner, ⅝ x 2", $12.00.

H-L-F sample, Polish for Automobiles and Fine Furniture, 1¼ x 2⅛ x 2", $20.00.

McAleer's sample, Quick Cleaner Paste, ⅝ x 1½", $25.00.

Imperial, Metal Polish, #5½, 1 x 3⅛", $15.00.

McAleer's sample, Quick-Wax, ⅝ x 1½", Am. Can 70-A, $20.00.

Johnson's, Automobile Wax, 1 x 2¾", Am. Can Mass., $18.00.

Kelwax, Polishing Wax, ⅝ x 1⅞", $5.00.

Presto, Stove Polish, 1 x 3½", $10.00.

Samoline sample, Cleaner, ¼ x 1⅛", $12.00.

Wiggins Wigg's, Cleanser, 2 x 1½", Hekin, $12.00.

Selaw sample, Cleanser, ¾ x 2", $25.00.

X-Cel #5 sample, Stove Polish Powder, 2⅛ x 2⅛", $50.00.

Silverine, Metal Polish, $.25, 2 x 3 x 1½", Somers, $50.00.

Sun-Ray sample, Metal Polish, ⅜ x 1⅛", $10.00.

Yankee sample, Nickel Polish, ⅜ x 1⅜", $25.00.

Dental

All-In-One, Dental Tablets, $.25, 1½ x 1½ x 2¼" Am. Can Co. 70-A, $50.00.

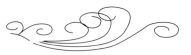

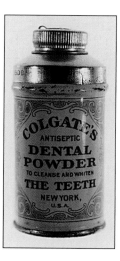

Colgate's sample, Dental Powder, 1 x 2¼", $55.00.

Arnica, Tooth Soap, ½ x 2 x 3⅛", H.F. Miller, Baltimore, $55.00.

Co•re•ga sample, Dental Powder, ¾ x 1¼ x 2", $40.00.

Avon sample, Smoker's Tooth Powder, ¾ x 1¼ x 2", $50.00.

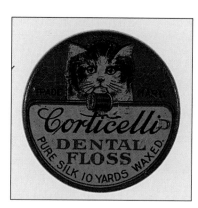

Corticelli, Dental Floss, ¼ x 1⅜", $40.00.

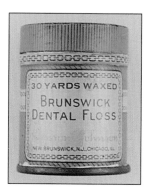

Brunswick, Dental Floss, 30 Yards, 1⅛ x 1½", $20.00.

CPC, Tooth Powder, 1 x 2¼", Metal Pkg. Co., Brooklyn, $45.00.

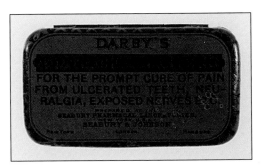

Darby's, Toothache Plasters, ¼ x 1⅛ x 2⅛", Mersereau Mfg., $35.00.

Drucker's Revelation sample Tooth Powder, 1 x 2⅜", $25.00.

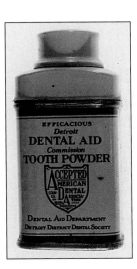

Dental Aid sample, Tooth Powder, 1 x 1¼ x 2½", Nat. Can, $20.00.

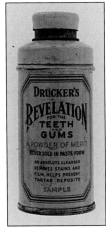

Drucker's Revelation sample, Tooth Powder, 1 x 2⅝", Tindeco, $20.00.

Dr. Bovel's, Rose Bud Tooth Soap, $.25, ⅝ x 1⅞ x 2½", MacDonald Mfg., $65.00.

The Druggists, Tooth Soap, ½ x 2 x 3⅛", Chicago Stamping Co., $80.00.

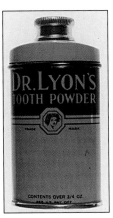

Dr. Lyon's, Tooth Powder, ⅞ x 1½ x 3", $30.00.

Evans's, Tooth Powder, 1 x 1¾ x 2⅞", Taite & Sisler, Philadelphia, $55.00.

Fasteeth sample, Denture Powder, ½ x 1½ x 2", $20.00.

Merritt's sample, Super-Plate Powder, ½ x ⅞ x 2", $30.00.

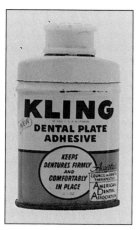

Kling sample, Dental Plate Adhesive, ¾ x 1¼ x 2⅛", $25.00.

Moy sample, Dental Powder, ¾ x 1½ x 2", $25.00.

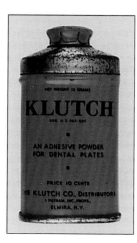

Klutch, Dental Adhesive Powder, $.10, ⅝ x 1¼ x 2⅜", $25.00.

P-Kay sample, Dental Plate, Cleaner, ¾ x 1¼ x 2", $60.00.

Klutch sample, Dental Powder, ¾ x 1⅝ x 2⅛", $30.00.

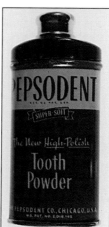

Pepsodent, Tooth Powder, ⅞ x 1⅝ x 3¼", $18.00.

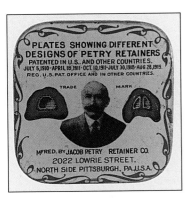

Petry, Retainers, Sq., ¾ x 2½ x 2½", $45.00.

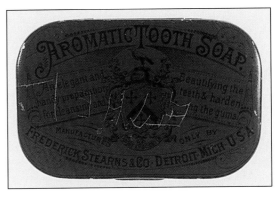

Stearns, Frederick, Aromatic Tooth Soap, ½ x 2 x 3⅛", Chicago Stamping Co., $75.00.

Purita, Tooth Powder, $.25, 1¾ x 2⅞ x 1", Somers, $80.00.

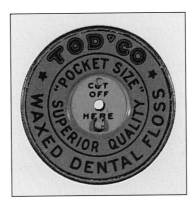

Tod Co, Dental Floss, ¼ x 1¼", $25.00.

Riker sample, Tooth Powder, 1 x 2⅝", $80.00.

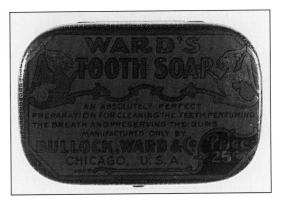

Ward's, Tooth Soap, $.25, ½ x 2 x 3", American Stopper, Brooklyn, $90.00.

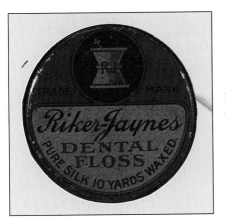

Riker-Jaynes, Dental Floss, ⅛ x 1⅜", $35.00.

Wernet's sample, Denture Powder, ¾ x 1¼ x 2¼", $30.00.

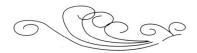 

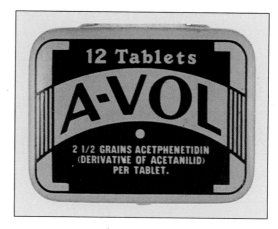

5 Drops, Salve, $.25, ⅝ x 1½", Am. Can Co. 71-A, $25.00.

A-Vol, Tablets, ¼ x 1¼ x 1¾", Am. Can 10-A, $12.00.

A-1 sample, Salve, ¼ x 1½", $6.00.

A.D.S., Arnica Salve, ⅞ x 1⅜", $18.00.

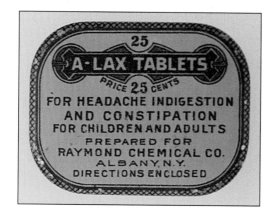

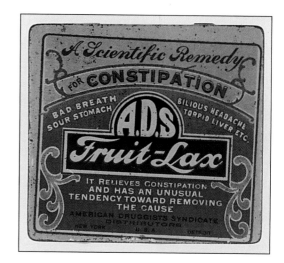

A-Lax, Tablets, $.25, ⅝ x 1¼ x 1½", $18.00.

A.D.S., Fruit-Lax, ⅜ x 3 x 3¼", A.S. Co., $30.00.

A.D.S., Fruit-Lax, $.10, ⅜ x 1¼ x 1¾", $18.00.

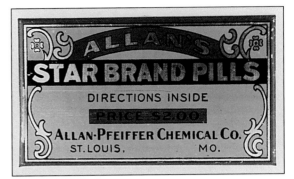

Allan's, Star Brand Pills, $2.00, 1⅝ x 3 x ⅞", Clark, Rockford, Ill., $50.00.

A.D.S., Fruit-Lax, $.10, ⅜ x 1⅝ x 1⅞", $18.00.

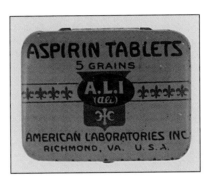

American Laboratories, Aspirin Tablets, ¼ x 1¼ x 1¾", $10.00.

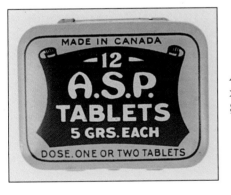

A.S.P., Tablets, ⅜ x 1¼ x 1¾", $12.00.

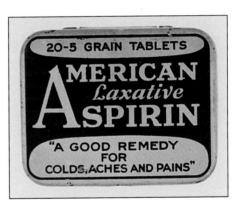

American, Laxative Aspirin, ¼ x 1½ x 2", $15.00.

Alba-Lax, Laxative Candy, $.10, ½ x 1¾ x 2¼", $22.00.

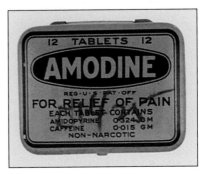

Amodine, Pain Pills, ⅜ x 1¼ x 1¾", $12.00.

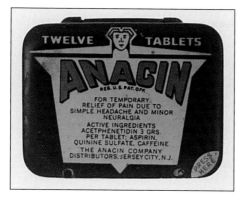

Anacin, 12 Tablets, ¼ x 1¼ x 1¾", N.C.C., $6.00.

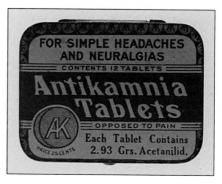

Antikamnia, Tablets, $.25, ¼ x 1¼ x 1¾", Am. Can 10-A, $25.00.

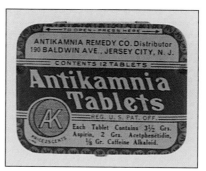

Antikamnia, Tablets, $.25, ¼ x 1¼ x 1¾", Am. Can Co. 10-A, $25.00.

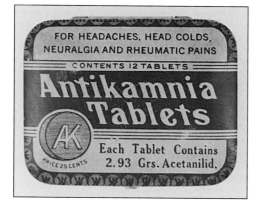

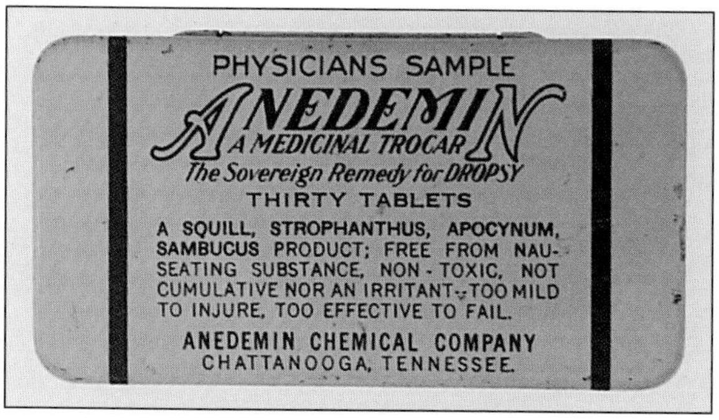

Anedemin sample, Tablets, ¼ x 1¾ x 3¼", $8.00.

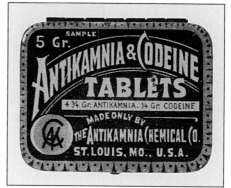

Antikamnia & Codeine sample, Tablets, ¼ x 1¼ x 1¾", Mersereau, $35.00.

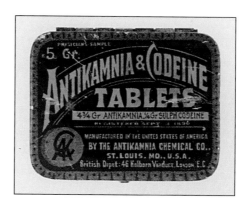

Antikamnia & Codeine sample, Tablets, ¼ x 1¼ x 1¾", Mersereau, $40.00.

Antikamnia, Headache Cold Tablets, $.25, ¼ x 1¼ x 1¾", $15.00.

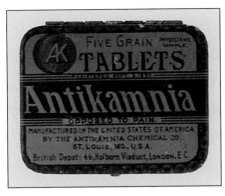

Antikamnia sample, Tablets, ¼ x 1¼ x 1¾", Mersereau, $45.00.

ASCO, Medicine, ¼ x 1¼ x 1¾", $15.00.

Aristos, Corn Salve, ¼ x 1⅛", $20.00.

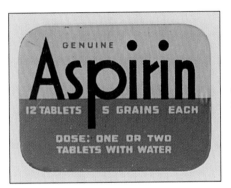

Aspirin, ⅜ x 1¼ x 1¾", $10.00.

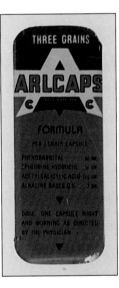

Arlcaps, Medicine, ¼ x ¾ x 2", $10.00.

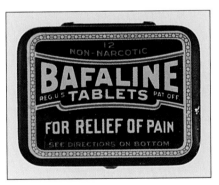

Bafaline, Tablets, ¼ x 1¼ x 1¾", Am. Can Co. 10-A, $18.00.

Arsenic, Medicine, ¼ x 1¼ x 1½", $12.00.

B C, Headache & Neuralgia Tablets, $.25, ¼ x 1¼ x 1¾", $6.00.

Balch's, Laxes, $.10, ½ x 1½ x 1½", $15.00.

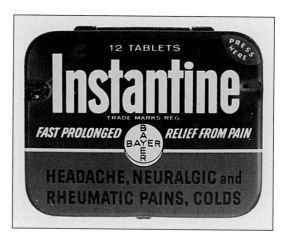

Bayer Instantine, Tablets, ¼ x 1½ x 2", $5.00.

Barrick's, Lazy Liver Lifters, $.25, ½ x ⅞ x 2⅛", $22.00.

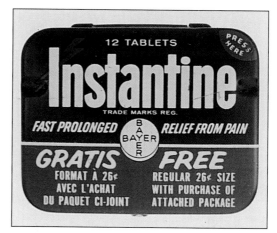
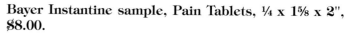

Bayer Instantine sample, Pain Tablets, ¼ x 1⅝ x 2", $8.00.

Bauer & Black, Ray's Adhesive Plaster, ⅜ x 1⅛ x 2⅛", $22.00.

Bauer & Black, Tirro Mending Tape, 1 x 1⅛", $15.00.

Bayer, Aspirin, ¼ x 2 x 2½", $10.00.

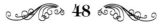

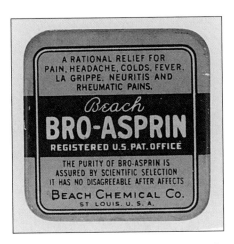

Beach, Bro-Aspirin, ¼ x 1⅝ x 1⅝", $8.00.

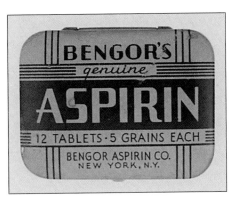

Bengor's, Aspirin, ¼ x 1¼ x 1¾", $8.00.

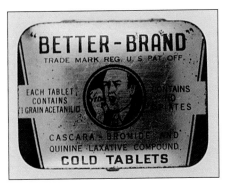

Better-Brand, Cold Tablets, ¼ x 1¼ x 1¾", Am. Can 10-A-K, $12.00.

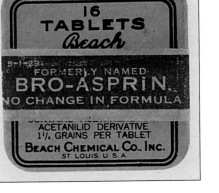

Beach, Bro-Aspirin, ¼ x 1⅝ x 1⅝", Am. Can Co. 89-A, $8.00.

Bile Beans, Biliousness, $.50, ⅝ x 1½", $8.00.

Bear's sample, Jack Frost Cream, ⅛ x ⅞", $20.00.

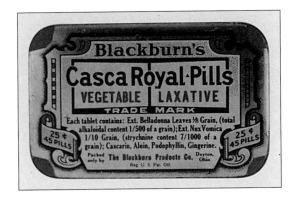

Blackburn's, Casca Royal Pills, $.25, ⅜ x 1½ x 2½", $22.00.

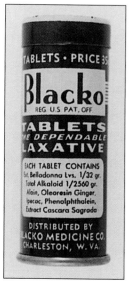

Blacko, Laxative, ¾ x 2",
$15.00.

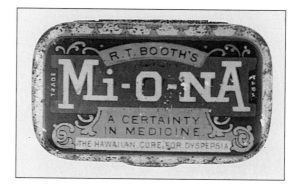

Booth's, R.T., Mi-O-Na, Hawaiian Cure, ⅜ x 1⅜ x 2½",
Am. Can Co. 10-A, $45.00.

Borbro, Aspirin
Tablets, 1 x 1½ x
1½", $12.00.

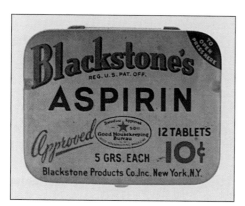

Blackstone's, Aspirin, $.10, ¼ x 1¼ x 1¾", Am. Can
Co. 10-A, $8.00.

Brater's sample, Asthma Powder, ⅞ x 1¾ x 3", Liberty Can, Lancaster, Pa., $40.00.

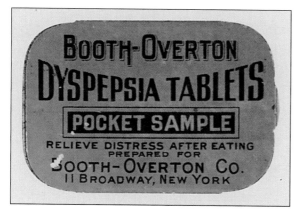

Brawntawns,
Tonic Tablets,
$.50, ½ x 1¾ x
3", Am. Can Co.
43-A, $80.00+.

Booth-Overton sample, Dyspepsia Tablets, ⅜ x 1 x
1½", American Stopper, Brooklyn, $30.00.

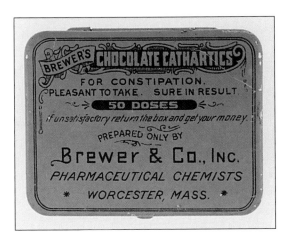

Brewer's, Chocolate Cathartics, ⅜ x 1⅞ x 2½", $25.00.

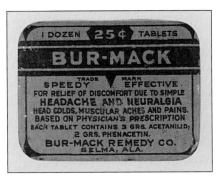

Bur-Mack, Headache Pills, $.25, ¼ x 1¼ x 1¾", $12.00.

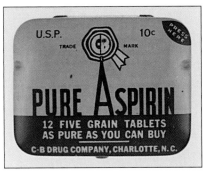

C-B Drug, Aspirin, ¼ x 1¼ x 1¾", Am. Can 10-A, $8.00.

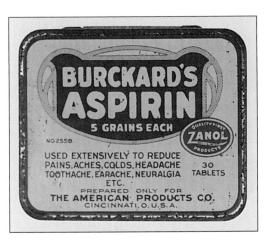

Burckard's, Aspirin, ⅜ x 1⅞ x 2⅜", $8.00.

Cadum, Ointment, ¼ x 2⅜", $12.00.

Buckley's, Cinnamated Capsules, $.35, ⅜ x 1½ x 2⅜", $15.00.

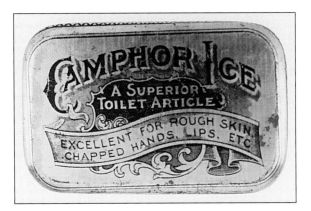

Camphor Ice, ⅞ x 1¾ x 2⅞", $12.00.

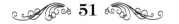

Carnation, Corn Caps, ⅝ x 1 x 2⅜", $30.00.

Cascarets, Candy Cathartic, $.10, ¼ x 1⅝ x 1⅞", $8.00.

Cascarets, Candy Cathartic, $.10, ⅜ x 1¼ x 1¾", $15.00.

Carter's, Little Liver Pills, $.10, ½ x 1⅜", $18.00.

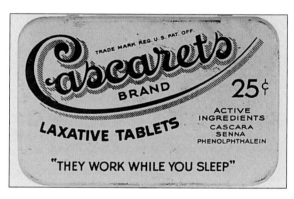

Cascarets, Laxative Tablets, $.25, ½ x 1½ x 2½", Am. Can 50-A, $10.00.

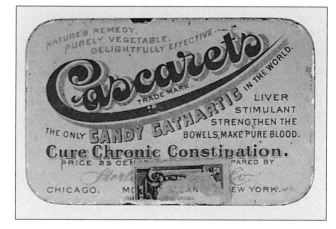

Cascarets, Candy Cathartic, ⅜ x 1½ x 2½", $18.00.

Castarlax, Chocolate Laxative, $.10, ⅜ x 1⅝ x 1⅝", $12.00.

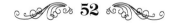

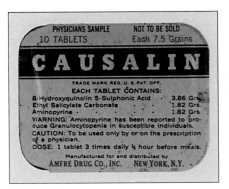

Causalins sample, Tablets, ¼ x 1¼ x 1¾", $10.00.

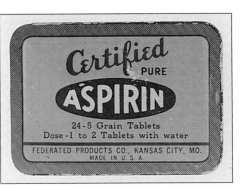

Certified, Aspirin, ⅜ x 1 x 1½", $5.00.

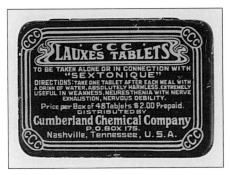

CCC, Lauxes Tablets, ⅜ x 1½ x 2¼", $30.00.

Certified Hospital, Aspirin, ¼ x 1¼ x 1¾", $8.00.

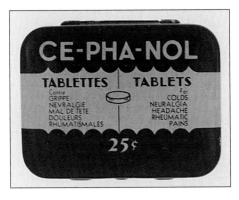

Ce-pha-nol, Tablets, $.25, ¼ x 1¼ x 1¾", $8.00.

Chamberlain's, Acetyl-Salicylic, $.25, ¼ x 1¼ x 1¾", MacDonald, Toronto, $15.00.

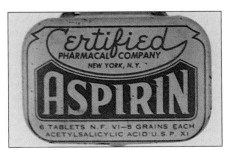

Certified Aspirin, ⅜ x 1⅞ x 2⅝", $10.00.

Champion, Adhesive Tape, ¾ x 1", $20.00.

Cheseborough Man'f'g., Vaseline, ⅞ x 2⅝", $12.00.

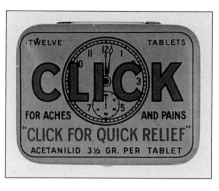

Click, Pain Pills, ⅜ x 1¼ x 1¾", Am. Can Co. 10-A, $15.00.

Clinic, Aspirin, ¼ x 1¼ x 1¾", $12.00.

Citrox sample, Salve, ⅜ x 1¾", $5.00.

Clover Farm Brand, Aspirin, ¼ x 1¼ x 1¾", Am. Can Co. 10-A, $20.00.

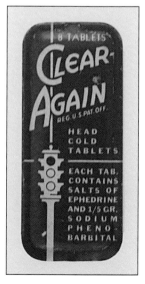

Clear-Again, Head Cold Tablets, ¼ x ¾ x 1¾", $20.00.

Cloverine, Salve, $.50, ¾ x 2½", $6.00.

Cocorets, Laxative, $.10, ⅜ x 1¼ x 2", Am. Can 50-A, $12.00.

Cressy, Family Remedies, ⅜ x 1½ x 2½", $15.00.

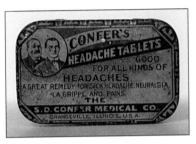

Confer's, Headache Tablets, ½ x 1½ x 2½", Am. Can Co. 70-A, $35.00.

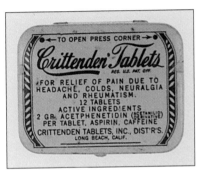

Crittenden, Headache Tablets, ¼ x 1¼ x 1¾", Am. Can 10-A, $10.00.

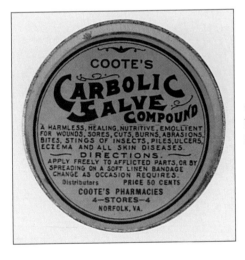

Coote's, Carbolic Salve, ¾ x 2¾", $12.00.

Crow Jim, Corn Salve, ½ x 1", Am. Can Co. 43-A, $18.00.

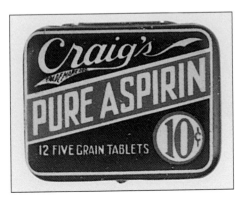

Craig's, Pure Aspirin, $.10, ¼ x 1¼ x 1½", $15.00.

Crow Jim, Corn Salve, $.10, ⅜ x 1", $20.00.

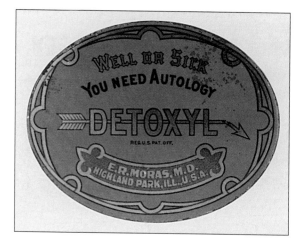

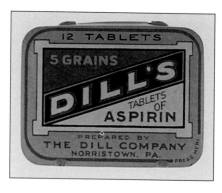

Dill's, Aspirin, ¼ x 1¼ x 1¾", Nat. Can Co., $15.00.

Detoxyl, Medicine, ⅝ x 2 x 2⅞", Am. Can 70-A, $18.00.

Diotex sample, Anti-gas, ¼ x 1 x 1¼", $6.00.

Doan's, Ointment, $.60, ⅝ x 1⅞", $50.00.

Diamond Brand Chi Ches Ters, Pills, 1⅝ x 2⅞ x 1", $25.00.

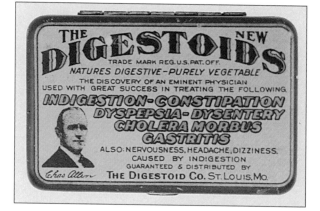

Doan's sample, Ointment, ¼ x 1⅛", $30.00.

Digestoids, Laxative, ⅝ x 1½ x 2⅝", Am. Can Co. 70-A, $25.00.

Doan's sample, Ointment, ¼ x 1⅛", $30.00.

Dr. Aldrich, Lung Salve, $1.00, 1⅜ x 3½", Am. Can Co. 70-A, $18.00.

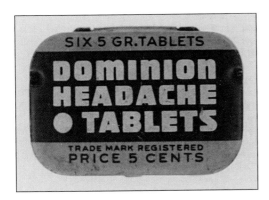

Dominion, Headache Tablets, $.05, ¼ x ⅞ x 1⅜", $10.00.

Dr. Bell's sample, Antiseptic Salve, ¼ x ⅞", $40.00.

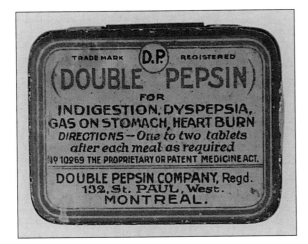

Double-Pepsin, Indigestion Tablets, ⅜ x 1¼ x 1¾", $12.00.

Dr. Bell's, Unguento, ¾ x 1⅞", CW-37", $25.00.

Dr. Brigadell's sample, Camphorole Cold Rub, ¼ x 1⅛", $12.00.

Dr. W.O., Coffee, Massage Ointment #4, ¼ x 1⅛", $15.00.

Dr. Butler's, Buckthorn Splits Laxative, $.10, ¼ x 1½ x 2", Am. Can Co. 89-A, $25.00.

Dr. W.O. Coffee, Prescription #48, ¼ x 1⅛", $15.00.

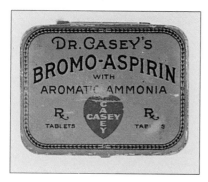

Dr. Casey's, Bromo-Aspirin, ¼ x 1¼ x 1¾", $12.00.

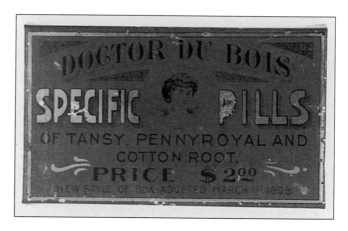

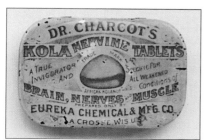

Dr. Charcot's, Kola Nervine Tablets, ½ x 1¾ x 2½", Norton Bros., $90.00+.

Dr. Du Bois, Specific Pills, $2.00, ⅝ x 1⅝ x 3", $50.00.

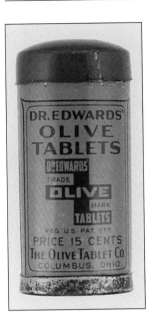

Dr. Edwards', Olive Tablets, $.15, ½ x ⅞ x 1¾", $8.00.

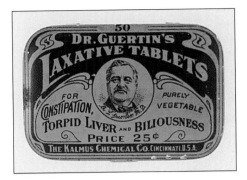

Dr. Guertin's, Laxative Tablets, $.25, ⅜ x 1½ x 2", Am. Can Co. 70-A, $30.00.

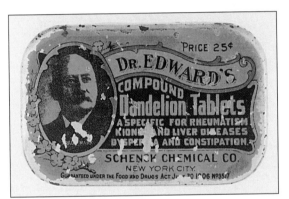

Dr. Edward's, Dandelion Tablets, $.25, ½ x 1⅝ x 2½", $50.00.

Dr. Hamilton's, Pills, $.25, ½ x 1½", $15.00.

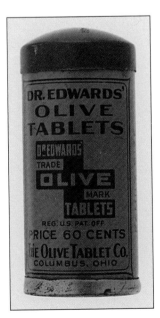

Dr. Edwards', Olive Tablets, $.60, ⅞ x 1⅛ x 2⅜", $12.00.

Dr. Hammonds, Nerve and Brain Pills, ½ x 1⅝ x 2⅞", American Stopper, $95.00.

Dr. Hand's, Chafing Powder, 1¼ x 3", $75.00+.

Dr. Hobson's, Laxative Cascara Tablets, $.25, ⅜ x 2¼ x 3½", American Stopper, $40.00.

Dr. Hough's, White Ointment, $.10, ⅜ x 1¼", $20.00.

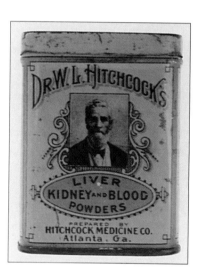

Dr. Hitchcock's, Liver, Kidney, and Blood Powders, $.25, 1⅛ x 2⅛ x 2¾", $25.00.

Dr. Hugo's, Health Tablets for Women, ½ x 1½ x 2½", Mac-Donald, $80.00+.

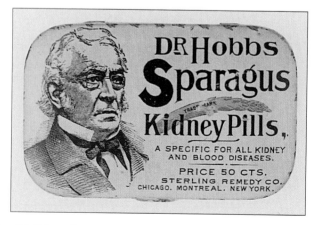

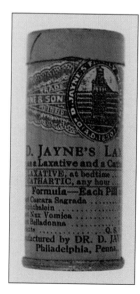

Dr. Jayne's, Laxative, ¾ x 1¾", $25.00.

Dr. Hobbs, Sparagus Kidney Pills, $.50, ½ x 1½ x 2½", Frank Diesel, $60.00.

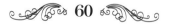

Dr. Jayne's, Expectorant Opium Tablets, ⅜ x 1¾ x 2¾", $150.00.

Dr. Luke's, Sarsaparilla, 2¼ x 3½ x 1¼", $70.00.

Dr. Jayne sample, Pildoras Sanativas, ¼ x ¾", $35.00.

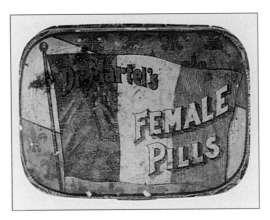

Dr. Martel's, Female Pills, $2.00, 1¼ x 1⅝ x 2½", $55.00.

Dr. Koch's, Corn Salve, ½ x 1¼", Am. Can 70-A, $25.00.

Dr. Koch's sample, Rolatum Healing Salve, ½ x 1⅛", Am. Can Co. 70-A, $30.00.

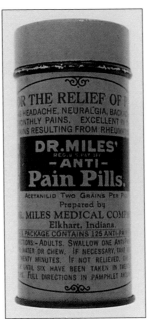

Dr. Miles, Anti-Pain Pills, 1½ x 3¼", $25.00.

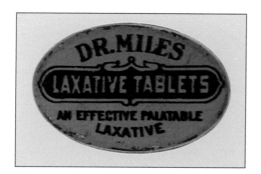

Dr. Miles, Laxative Tablets, ¼ x 1¼", $15.00.

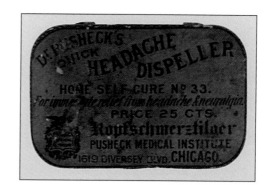

Dr. Pusheck's, Headache Dispeller #33, $.25, ½ x 1¼ x 2", Am. Can Co. 69-A, $35.00.

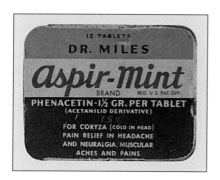

Dr. Miles, Aspir-Mint, $.15, ¼ x 1¼ x 1¾", $15.00.

Dr. Sayman's sample, Salve, ¼ x 1⅛", $25.00.

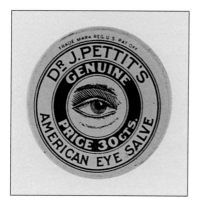

Dr. Pettit's, American Eye Salve, $.30, ¼ x 1⅛", $25.00.

Dr. Robert J. Pierce's, Empress Brand Tablets, 1⅝ x 2⅝ x 1", $35.00.

Dr. Sayman's, Healing Salve, ¼ x 1¼ x ¾", $18.00.

Dr. R. Schiffmann's, Asthmador, $.65, 1⅜ x 2¼ x 3½", Am. Can 98-A, $20.00.

Dr. Shoop's, Lax-ets Laxative, $.05, ⅜ x 1⅛ x 2½", $45.00.

Dr. Thacher's, Uterina Pills, $.50, ½ x 2 x 3⅛", Am. Can 10-A, $45.00.

Dr. Scholl's, Foot Powder, 1¼ x 3¾", Continental, $15.00.

Dr. Tutt's, Pills, $.25, ¼ x 1¼ x 1¾", $15.00.

Dr. Scholl's sample, Foot Balm, ½ x 1⅛", $18.00.

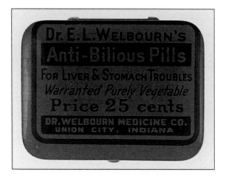

Dr. E.L. Welbourn's, Anti-Bilious Pills, $.25, ¼ x 1½ x 1¾", Am. Can Co. 10-A, $15.00.

Dr. William's, Aspirin, $.05, ¼ x ¾ x 1⅜", $12.00.

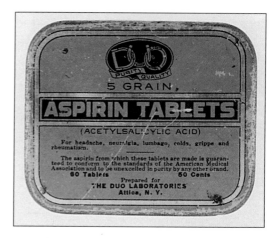

DUO, Aspirin Tablets, ¾ x 2 x 2½", $10.00.

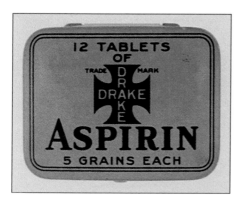

Drake, Aspirin, ¼ x 1¼ x 1¾", Am. Can Co. 10-A, $12.00.

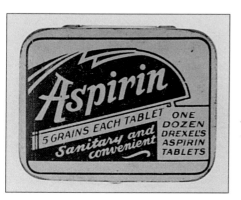

Drexel, Aspirin, ¼ x 1¼ x 1¾", Am. Can 10-A, $12.00.

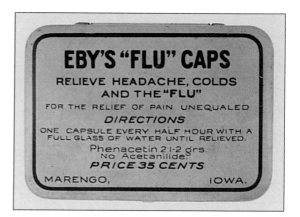

Eby's, Flu Caps, $.35, ¼ x 1¾ x 2½", $12.00.

Drury's, Vinco Plasters, $1.00, 1 x 2¼ x 3½", Somers Bros., $145.00.

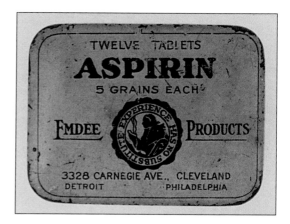

Emdee, Aspirin, ¼ x 1¼ x 1¾", $12.00.

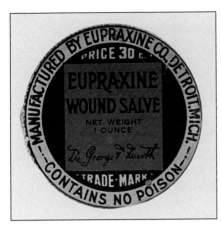

Eupraxine, Wound Salve, $.30, ¾ x 2", Am. Can 70-A, $15.00.

Ex-Lax sample, Chocolated Laxative, ⅜ x 1⅝ x 1⅝", $15.00.

Evans's, Charcoal Tablets, ⅝ x 2⅛ x 3½", $70.00.

Ex-Lax sample, Chocolated Laxative, ⅜ x 1⅝ x 1⅝", F.G. & Co., $18.00.

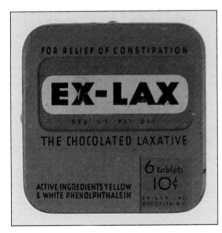

Ex-Lax, Chocolated Laxative, $.10, ¼ x 1⅝ x 1⅝", $10.00.

Ex-Lax sample, Chocolated Laxative, ¼ x 1½ x 1½", F.G. & Co., $12.00.

Ex-Lax, Chocolated Laxative, $.25, ⅜ x 2¼ x 3", MPC 411", $10.00.

Federa sample, Pain Ointment, ¼ x 1¼", $20.00.

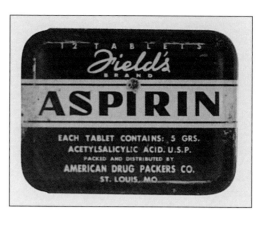

Field's, Aspirin, ¼ x 1¼ x 1¾", $10.00.

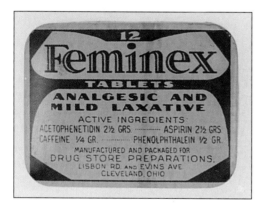

Feminex, Analagesic and Mild Laxative, ¼ x 1¼ x 1¾", $18.00.

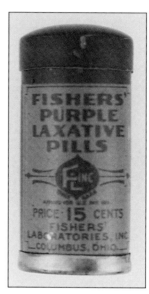

Fishers', Purple Laxative Pills, $.15, ⅝ x ⅞ x 1¾", $18.00.

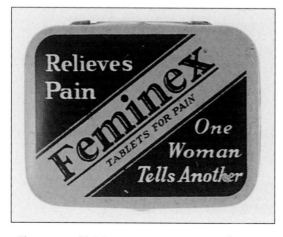

Feminex, Tablets, ¼ x 1¼ x 1½", $30.00.

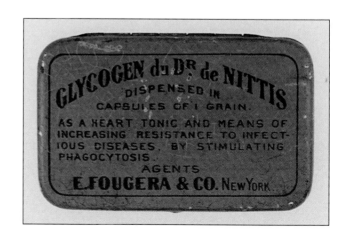

Fougera & Co., Glycogen du Dr. de Nittis, ⅜ x 1¼ x 2⅛", $30.00.

Frank's, Aspirin, ¼ x 1¼ x 1¾", $12.00.

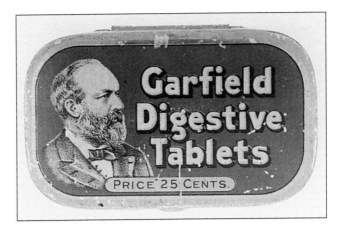

Garfield, Digestive Tablets, $.25, ½ x 1½ x 3", American Stopper, $75.00.

Fruit-Bran, Laxative Compound, ⅜ x 1¾ x 2½", Acme Can, Philadelphia, $25.00.

Germolene sample, Skin Ointment, ½ x 1⅛", $18.00.

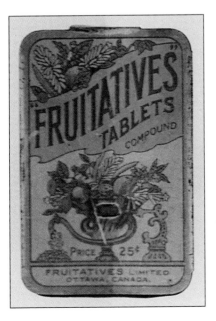

Fruitatives, Tablets, $.25, ⅜ x 1 x 1¾", $18.00.

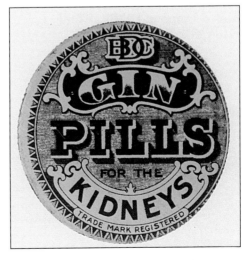

Gin, Kidney Pills, 1¼ x 2", $20.00.

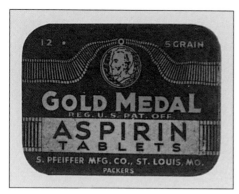

Gold Medal, Aspirin, ¼ x 1¼ x 1¾", $15.00.

Gotham "R" 8, Chocolate Laxative, $.10, ⅜ x 1⅝ x 1⅝", $8.00.

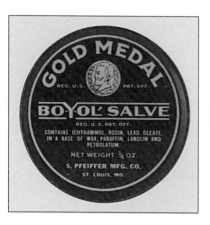

Gold Medal, Boyol Salve, ¾ x 2", $8.00.

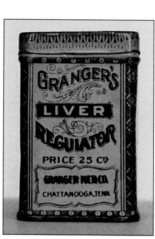

Granger's, Liver Regulator, $.25, 1¾ x 1¾ x 2⅝", $35.00+.

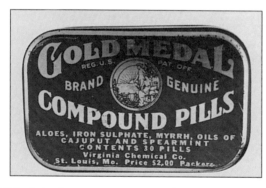

Gold Medal, Compound Pills, $2.00, 1 x 1¾ x 2⅞", Am. Can 70-A, $15.00.

Great Christopher, Corn Cure, $.35, ½ x 1¼", $40.00.

Good Hope, Herb Salve, ⅝ x 1⅞, Thomas Davis & Sons, Montreal, $15.00.

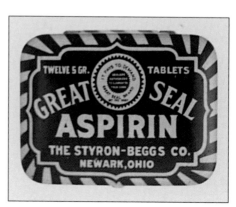

Great Seal, Aspirin, ¼ x 1¼ x 1¾", Am. Can Co. 10-A, $12.00.

Great Seal, Chocolate Laxative, ¼ x 1¾ x 2⅛",
National Can, $10.00.

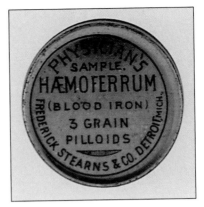

Haemoferrum sample, Iron Pills, ⅜ x 1¼", Wm. A. Gill Co., $15.00.

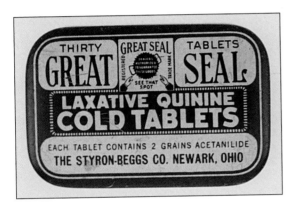

Great Seal, Laxative Quinine Cold Tabs, ⅜ x 1¼ x 2",
Am. Can 10-A, $12.00.

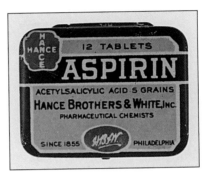

Hance, Aspirin, ¼ x 1¼ x 1½", $10.00.

Grove's, Sanare Cutis for Eczema, ¾ x 2⅜", Am. Can Co. 70-A, $60.00+.

Hance Bros. & White sample, Phenol Sodique Ointment, ¼ x ⅞", $20.00.

Gunnell's sample, Catarrh Cream, ¼ x ⅞", $20.00.

Hartz Mountain, Foot Balm, ⅜ x 1⅜", $22.00.

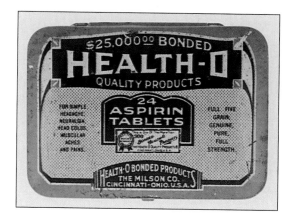

Health-O, Aspirin, ¼ x 1¾ x 2½", $12.00.

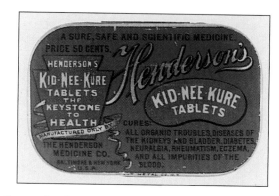

Henderson's, Kid-nee Kure, ½ x 2 x 3⅛", Art Metal Co. N.Y., $70.00.

Health-O, Carbolic Salve, ¾ x 2¾", Am. Can 70-A, $20.00.

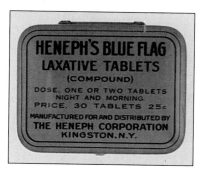

Heneph's, Blue Flag Laxative, $.25, ¼ x 1¼ x 1¾", Am. Can Co. 10-A, $8.00.

Heneph's Blue Flag, Laxative, $.50, ¾ x 2", $15.00.

Helex sample, Healing salve, ¼ x 1⅛", $15.00.

Hickman's Purifina, Salve, ¾ x 2⅛", Acme, $30.00.

Higgins, Aspirin, ¼ x 1¼ x 1¾", $8.00.

Home Remedy, Hazine Healing Ointment, 1 x 2⅜", $30.00.

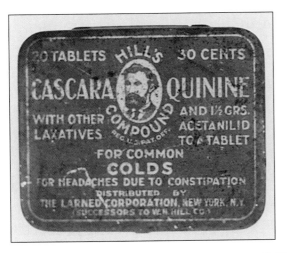

Hill's, Cascara Quinine, $.30, ¼ x 1¾ x 1¼", $15.00.

Home-Need, Adhesive Tape, 1⅛ x 1¼", $8.00.

HyGee, VD Preventitive, ¼ x 1¾ x 2½", $125.00.

Hobbs, Sparagus Kidney Pills, $.50, ⅜ x 1½ x 2½", Am. Can 70-A, $70.00.

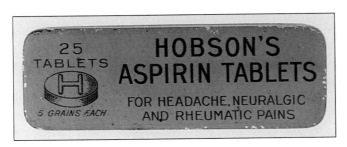

HyGee, VD Preventitive, ⅜ x 1½ x 2", $175.00.

Hobson's, Aspirin Tablets, ½ x ⅞ x 3", $12.00.

Idico, Cones, ½ x 1⅜", $8.00.

Johnson & Johnson, Band-Aid, $.10, ⅜ x 1⅝ x 3⅛", $8.00.

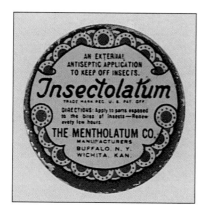

Insectolatum, Salve, ¼ x 1⅛", $8.00.

Joy-Walk, Corn Plasters, $.25, ¾ x 2¼ x 4", $70.00.

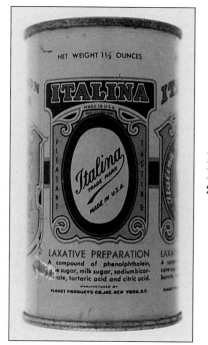

Italina, Laxative Preparation, $.15, 2 x 3⅜", $30.00.

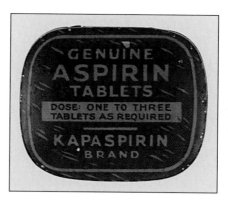

Kapaspirin, Aspirin, ½ x 1¼ x 1¾", $16.00.

Kemcolax, Peppermint Laxative, ¼ x 1½ x 2", $15.00.

Kickapoo Indian, Salve, $.25, ⅝ x 1⅞", $90.00.

Kleen sample, Foot Balm, ¾ x 1¾", $20.00.

Killakes, Relieves Headaches, $.50, ⅝ x 1⅝ x 2⅝", $15.00.

Kohler, One Night Corn Salve, ⅜ x 1⅛", $22.00.

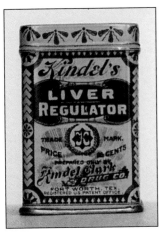

Kindel's, Liver Regulator, $.25, 1¾ x 1¾ x 2⅝", $45.00+.

Kohler Antidote, Headache Tablets, $.40, ¼ x 1½ x 2⅛", $20.00.

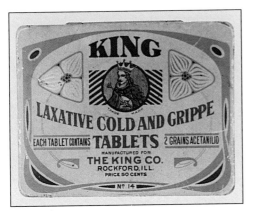

King, Laxative Cold & Grippe Tablets, ⅜ x 2¾ x 3½", $25.00.

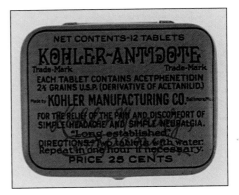

Kohler-Antidote, Pain Pills, $.25, ⅜ x 1¼ x 1¾", $15.00.

Kohler's, Corn Cure, $.10, ½ x 1⅛", $25.00.

Kondon's sample, Catarrhal Jelly, ¼ x ⅞", $40.00.

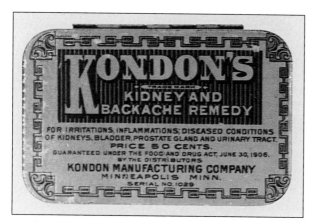

Kondon's, Kidney and Backache Remedy, ¼ x 1½ x 2½", $25.00.

Kondon's sample, Catarrhal Jelly, ¼ x ⅞", $45.00.

Krew-Pina sample, Cold Salve, ¼ x ⅞", $15.00.

Kondon's sample, Catarrhal Jelly, ¼ x ⅞", $18.00.

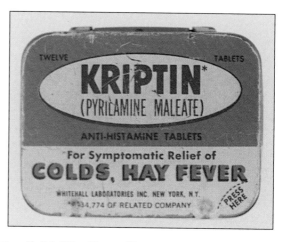

Kriptin, Cold, Hay Fever Tablets, ¼ x 1¼ x 1¾", $8.00.

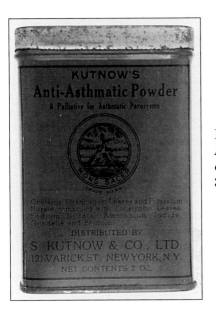

Kutnows, Anti-Asthmatic Powder, 1⅜ x 2¼ x 3⅛", $30.00.

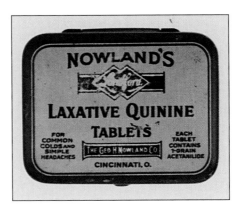

Landford Nowland's, Laxative Quinine Tablets, ¼ x 1¼ x 1¾", $8.00.

Lanikol sample, Skin Ointment, ⅜ x 1¼", Am. Can Co. 78-A, $18.00.

Lan-Tox, Witch Hazel Salve, ⅞ x 2¾", Am. Can 70-A, $35.00.

Larkin, Camphor Ice, 1 x 3¾", Am. Can 10-A-X, $12.00.

Lancaster's English, Celery Caffeine Headache Tablets, $.25, ½ x 1½ x 2½", $40.00.

Lavex, Mineral Powder, 1¼ x 1¾ x 2½", $20.00.

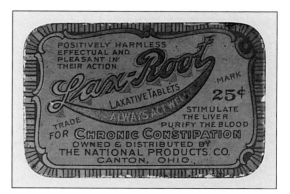

Lax-Root, Laxative Tablets, $.25, ⅜ x 1⅝ x 2½", American Stopper, $30.00.

Lax-ease, Laxative, $.10, ⅜ x ⅞ x 2½", $35.00.

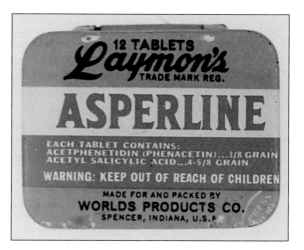

Laymon's, Asperline, ¼ x 1¼ x 1½", Canco 70-A, $10.00.

Lax-ola, Laxative, $.25, ⅜ x 1⅜ x 2⅛", $15.00.

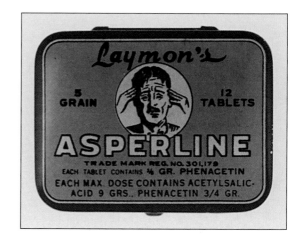

Laymon's, Asperline, ¼ x 1¼ x 1¾", Am. Can 10-A, $15.00.

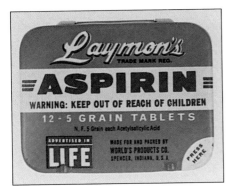

Laymon's, Aspirin, ¼ x 1¼ x 1¾", CANCO, In., $8.00.

Lazy, Liver Pills, ¼ x 1¼", $60.00.

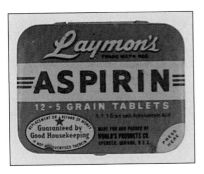

Laymon's, Aspirin, ⅜ x 1¼ x 1¾", CANCO 70-A, $10.00.

Len-Oint, Antiseptic Ointment, $.50, ¾ x 2", $10.00.

Laymon's Five-A-Lax, Laxative, $.05, ¼ x ¾ x 1¾", $8.00.

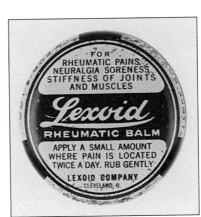

Lexoid, Rheumatic Balm, $.30, ⅝ x 1½", $18.00.

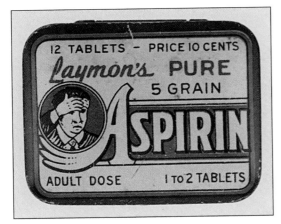

Laymon's Pure, Aspirin, $.10, ¼ x 1¼ x 1½", $25.00.

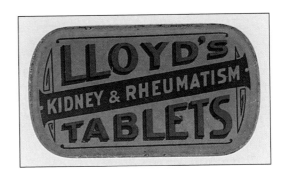

Lloyd's, Kidney & Rheumatism Tablets, ⅝ x 1⅜ x 2⅝", Am. Can Co. 70-A, $25.00.

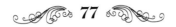

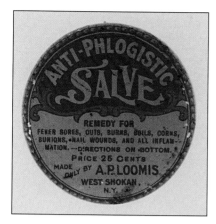

Loomis, A.P., Anti-Phlogistic Salve, $.25, ¾ x 2", $20.00.

Magic, Aspirin, ¼ x 1¼ x 1¾", $10.00.

Magic-Lax, Laxative Nuggets, $.10, ⅜ x 1⅞ x 1⅞", $15.00.

Maclean Brand, Stomach Tablets, ¼ x 2⅜ x 2¾", $10.00.

Magic-Lax, Laxative Nuggets, $.25, ⅜ x 2⅛ x 4¾", American Can, Phil., $12.00.

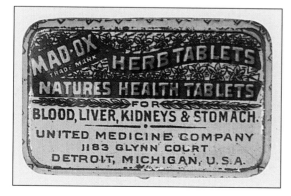

Mad-Ox, Herb Tablets, ¾ x 1¾ x 2⅞", $25.00.

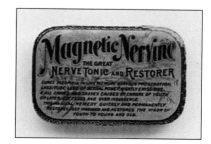

Magnetic Nervine, Nerve Tonic and Restorer, $1.00, ½ x 1½ x 2½", Chicago Stamping, $75.00+.

McClinton's, Hibernia Stick, 1½ x 3½", $25.00.

Maiden Herbs, Laxative, $2.00, ⅞ x 2⅛ x 3¼", $30.00.

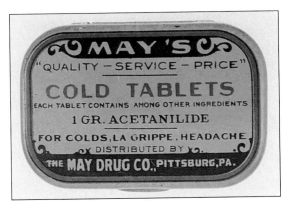

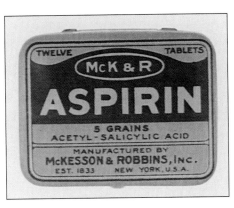

McKesson & Robbins, Aspirin, ¼ x 1¼ x 1¾", $8.00.

May's, Cold Tablets, ½ x 1⅝ x 2½", Am. Can Co. 11-A, $18.00.

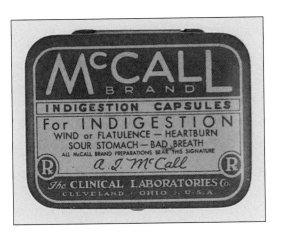

McKesson & Robbins, Surin Laxative, 1 x 1¾", $12.00.

McCall, Indigestion Capsules, ¼ x 1¼ x 1¾", Am. Can Co. 10-A, $8.00.

McKesson's, Copper-Iron Compound, ⅜ x 1½ x 2¼", $15.00.

Mecca sample, Ointment, ¼ x ⅞", $15.00.

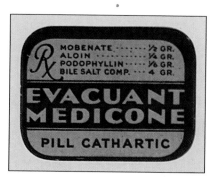

Medicone, Evacuant, sample, Pill Cathartic, ¼ x 1¼ x 1⅝", $8.00.

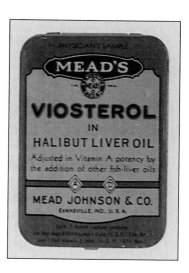

Mead's, Viosterol, ¼ x 1¼ x 1⅞", Am. Can Co. 10-A, $15.00.

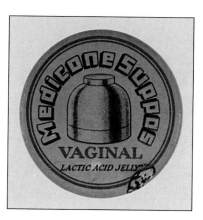

Medicone Suppos sample, Vaginal Jelly, ¾ x 1¾", $55.00.

Mecca Compound sample, Soothing Ointment, ⅜ x 1⅛", $20.00.

Mentho-Nova, Salve, ⅞ x 2¼", $20.00.

Mentho-Nova, Ointment, $.25, ¾ x 2⅜", $15.00.

Mexican, Corn Salve, $.15, ¼ x 1¼", Mersereau, $25.00.

Milkweed Cream sample, for All Skin Diseases, ¼ x ⅞", $40.00.

Mentholatum sample, Salve, ¼ x 1½", $12.00.

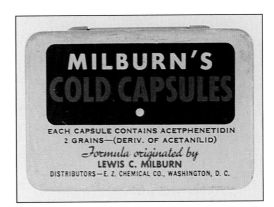

Milburn's, Cold Capsules, $.35, ⅜ x 1⅝ x 2⅜", $5.00.

Metcalf's, Coca Tablets, 2¼ x 3½ x 1½", Somers, $60.00.

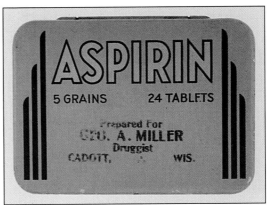

Miller, Geo. A., Aspirin, ⅜ x 1¾ x 2⅝", $8.00.

Montgomery Ward Peerless, sample Corn Wax, ½ x 1⅛", $15.00.

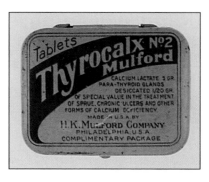

Mulford Thyrocalx No. 2, Tablets, ¼ x 1¼ x 1¾", $15.00.

Munyon's, Paw-Paw Pills, ⅜ x 1¼ x 1¼", $35.00.

Moscos, Great Peruvian Catarrh Cure, $.25, ½ x 1½", 100.00.

Munyon's sample, Corn Cure, ¼ x 1⅛", Mersereau, $35.00.

Moscos, Great Peruvian Catarrh Cure, $.25, ½ x 1½", $110.00.

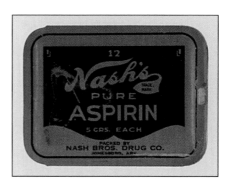

Nash's, Aspirin, ¼ x 1¼ x 1¾", $10.00.

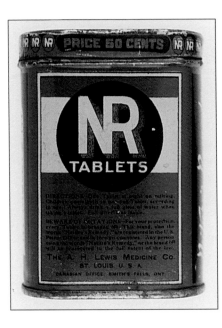

Nature's Remedy, Laxative, $.50, 1 x 2 x 2⅞", $12.00.

New Skin, Liquid Court Plaster, ⅝ x ⅞ x 2¼", $20.00.

Nature's Remedy Juniors, Laxative, $.50, 1 x 2⅛ x 1½", $6.00.

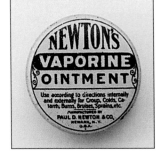

Newton's, Vaporine Ointment, ½ x 2⅛", $10.00.

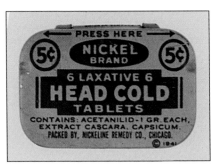

Nickel Brand, Head Cold Tablets, $.05, ¼ x 1 x 1⅜", $12.00.

Nelson Baker, Santonin Chocolates, ⅞ x 1⅝ x 3", $45.00+.

Nickel Brand, Laxative, $.05, ¼ x 1 x 1⅜", $12.00.

No-To-Bac, Intended to Assist in Overcoming Tobacco Habit, $1.00, ½ x 2¼ x 3½", $85.00.

No-To-Bac, Remedy for the Tobacco Habit, $1.00, ½ x 2¼ x 3¾", Am. Can Co. 34, $95.00.

No-To-Bac, Positive and Permanent Cure for the Tobacco Habit, $1.00, ½ x 2¼ x 3¼", $80.00.

No-To-Bac, Remedy for the Tobacco Habit, $1.00, ⅝ x 2⅜ x 3¾", Am Can Co. 70-A, $95.00.

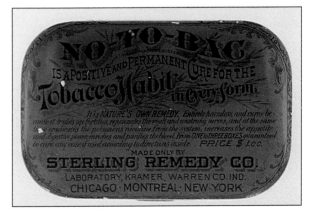

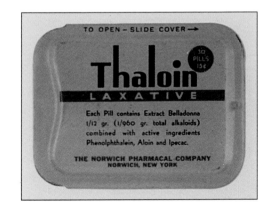

No-To-Bac, Positive and Permanent Cure for the Tobacco Habit, $1.00, ½ x 2¼ x 3¾", Chicago Stamping, $75.00.

Norwich Thaloin, Laxative, ¼ x 1¼ x 1¾", $10.00.

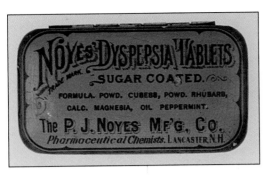

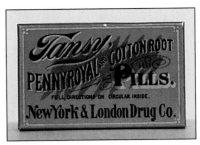

Nyal, Tansy, Penny-royal and Cotton Root Pills, ¾ x 2⅛ x 3½", $65.00+.

Noyes', Dyspepsia Tablets, ⅜ x 1⅛ x 2⅛", Somers Bros., $60.00.

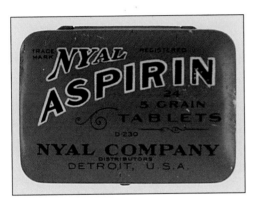

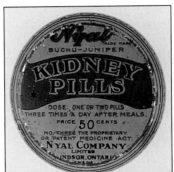

Nyal, Kidney Pills, $.50, ⅞ x 2¼", $15.00.

Nyal, Aspirin, ⅜ x 1¾ x 2½", MP, N.Y., $18.00.

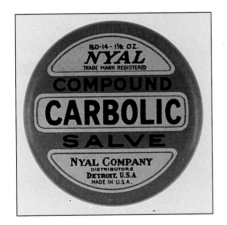

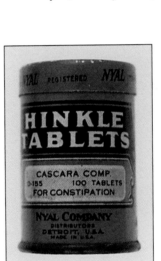

Nyal, Hinkle Tablets, 1 x 1½", $18.00.

Nyal, Carbolic Salve, 1 x 2⅜", MP, $10.00.

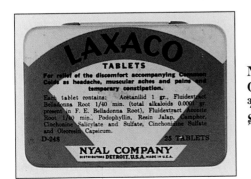

Nyal Laxaco Cold Tablets, ⅜ x 1½ x 2⅜", $15.00.

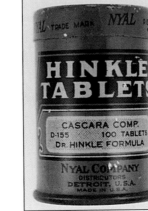

Nyal, Hinkle Tablets, 1 x 1½", $20.00.

Nyal's, Eye Salve, $.25, ⅝ x 1¾", $25.00+.

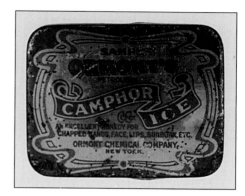

Ormont's sample, Camphor Ice, ¼ x 1¾ x 2", $15.00.

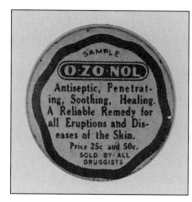

O-Zo-Nol sample, Antiseptic Salve, ¼ x ⅞", $18.00.

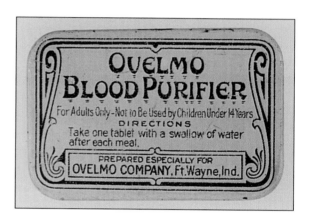

Ovelmo, Blood Purifier, ⅜ x 1⅝ x 2½", $20.00.

O'Neill's sample, Vegetable Remedy Tablets, ⅜ x 1½ x 1⅞", $20.00.

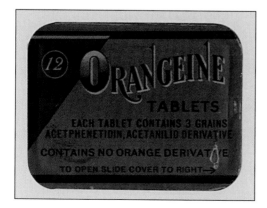

Orangeine, Tablets, ⅜ x 1¼ x 1¾", $15.00.

Owl Drug Purletts, Laxative, $.25, ¾ x 2¼ x 2¼", Am. Can 10-A, $15.00.

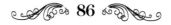

Page's sample, Ointment, ⅛ x 1⅛", $12.00.

Owl Drug, Scott Vegetable Tablets, $.50, ½ x 1⅝ x 2½", Am. Can Co. 10-A, $40.00.

Page's sample, Ready Relief Ointment, ¼ x ⅞", $40.00.

Owl Drug Co., Medicine, ½ x 1⅝", $8.00.

Parke, Davis & Co., Pepsinum Purum, 1 x 1¾ x 2½", Somers, $90.00+.

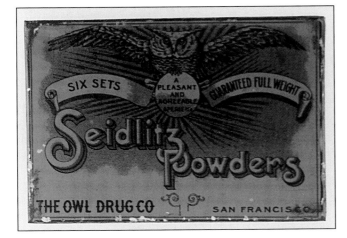

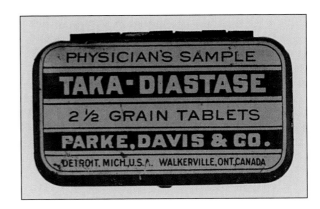

Owl Drug Co., Seidlitz Powders, 1½ x 2 x 3", $35.00.

Parke, Davis & Co., Taka-Diastase, ¼ x 1¼ x 2⅛", $12.00.

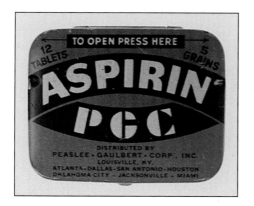

Peaslee-Gaulbery-Corp., Aspirin, ¼ x 1¼ x 1¾", Am. Can Co. 10-A, $8.00.

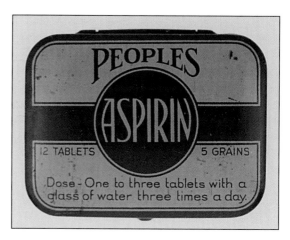

Peoples, Aspirin, ¼ x 1¼ x 1¾", $8.00.

Penetro sample, Salve, ⅜ x 1¼", $15.00.

Peppets, Laxative, $.25, ½ x 1¾ x 3¼", $10.00.

Penslar, Corn Salve, ¾ x 1½", $18.00+.

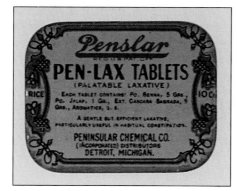

Penslar, Pen-Lax-Tablets, $.10, ⅜ x 1¼ x 1¾", $8.00.

Perkins, Onor-Maid Carbolic Salve, ⅞ x 2¾", $35.00.

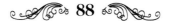

Peterson's, Ointment, $.75, ¾ x 2⅝", $10.00.

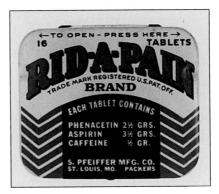

Pfeiffer Mfg. Co., Rid-A-Pain Tablets, $20.00.

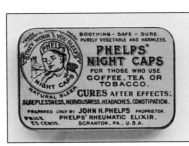

Phelp's, Night Caps, $.25, ½ x 1½ x 2½", Am. Can Co. 50-A, $80.00+.

Peterson's sample, Ointment, ¼ x ⅞", $35.00.

Phen-Amy-Caps, Capsules, $.25, ½ x 1¼ x 1¾", Am. Can Co., $15.00.

Pettit's, Eye Salve, ¼ x 1⅛", $8.00.

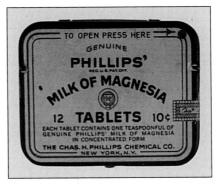

Phillips', Milk of Magnesia, $.10, ¼ x 1¾ x 1⅞", $8.00.

Pierce's, Empress Brand Pennyroyal Tablets, $1.50, 1¼ x 2¼ x 1¼", $45.00.

Pinex, Laxative, $.25, ⅜ x 1¾ x 3¼", Am. Can 2-A, $18.00.

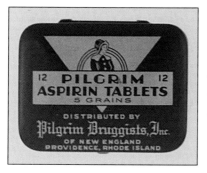

Pilgrim, Aspirin Tablets, ¼ x 1¼ x 1¾", Am. Can 10-A, $15.00.

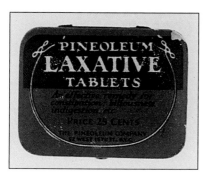

Pineoleum, Laxative Tablets, $.25, ¼ x 1¼ x 1¾", Am. Can Co. 10-A, $8.00.

Pinko-Laxin, Laxative, $1.00, ⅝ x 2⅛ x 2¾", Am. Can. Co. 70-A, $25.00.

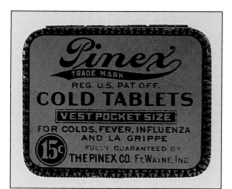

Pinex, Cold Tablets, $.15, ¼ x 1¼ x 1¾", 16.00.

Plough Mexican, Heat Powder, $.10, 1¼ x 2⅜", $18.00.

Ponca Compound, Uterine Alternative, $1.00, 1¼ x 1⅝ x 2¼", $35.00.

Poslam, Salve, $.10, ¼ x 1", $8.00.

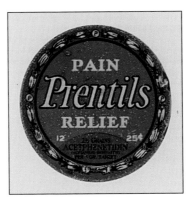

Prentils, Pain Relief, $.25, ¼ x 1⅝", $8.00.

Pond's, Digestans Tablets, $.15, ⅜ x 1½ x 2½", $18.00.

Preventa, Salve, ¼ x ⅞", $8.00.

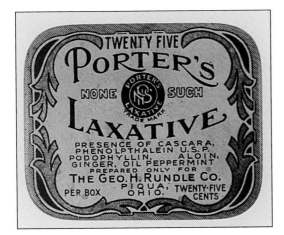

Prid Smile, Salve, ¾ x 1⅞", $10.00.

Porter's, Laxative, $.25, ⅜ x 1½ x 1⅞", National Can, $12.00.

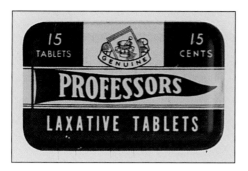

Professors, Laxative Tablets, $.15, ¼ x 1¼ x 2⅛",
$5.00.

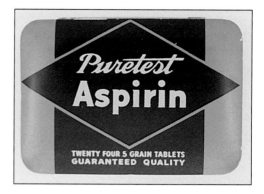

Puretest, Aspirin, ⅜ x 1¾ x 2½", $8.00.

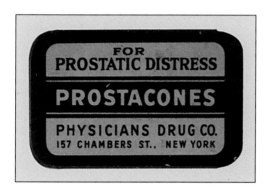

Prostacones sample, Suppositories, ½ x 1 x 1½",
$10.00.

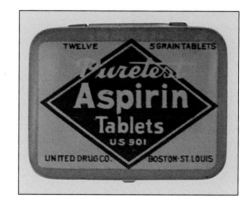

Puretest US 901, Aspirin, ⅜ x 1¾ x 2½", $12.00.

Prunets, Tonic Laxative\Liver Pellets, $.10, ¼ x ½ x
1½", $18.00.

Pyramid sample, Ointment, ¼ x ⅞", $35.00.

Puretest A.S.A., Aspirin, ⅜ x 1¾ x 2½", $10.00.

Quayle & Son, Medicine, ½ x 1", $15.00.

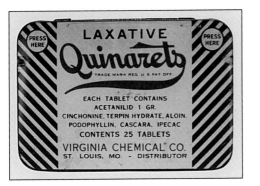

Ral-U-G, Liniment, ¾ x 2",
Am. Can Co. 27-A, $30.00+.

Quinarets, Laxative, ¼ x 1¾ x 2⅜", Am. Can 50-A,
$10.00.

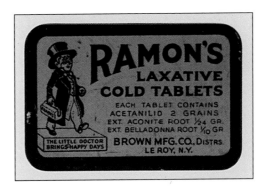

Ramon's, Laxative Cold Tablets, ⅜ x 1¼ x 2", $12.00.

Quinine Pills, ⅜ x 1⅛ x 1⅝", $15.00.

Ramon's, Co-Tabs, $.10, ⅜ x 1¼ x 1¾", $15.00.

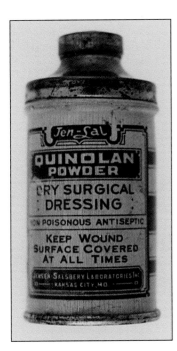

Quinolan Powder, Dry
Surgical Dressing, 1⅜ x
2¾", Am. Can 10-A,
$25.00.

Ramon's, Relief Aspirin, $.10, ¼ x 1¼ x 1¾", Am. Can
10-A, $15.00.

Ramses, Diaphragm, ¾ x 2⅞", $70.00.

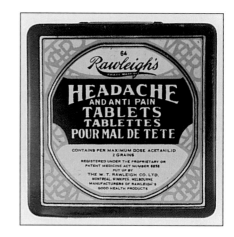

Rawleigh's, Headache Tablets, 64, ⅜ x 3⅛ x 3⅛",
Whittall Can Co., $10.00.

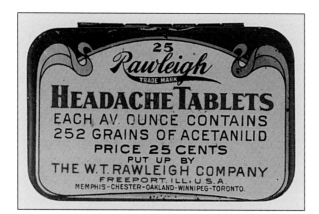

Rawleigh, Headache Tablets, $.25, ½ x 1½ x 2½",
$30.00.

Raymond's sample,
Wonderoil Antiseptic,
¼ x ⅞", $30.00.

Raymond's sample,
Wonderoil Antiseptic,
¼ x ⅞", $30.00.

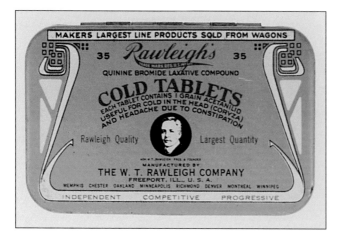

Rawleigh's, Cold Tablets 35, ½ x 1½ x 2½", $10.00.

Real-Lax, Laxative,
$.10, ¼ x 1½ x 1½",
$10.00.

Red-Cloverine sample, Salve, ¼ x ⅞", $20.00.

Red Cloverine, Salve, $.15, ¾ x 2½", Am. Can Co. 27-A, $15.00.

Reed & Carnrick sample, Pancrobilin Tablets, ¼ x 1¼ x 1¾", $15.00.

Red Cross, Salve, $.25, 1 x 2½", $25.00.

Reed's, Aspirin, ¼ x 1¼ x 1¾", $5.00.

Red Cloverine sample, Salve, ¼ x 1⅛", $25.00.

Regs, Laxative, ⅜ x 1⅝ x 2⅛", $8.00.

Regs sample, Laxative, ¼ x 1⅝ x 1⅝", $15.00.

Results, Laxative, $.10, ¼ x 1¼ x 1¾", $12.00.

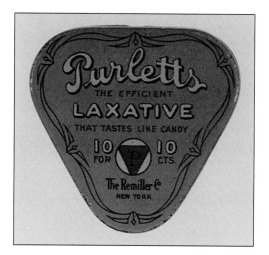

Remiller Co., Purletts Laxative, $.10, ½ x 1½ x 1½", $18.00.

Retlaw, Quick-Healing Salve, $.25, ⅞ x 2⅛", $18.00.

Rex sample, Ointrex, ⅜ x 1¼", Am. Can Co. 10-A, $18.00.

Remiller Co., Purletts Laxative, $.25, ¾ x 2⅛ x 2¼", $18.00.

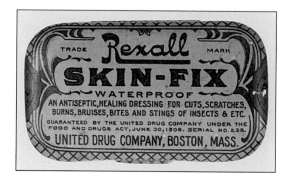

Rexall, Skin-Fix, ½ x 1⅜ x 2½", $35.00.

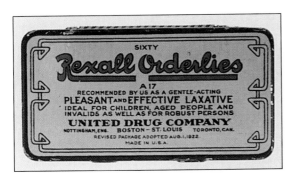

Rexall, Orderlies, ½ x 2 x 4", $15.00.

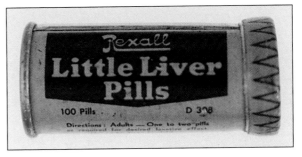

Rexall, Little Liver Pills, 1 x 1¾", $15.00.

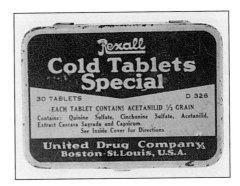

Rexall, Cold Tablets Special, ⅜ x 1½ x 2¼", $10.00.

Rexall, One Minute Headache Powders, ¼ x 1¾ x 2⅜", $12.00.

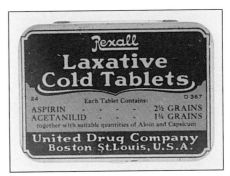

Rexall, Laxative Cold Tablets, ½ x 1½ x 2¼", $12.00.

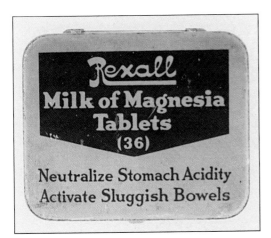

Rexall, Milk of Magnesia Tablets, ½ x 1½ x 1⅞", $15.00.

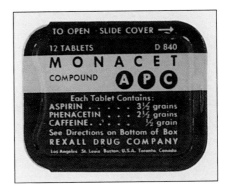

Rexall, Monacet Compound, ¼ x 1¼ x 1¾", $6.00.

Ring's, Witch Hazel Ointment, $.10, ¾ x 1½", H.F. Miller & Son, Baltimore, $25.00.

Rose-Vel, Salve, ¼ x 1⅛", $6.00.

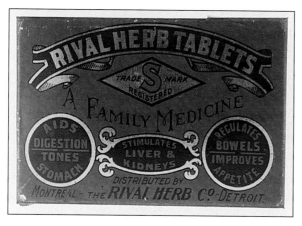

Rival, Herb Tablets, $1.00, 1¼ x 2⅛ x 3¼", $15.00.

Rosebud, Regulators, $.25, ½ x 1½ x 1½", $25.00.

Rose, Corn Salve, ½ x 1", $6.00.

Roseoline, Cream, ⅞ x 2¼, American Stopper, $18.00.

Rose-Vel, Great Healer, 1 x 2½", $10.00.

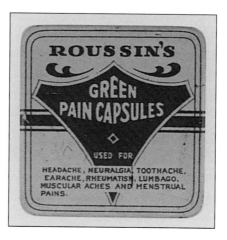

Roussin's, Green Pain Capsules, ¼ x 1⅝ x 1⅝", Buckeye Stamping Co., $18.00.

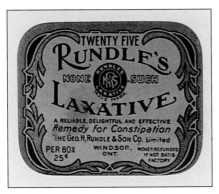

Rundle's, Laxative, $.25, ¼ x 1½ x 1⅞", $12.00.

Salo-Sedatus sample, Fever and Pain Tablets, ¼ x 1¼ x 1¾", Mersereau, $25.00.

Salva-cea, Ointment, ¾ x 2", Am. Can 10-A, $12.00.

Rundle's, Liniment Salve, $.35, 1 x 3⅜", C.C.Co. 90, $12.00.

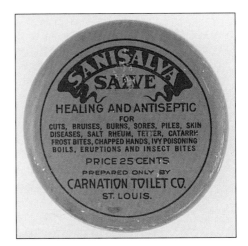

Sanisalva, Salve, $.25, ⅞ x 2¾", $18.00.

Saratoga sample, Ointment, ¼ x 1¼", $20.00.

Rydale's, Liver Tablets, $.25, ⅜ x 2⅛", $40.00.

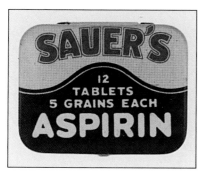

Sauer's, Aspirin, ¼ x 1¼ x 1½", $10.00.

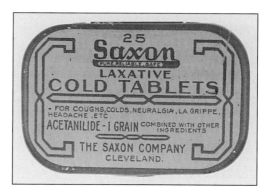

Saxon, Laxative Cold Tablets, ½ x 1⅝ x 2⅝", Am. Can Co. 11-A, $18.00.

Saxon, Sweetlax Chocolate Laxative, ⅜ x 2¼ x 3⅝", $15.00.

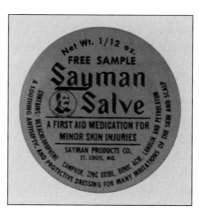

Sayman sample, Salve, ¼ x 1¼", $10.00.

Saxon, Sweetlax Chocolate Laxative, ¼ x 1¼ x 1¾", Am. Can Co. 10-A, $8.00.

Scott, Vegetable Tablets, $.25, ½ x 1⅜ x 2½", BUO-25", $50.00.

Saxon, Sweetlax Laxative, ⅜ x 1¼ x 1⅝", Am. Can Co. 10-A, $15.00.

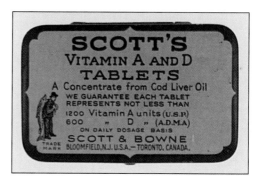

Scott's, Vitamin A & D, ¼ x 1½ x 2¼", $30.00.

Scott's Marvel, Salve, $.50, ¾ x 2⅜", $15.00.

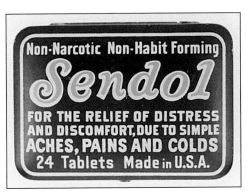

Sendol, Cold and Pain Tablets, ⅜ x 2½ x 1¾", Am. Can Co. 50-A, $6.00.

Seabury, Pharmacal Laboratories, ½ x 1⅜", $45.00.

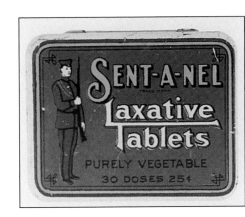

Sent-a-nel, Laxative, $.25, ¼ x 1⅞ x 2½", Tindeco, $22.00.

Seabury's, Bunion Plaster, ½ x 1¾ x 3⅛", Mersereau, $70.00.

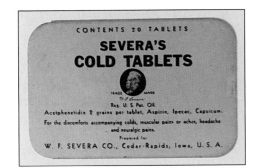

Severa's, Cold Tablets, ½ x 1⅝ x 2½", $8.00.

Seccotine, Medicine, ½ x 1 x 2¼", $8.00.

Sewickley $.15, Corn and Wart Exterminator, ⅜ x ⅞", $20.00.

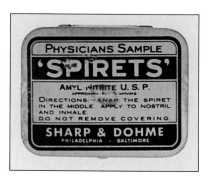

Sharp & Dohme sample, 'Spirets,' ¼ x 1¼ x 1¾", $12.00.

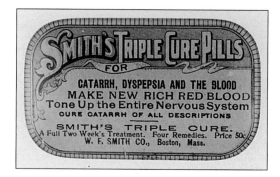

Smith's, W.F., Triple Cure Pills, $.50, ½ x 1⅝ x 2⅞", American Stopper, $65.00.

Simmons', Laxative Powder, 1½ x 2¼ x 2⅝", Am. Can 51-A, $35.00.

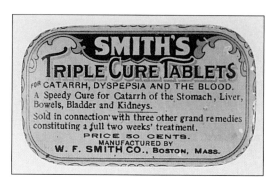

Smith's, W.F., Triple Cure Tablets, American Stopper, $.50, ¼ x 2 x 2⅞", $70.00.

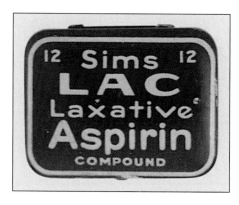

Sims, Laxative Asprin, ¼ x 1¼ x 1¾", $6.00.

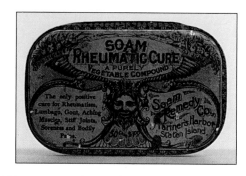

Soam, Rheumatic Cure, $.50, ⅝ x 2¼ x 3½", Somers Bros., $145.00+.

Smith's sample, Balsam of Rose Buds, ¼ x ⅞", $15.00.

Spartan, Aspirin, $.10, ⅜ x 1¼ x 1¾", $12.00.

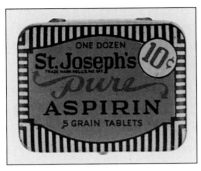

St. Joseph's, Pure Aspirin, $.10, ¼ x 1¼ x 1¾", $10.00.

Standard Laboratories, Bell's Salve, ⅞ x 2⅜", $10.00.

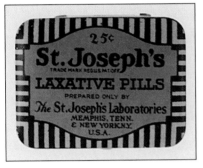

St. Joseph's, Laxative Tablets, $.25, ¼ x 1¼ x 1¾", MP Co., $7.00.

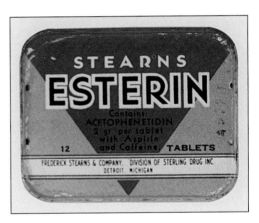

Stearns, Esterin, ¼ x 1¼ x 1¾", $12.00.

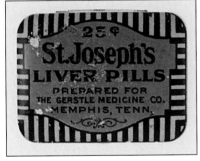

St. Joseph's, Liver Pills, $.25, ¼ x 1¼ x 1¾", MP Co., $8.00.

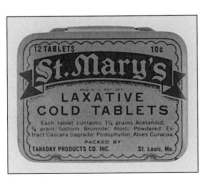

St. Mary's, Laxative Cold Tablets, $.10, ¼ x 1¼ x 1¾", National Can, $12.00.

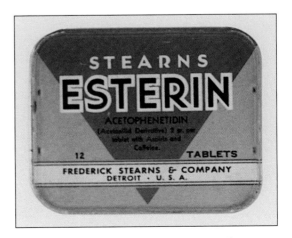

Stearns, Esterin, ¼ x 1¼ x 1¾", $12.00.

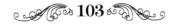

Sterling's sample, Vapor-Eze-Salve, ⅜ x 1¼", $20.00.

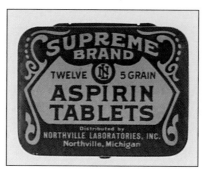

Supreme Brand, Aspirin Tablets, ¼ x 1¼ x 1½", National Can, $10.00.

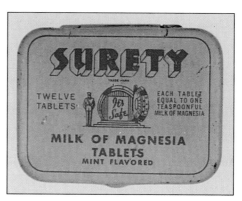

Surety, Milk of Magnesia, ⅜ x 1¼ x 1¾", $15.00.

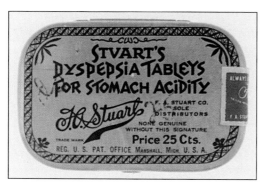

Stuart's, Dyspepsia Tablets, $.25, ½ x 2 x 3⅛", $22.00.

Surety-Lax, Chocolated Laxative, ⅜ x 1⅝ x 1⅝", $20.00.

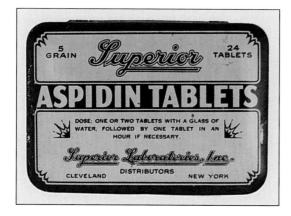

Superior, Aspidin Tablets, $.40, ¼ x 1¾ x 2½", $8.00.

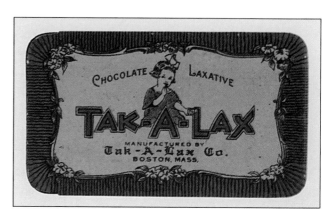

Tak-A-Lax, Chocolate Laxative, ⅜ x 1¼ x 2¼", Am. Can 10-A, $45.00.

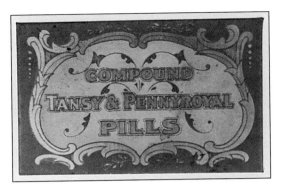

Tansy & Pennyroyal, Pills, ¾ x 1¾ x 2⅞", $45.00.

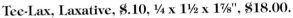

Tee-Lax, Laxative, $.10, ¼ x 1½ x 1⅞", $18.00.

Tholene, Salve, $.25, ⅞ x 2⅛", $20.00.

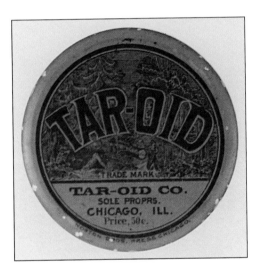

Tar-oid, Salve, $.50, ¾ x 2⅛, Norton Bros, Chicago, $30.00.

To-Mo-Lo, Foot Ointment, ¾ x 2", $12.00.

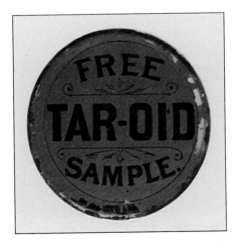

Tar-oid sample, Ointment, ½ x 1⅛", $40.00.

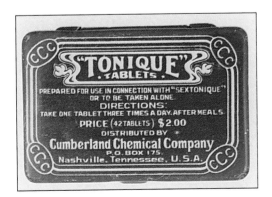

Tonique, Tablets, ⅜ x 1¾ x 2¾", $35.00.

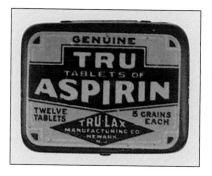

Tru-Lax, Aspirin, ¼ x 1¼ x 1¾", $10.00.

Tyrrell's, Rectal Soap, 1¾ x 3⅜", Liberty Can, $75.00.

Tru-Lax, Laxative, $.10, ¼ x 1⅛ x 1⅛", Am. Can 10-A, $15.00.

U C A, Vapor Balm, $.25, ¾ x 2⅜", Am. Can 70-AX, $8.00.

Tuberose, Ointment, ¾ x 2⅜", $18.00.

Umatilla, Indian Catarrh Cure, $.50, ⅝ x 1½ x 2⅝", Wm. A. Gill Co., $150.00.

Ung. Hyd., Eye Ointment, ½ x 1¼", $25.00.

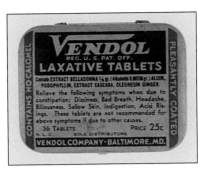

Vendol, Laxative Tablets, $.25, ⅜ x 1¼ x 1¾", $12.00.

Ung't sample, Aseptinol Comp., ¼ x 1⅛", $30.00.

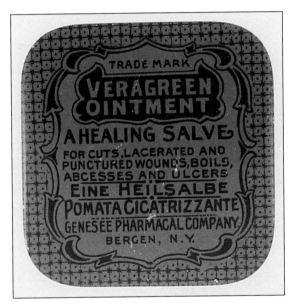

Veragreen, Ointment, ¾ x 2½ x 2½", $15.00.

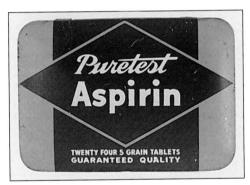

United Drug Co., Puretest Aspirin, ¼ x 1¼ x 1½", MP Co., $12.00.

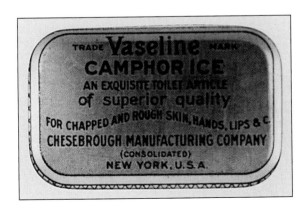

Vaseline, Camphor Ice, ¾ x 1¾ x 2⅞", $5.00.

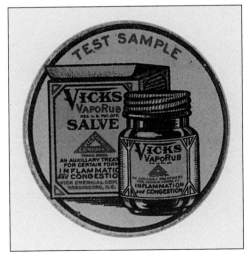

Vicks test sample, VapoRub, ¼ x 1⅝", $18.00.

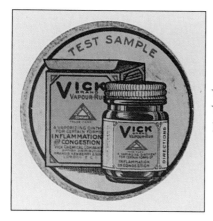

Vicks test sample, Vapour-Rub, ¼ x 1½", $12.00.

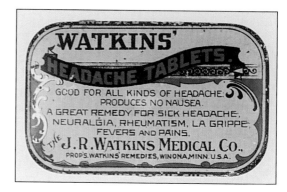

Watkins', Headache Tablets, ½ x 1½ x 2½", Am. Can 70-A, $45.00.

Vicks, VapoRub, ½ x 1⅝", $3.00.

Watkins, Corn Salve, ½ x 1½", $10.00.

Victor, Ointment, ¾ x 1⅞", $40.00.

Watkins sample, Menthol-Camphor Ointment, ¾ x 2⅜", Am Can Co 70-A, $8.00.

F. von Kennen, Salve, ¾ x 1⅞", Buckeye Stamping, $12.00.

Way's, Ointment, ¾ x 1¾", $40.00.

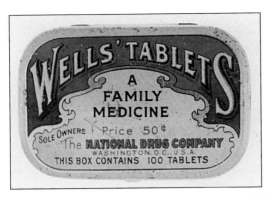

Wells', Tablets, ⅝ x 2 x 3", Metal Package, $25.00.

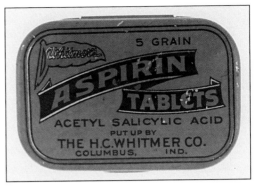

Whitmer's, Aspirin Tablets, ⅝ x 1⅝ x 2½", Am. Can Co. 10-A, $22.00.

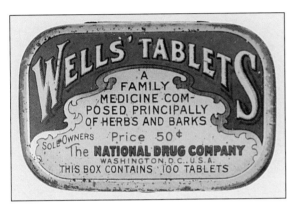

Wells, Tablets, $.50, ½ x 2 x 3", $22.00.

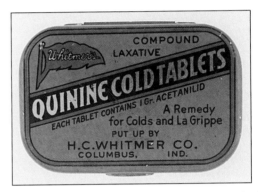

Whitmer's, Quinine Cold Tablets, ½ x 1⅝ x 2⅝", Am. Can Co. 10-A, $15.00.

White Wonder sample, Cold\Flu Salve, ⅛ x ⅞", $25.00.

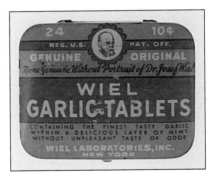

Wiel, Garlic Tablets, $.10, ¼ x 1¼ x 1¾", Am. Can 10-A, $15.00.

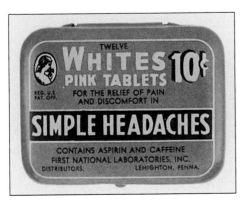

Whites, Pink Tablets, $.10, ¼ x 1¼ x 1¾", $15.00.

Wills, English Formula Pills, $.25, ⅜ x 1⅝ x 2½", Am. Can Co. 11-A, $50.00.

Zalva sample, Oint-
ment, ³⁄₈ x 1¼", $15.00.

Wyeth, Amphojel Tablets, ¼ x 1¼ x 1¾", $8.00.

Wyeth's Wyanoids sam-
ple, Hemorrhoidal Sup-
positories, ½ x 1⁵⁄₈ x
1⁵⁄₈", $8.00.

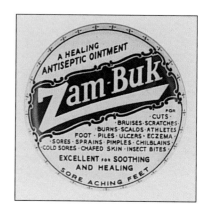

Zam-Buk, Healing Ointment, ¾ x 1⅞", $8.00.

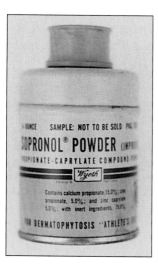

Wyeth sample, Sopronol
Powder, 1¼ x 2", $15.00.

Zam-Buk, Healing Ointment, ¾ x 1⅞", C.E. Fulford,
Toronto, $8.00.

Zaegel's sample,
Essence Pills, ¼ x
⅞", $10.00.

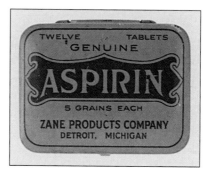

Zane Products,
Aspirin, ¼ x 1¼
x 1¾", $6.00.

Needles
(Phonographic)

Aegir, Needles, 200, ⅝ x 1⅝ x 2½", $18.00.

Britian's Best sample, Needles, ⅝ x 2", $50.00.

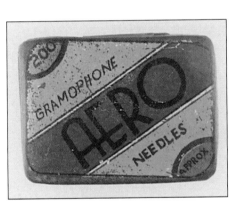

Aero, Gramophone Needles, 200, ⅜ x 1¼ x 1¾", $25.00.

Burchard's Salon, Needles, 200, ⅜ x 1¼ x 1¾", $40.00.

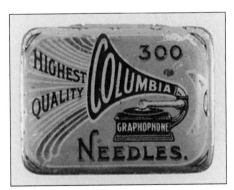

Columbia, Highest Quality Needles, 300, ⅜ x 1¼ x 1¾", $40.00.

Brilliantone, Needles, 300, ½ x 1¼ x 1¾", $30.00.

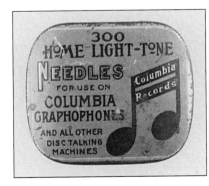

Columbia, Home-Light-Tone Needles, 300, ½ x 1¼ x 1½", $40.00.

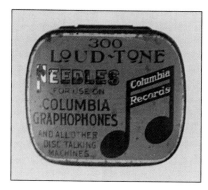

Columbia, Loud Tone Needles, 300, ½ x 1¼ x 1½", $35.00.

Columbia Superbe, Soft Tone Needles, 200, ¼ x 1⅜ x 1⅞", $35.00.

Columbia, Needles, 300, ½ x 1¼ x 1½", $30.00.

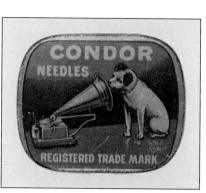

Condor, Phonograph Needles, ½ x 1¼ x 1½", $45.00.

Columbia, Gramophone Needles, 300, ½ x 1¼ x 1½", $35.00.

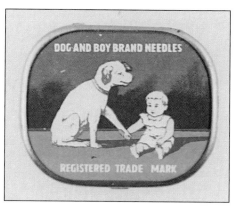

Dog and Boy, Needles, ½ x 1¼ x 1½", $30.00.

Columbia Ideal, Soft Tone Needles, ¼ x 1⅜ x 1⅞", $35.00.

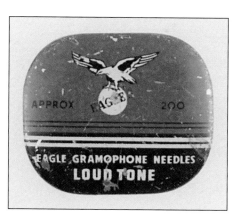

Eagle, Loud Tone Gramophone Needles, ½ x 1¼ x 1¾", $35.00.

Eaton, T., Soft Tone Gramophone Needles, 200, ⅝ x 2", $40.00.

Elkah Special, Needles, ⅜ x 1¼ x 1¾", $30.00.

Eaton, T. Co., Needles, 200, ¼ x 1¼ x 1¾", $25.00.

Herold-Doppelton, Needles, ⅜ x 1¼ x 1¾", $30.00.

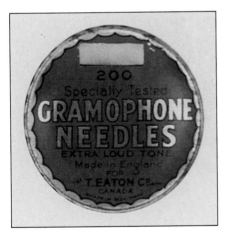

Eaton, T., Extra Loud Tone Phono Needles, ⅝ x 2", $35.00.

Herold-Nadeln, Needles, ⅜ x 1½ x 1½", $30.00.

Edison Bell, Chromic Needles, 100, ⅜ x 1¼ x 1¾", $35.00.

Herold-Wenglein, Needles, ⅜ x 1½ x 3½", $65.00.

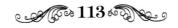

Herold-Zukunft, Needles, ⅜ x 1¼ x 1¾", $30.00.

Marschall, Needles, ½ x 1¼ x 1½", $35.00.

Jenkin's & Son, Grand Opera Needles, ⅝ x 2", $45.00.

Muza, Needles, ⅜ x 1¼ x 1¾", $30.00.

Klingsor-Nadeln, Needles, ⅜ x 1⅛ x 2¼", $25.00.

Natural Voice, Needles Phono, 200, ½ x 1¼ x 1½", $35.00.

Leisespieler, Needles, ⅜ x 1½ x 1½", $25.00.

S.S.S. Fursten, Needles, ⅜ x 1¼ x 1¾", $45.00.

Shell, Needles, 200, #16, ⅜ x 1¼ x 1¾", $35.00.

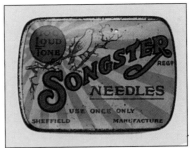

Songster, Loud Needles, 100, ¼ x 1¼ x 1¾", $35.00.

Shell, Extra Loud Needles, 200, #3, ⅜ x 1¼ x 1¾", $35.00.

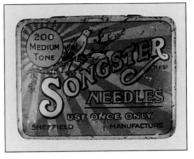

Songster, Medium Tone, 200, ⅜ x 1¼ x 1½", $35.00.

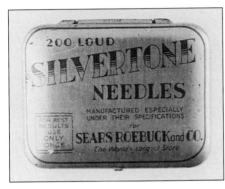

Silvertone, Loud Needles, 200, ⅜ x 1¼ x 1¾", $60.00.

Songster, Soft Needles, 200, ⅜ x 1¼ x 1¾", $35.00.

Silvertone, Soft Needles, 200, ¼ x 1¼ x 1½", $60.00.

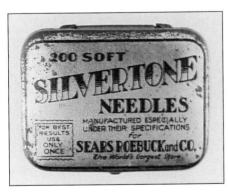

Stag Brand, Gramophone Needles, 200, ⅜ x 1¼ x 1¾", $40.00.

Songster, Trailer Needles, 100, ⅜ x 1¼ x 1¾", $40.00.

Sunder, Phono Needles, ⅜ x 1¼ x 1¾", $25.00.

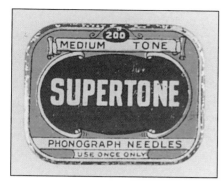

Supertone, Medium Tone Needles, 200, ⅜ x 1¼ x 1¾", $35.00.

Verona, Needles, ⅜ x 1½ x 1½", $40.00.

Taj Mahal, Needles, ½ x 1¼ x 1¾", $35.00.

Victor, Needles, ½ x 1¼ x 1½", $55.00.

Tansen, Gramophone Needles, ⅜ x 1¼ x 1¾", $30.00.

Victor, Needles 200, ½ x 1¼ x 1½", $60.00.

The Twin Needles, ¼ x 1¼ x 1½", $45.00.

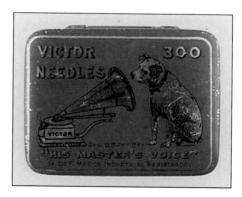

Victor, Needles, 300, ½ x 1¼ x 1¾", $50.00.

Victor, Extra Loud Needles, ½ x 1¼ x 1½", $45.00.

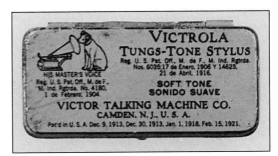

Victor, Soft Tone Tungs-Tone Needles, ¼ x 1 x 2", $40.00.

Victor, Half Tone Needles, ½ x 1½ x 2½", $55.00.

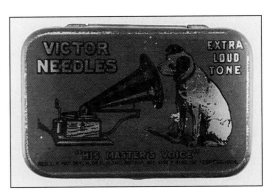

Victor, Extra Loud Tone Needles, ½ x 1½ x 2½", $45.00.

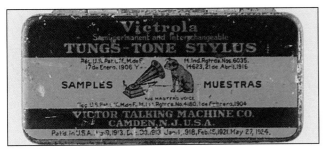

Victor sample, Tungs-Tone Stylus, ¼ x ⅞ x 2", $55.00.

Winner, Loud Needles, 200, ½ x 1¼ x 1½", $40.00.

Victor, Soft Tone Needles, ½ x 1¼ x 1¾", $45.00.

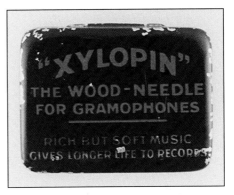

"Xylopin," Wood Needles, ¼ x 1¼ x 1¾", $30.00.

Shoe Polishes

American, Shoe Polish, ¾ x 2⅛", Am. Can Co. 3-A, $18.00.

Bixby's, Tan Paste, ¾ x 2¼", $20.00.

American 'Nova,' Shoe Polish, ⅞ x 2½", Am. Can 70-A, $25.00.

Black Cat Polish Co., Betsy Ross Polish, ⅞ x 1¾", R.C. Co. 11-A, $25.00.

Bixby's, "Satinola," ⅝ x 2¼", $25.00.

Daisy, Russet Polish, ⅜ x 1¾", $18.00.

Griffin Grifola, Shoe Polish, ⅝ x 1¾", $20.00.

Ermin, Boot Polish, 1 x 2½", $15.00.

Griffin ABC, Black Shoe Polish, 1 x 2½", $5.00.

Everett & Barron, Ever Ready
Suede Stick, 1 x 3¾", $15.00.

Griffin ABC, Black Shoe Polish, 1 x 2½", $5.00.

Griffin ABC, Tan Shoe Polish, 1 x 2½", $3.00.

Pasta Superior sample, Shoe Polish #2, ⅝ x 1¾", $20.00.

Hay, R., & Son, Shoe Polish, ¾ x 2¼", Fischer Mfg., Hamilton, Ohio, $25.00.

Ralston, Robt., Beauty Paste Polish, ¾ x 2⅛", $15.00.

Kelly's, Slide Shoe Polish, 1 x 2⅞", TINDECO, $150.00.

Shinola sample, Black Shoe Polish, 1 x 2", $18.00.

Tiger Brand, Red Shoe Polish, ¾ x 1¾", $30.00.

Tilleys, Suede Powder, 1⅜ x 2½ x 3¾", Am. Can Co. 31-A, $18.00.

Tiger Brand, Russet Shoe Polish, ¾ x 1¾", $30.00.

Whittemore's, Black Oil Paste, 1 x 2⅞", $12.00.

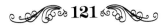

Cowan's sample, Instant Cocoa, 1 x 1⅜ x 1⅝", Mac-Donald, $175.00.

Mazawattee sample, Latariba Cocoa, ⅝ x 1½ x 2¼", $120.00.

Droste's sample, Cocoa, 1 x 1 x 1⅞", $90.00.

Neilson's sample, Cocoa, 1⅜ x 2", $30.00.

Rowntree's sample, Cocoa, 1 x 1⅜ x 1⅝", $65.00.

Ideal sample, Cocoa, 1¼ x 1⅝ x 2½", Liberty Can, $155.00.

Runkel's sample, Pure Cocoa, 1¼ x 1¼ x 2", $125.00.

Barrington Hall sample, Coffee, 2⅞ x 2⅛", Canco, $60.00.

Chase & Sanborn sample, High Grade Coffee, 2½ x 2¼", $60.00.

Edward's sample, Coffee, 2¾ x 2¾", $60.00.

Breakfast Cheer sample, Coffee, 2¼ x 2¾", Am. Can 10-A, $130.00.

High Point sample, Electric Perc Coffee, 3 x 2½", $30.00.

Millar's sample, Magnet Coffee, 2⅜ x 3", $110.00.

Chase & Sanborn sample, Coffee, 2½ x 2¼", Metal Pkg., Brooklyn, $65.00.

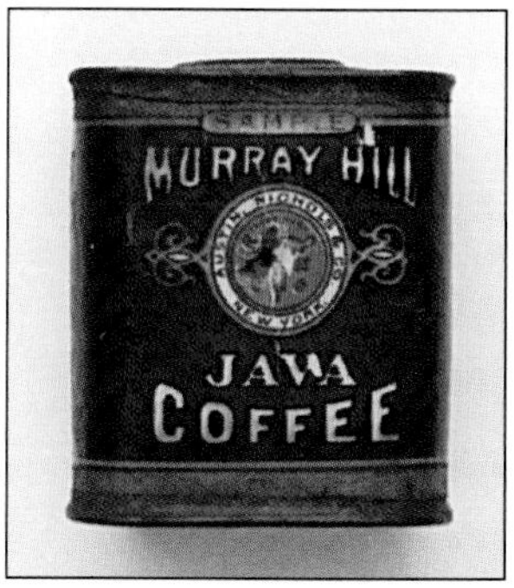

Murray Hill sample, Java Coffee, 1⅜ x 1⅞ x 2", $90.00.

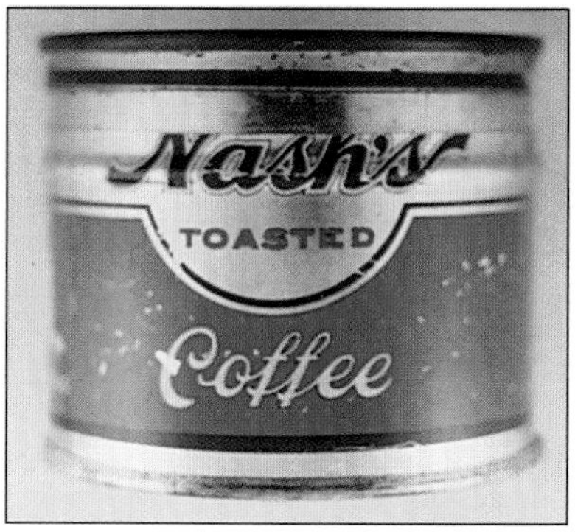

Nash's sample, Coffee, 2¾ x 3⅜", Am. Can 10-A, $80.00.

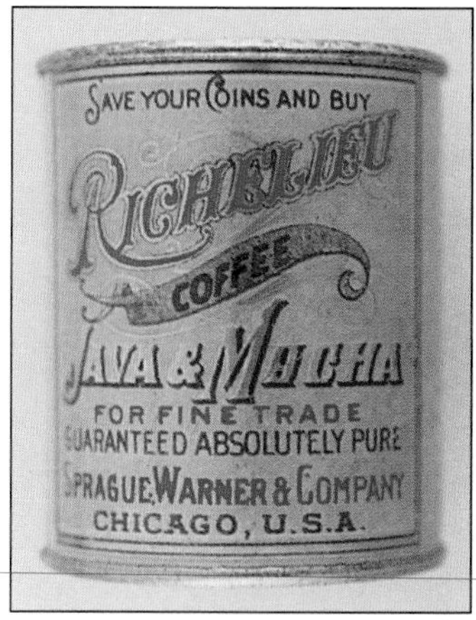

Richelieu sample, Java & Mocha, 2⅜ x 2", $115.00.

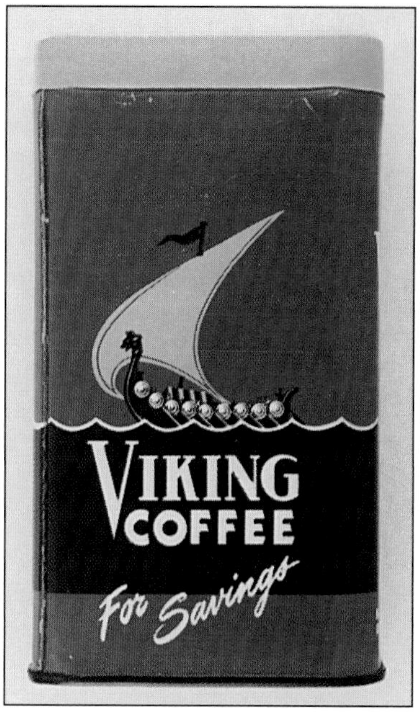

Viking sample, Coffee Bank, 1¾ x 2¼ x 4", $25.00.

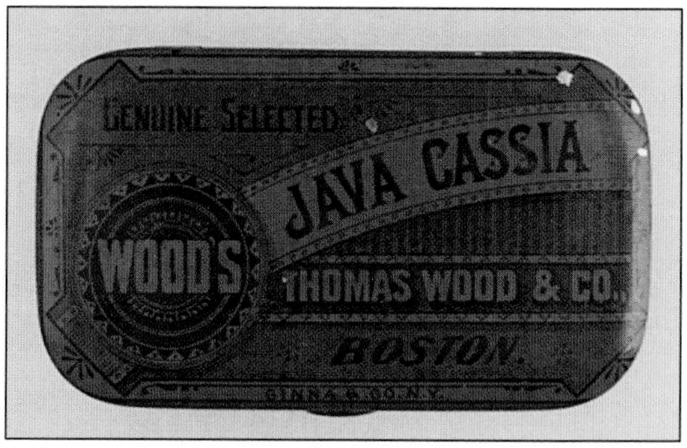

Wood's, Thomas, sample, Java Cassia Coffee, ⅜ x 1½ x 2½", Ginna, $175.00.

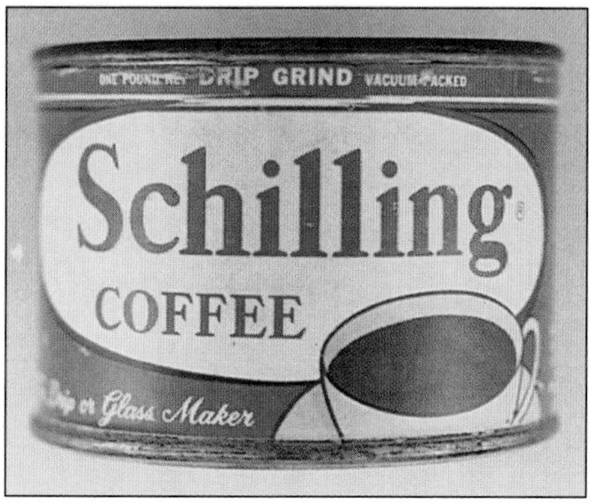

Schilling sample, Coffee, 1⅞ x 2½", $50.00.

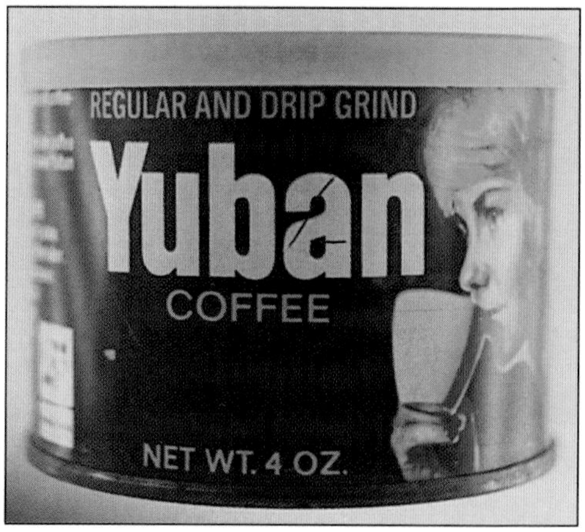

Yuban sample, Coffee, 4oz., 3⅜ x 2½", $20.00.

Cooks Friend sample, Baking Powder, 1⅛ x 1⅝ x 1", $30.00.

Lowney's sample, Cocoa Butter, ⅞ x 2¾", G.5 W 6, $15.00.

Eskay's sample, Albumenized Food, 1½ x 2⅜", $40.00.

Nestles sample, "Lactogen," 2⅞ x 2½", $30.00.

Gold Leaf sample, Baking Powder, 1⅜ x 1⅞", $35.00.

Nestle's sample, Food, 1¼ x 1¾", Am. Can Co. 10-A, $30.00.

Ocean Spray (bank), Cranberry Sauce, 2⅜ x 2⅝",
C.C.Co. B, $40.00.

Towles Log Cabin sample, Syrup, House, 1¼ x 1⅞ x
2½", $275.00.

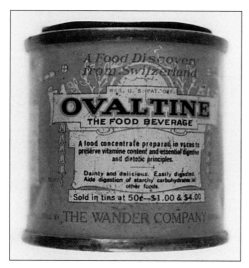

Watkin's trial size, Malted Milk, 1¾ x 2½",
C.C.Co. 30-10, $75.00.

Ovaltine sample, Food Beverage, 2 x 2", $45.00.

Snow King sample, Baking
Powder, 2 x 3¼", $60.00.

Whitman's, Choco-
late Syrup, 4¼ oz.,
2⅛ x 2⅞", $25.00.

3XB sample, Powder, ¾ x 1⅜ x 2½", $20.00.

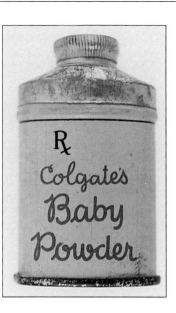

Colgate sample, Baby Powder, ¾ x 1¼ x 2", $60.00.

Armand sample, Cold Cream Talcum, ¾ x 1⅜ x 2⅛", $90.00.

Colgate sample, Violet Talc Powder, ⅝ x ⅞ x 1⅞", $100.00.

Armand sample, Talcum, ¾ x 1¼ x 2⅛", $75.00.

Corsage sample, Bouquet Talcum, ¾ x 1¼ x 2⅛", $140.00.

Cuticura sample, Talcum Powder, ¾ x 1¼ x 2", C.C. Co., $65.00.

Jergens sample, Eutaska Talcum Powder, ¾ x 1¼ x 2⅛", $60.00.

Hanson-Jenks sample, Violet Brut Talcum, ¾ x 1⅜ x 2⅛", $50.00.

Mennen sample, Flesh Tint Talcum, ¾ x 1¼ x 2⅛", $40.00.

Hinds Cre-mis sample, Talcum Powder, ¾ x 1⅜", $75.00.

Mennen sample, Kora-Konia Powder, ¾ x 1⅛ x 2", $30.00.

Mennen sample, Narangia Talcum Powder, ¾ x 1¼ x 2", $60.00.

Mulford's sample, Toilet Talcum, ¾ x 1¼ x 2", $70.00.

Mennen sample, Sen Yang Talcum Powder, ¾ x 1¼ x 2⅛", $125.00.

Parke, Davis & Co. sample, Euthymol Talcum Powder, ⅝ x ⅞ x 2", $30.00.

Mennen sample, Sen Yang Toilet Powder, ¾ x 1¼ x 2⅛", $110.00.

Regal sample, Talcum Powder, ¾ x 1¼ x 2", $65.00.

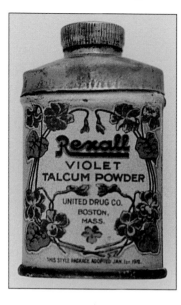

Rexall sample, Violet Talcum Powder, ¾ x 1⅜ x 2⅛", $60.00.

Squibb's sample, Carnation Talcum, 1 x 2⅛", $45.00.

Riker's sample, Violet Excelsis Talcum, ¾ x 1¼ x 2", $45.00.

Taylor's sample, Blue Bird Talcum, ½ x 1¼ x 2⅛", $195.00.

Royal Vinolia sample, Talcum Powder, ¾ x 1⅜ x 2⅛", $125.00.

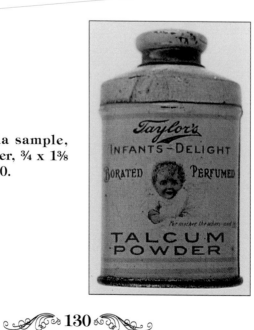

Taylor's sample, Infant Talcum Powder, ¾ x 1¼ x 2⅛", $125.00.

Taylor's sample, Valley Violet Talcum Powder, ¾ x 1¼ x 2⅛", $115.00.

Williams' sample, Baby Talc, ¾ x 1¼ x 2¼", $75.00.

Vantine's sample, Sana-Dermal Talcum Powder, 1 x 2⅛", $450.00.

Williams' sample, Carnation Talc, ¾ x 1¼ x 2¼", $60.00.

Violet Sec sample, Talcum Powder, ¾ x 1¼ x 2⅛", N.Y., $80.00.

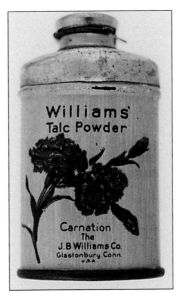

Williams' sample, Carnation Talc Powder, ¾ x 1¼ x 2¼", $55.00.

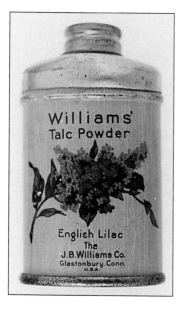

Williams' sample, English Lilac Talc Powder, ¾ x 1⅜ x 2¼", $65.00.

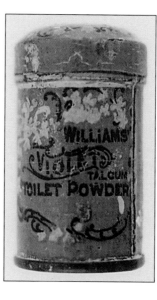

Williams' sample, Violet Talcum Powder, ¾ x 1⅜ x 2¼", $75.00.

Williams' sample, La Tosca Rose Talc Powder, ¾ x 1¼ x 2⅛", $75.00.

Williams' sample, Violet Talcum Powder, 1 x 1⅞", $80.00.

Williams sample, La Tosca Rose Talc, ¾ x 1⅜ x 2¼", $55.00.

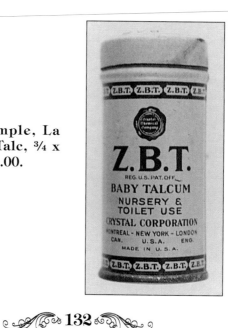

Z.B.T. sample, Baby Talcum, 1 x 2⅛", $25.00.

Gold Shield sample, Tea, 2 x 2½", $40.00.

Martinson's sample, Tea Bags, 1¾ x 2¼ x 3", Am. Can 10-A, $25.00.

Horniman's sample, Boudoir Tea, 1¼ x 2⅛ x 1⅜", $60.00.

McCormick Banquet sample, Tea, 1¾ x 2¼ x 2½", $30.00.

Horniman's sample, Pure Tea, 1½ x 1½ x 1½", $80.00.

Premier sample, Tea, 1½ x 2½ x 2⅞", $30.00.

Kolona sample, Ceylon Tea, ¾ x 1⅞ x 2½", Toronto, $35.00.

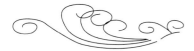

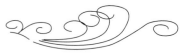

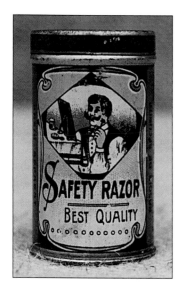

Best Quality, Safe-
ty Razor, 1½ x
2⅜", $250.00.

Fairy, Safety Razor, 1¼ x 2¼",
$375.00+.

Colgate's, Rapid Shave Powder, 1¼ x 2¼", $20.00.

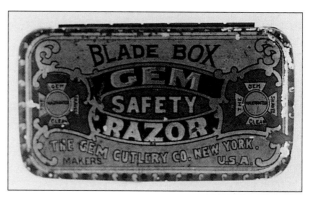

Gem, Blade Box, ¼ x 1⅛ x 2⅛", $45.00.

Ever-Ready,
Blade Bank, 1
x 1⅞ x 2¾",
$25.00.

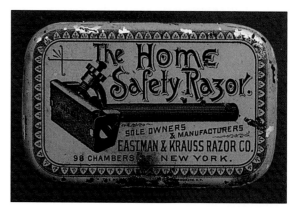

Home, Safety Razor, $2.00, 1⅞ x 3 x 1⅝", $275.00.

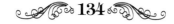

Kropp, Razor Strop Paste, ¾ x 1", $20.00.

Laurel Vest Pocket, Safety Razor, ½ x 1½ x 2", $25.00.

Lakeside, Strop Dressing, ⅝ x 1½", $20.00.

Magna, Razor Blade Case, ¼ x 1⅛ x 2⅛", $90.00.

Langlois, Shaving Cream, 1⅜ x 2¼ x 2½", $35.00.

Raleigh's sample, Shaving Cream, ¼ x 1⅛", $6.00.

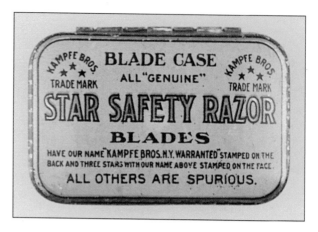

Razorkeen, Sharpens Razors, $.10, ¼ x 1¼", $25.00.

Star, Safety Razor Blades, ¼ x 1⅛ x 1¾ ", $60.00.

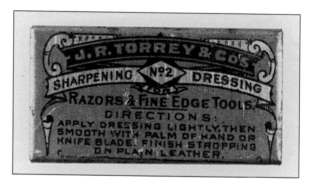

Sharp-O No. 3, Strop Dressing, $.10, ½ x 1¼ ", $25.00.

Torrey, J.R., Sharpening Dressing, ⅞ x 1¾ x ½, $60.00.

Star, Safety Razor, 1¼ x 2⅛ ", $185.00.

Torrey's, Strop Dressing, ½ x 1½", $40.00.

Spices

Advance, Ground Pepper, 4½ x 3 x 1½", $25.00+.

Arbuckles', Cream Tartar, 1¼ x 2¾", $30.00+.

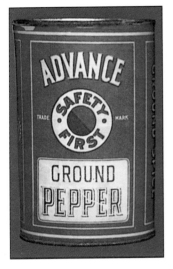

Aircraft Brand, Cayenne Pepper, 3½ x 2¼ x 1¼", $35.00+.

Aristo Brand, Whole Cloves, 3½ x 2⅜ x 1¼", $30.00+.

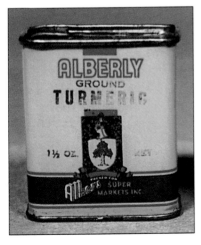

Alberly, Turmeric, 2½ x 2¼ x 1¼", American Can 62-A", $15.00+.

Arsenal Brand, Spices, 3¼ x 2¼ x 1½", $45.00+.

Aunt Jane's, Red Pepper, 1½ x 2¼ x 3¼", $45.00+.

Baker's, Mustard, $.10, 4 x 2¼ x 1¾", $40.00+.

Baby Edith, Allspice, 3¾ x 2 x 1⅛", $20.00+.

Baby Stuart, Nutmegs, 3¼ x 2¼ x 1⅜", $70.00+.

Banner Boy Brand, All-spice, 3¾ x 2¼ x 1¼", Continental, $45.00+.

Baker's, Cinnamon, 4 x 2¼ x 1¾", $45.00+.

Batavia Brand, Ginger, 4½ x 1¾ x 1¼", $30.00+.

Bacon, Stickney & Co.'s, All-spice, 3 x 2¼ x 1¼", $25.00.

Ben-Hur, Curry Powder, 1¼ x 2¼ x 3¼", $20.00.

Bacon, Stickney, Sage, 2¾ x 2¼ x 1¼", CANCO, $20.00+.

Bennett Simpson & Co., Nutmeg, 1¾ x 2½ x 4", $45.00+.

"Best Ever," Sage, 3¼ x 2¼ x 1¼", Columbia Can Co, $50.00+.

Bells, Poultry Season-ing, ½ x 1⅜ x 2½", $70.00.

Best Value Sales, Cloves, 3½ x 2¼ x 1¼", $35.00+.

Big Horn, Ground Sage, 1¼ x 2⅜ x 3", $50.00.

Bluebird Brand, Ground Mustard, 3¼ x 2¼ x 1¼", $25.00+.

Black Hills Brand, Paprika, 3½ x 2¼ x 1¼", $25.00+.

Brimfull Brand, Mustard, 3⅞ x 2⅜ x 1", Am. Can Co. 62, $15.00+.

Blue Ribbon Brand, Black Pepper, 3 x 2¼ x 1¼", $25.00+.

Blue Seal Brand, Cloves, 2½ x 2¼ x 1½", Am. Can Co. 43-A, $20.00+.

Burma, Cinnamon, 3 x 2¼ x 1", $30.00+.

Busch Mills, Nutmeg, 4 x 2½ x 1¾", Am. Can Co. 10-A, $22.00+.

Busy Biddy, Mustard, 3¾ x 2¼ x 1¼", $75.00+.

Busy Biddy, Turmeric, 1¼ x 2¼ x 3", $75.00+.

Buster Brown, Allspice, 1⅜ x 1⅜ x 2⅝", $45.00+.

Canova Brand, Ginger, 3½ x 2¼ x 1¼", American Can 70-A, 40.00+.

Buster Brown, Paprika, 2¾ x 2¼ x 1¼", $60.00+.

Century, Spices, 3½ x 2¼ x 1¼", $25.00+.

Clover Farm, Mace, 3 x 2¼ x 1¼", Continental, $22.00+.

Crown Brand, Allspice, 3½ x 2 x 1", $25.00+.

Colburn, Paprika, 1⅝ x 2½", $25.00+.

CW, Ground Mustard, 3⅝ x 2⅜ x 1⅛", $15.00.

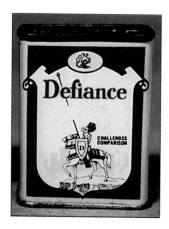

Defiance, Spice, 3 x 2¼ x 1¼", $30.00+.

Colonial Brand, Allspice, 3¾ x 2¼ x 1¼", $45.00.

Dove, Pumpkin Pie Spice, 2 x 2¼ x 1¼", $22.00+.

Dove Brand, Allspice, 1⅜ x 1¾ x 3½", $40.00+.

Dove Brand, Turmeric, 3⅛ x 2¼ x 1¼", $40.00+.

Dove Brand, All-spice, 2½ x 2 x 1¼", $35.00+.

Dove Brand, Whole Cinnamon, 2 x 4", $60.00+.

Dr. Koch's, Allspice, 3¼ x 2¼ x 1⅜", American Can 82-A, $55.00+.

Dove Brand, Paprika, 2 x 4", $60.00+.

DuMont, Red Pepper, 3½ x 2¼ x 1¼", $15.00+.

Durkee's, Paprika, 2 x 3¾", $20.00+.

Empress Brand, Nutmeg, 3¼ x 2¼ x 1¼", American Can 2-L-O, $55.00+.

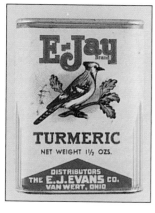

E-Jay, Turmeric, 1¼ x 2¼ x 2⅞", $20.00.

Empress Brand, Paprika, 3¼ x 2¼ x 1", $35.00+.

Edjol, Cloves, 4½ x 2½ x 1½", $25.00+.

Ellis, Chile Powder, 2¾ x 2¼ x 1¼", $25.00+.

Evans, Black Pepper, 3¼ x 2¼ x 1¼", Columbia Can, 30.00+.

Fairmont Brand, Turmeric, 3¼ x 2¼ x 1¼", $40.00+.

Fern, Red Pepper, 3 x 2¼ x 1¼", $35.00+.

Fairway Brand, Allspice, 3¼ x 2¼ x 1½", $75.00+.

Festal Hall, Whole Cinnamon, 2 x 3¾", $25.00+.

Fairway Brand, Red Pepper, 2½ x 1¾ x 1¼", $30.00.

Favorite Brand, Cream of Tartar, 1 x 2¼ x 4", $20.00+.

Festival Brand, White Pepper, 3½ x 2¼ x 1¼", $30.00.

Fiesta Brand, Mustard, 3¾ x 2¼ x 1¼", $35.00+.

Finer Foods, Cinnamon, 4¼ x 2½ x 1½", $15.00+.

Fisher's, Ground Ginger, 4¾ x 2¼ x 1¼", American Can 53-A, $35.00+.

Florence Nightingale, Paprika, 1¾ x 3½", Am. Can Co. 70-A, $15.00+.

Folger's, Curry Powder, 3¼ x 2¼ x 1¼", $30.00+.

Folger's, Ginger, 1¼ x 2¼ x 3¼", $35.00+.

Fort Hamilton, Allspice, 3 x 2¼ x 1¼", $55.00+.

French's, Ketchup Spice,
1½ x 2¼ x 3¼", $45.00+.

Gold Bond, Red Pepper,
3½ x 2¼ x 1¼", $25.00+.

French's, Nutmeg, 1¾ x
4", Liberty Can, $35.00+.

Gold Medal Brand,
Cloves, 3 x 2¼ x 1¼",
Continental, $20.00+.

Gillett's, Cloves, 2¾ x 2¼ x
1¼", $25.00+.

Gillett's, Paprika, 1¾ x 3¾",
$35.00+.

Golden Drip, Red
Pepper, 3¾ x 2¼ x
1¼", $30.00+.

Golden Sheaf, Ginger, 3 x 2¼ x 1¼", $35.00+.

Great American, Pepper, 1⅞ x 3¼", American Can 14-A, $25.00+.

Golden Sun, Cloves, 1¼ x 2¼ x 3", $20.00.

Grisdale Brand, White Pepper, 4 x 2½ x 1", American Can 10-A, $30.00+.

H & H Brand, Red Pepper, 3½ x 2¼ x 1¼", Federal Tin Co., $30.00+.

Golden West, Sage, 3¼ x 2¼ x 1¼", American Can 92-A, $40.00+.

Happy Hour Brand, Pickling Spice, 2 x 4", $30.00+.

Harley Brand, Pepper, 2½ x 2½ x 4⅞", Am. Can 70-A, $25.00+.

Hoyt's, Ground Cinnamon, 1 x 2¼ x 4⅛", $22.00.

Hillman's, Allspice, 1⅜ x 2⅜ x 3⅝", $45.00+.

Home Brand, Red Pepper, 3 x 2¼ x 1¼", $35.00+.

Hoyt's, Poultry Seasoning, 2 x 3½", $25.00+.

Hostess, Mustard, 4⅛ x 2¼ x 1¼", American Can 62, $70.00+.

Hudson Brand, Cloves, 3 x 1¾ x 1¼", $35.00+.

IGA Brand, Allspice, 3¼ x 2¼ x 1¼", $25.00+.

Jewel Tea Co., Allspice, 2¼ x 2¼ x 2¾", CANCO, $25.00+.

Indian Mills, Ginger, 2 x 3¾", $80.00+.

Iris, Cloves, 2¼ x 2¼ x 1¼", Am. Can Co. 74-A, $15.00+.

Jewel Tea Co., Black Pepper, 2¼ x 2¼ x 2¾", CANCO, $30.00+.

Jack Sprat, Celery Salt, 3 x 2¼ x 1¼", $25.00+.

Jewel Tea Co., Cinnamon, 2¼ x 2¼ x 2¾", CANCO, $30.00+.

Jo Beth Co. Brand, Rubbed Sage, 2 x 4", $50.00+.

King Crop Brand, Allspice, 3¾ x 2¼ x 1¼", American Can 62, $55.00+.

Juno Brand, Allspice, 3¼ x 2¼ x 1¼", $40.00+.

Knickerbocker, Ginger, 3⅜ x 2⅜ x 1⅜", American Can 10-A, $35.00+.

Ko-we-ba Brand, Caraway Seed, 3½ x 2¼ x 1¼", American Can 70-A, $30.00+.

King, Cinnamon, 4¼ x 2½ x 1¾", $45.00+.

Ko-we-ba Brand, Mustard, 3½ x 2¼ x 1¼", American Can 70-A, $30.00+.

Lake View, Whole Allspice, 2 x 3⅞", $25.00+.

Lee & Cady, Turmeric, 3 x 2½ x 1¼", $30.00+.

Lake View, Whole Cinnamon, 2 x 3¾", $25.00+.

Lehn & Fink's, Black Pepper, 4 x 2½ x 1¼", $45.00+.

Lily, Black Pepper, 4 x 2¾ x 1¾", $30.00+.

Lecroy's, Poultry Seasoning, 3 x 2¼ x 1¼", American Can 27-A, $15.00+.

Lily, Mace, 2¾ x 2 x 1", $25.00+.

Little Elf Brand, White Pepper, 3½ x 2¼ x 1¼", $35.00+.

Manhattan, Allspice, 3¼ x 2¼ x 1¼", Continental, $30.00+.

Luxurie, Rubbed Sage, 3¾ x 2¼ x 1¼", Am. Can Co. 62, $25.00+.

Manischewitz, Ginger, 3¼ x 2 x 1", Continental Can Co., $15.00+.

Malco, Pickling Spice, 2 x 3¾", $25.00+.

Maltese Cross, Allspice, 3 x 2¼ x 1¼", $50.00+.

Manischewitz's, White Pepper, 3½ x 2 x 1", $35.00+.

McConnon, Pepper, 4½ x 2½ x 1½", Am. Can, $20.00+.

Millar's, Poultry Seasoning, 3¼ x 2¼ x 1¼", $55.00+.

McCormick's Bee Brand, Turmeric, 3½ x 2¼ x 1¼", $35.00+.

Mohican, Red Pepper, 3¾ x 2¼ x 1¼", Am. Can Co. 10-A, $40.00+.

Monday's, Allspice, 4½ x 2¼ x 1½", $22.00+.

Millar's, Chili Powder, 3¼ x 2¼ x 1¾", $30.00+.

Monitor Brand, Mace, 2⅞ x 2½", $35.00+.

Monsoon, Allspice, 1¼ x 2¼ x 3⅜", Am. Can Co. 70-A, $25.00.

Newton's, Allspice, 3¼ x 2¼ x 1½", American Can 70-A, $35.00+.

Nabob, Mint, 3¼ x 2¼ x 1", Am. Can Co. 2LA, $45.00+.

None-Such, Paprika, 1⅝ x 3⅝", $30.00+.

Nun-Better, Cayenne Pepper, 3⅛ x 2¼ x 1⅜", $45.00+.

Nebia, Turmeric, 3½ x 2¼ x 1¼", $40.00+.

Oak Hill, Nutmeg, 1½ x 4½", Am. Can Co., $60.00+.

Okade, Turmeric, 1⅛ x 2⅛ x 3⅛", $35.00+.

Park Newport, Allspice, 1¾ x 4", Federal Can Co., $45.00+.

Opal, Red Pepper, 3¼ x 2¼ x 1¼", $25.00+.

Perfect, Allspice, 3¼ x 2¼ x 1¼", Columbia Can, $55.00+.

Peyton Palmer, Red Pepper, 2½ x 2¼ x 1¼", $15.00+.

Paradise Brand, Pepper, 3¼ x 2¼ x 1¼", $25.00+.

Pioneer, Red Pepper, 3¾ x 2½ x 1¾", $22.00+.

Pitkin's Old Home, Paprika, 3¾ x 2⅛ x 1¼", $30.00+.

Printz & French, Cream Tartar, 1¼ x 3⅝", $20.00.

Premier, Allspice, 2¾ x 2¼ x 1¼", $18.00+.

Prize Medal, Ginger, 4¼ x 2¼ x 1¼", $18.00+.

Price's Spices, Ginger, 3¾ x 2 x 1¼", American Can 70-A, $45.00+.

Pure Quill, Curry Powder, 3½ x 2¼ x 1¼", Missouri Can Co., $45.00+.

Red & White, Allspice, 3¾ x 2¼ x 1¼", American Can 62, $15.00+.

Red Ribbon, Ginger, 3¾ x 2¼ x 1¼", Am. Can Co. 62, $25.00+.

Red Arrow, Mustard, 5⅛ x 2⅜ x 1⅜", $20.00+.

Red Star, Mace, 3⅝ x 2⅜ x 1⅛", $25.00+.

Regoes, Rubbed Sage, 3½ x 4¼", Continental Can, $35.00+.

Red Monogram, Ginger, 3¼ x 2¼ x 1¼", $25.00+.

ReJoyce, Black Pepper, 5¼ x 2¼ x 1¼", Am. Can Co. 62, $75.00+.

Ries & Porter, Red Pepper, 3¼ x 2¼ x 1¼", $25.00+.

Rosemary, White Pepper, 3⅜ x 2⅜ x 1¼", $15.00+.

Rob-Roy, Mace, 3¼ x 2¼ x 1¼", $35.00+.

Rosemary Brand, Sage, 3 x 2¼ x 1¼", Continental Can Co., $50.00+.

Roosa & Ratliff, Red Pepper, 3 x 2⅛ x 1⅛", $20.00+.

Rose Bud, Ginger, 1⅛ x 2¼ x 3⅝", $20.00+.

Roosevelt Brand, Ginger, 3¾ x 2¼ x 1¼", Continental Can Co., $60.00+.

Royal Blue, Turmeric, 3 x 2¼ x 1¼", Continental, $20.00+.

S & F, Ginger, 3¼ x 2¼ x 1¼", $15.00+.

Royal King, Red Pepper, 1½ x 2¼ x 3¼", $65.00+.

Safe Owl, Mace, 3 x 1⅞ x 1", $30.00+.

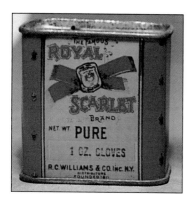

Royal Scarlet, Cloves, 2⅛ x 2⅛ x 1¼", $20.00+.

Royal Tiger, Cinnamon, 1¾ x 2½ x 3¾", $70.00+.

Sante Fe Brand, Red Pepper, 3¼ x 2¼ x 1¼", $40.00+.

Savoy, Cloves, 4 x 2¼ x 1¼", Continental, 30.00+.

Security Brand, Cloves, 3¾ x 2¼ x 1¼", Continental, $50.00+.

Savoy, Sage, 3½ x 2¼ x 1¼", Am. Can Co. 70-A, 40.00+.

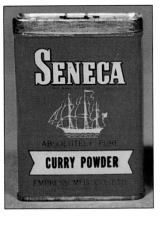

Seneca, Curry Powder, 3¼ x 2¼ x ¾", Am. Can Co. 2-L, $35.00+.

Shores, Black Pepper, 1¼ x 2⅛ x 3¼", American 82A, $65.00.

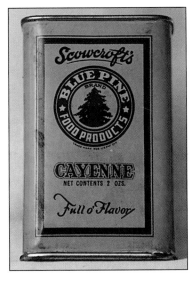

Scowcroft's, Cayenne, 3½ x 2¼ x 1¼", $30.00+.

Shores, Jamaica Ginger, 2 x 3 x 4¾", American Can Co. 82-A, $60.00.

Shurfire Brand, Nutmeg, 3¼ x 2¼ x 1¼", Continental, $15.00+.

Smith, James P., Co., Curry Powder, 1¾ x 1⅜ x 4", American Can 15-A, $30.00+.

Silver Sea, Whole Allspice, 2 x 4", $60.00+.

Stuart's Handy, Ginger, 3¾ x 2¾ x 1¼", Am. Can Co. 62, $60.00+.

Slades', Oxford Mustard, 3¾ x 2¼ x 1", Am. Can Co. 2-L, $20.00+.

Slade's, Turmeric, 1¼ x 1¾ x 2¾", $25.00.

Sweet Life, Cloves, 5¼ x 2¼ x 1¼", Owens Illinois Can, $45.00+.

Sweetheart, Allspice, 1¼ x 2¼ x 3¼", Continental Can, $25.00+.

Three Crow, Allspice, 3 x 2¼ x 1", $40.00+.

Symns, Red Pepper, 3¼ x 2¼ x 1¼", $35.00+.

Three Crow, Ginger, 1 x 1⅜ x 3⅜", $30.00.

Tamco, Allspice, 1⅛ x 2¼ x 1¼", Am. Can Co. 62, $45.00+.

Tech, Turmeric, 3½ x 2¼ x 1¼", $15.00+.

Three Crow Brand, Mustard, 4⅝ x 3¼ x 2⅛", Federal Tin Co., $70.00+.

Time O'Day, Sage, 3 x 2¼ x 1¼", $18.00+.

Van Curler, Ginger, 3½ x 2¼ x 1¼", $40.00+.

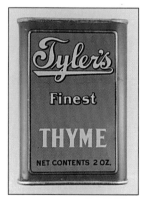

Turkey Red, Red Pepper, 3 x 2⅛ x 1¼", $45.00+.

Van Roy, Mustard, 5¼ x 2⅜ x 1⅜", $25.00+.

Tyler's, Thyme, 1¼ x 2¼ x 3¼", $15.00.

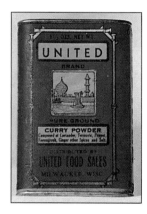

United, Curry Powder, 3¼ x 2¼ x 1¼", $40.00+.

Walker's, Chile Powder, 1½ x 3⅝", $15.00.

Weikel's, Allspice, 3¾ x 2⅜ x 1⅝", $35.00+.

White Goose Brand, Cinnamon, 3¼ x 2¼ x 1½", $30.00+.

Wellman, Allspice, 1¼ x 2¼ x 3¼", $25.00.

White Swan, Cinnamon, 2¾ x 2¼ x 1¼", CANCO, $35.00+.

West Point, Cloves, 3 x 2 x 1¼", Continental Can Co., $40.00+.

Widlar's, Turmeric, 3⅝ x 2¼ x 1", $25.00+.

White Bear Brand, Nutmeg, 3¼ x 1¾ x 1½", $40.00+.

Wigwam, Ginger, 2½ x 2¼ x 1¼", $60.00+.

Willson's Monarch, Cloves, 3¾ x 2¼ x 1⅜", $70.00+.

Wixon Brand, Ginger, 3⅞ x 2½ x 1⅞", $25.00+.

Willson's Monarch, Nutmeg, 3¾ x 2¼ x 1⅜", $70.00+.

Yerkes, Pure Nutmeg, 1¼ x 2¼ x 3¼", $25.00+.

Zanol, Allspice, 4 x 2¼ x 1¼", $40.00+.

Wixom Spice Co., Paprika, 2 x 4¼", CANCO, $35.00+.

Zanol, Paprika, 1¾ x 3¼, Metal Package, $35.00+.

Boro Salicine, Julep Mints, ½ x 1 x 2¾", $25.00.

Frozen Mints, Chewing Gum, 1⅜ x 2½ x 4", $115.00.

Brandle & Smith, Butter Scotch Waffles, $.10, 1⅛ x 2¼ x 3¾", $25.00.

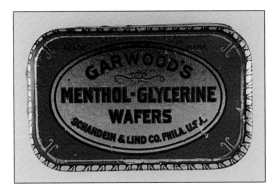

Garwood's, Menthol Glycerine Wafers, ¾ x 1¾ x 3", $18.00.

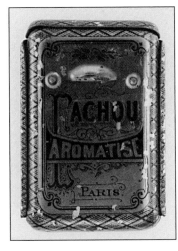

Cachou, Aromatise, ⅜ x 1⅛ x 1¾, Somers Brothers, $45.00.

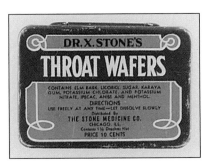

Dr. X. Stone's, Throat Wafers, $.10, ¼ x 1½ x 1¾'", $15.00.

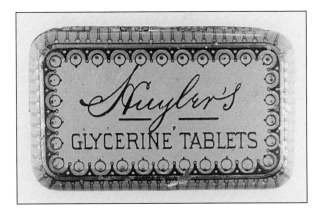

Huyler's, Glycerine Tablets, ⅜ x 2⅛", $40.00.

Huyler's, Glycerine Tablets, ⅞ x 1¾ x 3", Ginna, $40.00.

Mulford, Aromatics, ¾ x ¾ x 2¾", $40.00.

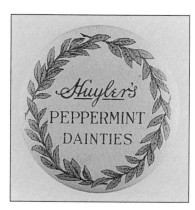

Huyler's, Peppermint Dainties, ½ x 1⅞", Am. Can Co. 10-A, $15.00.

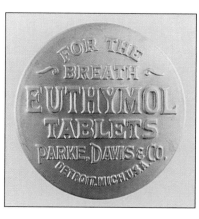

Parke, Davis & Co., Euthymol Tablets, ½ x 2¼", $15.00.

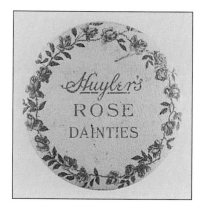

Huyler's, Rose Dainties, ½ x 1⅞", Am. Can Co. 13-A, $30.00.

Radiator, Menthol Licorice, ½ x 1¼ x 1¾", $20.00.

Imps, Licorice & Menthol, ½ x 1½ x 2⅛", $20.00.

U-All-No, Campus Mints, 1½ x 1½ x 2", $30.00.

Fixaco, Cough Drops, $.10, ¼ x 1¼ x 1¾", $15.00*.

After the Ball, Throat Lozenges, ¾ x 1¼ x 2½", Somers Brothers, $75.00.

Campho-Menthol sample, Lozenges, ¼ x 1¼", $30.00.

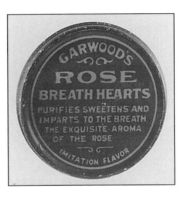

Garwood's, Rose Breath Hearts, ½ x 1½", $20.00.

Evans's, Menthol & Glycerine Lozenges, ⅞ x 1¾ x 2¾", American Stopper, $12.00+.

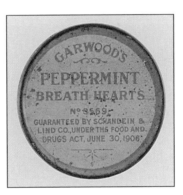

Garwood's, Peppermint Breath Hearts, ½ x 1⅝", $25.00.

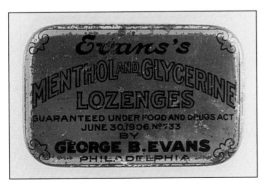

Evans's, George B., Menthol & Glycerine Lozenges, ¾ x 1¾ x 2¾", Metal Package, $20.00+.

Gunther's, Cough Drops, ½ x 2¼ x 3½", $95.00.

Klein's Japanese, Cough Drops, $.15, ⅞ x 3 x 3",
$40.00.

Nigroids, Throat and Voice Lozenges, ¼ x 1¼ x 1¾",
$20.00.

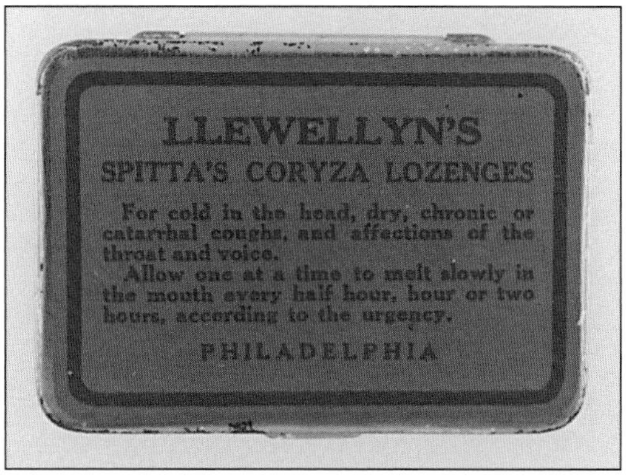

Llewellyn's, Spitta's Coryza Lozenges, ⅜ x 1½ x 2¼",
$10.00.

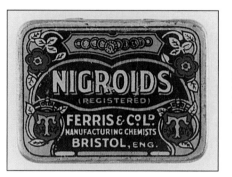

Nigroids, Throat
Lozenges, ⅜ x 1¼
x 1¾", $15.00.

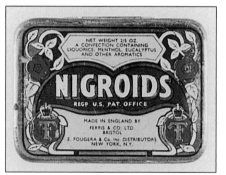

Nigroids, Throat
Lozenges, ⅜ x 1¼
x 1¾", $18.00.

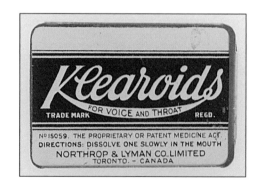

Moore's, Throat & Lung Lozenges, ½ x 2 x 3⅛",
Somers, $75.00.

Northrop & Lyman, Klearoids Throat Lozenges, ⅜ x
1½ x 2½", $15.00.

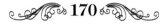

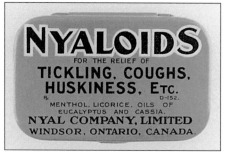

Nyal, Nyaloids Cough, ⅜ x 1½ x 2⅞", $15.00.

Sonorets, Familex Licorice, $.25, ⅜ x 1½ x 2½", $12.00.

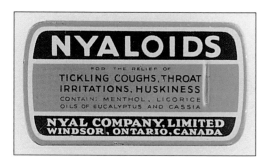

Nyal, Nyaloids Throat, ⅜ x 1½ x 2½", $15.00.

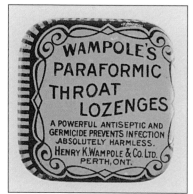

"Trix," Breath Perfume, $.10, ⅜ x 1⅛", $12.00.

Opera Stars, Throat Lozenges, $.10, ¼ x 1¾ x 2¾", $75.00.

Wampole's, Paraformic Throat Lozenges, ⅜ x 1¼ x 1¼", $15.00.

Orlis, Throat Lozenges, ½ x 2½ x 3¼", $5.00.

Welco, Troches, ½ x 2 x 3⅛", American Stopper, $45.00.

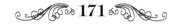

Buy-Roz, Gum, ¾ x 1½"
$25.00.

Huyler's, Pepsin Gum, ½ x 1⅛ x 2¼", $25.00.

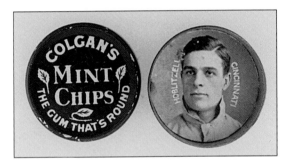

Colgan's, Mint Chips, with baseball card, ⅝ x 1½",
$60.00.

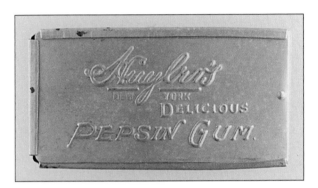

Huyler's N.Y., Pepsin Gum, ½ x 1 x 2¼", $25.00.

Colgan's, Violet Chips Gum, ¾ x 1½", $35.00.

Hyman, Gum, 1 x 2¼", Germany, $80.00.

Huyler's, Gum Imperials, ½ x 2⅛", $15.00.

Kenny, C.D., heart shaped, ⅝ x 1½ x 1¾", $75.00.

Luken's Peggy, Gum Holder, 1¼", $110.00.

Zig Zag, Gum, 1 x 2½", $130.00.

Schieffelin, Violet Gum, ⅜ x 1½ x 2⅜", $30.00.

Zig Zag, Gum, 1 x 2⅜", $140.00.

Zeno Forbidden Fruit, Peppermint Gum, ⅝ x 1 x 3⅛", $225.00.

Zig Zag, Gum, ¾ x 1⅝", $60.00.

Zig Zag, Gum, 1 x 2⅝", $120.00.

Zig Zag, Gum, ⅞ x 2⅜", $120.00.

Typewriter & Machine Ribbons

Aero Brand, Typewriter Ribbon, ¾ x 2½", $18.00.

American, Storms, H. M., Typewriter Ribbon, ¾ x 2¼ x 2¼", $90.00.

American, Storms, H. M., Typewriter Ribbon, 1¾ x 1⅝ x 2", Decorated Metal, $95.00.

Allied Flagship, Typewriter Ribbon, ¾ x 2½", $12.00.

Anchor Brand, Typewriter Ribbon, 1¾ x 1¾ x 1⅞", $55.00.

American, Storms, H. M., Typewriter Ribbon, ¾ x 2½ x 2½", $95.00.

Arrow Brand, Typewriter Ribbon, ¾ x 2½ x 2½", Decorated Metal, $20.00.

Aux Cayes, Typewriter Ribbon, ¾ x 2⅛ x 2⅛", Am. Can Co. 11-A, $15.00.

Bell, Typewriter Ribbon, ¾ x 2½", $12.00.

Beaver Economo, Typewriter Ribbon, ¾ x 2½ x 2½", $30.00.

Ben Franklin, Typewriter Ribbon, ¾ x 2½", $25.00.

Beaver Yankee, Typewriter Ribbon, ¾ x 2½", $45.00.

Beck Duplicator, Duplicating Ribbon, ¾ x 2½ x 2½", $15.00.

Bucki Supreme, Typewriter Ribbon, ⅞ x 2½", $15.00.

Bucki Supreme, Typewriter Ribbon, ⅞ x 2½ x 2½", $12.00.

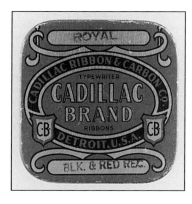

Cadillac, Typewriter Ribbon, ¾ x 2½ x 2½", $18.00.

Carnation, Typewriter Ribbon, 1⅝ x 1⅝ x 1⅞", $55.00.

Bundy, Typewriter Ribbon, ⅝ x 2¼", $18.00.

Carter's Cavalier, Typewriter Ribbon, ⅞ x 2¼ x 2¼", $15.00.

Burroughs, Adding Machine Ribbon, 1⅝ x 1⅝ x 2⅜", $20.00.

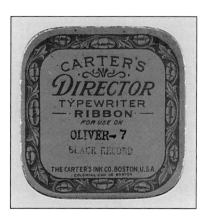

Carter's Director, Typewriter Ribbon, ¾ x 2¼ x 2¼, Colonial Can, Boston, $18.00.

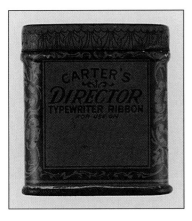

Carter's Director, Typewriter Ribbon, 1¾ x 1¾ x 1⅞, Colonial Can, Boston, $45.00.

Cenco, Typewriter Ribbon, ¾ x 2½ x 2½", $12.00.

Carter's Ideal, Typewriter Ribbon, ¾ x 2½", $6.00.

Clary, Adding Machine Ribbon, ¾ x 1¾ x 1¾", $12.00.

Carter's Ideal, Typewriter Ribbon, 1¾ x 1¾ x 2", Colonial Can, $45.00.

Carter's Nylon, Typewriter Ribbon, ¾ x 2¼", $12.00.

Codo Stenocraft, Typewriter Ribbon, ¾ x 2½ x 2½", $15.00.

Conquest, Typewriter Ribbon, ¾ x 2½ x 2½", $8.00.

Columbia, Typewriter Ribbon, ⅝ x 2¼", $12.00.

Cook Old Reliable, Typewriter Ribbon, ¾ x 2½ x 2½", $20.00.

Columbia Carbon, Duplicating Ribbon, ⅞ x 2½ x 2½", $18.00.

Copy-Right Brand, Typewriter Ribbon, ⅞ x 2¼ x 2¼", $45.00.

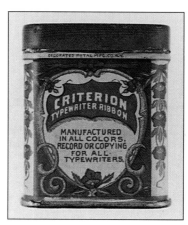

Criterion McDonovan, Typewriter Ribbon, 1⅝ x 1⅝ x 2", Decorated Metal, $55.00.

Columbia Economique, Typewriter Ribbon, ⅞ x 2½", $8.00.

Crowfoot, Typewriter Ribbon, ⅞ x 2¼ x 2¼", $20.00.

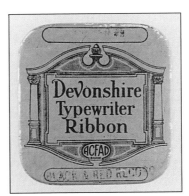

Devonshire, Typewriter Ribbon, ¾ x 2½ x 2½", $20.00.

Crown, Typewriter Ribbon, ¾ x 2½", $12.00*.

Ditto, Typewriter Ribbon, ⅞ x 2½", $8.00.

De-Fi, Typewriter Ribbon, 1 x 2½ x 2½", $18.00.

Ditto, Typewriter Ribbon, ¾ x 2½ x 2½", $8.00.

Derwood, Typewriter Ribbon, ⅞ x 2½", $6.00.

Du-Ra-Bul, Typewriter Ribbon, 1⅝ x 2⅛ x 1¾", $55.00.

Eagle Brand, Typewriter Ribbon, $1.00, ¾ x 2½ x 2½", Decorated Metal, $20.00.

Fisher, Typewriter Ribbon, ¾ x 2½ x 2½", Decorated Metal, $15.00.

Elk Brand, Typewriter Ribbon, $1.00, ¾ x 2¼", Clark Mfg., Rockford, Ill., $20.00.

Flexo, Typewriter Ribbon, ¾ x 2¼", $12.00.

Faultless, Typewriter Ribbon, 1¾ x 1¾ x 2", Mersereau, $45.00.

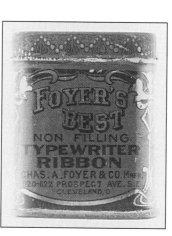

Foyer's Best, Typewriter Ribbon, 1⅝ x 1⅝ x 2", $55.00.

Fine Service Brand, Typewriter Ribbon, ⅞ x 2½", $10.00.

Frederick, Typewriter Ribbon, ¾ x 2½ x 2½", $20.00.

Frye Mfg., Typewriter Ribbon, ¾ x 2½", $18.00.

Gold Medal Brand, Typewriter Ribbon, 1⅝ x 1⅝ x 2", $45.00.

Gamulco, Typewriter Ribbon, 1¾ x 1¾ x 2", $45.00.

Grand Prize Brand, Typewriter Ribbon, ¾ x 2½ x 2½", Decorated Metal, $20.00.

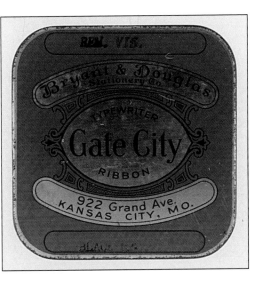

Gate City, Typewriter Ribbon, ¾ x 2½ x 2½", $20.00.

Hazel-Atlas Glass, Typewriter Ribbon, ¾ x 2½", $15.00.

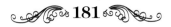

Herald Square, Typewriter Ribbon, ¾ x 2½ x 2½",
$12.00.

ICR, Typewriter Ribbon, ⅞ x 2½", $15.00.

Hess Hawkins, Typewriter Ribbon, ¾ x 2½ x 2½",
Decorated Metal, $18.00.

Imperial, Typewriter Ribbon, 1⅝ x 1⅝ x 1⅞",
Mersereau, $60.00.

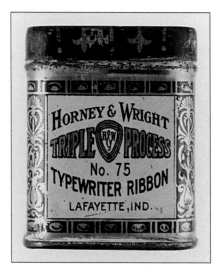

Horney & Wright, Triple Process Typewriter Ribbon,
1⅝ x 1⅝ x 2", Am. Can Co. 11-A, $65.00.

International Committee, Typewriter Ribbon, ¾ x 2½
x 2½", Decorated Metal, $18.00.

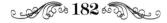

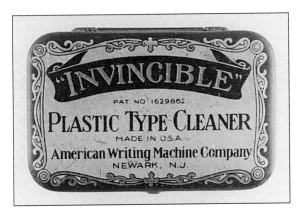

Klean-Write, Typewriter Ribbon, 1 x 2½", $18.00.

Invincible, Plastic Type Cleaner, ¾ x 1½ x 2½", $15.00.

Kolok, Typewriter Ribbon, ⅞ x 2½", $18.00.

Kreko, Typewriter Ribbon, ¾ x 2½", $18.00.

KaBell Brand, Typewriter Ribbon, ¾ x 2½", $15.00.

Leete, Robert S., Typewriter Ribbon, ¾ x 2½ x 2½", $15.00.

Kee-Lox, Typewriter Ribbon, 1⅝ x 1⅝ x 1½", Am. Can 11-A, $25.00.

Liberty Brand, Typewriter Ribbon, 1¾ x 1¾ x 2", Decorated Metal, $60.00.

Miller Line, Typewriter Ribbon, 1⅝ x 1⅝ x 2¼", $45.00.

Lion Brand E F, Typewriter Ribbon, 1¾ x 1½", $80.00.

Little's Gold Seal, Typewriter Ribbon, ¾ x 2½ x 2½", Decorated Metal, $15.00.

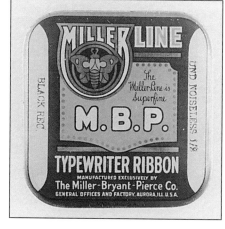

Miller Line M.B.P., Typewriter Ribbon, ¾ x 2½ x 2½", $10.00.

McGregor, Typewriter Ribbon, ⅞ x 2½", $12.00.

Miller Line M.B.P., Typewriter Ribbon, ¾ x 2½ x 2½", $8.00.

Monarch, Typewriter Ribbon, ¾ x 2¼ x 2¼",
Am. Can 11-A, $15.00.

Old Dutch Line, Typewriter Ribbon, ¾ x 2½ x 2½",
Decorated Metal, $25.00.

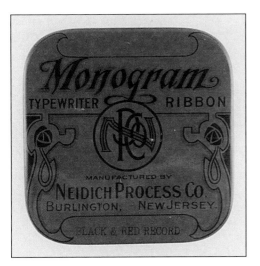

Old English, Typewriter Ribbon, ¾ x 2½", $15.00.

Monogram, Typewriter Ribbon, ¾ x 2½ x 2½",
$20.00.

Natural Bridge, Typewriter Ribbon, ¾ x 2½ x 2½",
Decorated Metal, $35.00.

Old Town, Typewriter Ribbon, 1¾ x 2½", $15.00.

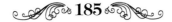

Oliver, Typewriter Ribbon, ¾ x 2¼ x 2¼", $20.00.

Pigeon Brand, Typewriter Ribbon, ¾ x 1⅝", $12.00.

Oliver, Typewriter Ribbon, ¾ x 2¼ x 2¼", $12.00.

Pigeon Brand, Typewriter Ribbon, ¾ x 2 x 2", $15.00.

Paragon, Typewriter Ribbon, 1¾ x 1¾ x 2", Am. Can 10-A, $50.00.

Pilot, Typewriter Ribbon, ¾ x 2½", $18.00.

Paramount, Typewriter Ribbon, ¾ x 2½", $15.00.

"Pinnacle," Typewriter Ribbon, 1⅝ x 1⅝ x 2", Decorated Metal, $55.00.

Pioneer Brand, Typewriter Ribbon, ¾ x 2¼ x 2¼", $18.00.

Queen, Typewriter Ribbon, ¾ x 2½", $15.00.

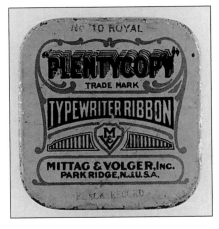

"PlentyCopy," Typewriter Ribbon, ¾ x 2½ x 2½", $8.00.

Premier Brand, Typewriter Ribbon, ¾ x 2¼ x 2¼", Hudson Co., $30.00.

Queen Brand, Typewriter Ribbon, ¾ x 2½ x 2½", $18.00.

Protype, Phillip's, Typewriter Ribbon, ¾ x 2½ x 2½", $15.00.

Rail Road 3R, Typewriter Ribbon, 1¾ x 1¾ x 2", $65.00.

Regal, Typewriter Ribbon, ¾ x 2⅝ x 2⅝", $20.00.

Schaum-Vaugham Corp., Typewriter Ribbon, ¾ x 2½ x 2½", Decorated Metal, $15.00.

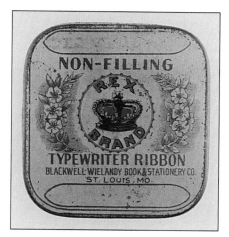

Rex Brand, Typewriter Ribbon, ¾ x 2¼ x 2¼", $20.00.

Scout Brand, Typewriter Ribbon, ⅞ x 2½", $10.00.

Royal, Typewriter Ribbon, ¾ x 2½ x 2½", Decorated Metal, $20.00.

Siltex Egyptian, Typewriter Ribbon, ¾ x 2½ x 2½", $15.00.

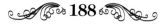

Solrite, Typewriter Ribbon, ¾ x 2½ x 2½", $18.00.

Stock, Typewriter Ribbon, ⅞ x 2½", $8.00.

Stormtex, Typewriter Ribbon, ¾ x 2½ x 2½", $15.00.

Stafford's Superfine, Typewriter Ribbon, ¾ x 2½ x 2½", $18.00.

Sundstrand, Adding Machine Ribbon, ¾ x 1⅝", $25.00.

"Superior," Typewriter Ribbon, ⅞ x 2½", $10.00.

Stamco, Typewriter Ribbon, ¾ x 2½ x 2½", $12.00.

Sure-Rite, Typewriter Ribbon, ⅞ x 2½", $15.00.

Typal, Typewriter Ribbon, ¾ x 2½ x 2½", Decorated Metal, $15.00.

Swallow Brand, Typewriter Ribbon, ¾ x 2¼ x 2¼", $25.00.

Ultimo, Typewriter Ribbon, ¾ x 2½ x 2½", $25.00.

"Tagger," Typewriter Ribbon, ¾ x 2¼ x 2¼", $10.00.

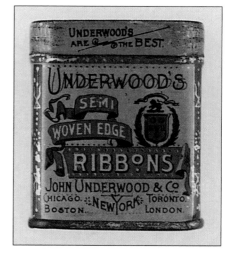

Underwood's, Typewriter Ribbon, 1⅝ x 1⅝ x 1⅞", Mersereau Bros., $35.00.

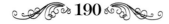

Underwood, Typewriter Ribbon, Noiseless, ¾ x 2½ x 2½", $8.00.

Utility, Typewriter Ribbon, ¾ x 2½ x 2½", Decorated Metal, $15.00.

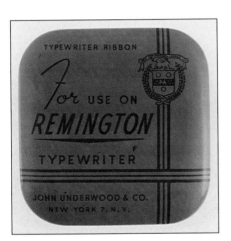

Underwood, Typewriter Ribbon, Remington, ⅞ x 2½ x 2½", $10.00.

Viking Line, Typewriter Ribbon, ¾ x 2½ x 2½", $25.00.

Vis-Quin, Typewriter Ribbon, 1¾ x 1¾ x 2", $40.00+.

Underwood, Typewriter Ribbon, Royal, ¾ x 2½ x 2½", $6.00.

XLNT Brand, Typewriter Ribbon, ¾ x 2½", $12.00.

American Brand, Bird Salve, ¼ x 1⅝", Am. Can 10-A, $18.00.

Dr. Roberts, Hard Milking Outfit, 1 x 2¼ x 3½", $55.00.

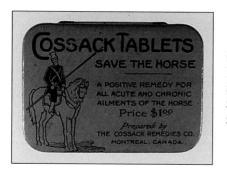

Cossack Tablets, Horse Medicine, $1.00, ¾ x 2⅛ x 3⅛", McDonald, $80.00.

Dr. LeGear's, Pepsin Compound Tablets, ¾ x 1⅝ x 2⅛", $45.00.

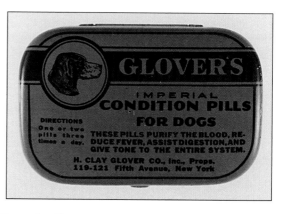

Glover's, Condition Pills, ½ x 2 x 3⅛", $35.00.

Dr. LeGear's, Head Lice Remedy, $.25, 1 x 2¾", Am. Can Co. 70-A, $70.00.

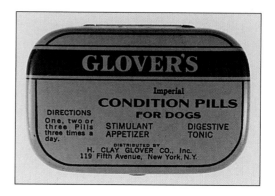

Glover's, Condition Pills, ½ x 2 x 3⅛", $55.00.

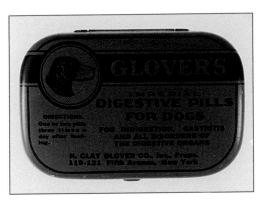

Glover's, Digestive Pills, ½ x 2 x 3", $25.00.

Pussy Scat, Powder, $.25, ⅞ x 2 x 2⅞", $80.00.

Hartz Mountain, Bird Song Food, 1⅛ x 2 x 2¾", $15.00.

Spratt, Sing Song, ¾ x 1¼ x 2", $20.00.

Helex, Healing Powder, 1 x 1⅞", $45.00.

Wheelock's, Veterinary Healing Salve, $.25, 1 x 2⅝", Buckeye Stamping Co., $40.00.

North Star sample, Wool Fat, ¾ x 1½", Am. Can Co. 27-A, $18.00.

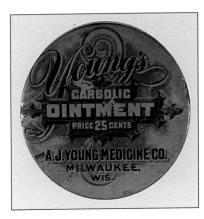

Young's, Carbolic Ointment, $.25, 1⅛ x 2½", $25.00.

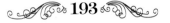

Watch Parts

A-K Special, Main-springs, ¾ x 2¾ x 2¾", $35.00.

Globe, Mainsprings, ¾ x 2¾ x 2¾", $60.00.

Ajax, Main Springs, ⅝ x 2¾ x 2¾", $50.00.

Overland, Mainsprings, ⅝ x 2¾ x 5⅛", $125.00+.

Columbia, Main Springs, ¾ x 2¾ x 2¾", $75.00.

Elgin, Main Springs, 1 x 2¾ x ½", $15.00.

Wizard, Mainsprings, ⅝ x 3 x 3⅜", Am. Can 11-A, $60.00.

AG & C, Adhesive Plaster, ⅞ x ⅞", $15.00.

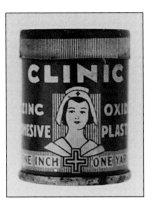

Clinic, Zinc Oxide, 1 x 1¼", $35.00.

Benson's, Rubber Adhesive Plaster, 1 x 1¾", $25.00.

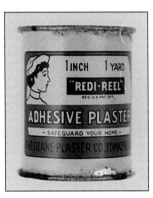

Deane "Redi-Reel," Adhesive Plaster, 1 x 1¼", $25.00.

Blue Seal, Zinc Plaster, 1 x 1⅜", $22.00.

Dean's, Zinc Plaster, ¾ x 1", $25.00.

Blue Seal, Zinc Plaster, ⅞ x 1", $25.00.

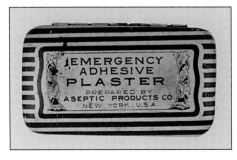

Emergency, Adhesive Plaster, ¼ x 1⅛ x 2¼", $35.00.

Gotham, Adhesive Plaster, ¾ x 2⅜", $8.00+.

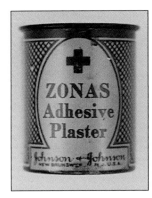

Johnson & Johnson, Zonas Adhesive Plaster, ¾ x 1⅝", $25.00.

Gotham, Adhesive Plaster, 1 x 1¼", $25.00+.

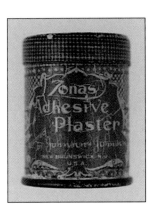

Johnson & Johnson, Zonas Adhesive Plaster, 1 x 1¼", $15.00.

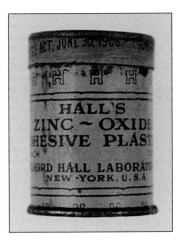

Hall's, Zinc Oxide, 1 x 1¼", $18.00.

Johnson & Johnson, Zonas Adhesive Plaster, 1 x 1¼", $25.00.

Home-Need, Adhesive Plaster, 1 x 1¼", $18.00.

Lee's, Rubber Adhesive, 1 x 1⅝", $25.00.

Paragon, Adhesive Plaster, 1 x 1¼", $25.00.

Supreme, Adhesive Plaster, 1 x 1¼", $30.00+.

Perrigo's, Adhesive Plaster, 1⅛ x 1⅛", $15.00.

Surgeon's, Rubber Adhesive Plaster, ⅝ x 2", $35.00.

Walgreen, Adhesive Plaster, 1⅛ x 1¼", $18.00.

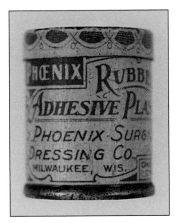

Phoenix, Rubber Adhesive Plaster, 1 x 1¼", Am. Can 70-A, $30.00.

Willard's, Adhesive Plaster, 1 x 1¼", $18.00.

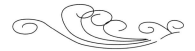

Al. Foss, Pork Rind Minnow, 1 x 1¼ x 4", Am. Can 70-A, $40.00.

Marshall Wells, Split Shot, ⅜ x 1½", $20.00.

Gladding's, Line Tonic, ¾ x 2¾", $8.00.

Lew Morrison, Dry-Pak Pork Rind, ½ x 2½ x 3⅝", $18.00.

Marathon, Dry Line Dope, ¾ x 2¾", $8.00.

Rainbow Quality, Silkworm Gut Leader, 1 x 3⅜", Am. Can 10-A, $60.00.

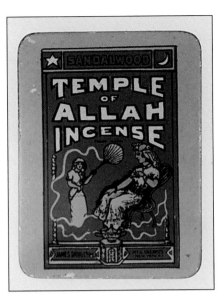

James Drug Co., Temple of Allah Incense, ⅜ x 2⅜ x 3⅛", $18.00.

Vantine's, Sandalwood Incense, ¼ x 1⅜ x 4", $15.00.

Vantine's, Incense, ¼ x 1¼ x 1⅛", MP, $10.00.

Vantine's, Rose Incense, ¼ x 1⅜ x 4", $15.00.

Vantine's sample, Temple Incense Cones, ¼ x 1⅛ x 2", $12.00.

American X, Ink Pad, ⅝ x 2 x 3¼", $10.00.

Junior XXX, Stamp Pad, ⅜ x 1 x 1¾", $18.00.

Fulton, Stamp Pad, #0, ⅜ x 2¼ x 3½", $12.00.

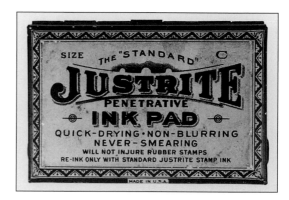

Justrite, Ink Pad, ⅝ x 2¼ x 3½", $12.00.

Fulton, Ink Pad, No. XX, ⅜ x 1¼ x 2¼", $8.00.

Peerless, Ink Pad, #0, ½ x 2¼ x 3¾", $8.00.

Fulton, Ink Pad, No. XX, ¼ x 1¼ x 2¼", $8.00.

Superb, Stamp Pad, Size A, ½ x 1⅝ x 2¾", $12.00.

Amolin sample, Deodorant Powder, 1 x 2⅝", Am. Can 10A, $35.00.

Ce-Co Diamond Brand sample, Deodorant Powder, 1 x 2⅛", $35.00.

Anafung sample, Foot Powder, 1 x 1¼ x 2½", $15.00.

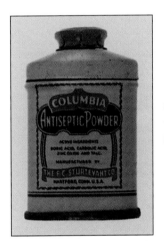

Columbia sample, Antiseptic Powder, ⅝ x 1⅜ x 2⅛", $35.00.

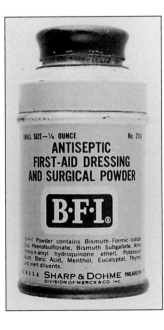

B-F-I sample, Antiseptic Powder, 1¼ x 2¼", $10.00.

Deodo sample, Deoderant Powder, ¾ x 1¼ x 2¾", $30.00.

Paislay's sample, Lavender Styptic Powder, ¾ x 1¼ x 2", C.C. Co. 30.66, $25.00.

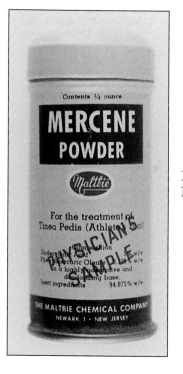

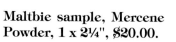

Maltbie sample, Mercene Powder, 1 x 2¼", $20.00.

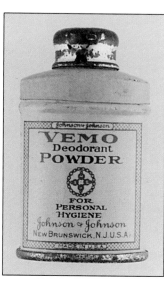

Vemo (J&J), Deodorant Powder, ¾ x 1¼ x 2¼", $50.00.

Odorono sample, Deodorant Powder, ¾ x 1⅛ x 1⅞", $30.00.

White Cross sample, Foot Powder, ⅞ x 1½ x 2⅜", $35.00.

De Luxe, Spanish Saffron, ⅜ x 1½ x 2½", $15.00.

Hudson, Spanish Saffron, ⅜ x 1½ x 2½", $12.00.

Frank's, Spanish Saffron, ¼ x 1¼ x 1¾", $4.00.

Kleckner's, Saffron, ⅜ x 1½ x 2½", $30.00.

S.W.C., Saffron, 1¼ x 1¾ x 1¼", $8.00.

Gillett's, Saffron, 1¼ x 1¾ x 1⅞", $20.00.

Sunred, Spanish Saffron, ⅜ x 1⅝ x 1⅝", $8.00.

12, Thumb Tacks, ⅝ x 1",
$10.00.

"Boye," Egg Eyed Needles, ⅛ x 1 x 2", $10.00.

American Can sample, Giveaway, ⅜ x 2",
$275.00.

Ansco, Re-Developer,
⅞ x 3¼ x 3¼",
$30.00.

Boy's Harp, Harmonica, ⅞ x 1¼ x 4", $15.00.

Barrett's, Roachsaultt Insecticide, 1⅝ x 3½", MP Co., N.Y.,
$30.00.

Bruton's, Scotch Snuff, 1¼ x 1¾", 22.00.

Bryant and Mays, Match Safe, ⅜ x 1¼ x 1¾", $60.00.

Carhart's, Scotch Snuff, 2⅜ x 1¾", $22.00.

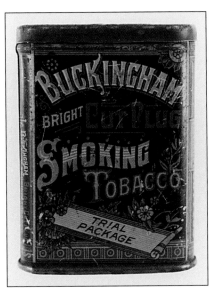

Buckingham Sample, Smoking Tobacco, ¾ x 2¼ x 3", $90.00.

Casterline Co., Cigarette Paper, ¼ x 1⅝ x 3", $35.00.

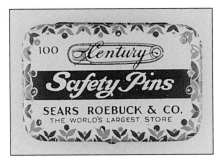

Century (Sears), Safety Pins, ¾ x 1½ x 2½", $20.00.

"Budget," Flints, ¼ x ⅞ x 1⅜", $8.00.

Consolidated Fireworks, Fireworks Powder, 1⅜ x 3½", $200.00.

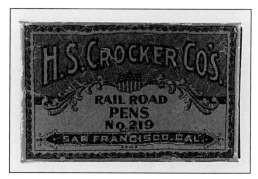

Crocker, H.S., Co., Railroad Pens #219, ¾ x 1¾ x 2⅞", Somers Bros, Brooklyn, $35.00.

Dixon's sample, Silica Graghite, ¾ x 1¼", J.B. Carroll, Chicago, $25.00.

Cushman & Denison sample, Pinch Fastners, ¼ x ⅞", $15.00.

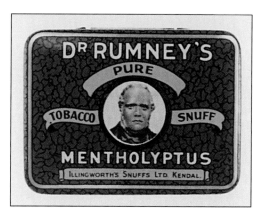

Dr. Rumney's, Mentholypus Snuff, ⅜ x 1¼ x 1¾", $15.00.

Dean, Snuff, ½ oz., 2 x 2½ x ⅜", $20.00.

Dietzgen, VanDyke Salt, 2⅜ x 1¾", Am. Stopper, $15.00.

Eastman's, Flash Cartridge, #3, $.25, 1¼ x 3", $30.00.

Esterbrook's, Business Steel Pens, ½ x 1¼ x 1¾", $25.00.

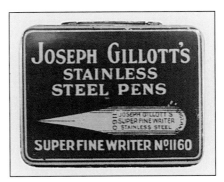

Gillott's, Joseph, 1160, Steel Pen Nibs, ¼ x 1¼ x 1¾", $25.00.

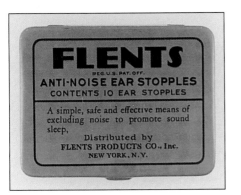

Flents, Ear Plugs, ½ x 2 x 2¾", $5.00.

Globe, Horseshoe Nail, ⅝ x 1⅞ x 3", $25.00.

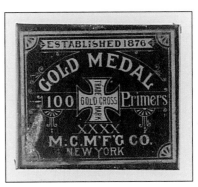

Gold Medal, Gold Cross Primers, 1¼ x 2 x 2½", $45.00.

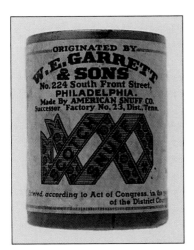

Garrett, Scotch Snuff, 1¾ x 2¼", $20.00.

Hamilton Beach, Motor Oil, 1⅞ x 2", $35.00.

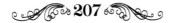

Handy Roll, Air Mail Stamps, ½ x 2 x 3", $5.00.

Hicks', Precussion Caps, No. 12, ½ x 1½", $40.00.

Harris, Bouillon Cubes, ⅝ x 1⅞ x 2⅝", $10.00.

Hold Fast, Chain Lubricant, ⅞ x 3⅜", Mersereau Mfg., $35.00.

Hi-Volt, Synthetic Crystal, ⅜ x ⅞", $15.00.

Hick's, Precussion Caps, No. 11, ⅝ x 1½", $30.00.

Hy-Grade, Tropical Fish Food, 1¼ x 2⅞", $18.00.

Imperial, Cut Plug Tobacco, 1 x 2⅝", $55.00.

Key sample, Graphite Paste, 1⅛ x 2⅛", Am. Can 70-A, $10.00.

Jackson's, Line Level, ¾ x 1¾ x 2¼", $18.00.

Lenk, Soldering Paste, ½ x 1⅜", $6.00.

"Justrite," Natural Fish Food, 1⅜ x 1¾ x 2½", $10.00.

Lifebuoy, First Aid Set, ⅝ x 1¼ x 1½", $50.00.

Kester, Aluminum Solder, ⅞ x 2¼", Am. Can Co. A-33, $8.00.

Magic, Song Restorer, 1¼ x 1¾ x 3", 15.00.

Marshall Co., Jewelers Material, ¼ x 1⅛", $5.00.

Montclair Brand, Bouillon Cubes, ¾ x 2 x 2¾", $15.00.

Metol Quinol, Developer, $.75, ¾ x 3 x 3", $30.00.

Montclair Brand, Bouillon Cubes, ⅞ x 1¾ x 3", $15.00.

Miller Bros. U S, Steel Pens, ½ x 1¼ x 1½", $22.00.

Monarch, Mending Kit, ⅝ x 2⅛ x 2⅞", $20.00.

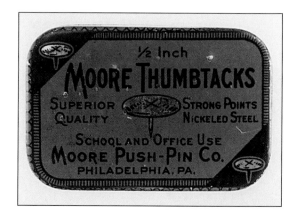

Moore, Thumbtacks, ⅜ x 1¼ x 2", $8.00.

Nepera, Developer, $.50, 1⅛ x 1½ x 2⅛", Mersereau, $30.00.

Old Woman, unknown, 3 x 5", 120.00.

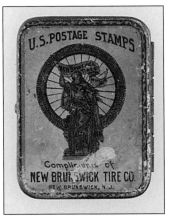

New Brunswick Tire Co., Postage Stamp Holder, ¼ x 1¼ x 1¾", $100.00.

Nu-Enamel sample, Enamel Paint, 2 x 1⅞", Am. Can. Co. 53-A, $6.00.

Patton's, Sun Proof Paints, 1⅝ x 2¼ x 2", Am. Can Co. 70-A, $30.00.

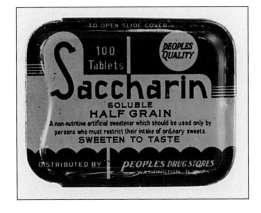

Old Mariner sample, Smooth Tobacco, 1½ x 2¼ x 1¾", $25.00.

Peoples, Saccharin, ¼ x 1¼ x 1½", $12.00.

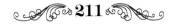

Philmore, "X"tra Loud Crystal, ½ x 1¼", $15.00.

Priscilla, Stamping Paste, ¾ x 3⅛", $15.00.

Pine Tree, Ribbons, ½ x 1⅛ x 1⅝", $15.00.

Piper Heidsieck, Chewing Tobacco, ⅜ x 2¾ x 2¾", $10.00.

Ready Light, Portable Light, ⅜ x 2¼ x 2¼", Somers Brothers, $35.00.

Premier Golden, Snuff, ½ x 1¾ x 2⅜", England, $20.00.

Red Seal, Sweet Snuff, 2⅜ x 1¾", $25.00.

Rolon No. 1, Clip, ¾ x 1½", $25.00.

Spencerian, Steel Pens, ¼ x ¾ x 2", Somers Bros., $40.00.

Rooster, Snuff, 1¼ x 2", $35.00.

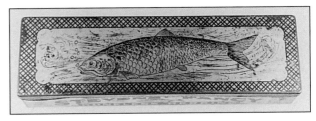

Steven's Fancy, Boneless Herring, 4oz., ⅞ x 1¾ x 6", Am. Can 32-A, $40.00.

Superb, Rubber Type Dates, ½ x 2¼ x 3½", $8.00.

Schlett, A.A., Liliput-Harmonica, ⅜ x ½ x 1¾", $40.00.

Sears Roebuck Co., Dry Ink, ¼ x 1⅛ x 2⅜", $40.00.

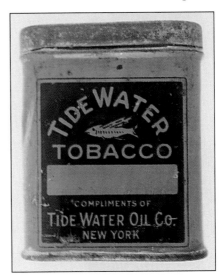

Tide Water, Tobacco, 2¼ x 2¼ x 2½", Am. Can 10-A, $30.00.

Tintograph, Color Box, ¼ x 1⅝", $10.00.

"Webley," Rifle Pellets, 500, ¾ x 2⅜ x 4", $30.00.

Tops, Sweet Snuff, 1¾ x 2¼", $20.00.

White, Fastners, 100, 1⅛ x 1½", $10.00.

Univex, Safety Film, ½ x 1⅞", $5.00.

Virginia Plug, Tobacco, ¾ x 1¾ x 2¼", $18.00.

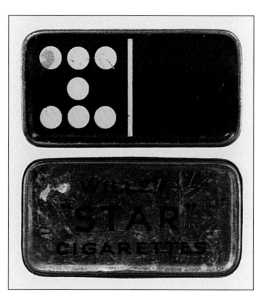

Willis "Star," Cigarette Domino, ¼ x 1 x 2", $25.00.

V2 = Volume 2
p204–1 = Page 204, photo 1

Index

(including updated
prices for Volumes
1 & 2)

12, Thumb Tacks, ⅝ x 1", V2p204–1, $10.00.

18K Brand (bank), Coffee, 2½ x 4", V1p224–1, $70.00.

20th Century, Tire Repair Outfit, ¾ x 1¼ x 4½", V1p12–8, $30.00.

3-M Brand sample, Valve Grinding Comp., ½ x 1½", no photo, $15.00.

3\F sample, Coffee, 2 x 3¾", V1p224–2, $70.00.

3XB sample, Powder, ¾ x 1⅜ x 2½", V2p127–1, $20.00.

5 Drop $.25, Salve, ⅝ x 1½", V2p44–1, $25.00.

6-O'clock, Bouillon Cubes, ¾ x ¾ x 2½", V1p19–1, $10.00.

666 $.10, Salve, ½ x 1½", V1p67–1, $8.00.

666 sample, Salve, ½ x 1½", V1p67–4, $8.00.

666 sample, Salve, ¼ x 1⅛", V1p67–2, $8.00.

666 sample, Salve, ¼ x 1⅛", V1p67–3, $8.00.*

A H Co. FH, Rivets 100, 1¼ x 1½", no photo, $5.00.

A-1 Sample, Salve, ¼ x 1½", V2p44–3, $6.00.

A-Corn, Salve, ¼ x 1¼", V1p67–7, $20.00.

A-Corn, Salve, ¼ x 1¼", V1p67–6, $20.00.

A-Corn, Salve, ⅜ x 1¼", V1p67–5, $20.00.

A-Corn, Salve, ½ x 1¼", no photo, $20.00.

A-K Special, Mainsprings, ¾ x 2¾ x 2¾", V2p194–1, $35.00.

A-Lax $.25, Tablets, ⅝ x 1¼ x 1½", V2p44–5, $18.00.

A-Vol, Tablets, ¼ x 1¼ x 1¾", V2p44–2, $12.00.

A.B.C., Gauzband, ½ x 2 x 2½", no photo, $15.00.

A.C., Troches, ¼ x 2⅛ x 3¼", V1p290–4, $10.00.

A.C.M.I., Grease, ⅞ x ¾", V1p11–1, $5.00.

A.D.S., Arnica Salve, ⅞ x 1⅜", V2p44–4, $18.00.

A.D.S., Aspirin, ¼ x 1¾ x 2⅝", V1p67–8, $15.00.

A.D.S., Aspirin 24, ¼ x 1¾ x 2⅝", V1p67–9, $10.00.

A.D.S., Croup Ointment, ⅞ x 2⅜", V1p67–10, $20.00.

A.D.S., Dental Soap, no photo, $75.00.

A.D.S., Floral Breathoids, ½ x 1 x 1⅝", V1p286–1, $20.00.

A.D.S., Fruit-Lax, ⅜ x 3 x 3¼", V2p44–6, $30.00.

A.D.S., Gastro Tonic Tablets, ⅜ x 1 x 1⅝", V1p67–11, $30.00.

A.D.S., Quick Healing Salve, ⅞ x 1⅜", V1p67–12, $18.00.

A.D.S., Tronk-Lets, ⅝ x 2 x 2⅝", no photo, $18.00.

A.D.S. $.10, Fruit-Lax, ⅜ x 1¼ x 1¾", V2p45–1, $18.00.

A.D.S. $.10, Fruit-Lax, ⅜ x 1⅝ x 1⅞", V2p45–3, $18.00.

A.D.S. $.50, Pile Remedy, 1½ x 2⅛ x 2⅛", V1p68–1, $30.00.

A.P.C., Mustard Plaster, ⅝ x 3⅝ x 4½", V1p68–2, $30.00.

A.P.C., Zinc Oxide Plaster, 1 x 1⅜", V1p344–1, $12.00.

A.P.C., Zinc Oxide Plaster, 1 x ¾", V1p344–2, $15.00.

A.S.B., Mainsprings, no photo, $25.00.

A.S.P., Tablets, ⅜ x 1¼ x 1¾", V2p45–5, $12.00.

Abbott sample, Desbutal, ¼ x ⅞ x 1⅜", V1p68–3, $4.00.

Abbott sample, Nembu-donna, ¼ x ⅞ x 1⅜", V1p68–4, $4.00.

Abbott sample, Nembutal-Bell, ¼ x ⅞ x 1⅜", V1p68–5, $4.00.

Abbott's, Corn Cure, ½ x 1¼", no photo, $25.00.

Abbott's, Menthol Plaster, 1⅜ x 6 ¼", V1p68–6, $50.00.

Abercrombie & Fitch, Shot Sinkers, ⅜ x 1½", V1p175–3, $20.00.

Ace High Sample, Cocoa, no photo, $110.00.

Ace High sample, Pomade, ½ x 1¼", V1p33–1, $20.00.

Acetidine, Pain Relief Tablets, ¼ x 1¼ x 1¾", V1p68–8, $7.00.

Acetidine, Tablets, ¼ x 1¼ x 1¾", V1p68–7, $8.00.

Acetophen, Medicine, ¼ x ⅞ x 2½", V1p68–9, $8.00.

Ackers, Dyspepsia Tablets, ½ x 2 x 3½", no photo, $35.00.

Acme, Tire Valve Cores, ¼ x 1 x 1¼", V1p16–6, $12.00.

Acme, Zinc Oxide, 1 x ¾", V1p344–3, $35.00.

Acme # 1, Tire Repair Kit, ½ x 2¼ x 3½", no photo, 80.00.

Acme # 2, Tire Repair Kit, ½ x 2¼ x 3½", V1p12–9, $80.00.

Acme $.10, Licorice Pellets, ½ x 1½ x 2¼", V1p290–5, $115.00.

Acme 20, Auto Fuses, ¼ x 1¼ x 1¾", V1p7–4, $10.00.

Acme 30, Auto Fuses glass, ¼ x 1¼ x 1¾", V1p7–3, $10.00.

Acme Air Appliance, Tire Valve Insiders, ¼ x 1 x 1⅜", V1p16–7, $12.00.

Acolite, Dentist Powder, ¼ x 1¼ x 1¾", V1p56–7, $8.00.

Acquin, Medicine, ¼ x 1 x 2", no photo, $20.00.

Adams, Type Ribbon, ¾ x 2½ x 2½", V1p301–1, $25.00.

Adams S.G. #0, Ink Pad, ½ x 2⅜ x 3⅝", V1p178–10, $30.00.

Addison, Type Ribbon, ¾ x 2½", no photo, $15.00.

Addressograph, Type Ribbon, 1¾ x 1¾ x 2", V1p301–4, $30.00.

Addressograph, Type Ribbon, 1⅝ x 1⅝ x 2", V1p301–3, $30.00.

Addressograph, Type Ribbon, 1⅝ x 1⅝ x 2", V1p301–2, $25.00.

Adelphi, Pins Drawing, ⅜ x 1⅞ x 3", V1p192–1, $8.00.

Adgene 2oz. sample, Coffee Food Beverage, 1⅝ x 2⅜", V1p243–1, $20.00.

Admiral, Phonograph Needles, no photo, $35.00.

Advance, Ground Pepper, 4½ x 3 x 1½", V2p137–1, $25.00.

Advo Gold Medal sample, Coffee, 3 x 2½", V1p224–4, $85.00.

Aegir, Phonograph Needles, no photo, $25.00.

Aegir 200, Needles, ⅝ x 1⅝ x 2½", V2p111–1, $18.00.

Aero, Phonograph Needles, no photo, $35.00.

Aero 200, Phono Needles, ⅜ x 1¼ x 1¾", V2p111–4, $25.00.

Aero Brand, Type Ribbon, ¾ x 2½", V2p174–1, $18.00.

Aetna Powder, Detonators, 1⅜ x 2⅛ x 2½", no photo, $20.00.

Afford Prompt Relief, Itch Ointment, ⅝ x 1⅞", V1p68–11, $8.00.

After Shave sample, Talcum Powder, no photo, $65.00.

After the Ball, Throat Lozenges, ¾ x 1¼ x 2½", V2p169–1, $75.00.

AG & C, Adhesive Plaster, ⅞ x ⅞", V2p195–1, $15.00.

AG & C, Zinc Oxide, 1 x 1", no photo, $18.00.

AG & C (Seabury & Johnson), Adhesive Plaster, 1 x 1¼", V1p344–4, $18.00.

Agavan, Medicine, ¼ x 1¼ x 1¾", V1p68–12, $15.00.

Aidol sample, Relives Pain, ¼ x 1⅝, no photo, $8.00.

Air Float sample, Talcum, ¾ x 1¼ x 2", V1p256–1, $140.00.

Air Float Sample, Wisteria Talcum, no photo, $90.00.

Air Seal, Valve Cores, ¼ x 1⅛ x 1½", no photo, $10.00.

Airco 6, Sparklighters, ¼ x 1 x ¼", V1p192–2, $6.00.

Aircraft Brand, Pepper, 3½ x 2¼ x 1¼", V2p137–3, $35.00.

Ajax, Watch Main Spring, ⅝ x 2¾ x 2¾", V2p194–3, $50.00.

Ajax sample, Cleanser, 1¾ x 2½", V1p21–1, $25.00.

Ajax Tablets, Tablets, ½ x 1½ x 2½", V1p69–1, $40.00.

Akalyn, Tablets, ¼ x 1¼ x 1¾", V1p69–2, $10.00.

Akron Tourist Tubes, Condom, no photo, $350.00.

Alba-Lax $.10, Laxative Candy, ½ x 1¾ x 2¼", V2p45–7, $22.00.

Albano, Shoe Dressing, 1¼ x 2½", V1p276–1, $10.00.

Alberly, Turmeric, 2½ x 2¼ x 1¼", V2p137–5, $15.00.

Albodon sample, Tooth Powder, 1¼ x 2⅝", V1p56–8, $25.00.

Albolene sample, Skin Cleanser, ¼ x 1⅝", V1p49–4, $15.00.

Alcan, Musket Caps, ¾ x 2½", V1p64–1, $25.00.

Alert Tabs $.10, Tablets, ¼ x 1 x 1¼", V1p69–3, $6.00.

Alibis sample, Breath Mints, ¼ x 1½ x 2", no photo, $15.00.

All-In-One $.25, Dental Tablets, 1½ x 1½ x 2¼", V2p40–1, $50.00.

Alladin Gems, Pennyroyal Tablets, 1 x 1½ x 3", no photo, $40.00.

Allan's $2.00, Star Brand Pills, 1⅝ x 3 x ⅞", V2p45–2, $50.00.

Allen Benjamin Co., Watch Parts, ⅜ x 1⅛", V1p334–1, $10.00.

Allenbury's, Glycerine Pastilles, 1 x 2 x 3¼", $15.00.

Allen's, Face Powder, 3 x 3 x 1¼", V2p22–1, $55.00.

Allen's $.05, Aspirin, ¼ x ⅞ x 1⅜", V1p69–4, $10.00.

Allerton's, Chain Compound, 1 x 4", V1p174–1, $45.00.

Allerton's, Chain Lubercant, 1 x 4", V1p174–2, $45.00.

Allied Flagship, Type Ribbon, ¾ x 2½", V2p174–4, $12.00.

Allonal "Roche" sample, Insomnia Pills, ¼ x 1¼ x 1¾", V1p69–5, $15.00.

Allwrite, Type Ribbon, ¾ x 2½ x 2½", V1p301–5, $15.00.

Almonized sample, Cocoa Cream, ¼ x 1⅜, no photo, $15.00.

Almonized sample, Skin Cream, ¼ x 1⅜", V1p28–1, $12.00.

Aloha sample, Coffee, no photo, $120.00.

Alpine, Lozenges, ⅜ x 1½ x 2½", V1p290–6, $40.00.

Alpine sample, Witch Hazel, ¼ x ⅞, no photo, $25.00.

Altex $.50, Condoms, ⅜ x 1⅝ x 2⅛, no photo, $70.00.

A'Lure sample, Complexion Powder, ¼ x 1½", V1p250–1, $35.00.

A'Lure sample, Rouge Compact, ¼ x ⅞", V1p47–1, $25.00.

Amami sample, Bath Crystal Powder, 1 x 2¼", V1p264–1, $60.00.
Amami sample, Emollient, ½ x 1 x 1½", V1p28–2, $12.00.
Amami sample, Talcum, ¾ x 1¼ x 2⅛", V1p256–2, $100.00.
Ambergloss $.10, Cuticle Remover, ¼ x ½ x 1½", V1p42–1, $25.00.
Amer-Jap, Fish Food, ⅞ x 2½", V1p192–3, $25.00.
American, Bird Salve, ⅛ x 1⅝, no photo, $15.00.
American, Ink Pads, ⅜ x 1⅝ x 1⅝", V1p178–11, $8.00.
American, Inked Pads, ⅜ x 1⅝ x 1⅝", V1p178–12, $10.00.
American, Shoe Polish, ¾ x 2⅛", V2p118–1, $18.00.
American #4, Shoe Polish, 1 x 3½", V1p276–2, $30.00.
American (Nova), Shoe Polish, ⅞ x 2½", V2p118–3, $25.00.
American (White Cross), Zinc Oxide Plaster, 1 x 1¼", V1p344–5, $15.00.
American Ace, Music Needles, no photo, $40.00.
American Beauty, Type Ribbon, ¾ x 2½ x 2½", no photo, $15.00.
American Brand, Bird Salve, ¼ x 1⅝", V2p192–1, $18.00.
American Brand, Type Ribbon, 1⅝ x 1¾ x 2", V1p301–7, $90.00.
American Brand, Type Ribbon, ¾ x 2½", no photo, $95.00.
American Brand, Type Ribbon, ¾ x 2½ x 2½", V1p301–6, $8.00.
American Can sample, Giveaway, ⅜ x 2", V2p204–3, $275.00.
American Chain, Cotter Pins, 1⅜ x 2⅛", V1p192–4, $4.00.
American Co, Zinc Oxide Oint., ¾ x 2", V1p344–6, $10.00.
American Drug, see Dr. Hunter's Sure Relief.
American Laboratories, Aspirin Tablets, ¼ x 1¼ x 1¾", V2p45–4, $10.00.
American National, Patent Leather Paste, no photo, $18.00.
American Parts, Auto Fuses, ⅜ x 1⅜ x 1½", no photo, $8.00.
American Remedy Co., Laxative\Aspirin, ¼ x 1½ x 2", V2p45–6, $15.00.
American Ribbon, Type Ribbon, ¾ x 2¼ x 2¼", V1p301–9, $20.00.
American Storm H.M., Type Ribbon, no photo, $95.00.
American Storm H.M., Type Ribbon, 1¾ x 1¾ x 2", no photo, $115.00.
American Storm H.M., Type Ribbon, 1¾ x 1¾ x 2", no photo, $95.00.
American Storm H.M., Type Ribbon, 1¾ x 1⅝ x 2", V2p174–3, $95.00.
American Storm H.M., Type Ribbon, ¾ x 2½ x 2½", V2p174–6, $95.00.
American Storm H.M., Type Ribbon, ¾ x 2¼ x 2¼", V2p174–2, $90.00.
American Waltham, Watch parts, ½ x 1¼", V1p334–2, $15.00.
American X, Ink Pad, ⅝ x 2 x 3¼", V2p200–1, $10.00.
Ames' sample, A B C Salve, ⅜ x 1⅛, no photo, $15.00.
Amesco, Type Ribbon, ¾ x 2½ x 2½", V1p301–10, $18.00.
Amitone, Antacid Tablets, ¼ x 1⅞ x 2¾", V1p69–6, $8.00.
Amity, Type Ribbon, ¾ x 2¼ x 2¼", no photo, $18.00.
Ammen sample, Antiseptic Powder, 1 x 2", V1p248–1, $65.00.
Ammens sample, Antiseptic Powder, 1 x 2½", V1p248–2, $22.00.
Amneco, Type Ribbon, ¾ x 2½ x 2½", V1p301–11, $15.00.
AMO, Auto Fuses, ⅜ x 1¼ x 1¾", V1p7–5, $15.00.
Amodine, Pain Pills, ⅜ x 1¼ x 1¾", V2p45–8, $12.00.
Amolin sample, Deodorant Powder, 1⅜ x 3¼", V1p249–4, $22.00.
Amolin sample, Deodorant Powder, 1 x 2¾", V1p249–2, $35.00.
Amolin sample, Deodorant Powder, 1 x 2⅝", V1p249–1, $30.00.
Amolin sample, Deodorant Powder, 1 x 2⅝", V2p201–1, $35.00.
Ampts, Shoe Polish, ¾ x 2⅛", V1p276–6, $25.00.
Anacin, Analgesic Tablets, ¼ x 1¼ x 1½", V1p69–8, $6.00.
Anacin, Analgesic Tablets, ¼ x 1¼ x 1¾", no photo, 2.00.
Anacin, Tablets, ¼ x 1¼ x 1¾", V1p69–10, $10.00.
Anacin, Tablets, ¼ x 1¼ x 1¾", V1p69–11, $6.00.
Anacin, Tablets, ¼ x 1¼ x 1¾", V1p69–9, $5.00.
Anacin, Tablets 12, ¼ x 1¼ x 1¾", V2p46–1, $6.00.
Anacin, Tablets 25, ¼ x 2⅛ x 2½", V1p69–12, $8.00.
Anacin, Tablets 30, ¼ x 2⅛ x 2½", V1p70–1, $8.00.
Anademin, Tablets 100, 1⅝ x 1⅝ x 2½", V1p70–2, $20.00.
Anafung sample, Foot Powder, 1 x 1¼ x 2½", V2p201–3, $15.00.
Analgia, Tablets, ¼ x 1¼ x 1¾", V1p70–3, $15.00.
Analka sample, Wafers, ½ x 1¾", V1p70–4, $6.00.
Anasarcin, Tablets, 1¼ x 1⅝ x 2⅜", V1p70–5, $70.00.
Anasarcin, Tablets (100), 1 x 1⅜ x 2¼", V1p70–6, $35.00.
Anasarcin $2.00, Tablets, 1 x 1⅜ x 2¼", V1p70–7, $30.00.
Anasarcin 100, Tablets, 1 x 1⅜ x 2¼", V1p70–8, $20.00.
Anchor Brand, Type Ribbon, 1¾ x 1¾ x 1⅞", V2p174–5, $55.00.
Andro Medicone sample, Ointment, ¼ x 1", V1p70–9, $8.00*.
Andro Medicone sample, Three Tablets, ¼ x 1⅛", V1p70–10, $6.00.
Anedemin Sample, Tablets, ¼ x 1¾ x 3¼", V2p46–3, $8.00.
Angelus, Shoe Polish, 1 x 3½", V1p276–4, $10.00*.
Angelus Poppy 455, Rouge Incarnat, ¼ x 1⅛", V1p47–2, $22.00.
Angelwhite, Shoe Cleaner, 1 x 2¼", no photo, $5.00.
Anidon, Tablets, ¼ x 1¼ x 1¾", V1p70–11, $8.00.
Annett's, Perfect Cleanser, 1½ x 2", V1p21–2, $15.00.
Ansco, Developer, 1x 3⅛ x 3⅛", V1p184–1, $30.00.
Ansco, Re-Developer, ⅞ x 3¼ x 3¼", V2p204–5, $30.00.
Anti-Headache, Pain Pills, ¼ x 1½ x 1¾", no photo, $12.00.
Anti-Dim, Cloth, 1¼ x 2⅜", V1p192–5, $5.00.
Anticor, Shaver for Corns, 1⅛ x 1⅛ x 3¼", V1p274–1, $20.00.
Anticor Perfect, Safety Corn Razor, ¾ x ¾ x 2½", no photo, $40.00.
Antifebrin, see Acetanilid.
Antikamnia, Quinine & Salo Tabs, 1¼ x 2⅜, no photo, $30.00.
Antikamnia, Salo Tablets, 1⅝ x 2⅜, no photo, $40.00.
Antikamnia, Salo Tablets, 1⅝ x 2⅜, no photo, $45.00.
Antikamnia, Tablets, ¼ x 1¼ x 1¾", V1p71–1, $25.00.
Antikamnia $.10, Vest Pocket Tablets, ¼ x 1 x 1", V1p71–5, $15.00.
Antikamnia $.25, Headache Cold Tablets, ¼ x 1¼ x 1¾", V2p46–6, $15.00.
Antikamnia $.25, Tablets, ¼ x 1¼ x 1¾", V1p70–12, $25.00.
Antikamnia $.25, Tablets, ¼ x 1¼ x 1¾", V1p71–3, $25.00.
Antikamnia $.25, Tablets, ¼ x 1¼ x 1¾", V1p71–4, $38.00.
Antikamnia $.25, Tablets, ¼ x 1¼ x 1¾", V2p46–2, $25.00.
Antikamnia $.25, Tablets, ¼ x 1¼ x 1¾", V2p46–4, $25.00.
Antikamnia 1 oz., Tablets, 1⅝ x 2⅜", V1p71–2, $40.00.
Antikamnia sample, Codeine Tablets, ¼ x 1¼ x 1¾", V2p46–5, $35.00.
Antikamnia sample, Codeine Tablets, ¼ x 1¼ x 1¾", V2p46–7, $40.00.
Antikamnia sample, Tablets, ¼ x 1¼ x 1¾", V2p47–1, $45.00.
Antiseptic Ready, Razor, 1½ x 2⅜", V1p270–1, $215.00.
Anusol, Suppositories, ¼ x 1¼ x 1¾", no photo, 2.00.
Anusol sample, Hemorrhoidal Suppository, ⅜ x 1¼ x 1½", V1p71–6, $8.00*.
Anusol sample, Hemorrhoidal Suppository, ½ x 1¼ x 1½", V1p71–7, $6.00.
Anusol sample, Unguent, ⅜ x 1⅝", V1p71–8, $8.00.
Apex sample, Pomade, ¼ x 1¼", V1p33–2, $18.00.
Appelton's, Tea, ⅞ x 1⅞ x 2¼", V1p267–1, $35.00.
April Showers sample, Face Powder, ¼ x 1½ x 1⅞", V1p250–2, $22.00.
Apris, Condom, ¼ x 1⅝ x 2", V1p23–1, $50.00.
Arabian, Gall Salve, 1¾ x 2¼ x 2", V1p330–1, $20.00.
Arabian, Healing Balm, ½ x 2", no photo, $40.00.
Araby (B&B), Incense, ⅞ x 2⅜ x 2⅜", V1p178–1, $20.00.
Arbuckles', Cream Tartar, 1¼ x 2¾", V2p137–2, $30.00.
Arcade Brand, Type Ribbon, ¾ x 2½ x 2½", no photo, $15.00.
Arco, Type Ribbon, no photo, $12.00.
Ardath Loud Tone, Needles Phono, ¼ x 1¼ x 1¾", V1p203–1, $30.00.
Argotane, Laxative, ¼ x 1¼ x 1¾", V1p71–9, $8.00.
Ariel, Needles Phono, no photo, $30.00.
Ariphon sample, Diuretic Pills, ¼ x 1¼ x 1¾", V1p71–10, $20.00.
Arista, ¼ x 1¾ x 2⅝", V1p71–11, $15.00.
Aristo, Corn Salve, ¼ x 1⅛", V2p47–3, $20.00.

Aristo Brand, Whole Cloves, 3½ x 2⅜ x 1¼", V2p137–4, $30.00.
Aristocrat, Condom, ⅝ x 1⅝", V1p23–2, $85.00.
Arium, Radium Tablets, ⅞ x 1¾ x 2⅞", V1p71–12, $10.00.
Arko sample, Herbs, ¼ x ⅞", V1p72–1, $15.00.
Arlcaps, Medicine, ¼ x ¾ x 2", V2p47–5, $10.00.
Arm & Hammer sample, Baking Soda, 1 x 2¼ x 2⅛, no photo, $30.00.
Armand, Rogue, ¼ x 1½", V1p47–3, $12.00.
Armand $.25, Rouge, ⅜ x 1½", V1p47–4, $15.00.
Armand sample, Blended Face Cream, ¼ x 1⅝", V1p28–3, $15.00.
Armand sample, Bouquet Complexion Powder, ¼ x 1¾", V2p22–3, $15.00.
Armand sample, Bouquet Complexion Powder, ¼ x 1⅝", V2p22–5, $25.00.
Armand sample, Cold Cream Powder, ¼ x 1½", V2p22–2, $15.00.
Armand sample, Cold Cream Powder, ¼ x 1⅝", V1p250–5, $18.00.
Armand sample, Cold Cream Powder, ¼ x 1⅞", V1p250–4, $18.00.
Armand sample, Cold Cream Talcum, ¾ x 1⅜ x 2⅛", V2p127–3, $90.00.
Armand sample, Cold Cream Powder, ¼ x 1⅝", V1p250–3, $22.00.
Armand sample, Cream Rouge, ¼ x 1", V1p47–5, $18.00.
Armand sample, Talcum, ¾ x 1¼ x 2⅛", V2p127–5, $75.00.
Armand sample, Vanishing Cream, ¼ x 1⅝", V2p27–1, $15.00.
Armand sample, Wind Blown Rose, ¼ x 1¼", V2p22–4, $18.00.
Armand Symphonie sample, Face Powder, ¼ x 1⅝, no photo, $15.00.
Armand Symphonie sample, Face Powder, ¼ x 1⅝", V1p254–3, $18.00.
Armand Symphonie sample, Face Powder, ⅜ x 1½", V2p22–6, $15.00.
Armanko, Type Ribbon, ¾ x 2½ x 2½", no photo, $15.00.
Armor, Shoe Polish, 1 x 2¾", V1p276–4, $15.00.
Armour, Ovol, ¾ x 3⅞", V1p19–2, $6.00.
Armour's sample, Motorist\Mechanical Soap, ⅝ x 1¾", V2p13–1, $35.00.
Armour's Veribest, Bouillon Cubes, ¾ x 1¾ x 2⅝", V1p19–4, $20.00.
Armour's Veribest, Bouillon Cubes, ⅝ x 1¾ x 2⅝", V1p19–3, $20.00.
Armstrong's, Wax, 1½ x 2⅜ x 2¼", V1p343–1, $15.00.
Armstrong's sample, Croup Ointment, ¼ x 1⅝", no photo, $8.00.
Arnaldi, Cachets, sample 1 x 3 x 2", $8.00.
Arnica, Tooth Paste, ½ x 2 x 3¼", V1p60–1, $70.00.
Arnica, Tooth Soap, ½ x 2 x 3⅛", V2p40–3, $55.00.
Arnolds Perfect, Type Ribbon, 1⅝ x 1⅝ x 2", V1p301–12, $55.00.
Arrow Brand, Type Ribbon, ¾ x 2½ x 2½", V2p174–7, $20.00.
Arrows, Condom, ¼ x 1¼ x 1¾", V2p17–1, $75.00.
Arsenal Brand, Spices, 3¼ x 2¼ x 1½", V2p137–6, $45.00.
Arsenic, Medicine, ¼ x 1¼ x 1½", V2p47–7, $12.00.
Arthur's Peroxide sample, Tooth Powder, no photo, $35.00.
As the Pedals sample, Face Powder, ¼ x 1½", V1p250–6, $40.00.
As the Pedals sample, Talcum, ¾ x 1¼ x 2", V1p256–3, $50.00.
Ascherberg Loud Tone, Needles, ½ x 2", no photo, $30.00.
ASCO, Medicine, ¼ x 1¼ x 1¾", V2p47–2, $15.00.
Aseptinol Mfg., see Ungt Co., V1p161–9, $40.00.
Aspeco, Tablets, ¼ x 1¼ x 1¾", V1p72–2, $12.00.
Asper-Lax, Laxative, 1 x 1¼ x 1¾", V1p72–3, $15.00.
Asperform, Tablets, ¼ x 1¼ x 1¾", no photo, $12.00.
Aspertane, Tablets, ¼ x 1¼ x 1¾", V1p72–4, $12.00.
Aspertane, Tablets 30, ¼ x 2¼ x 2½", V1p72–5, $8.00.
Aspirets $.25, Aspirin, ½ x 1⅜ x 2⅛", V1p72–6, $15.00.
Aspirin, Aspirin, ¼ x 1¼ x 1¾", V1p72–7, $10.00.
Aspirin, Aspirin, ⅜ x 1¼ x 1¾", V2p47–4, $10.00.
Aspirol Aromatic, Ammonia, ¼ x 2 x 2½", no photo, $10.00.
Associated Pharmacist, Laxative Quinine, ⅜ x 1½ x 2½", V1p72–8, $12.00.
Aster, Adhesive Plaster, 1⅛ x 1¼", V1p344–6, $20.00.
Aster, Laxative Cascara, no photo, $18.00.
Aster Brand, Adhesive Plaster, 1 x 1⅜", V1p344–7, $20.00.
Athlete Pepsin, Gum, ½ x 1¾", V1p296–1, $90.00.
Atlas, Auto Fuses, ¼ x 1⅜ x 1½", V1p7–6, $10.00.
Atlas, Shoe Polish, 1 x 2½", V1p276–5, $15.00.
Atlas # 6, Blasting Caps 100, 1½ x 2 x 2½", V1p64–2, $30.00.
Atlas Tack, Cobblers' Nails, ¾ x 2", V1p192–6, $6.00.
Atophan, Tablets (20), ½ x 1 x 2⅛", V1p72–9, $12.00.
Atophan sample, Tablets (10), ½ x 1⅛ x 2⅝", V1p72–10, $18.00.
Attila, Type Ribbon, 2 x 2 x ½", no photo, $20.00.
Aubry Sisters, Beautifier, ¼ x 1¼", V2p32–1, $22.00.
Aubry Sisters sample, Cold Cream, ¼ x 1¼", V1p28–4, $35.00.
Auerhann Nadeln, Needles, no photo, $30.00.
Ault & Wiborg, Type Ribbon, ¾ x 2¼ x 2¼", V1p302–1, $22.00.
Ault & Wiborg Aulta, Type Ribbon, 1 x 2¾", V1p302–3, $12.00.
Ault & Wiborg Silk, Type Ribbon, ¾ x 2½", V1p302–4, $10.00.
Ault Wiborg, Type Ribbon, 1⅝ x 1⅝ x 2", V1p302–5, $50.00.
Aunt Jaynes, Pure Spices, 1½ x 2¼ x 3¼", V2p138–1, $45.00.
Aurora, Type Ribbon, 1½ x 1½ x 2", no photo, $50.00.
Aurora, Type Ribbon, ¾ x 2½ x 2½", V1p302–6, $25.00.
Auto Brand, Type Ribbon, ¾ x 2½ x 2½", no photo, $90.00.
Auto-Laks $.10, Chocolate Laxative, ⅜ x 1½ x 2½", V1p72–11, $50.00.
Auto-Laks $.10, Chocolate Laxative, ⅜ x 1⅝ x 2½", V1p73–1, $100.00.
Auto-Laks $.25, Chocolate Laxative, ¼ x 2⅞ x 3¼", V1p72,#12, 170.00.
Auto-Tab, Constipation, ¼ x 1⅜ x 1⅜", V1p73–2, $12.00.
Auto Insurance, Registration Kit, ¼ x 3⅛ x 3½", V1p192–7, $15.00.
Autocrat sample, Coffee, no photo, $130.00.
Autocrat sample, Coffee, 2⅜ x 3⅛", V1p224–4, $115.00.
Automobile, Accessories\Supplies, 1 x 3 x 2", V1p18–7, $6.00.
Aux Cayes, Type Ribbon, ¾ x 2⅛ x 2⅛", V2p175–1, $15.00.
Aux Cayes, Type Ribbon, ¾ x 2 x 2", V1p302–8, $15.00.
Aux Cayes, Type Ribbon, ⅝ x 2¼", V1p302–7, $8.00.
Aux Cayes, Type Ribbon, ⅝ x 2⅛ x 2⅛", V1p302–9, $15.00.
Avon, Boot Polish, ⅝ x 2", V1p276–6, $25.00.
Avon sample, Smoker's Tooth Powder, ¾ 1 1¼ x 2", V2p40–5, $50.00.
Avon sample, Talcum, no photo, $50.00.
AxAr, Pain Pills, ¼ x 1¼ x 1¾", V1p73–3, $6.00.
Ayre's Hubbard Har sample, Rose Skin Tissue, ⅜ x ⅞", V1p49–5, $25.00.
Azeada, Skin Whitner, ¾ x 1⅞", V2p27–3, $20.00.
Azomis sample, Toilet\Nursery Powder, no photo, $35.00.
Azuro, Blue Print Paper, 1⅝ x 4 ⅜", V1p192–8, $15.00.
B & B (Bauer & Black), Rubber Adhesive, no photo, $15.00.
B & G sample, Sterile Baby Powder, no photo, $65.00.
B C, Cold Tablets, ¼ x 1¼ x 1¾", V1p73–5, $10.00.
B C $.25, Headache Aspirin, ¼ x 1¼ x 1¾", V2p47–8, $6.00.
B C $.25, Tablets, ¼ x 1¼ x 1¾", V1p73–4, $15.00.
B-F-I sample, Antiseptic Powder, 1¼ x 2¼", V2p201–5, $10.00.
B-K, Auto Fuses, no photo, $10.00.
B-K, Auto Fuses, ⅜ x 1⅜ x 1½", no photo, $8.00.
B.F.I. sample, Antiseptic Dressing, 1 x 2", V1p248–5, $20.00.
B.F.I. sample, Antiseptic Powder, 1¼ x 2", V1p248–3, $20.00.
B.F.I. sample, Compound, 1¼ x 2⅝", V1p248–4, $18.00.
B.F.I. sample, First Aid Dressing, 1¼ x 2¼", no photo, $15.00.
B.P., Zinc Oxide, ½ x 1¾", no photo, $20.00.
BAB Tablets $1.00, Lozenges, ⅝ x 2½ x 4¼", V1p290–7, $22.00.
Babcock's sample, Cho Cho San Talcum, ¾ x 1⅛ x 2", no photo, $60.00.
Babcock's sample, Corilopsis Talcum, ⅞ x 1⅛ x 2", V1p256–4, $80.00.

Baby Edith, Allspice, 3¾ x 2 x 1⅛", V2p138–3, $20.00.
Baby Stuart, Nutmeg, 3¼ x 2¼ x 1⅜", V2p138–5, $70.00.
Baco-Curo, Cures Tobacco, ½ x 2¼ x 3⅜", V1p73–6, $95.00.
Bacon & Stickney, Allspice, 3 x 2¼ x 1¼", V2p139–1, $25.00.
Bacon, Stickney, Sage, 2¾ x 2¼ x 1¼", V2p139–3, $20.00.
Badger Brand, Type Ribbon, ¾ x 2½ x 2½", no photo, $45.00.
Badger Brand, Type Ribbon, ¾ x 2½ x 2½", V1p302–10, $40.00.
Bafaline, Tablets, ¼ x 1¼ x 1¾", V2p47–6, $18.00.
Bag Balm, Dilators, 1½ x 2½ x 1⅞", V1p330–2, $15.00.
Bag Balm sample, Ointment, 1½ x 1½ x 1½", V1p330–3, $45.00.
Bagshaw's 200, Brilliantone Needles, ¼ x 1¼ x 1¾", V1p203–2, $30.00.
Bahlsen, Cookies, 1⅛ x 1¼, no photo, $15.00.
Bailey's $1.50, Bath Brush, 1 x 3¾ x 5", V1p192–9, $90.00.
Baker W. sample, Cocoa, 1¼ x 1¾", V1p220–1, $150.00.
Baker W.H. sample, Cocoa ¼ Lb., 2½ x 2½ x 2¾", V1p220–2, $145.00.
Baker Walter sample, Cocoa, 1 x 1⅜ x 1¾", V1p220–3, $140.00.
Baker's, Cinnamon, 4 x 2¼ x 1¾", V2p138–2, $45.00.
Baker's, Lozenges, ⅜ x 1⅝ x 2½", V1p290–8, $18.00.
Baker's, Polish Silver, ¾ x 1½", V1p217–1, $30.00.
Baker's $.10, Mustard, 4 x 2¼ x 1¾", V2p138–4, $40.00.
Baker's Century, Vanilla Chocolate, 1⅛ x 2⅜", V1p220–4, $45.00.
Baker's sample, Cocoa Butter, ⅝ x 1¾ x 2¾", V1p243–2, $60.00.
Balch's $.10, Laxatives, ½ x 1½ x 1½", V2p48–1, $15.00.
Baldauf's, Healing Salve, ¾ x 1⅞", V1p73–7, $35.00.
Baldauf's $.25, Healing Salve, ¾ x 1⅞", V1p73–8, $25.00.
Ball, Watch Parts, ⅞ x 2⅛", V1p334–3, $15.00.
Ballroom Scene, no photo, $150.00.
Balsa Pine sample, Cold Salve, ⅜ x 1⅛", V1p73–9, $15.00.
Baltic Harmless, Rust\Stain Remover, ⅞ x1½", V1p21–3, $25.00.
Bamacea, Salve, ¾ x 1½", V1p73–10, $10.00.
Banker's No.2 RH, Paper Fastners, 1¼ x 1½", V1p62–1, $20.00.
Bankers Pen Co., Type Ribbon, no photo, $25.00.
Banner, Solder Cement, ¾ x 1¾", V1p285–1, $15.00.
Banner, Watch Mainsprings, ¾ x 3 x 3", V1p334–4, $40.00.
Banner Boy Brand, Allspice, 3¾ x 2¼ x 1¼", V2p138–6, $45.00.
Baralgin, Pain Tablets, ¼ x 1¼ x 1¾", V1p73–11, $12.00.
Bark-Lax, Dog Laxative, ½ x 2 x 2½", no photo, $70.00.
Barker's sample, Chocolate, no photo, $60.00.
Barlow's $.10, Wash Blue, ⅛ x 2⅛ x 2⅛", V1p192–10, $22.00.
Barnard's Universal, Type Ribbon, ¾ x 2¼ x 2¼", V1p302–11, $18.00.
Barracuda #BB, Sinkers, ½ x 1 x 1½", V1p175–4, $30.00.
Barrett's, Roachsaultt, 1⅝ x 3½", V2p204–6, $30.00.
Barrick's $.25, Lazy Liver Lifters, ½ x ⅞ x 2⅛", V2p48–3, $22.00.
Barrington Hall 4oz., Coffee, 3⅜ x 2½", V1p224–6, $65.00.
Barrington Hall sample, Coffee, 2⅞ x 2⅛", V2p123–1, $60.00.
Barrington Hall sample, Coffee, ⅝ x 2", V1p224–5, $15.00.
Bassett's, Shampoo Cream, 1¾ x 2¾", V1p49–6, $50.00*.
Batavia Brand, Ginger, 4½ x 1¾ x 1¼", V2p139–1, $30.00.
Bates, Stapler Refill, ⅞ x 1¾ x 1¾", V1p192–11, $18.00.
Battelship, Type Ribbon, ¾ x 2½ x 2½", V1p303–1, $15.00.
Battelship, Type Ribbon, ¾ x 2⅛ x 2⅛", V1p302–12, $30.00.
Battelship, Type Ribbon, ⅞ x 2½ x 2½", V1p303–2, $10.00.
Bauer & Black, Adhesive Plaster, 1 x ¼", V1p344–11, $15.00.
Bauer & Black, Adhesive Plaster, 1⅛ x 1¾", V1p344–12, $22.00.
Bauer & Black, Adhesive Plaster, ⅞ x 1¼", V1p344–10, $18.00.
Bauer & Black, Adhesive Plaster, ⅞ x 1⅛", V1p344–9, $18.00.
Bauer & Black, Adhesive Tape 4yds., ¾ x 2", V1p73–12, $6.00.
Bauer & Black, Adhesive Tape ⅝ x ¾ x 2", V1p74–3, $5.00.
Bauer & Black, First Aid Kit, ⅝ x 2¾ x 4⅛", V1p74–1, $15.00.
Bauer & Black, Handi-Tape, 1 x 2⅜ x 3¾", V1p74–2, $10.00.
Bauer & Black, Jap Dental Floss, ¼ x 1⅛", V1p55–1, $25.00.
Bauer & Black, Jap Tooth-Silk, ¼ x 1¼", V1p55–2, $20.00.
Bauer & Black, see Mother's Mustard Plaster, V1p124–7, $40.00.
Bauer & Black, Ray's Adhesive Plaster, ⅜ x 1⅛ x 2⅛", V2p48–5, $22.00.
Bauer & Black, Tirro Mending Tape, 1 x 1⅛", V2p48–7, $15.00.
Bauer & Black sample, Baby Talc, ⅞ x 1½ x 2¼", V1p264–2, $85.00.
Bauer & Black sample, Baby Talc, ⅞ x 1½ x 2¼", V1p264–3, $60.00.
Baume #55 sample, Old Surgeon's Remedy, ⅜ x ⅞", V1p74–4, $12.00.
Bayer, Aspirin, ¼ x 1¼ x 1¾", V1p74–5, $6.00*.
Bayer, Aspirin, ¼ x 2 x 2½", V2p48–7, $10.00.
Bayer $.15, Aspirin, ¼ x 1¼ x 1¾", V1p74–6, $6.00.
Bayer $.25, Aspirin, ¼ x 1¾ x 2½", V1p74–7, $8.00.
Bayer Instantine, Tablets, ¼ x 1½ x 2", V2p48–2, $5.00.
Bayer Instantine sample, Pain Tablets, ¼ x 1⅝ x 2", V2p48–4, $8.00.
Bay's, Adhesive Plaster, 1 x 1", V1p345–1, $22.00.
Beach, Bro-Aspirin, ¼ x 1⅝ x 1⅝", V2p49–1, $8.00.
Beach, Bro-Aspirin, ¼ x 1⅝ x 1⅝", V2p49–3, $8.00.
Bear's Jack Frost, Ointment, ⅝ x 1½", V1p74–9, $20.00.
Bear's Jack Frost sample, Head Colds, ⅜ x ⅞", V1p74–8, $35.00.
Bear's sample, Jack Frost Cream, ⅛ x ⅞", V2p49–6, $20.00.
Beau Brummel, Shoe Polish, 1 x 2¾", no photo, $18.00.
Beau Brummel, Shoe Polish, 1 x 3⅜", V1p276–7, $18.00.
Beaute-Salon, Pressing Compound, ¾ x 2½", V1p33–3, $8.00.
Beauty, Shoe Polish Wax, 1 x 2¾", V1p276–9, $15.00.
Beauty, Tooth Powder, no photo, $45.00.
Beauty, Tooth Soap, ½ x 2 x 3⅛", V1p60–2, $90.00.
Beauty Maid, Hair Pins, ½ x 2", V1p33–4, $4.00.
Beauvais, Type Ribbon, ¾ x 2½ x 2½", V1p303–3, $25.00.
Beaver Brand, Type Ribbon, ¾ x 2½ x 2½", V1p303–4, $35.00.
Beaver Economo, Type Ribbon, ¾ x 2½ x 2½", V2p175–3, $30.00.
Beaver Yankee, Type Ribbon, ¾ x 2½", V2p175–5, $45.00.
Bechtel's, Material, ⅜ x 1¼", V1p334–5, $3.00.
Beck Duplicator, Type Ribbon, ¾ x 2½ x 2½", V2p175–6, $15.00.
Bedford sample, Cocoa, no photo, $95.00.
Bee Brand, Aspirin, ¼ x 1¼ x 1¾", V1p74–10, $30.00.
Bee Brand, Insect Powder, 1⅝ x 4", V1p192–12, $18.00.
Bee Brand, Laxative Quinine Tabs, ⅜ x 1½ x 2", V1p74–11, $35.00.
Bee Brand 24, Laxative Quinine Tabs, ¼ x 1¾ x 2⅝", V1p74–12, $35.00.
Bee Brand sample, Tea, 3" tall, no photo, $35.00.
Beech-Nut sample, Coffee, 2¾ x 2¼", V1p225–2, $55.00.
Beech-Nut sample, Coffee, 3¼ x 2¾", V1p225–3, $55.00.
Beech-Nut sample, Coffee, 3⅜ x 2½", V1p225–1, $55.00.
Beef Peptonoids sample, see Physician's, V1p134–5, $75.00.
Beekist, Honey, no photo, $25.00.
Beekman, Seidlitz Powder, 1½ x 3¼ x 5 ½", no photo, $20.00.
Begy's, Mustarine Ointment, 1¼ x 2¾", V1p75–1, $20.00.
Begy's, Mustarine Ointment, ¾ x 2½", V1p75–3, $25.00.
Begy's, Mustarine Ointment, ¾ x 2⅜", V1p75–2, $16.00.
Begy's sample, Mustarine Ointment, ¼ x 1⅛", V1p75–4, $25.00.
Bel-Bon sample, Violet Talcum, ¾ x 1¼ x 2⅛", V1p256–5, $60.00.
Belcano sample, Skin Firm Cream, ¼ x ⅞", V2p27–5, $15.00.
Belgum, Ointment, 1 x 2¾", no photo, $18.00.
Bell, Type Ribbon, no photo, $18.00.
Bell, Type Ribbon, ¾ x 2½", V2p175–2, $12.00.
Bell Tower, Needles Gramaphone, ¼ x 1¼ x 1¾", V1p203–3, $30.00.
Bell-ans, Indigestion Pills, ¼ x ½ x 1", no photo, 4.00.
Belladona, Plaster, no photo, $25.00.
Belladona, Salve, ½ x 1⅜, $8.00.
Belle DeNuit Watkins, Cleansing Cream, ¼ x 1⅝", V1p28–5, $14.00.
Bello sample, Paste, ¼ x ⅞", V1p217–2, $25.00.
Bell's, Camphor Ice, 1 x 3½", V1p75–5, $15.00.
Bells, Poultry Seasoning, ½ x 1⅜ x 2½", V2p139–6, $70.00.
Bell's, Salve, ½ x 1¼", no photo, $18.00.

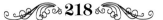

Bell's, Wax Vestas, ¾ x 1½ x 2¾", V1p193–1, $6.00.

Belmont, Type Ribbon, ¾ x 2½", V1p303–5, $8.00.

Beltel Massettes, Throat Lozenges, ¼ x 1¼ x 1¾", V1p290–9, $15.00.

Belva sample, Hair Pressing Oil, ¼ x 1½", V1p33–5, $5.00.

Belva sample, Hair Rep, ¼ x 1½", V1p33–6, $5.00.

Belva sample, Solid Hair Care, ¼ x 1⅝", V1p33–7, $8.00.

Ben Franklin, Type Ribbon, ¾ x 2½", V2p175–4, $25.00.

Ben-Hur, Curry Powder, 1¼ x 2¼ x 3¼", V2p139–2, $20.00.

Benford's Monarch, Spark Plugs, 1¼ x 1¼ x 4½", V1p12–1, $45.00.

Bengor's, Aspirin, ¼ x 1¼ x 1¾", V2p49–2, $8.00.

Benjamin, Rifle Shot, 1 x 3¼", V1p66–6, $5.00*.

Bennedict $2.00, Safety Razor, ¾ x 1¼ x 2⅜", V1p270–2, $225.00.

Bennett Simpson, Nutmeg, 1¾ x 2½ x 4", V2p139–4, $45.00.

Bennetts, Metal Polish Paste, ¾ x 2⅝", V1p217–3, $40.00.

Benson's, Porous Plaster, 1 x 1¼", V1p345–2, $20.00.

Benson's (Seabury), Pourse Plaster, 1 x 1¼", V1p345–3, $25.00.

Benson's S\J, Rubber Adhesive Plaster, 1 x 1¾", V2p195–3, $25.00.

Benzoto, Tooth Powder, 1⅝ x 4, no photo, $45.00.

Bergman, Watch Material, ½ x 1⅛", V1p334–4, $8.00.

Bermarine, Quinine Pomade, 1⅜ x 2½ x 3", V1p33–8, $35.00.

Bermarine $.25, Skin Brightner, ¾ x 1⅞", V1p50–1, $50.00.

Bermarine sample, Quinine Pomade, ¼ x 1½", V1p33–9, $45.00.

Berry's Creloe sample, Tea Tablets, ½ x 2 x 3", no photo, $18.00.

Best, Needles Gramaphone, ½ x 1¼ x 1½", V1p203–4, $35.00.

Best, Talking Needles, ⅜ x 1¼ x 1¾", V1p203–5, $35.00.

Best Aspirin Co., Aspirin Genuine 6, ¼ x 1 x 1⅜", V1p75–6, $10.00.

Best Crescent Quality, Stiffened Wire, ¾ x 1¾", V1p193–2, $28.00.

Best Ever, Sage, 3¼ x 2¼ x 1¼", V2p139–5, $50.00.

Best Quality, Safety Razor, 1½ x 2⅜", V2p134–1, $250.00.

Best Value, Cloves, 3½ x 2¼ x 1¼", V2p139–7, $35.00.

Bestfit, Watch Parts, ½ x 1⅛", V1p334–7, $5.00.

Betsy Ross, Polish Shoe, ⅞ x 2¾", V1p276–10, $30.00.

Better Brand, Aspirin, ¼ x 1 x 1¼", V1p75–7, $12.00.

Better Needle 200, XLoud Tone Needles, ¼ x 1⅛ x 2⅜", V1p203–6, $30.00.

Better Needles 200, Soft Tone, ⅜ x 1⅛ x 2¼", no photo, $30.00.

Better New, Super Gloss, no photo, $18.00.

Better-Brand, Cold Tablets, ¼ x 1¼ x 1¾", V2p49–3, $12.00.

Betterway sample, Lavender Wax Polish, ½ x 1¼", V1p343–2, $30.00.

Betterwear sample, Lavender Wax Polish, ½ x 1¼", V2p37–1, $18.00.

Betterwear sample, Wax Polish, ⅜ x 1¼", V2p37–3, $25.00.

Bibb's, Tire Repair Outfit, no photo, $55.00.

Bickmore, Gall Salve, ⅞ x 2⅝", V1p330–4, $25.00.

Bickmore, XYZ Skin Ointment, ½ x 1⅜", V1p330–5, $25.00.

Bickmore $.25, Exodr, ¾ x 1½ x 2¾", V1p330–6, $45.00.

Bickmore 2oz., Gall Salve, ⅞ x 2½", V1p330–7, $60.00.

Bickmore sample, Fly Salve, ¼ x 1¼", V1p75–9, $18.00.

Bickmore sample, Gall Salve, ¾ x 2", V1p330–8, $28.00.

Bickmore sample, Gall Salve, ⅜ x 1¾", V1p330–9, $35.00.

Bickmore sample, Gall Save, ⅜ x 1¾", V1p330–10, $30.00.

Bickmore sample, XYZ Ointment, ¼ x 1⅛", V1p330–11, $30.00.

Bickmore sample, XYZ Skin Ointment, ¼ x 1⅛", V2p35–1, $30.00.

Bifurcated, Rivets, ½ x 1⅞ x 1¾", V1p62–2, $30.00.

Big Boy Red\Head, Spark Plugs, 1⅞ x 2 x 4¼", V1p12–2, $115.00.

Big Horn, Ground Sage, 1¼ x 2⅜ x 3", V2p140–1, $50.00.

Big Policeman, Pile Cure, no photo, $35.00.

Bile Beans $.50, Biliousness, ⅝ x 1½", V2p49–5, $8.00.

Bing's, Watch Mainsprings, ⅞ x 2¾ x 5⅛", V1p334–8, $40.00.

Binney & Smith, Crayons, ⅜ x 2¾ x 3¾", V1p181–7, $15.00.

Birkmeyer's sample, Cough Drops, no photo, $55.00.

Bischoff's sample, Cocoa Breakfast, 2½ x 3¼", V1p220–5, $120.00.

Bishop's, Chocolate Gum, no photo, $90.00.

Bismadine, Alkalizer Tablets 30, ¼ x 2⅜ x 2¾", V1p75–10, $10.00.

BiSoDol, Mints (antacid), ¼ x 2⅜ x 2¾", V1p75–11, $8.00.

BiSoDol, Powder, 1⅜ x 1⅜ x 2⅛", V1p75–12, $10.00.

Bison Brand sample, Farm Shoe Dressing, ¾ x 1¾", V1p276–11, $22.00.

Biston's sample, Coffee Burmoca, 1½ x 3", V1p225–4, $85.00.

Bixby's, Satinola, ⅝ x 2¼", V2p118–5, $25.00.

Bixby's, Satinola Polish, ⅝ x 2⅛", V1p276–12, $30.00.

Bixby's, Shoe Jet-Oil, 1 x 2¾", V1p277–1, $18.00.

Bixby's, Tan Paste, ¾ x 2¼", V2p118–2, $20.00.

Bixby's No. 2, Satinola, ¾ x 1¾", V1p277–2, $25.00.

Black & White, Ointment, ½ x 1¾", V1p76–1, $8.00.

Black Beauty, Stove Polish, 1 x 3¼", V1p217–4, $22.00.

Black Boy, Type Ribbon, ¾ x 2½ x 2½", no photo, $50.00.

Black Boy Slugs, Gun Powder, no photo, $75.00.

Black Cat, Stove Cream, no photo, $25.00.

Black Cat Polish, Betsy Ross Polish, ⅞ x 1¾", V2p118–4, $25.00.

Black Cross, Rubber Adhesive Plaster, ¾ x ⅝", V1p345–4, $30.00.

Black Hills Brand, Paprika, 3½ x 2¼ x 1¼", V2p140–3, $25.00.

Black Jack, Type Ribbon, no photo, $100.00.

Blackburn's $.25, Casca Royal Pills, ⅜ x 1½ x 2½", V2p49–7, $22.00.

Blackburn's $.30, Casca Royal Pills, ⅜ x 1½ x 2½", V1p76–2, $20.00.

Blackburn's $.30, Casca Royal Pills, ⅜ x 1½ x 2½", V1p76–3, $20.00.

Blackburn's sample, Sulpherb Cream, ⅝ x 1⅛", V1p76–4, $8.00.

Blackhawks, Blood Body Tonic, no photo, $35.00.

Blacko, Laxative, ¾ x 2", V2p50–1, $15.00.

Blacko $.25, Laxative, ⅝ x ⅞ x 2⅜", V1p76–6, $15.00.

Blacko $.25, Stomach\Liver, ⅝ x ⅞ x 2⅜", V1p76–5, $15.00.

Blackola, Shoe Polish, ¾ x 2", V1p277–3, $10.00.

Blackstone's, Aspertain, ¼ x 1¼ x 1¾", V1p76–7, $10.00.

Blackstone's, Quinine Cascara, ¼ x 1¼ x 1¾", V1p76–9, $10.00.

Blackstone's, Quinine Cascara Bro, ¼ x 1¼ x 1¾", V1p76–10, $10.00.

Blackstone's, Tasty-Lax, ¼ x 1⅝ x 1⅝", V1p76–11, $10.00.

Blackstone's $.05, Aspirin, ¼ x 1 x 1½", V1p76–8, $8.00.

Blackstone's $.05, Aspirin 6, ¼ x 1 x 1⅜", V1p76–12, $12.00.

Blackstone's $.10, Aspertane, ¼ x 1¼ x 1¾", V1p77–1, $15.00.

Blackstone's $.10, Aspirin, ¼ x 1¼ x 1¾", V2p50–3, $8.00.

Blackstone's $.10, Laxative Cold Tablets, ¼ x 1¼ x 1¾", V1p77–2, $15.00.

Blackstone's $.10, Magnesia Tablets, ¼ x 1½ x 2", V1p77–3, $12.00.

Blackstone's $.10, Magnesia Tablets 12, ¼ x 1½ x 1⅞, no photo, $12.00.

Blackstone's $.10, Milk of Magnesia, ¼ x 1½ x 2", no photo, $10.00.

Blackstone's $.10, Tasty-Lax, ⅜ x 1⅝ x 1⅝", V1p77–4, $12.00.

Blackstone's sample, Tasty-Lax, ¼ x 1½ x 1½", V1p77–5, $18.00.

Blackstone's sample, Tasty-Lax, ⅜ x 1⅝ x 1⅝, no photo, $10.00.

Blaiddell's, Honette, ¼ x 1 x 2¼", V1p193–3, $15.00.

Blair's $.25, I B S Salve, ⅞ x 2¾", V1p77–6, $10.00.

Blair's N.B.O., Deodorant Cream, ⅝ x 2¼", V2p32–3, $8.00.

Blair's Snow White, Hair Beautifier, 1 x 3½", V1p34–4, $25.00.

Blake's, Mentholatum, ⅝ x 2", V1p77–7, $6.00.

Blanke's Faust sample, Coffee, no photo, $75.00.

Blanke's sample, Tea, no photo, $35.00.

Bliss $.25, Native Herbs 20, ⅜ x 1¼ x 1¾", V1p77–8, $20.00.

Blood & Stomach, Pills, ⅝ x 1½", V1p77–9, $55.00.

Blood Orange, Forbiden Fruit Gum, no photo, $125.00.

Bloodworth Drug, Aspirin, ½ x 1⅜, no photo, $5.00.

Blossom sample, Tea, ½ x 2 x 3¼", no photo, $45.00.

Blue Beard, Razor Hone, no photo, $120.00.

Blue Cross, Adhesive Plaster, 1 x 1¼", V1p345-5, $15.00.

Blue Goose, Condom, ⅜ x 1¾ x 2¼", no photo, $70.00.

Blue Ointment, Medicine, ⅝ x 1½", V1p185-2, $25.00.

Blue Ointment, Poison, ¼ x 1¼", V1p185-4, $35.00.

Blue Ointment, Poison, ⅝ x 1½", V1p185-3, $30.00.

Blue Ointment, Poison, ⅝ x 1¾", V1p185-1, $40.00.

Blue Ointment, U.S.P. Poison, ½ x 1½", V1p185-5, $35.00.

Blue Ribbon, Bouillon Cubes, 1 x 3½", V1p19-5, $10.00.

Blue Ribbon, Bouillon Cubes, 1 x 3½", V1p19-6, $6.00.

Blue Ribbon, De-Luxe Condoms, ¼ x 1¾ x 2¼", V2p17-4, $180.00.

Blue Ribbon $.50, De-Luxe Condom, ¼ x 1⅝ x 2⅛", V2p17-5, $275.00.

Blue Ribbon Brand, Black Pepper, 3 x 2¼ x 1¼", V2p140-5, $25.00.

Blue Ribbon sample, Baking Powder, 2½ x 2¼", no photo, $35.00.

Blue Ribbon sample, Metal Polish, 1⅛ x 1¾", V1p217-5, $70.00.

Blue Rose, Compact, ⅜ x 1⅝", V1p50-2, $10.00.

Blue Seal, Zinc Plaster, 1 x 1⅜", V2p195-5, $22.00.

Blue Seal, Zinc Plaster, ⅞ x 1", V2p195-7, $25.00.

Blue Seal Brand, Cloves, 2½ x 2¼ x 1½, V2p140-6, $20.00.

Blue Seal sample, Vaseline, ¼ x 1½", no photo, $6.00.

Blue Star sample, Coffee, 1½ x 2½ x 3¼", V1p225-5, $80.00.

Bluebird Brand, Ground Mustard, 3¼ x 2¼ x 1¼", V2p140-2, $25.00.

Blur-Less, Type Ribbon, ¾ x 2½ x 2½", no photo, $18.00.

Bo-Kay sample, Perfume, ¼ x 1", V2p32-5, $18.00.

Bocan's, Endex Pain Relief, ¼ x 1½ x 1¾", V1p77-10, $10.00.

Bocan's $.25, Knight Caps, ⅝ x 1⅜ x 2¾", V1p77-11, $35.00.

Boda, Type Ribbon, no photo, $15.00.

Bogle American, Watch Mainsprings, ¾ x 2¾ x 2¾", V1p334-9, $35.00.

Bogle Bros., Jewelers Supply, ⅜ x 1⅜, no photo, $15.00.

Bogle Bros., Watch Mainsprings, ¾ 2¾ x 2¾", no photo, $20.00.

Bohm F.A., Violin King, ⅞ x 1¼ x 4", V1p181-1, $20.00.

Bokar (bank), Coffee, 2½ x 3½", V1p225-6, $40.00.

Bokar sample, Coffee, 2½ x 4 ¾", no photo, $35.00.

Bokar sample, Coffee bank, 1¾ x 2¼ x 4", no photo, $25.00.

Boker's Henry 200, Loud Needles, ½ x 1¼ x 1½", V1p203-8, $35.00.

Boker's Henry 200, XLoud Needles, ¼ x 1¼ x 1¾", V1p203-9, $30.00.

Bon Ton sample, Coffee, no photo, $55.00.

Bonded, Aspirin, ¼ x 1¼ x 1¾", no photo, $8.00.

Bonds Ivory Cream, Tooth Soap, ½ x 1½ x 3", no photo, $60.00.

Boot Jack Plug, Tobacco Chew, ⅜ x 1⅝ x 3⅛", V1p191-1, $40.00.

Booth-Overton sample, Dyspepsia Tablets, ⅜ x 1 x 1½", V2p50-6, $30.00.

Booth's R.T., Mi-O-Na Hawaiian Cure, ⅜ x 1⅜ x 2½", V2p50-2, $45.00.

Booth's R.T., Mi-o-na Tablets, ½ x 1¾ x 3", V1p77-12, $30.00.

Booth's R.T., Mi-O-Na Tablets, ⅝ x 1¾ x 3", V1p78-1, $30.00.

Booth's sample, Balm Ointment, ⅜ x 1¼", V1p78-2, $30.00.

Booth's sample, Hyomei Balm, ¼ x 1⅛", V1p78-3, $35.00.

Booth's sample, Powder, no photo, $60.00.

Bootmaster, Cream Boot Polish, 1 x 3½", V1p277-4, $18.00.

Bootone, Polish, no photo, $18.00.

Boot's, Bronchial Lozenges, 1 x 2 x 3⅛", V1p291-1, $25.00.

Borbro, Aspirin Tablets, 1 x 1½ x 1½", V2p50-3, $12.00.

Borden's sample, Coffee, 2½ x 2¾", V1p226-1, $30.00.

Bordens sample, Milk, 1¼ x 2¼", V1p243-3, $25.00.

Borel Jules Co., Watch Crystals, ⅜ x 1¼", V1p334-10, $8.00.

Boro Salicine, Julep Mints Laxative, ½ x 1 x 2¾", V2p167-1, $25.00.

Boscul (bank), Coffee, 2½ x 2¼", V1p226-2, $95.00.

Boscul (bank), Coffee, 2¾ x 2¼", V1p226-3, $95.00.

Bostwick's, Aspirin, ¼ x 1¼ x 1½", no photo, $20.00.

Bourjois sample, Face Powder, ⅛ x 1½", V2p23-1, $20.00.

Bournville sample, Cocoa, ½ x 1¾ x 2½", V1p220-6, $75.00.

Bournville sample, Cocoa, ½ x 1⅞ x 2½", V1p220-7, $80.00.

Bower's, Mystic Salve, ¾ x 2⅜", V1p78-4, $15.00.

Bowes Seal Fast, Auto Fuses, ¼ x 1¼ x 1¾", V1p7-7, $8.00.

Bowman & Musser, Watch Mainsprings, 1 x 2¾ x 5 ¼", V1p334-11, $40.00.

Bowman Ezra F., Watch Mainsprings, 1¼ x 2¾ x 5 ⅜", V1p334-12, $35.00.

Boye, Egg Eyed Needles, ⅛ x 1 x 2", V2p204-2, $10.00.

Boye, Hair Pins, ⅝ x 1 x 3⅛", V1p33-10, $10.00.

Boyer sample, Face Powder, ⅜ x 1⅜", V1p250-7, $18.00.

Boyer sample, Flowers of Beauty, ⅜ x 1⅜, no photo, $18.00.

Boyer's No.5, Blacking, ⅞ x 4", V1p277-5, $70.00.

Boy's Harp, Harmonica, ⅞ x 1¼ x 4", V2p204-4, $15.00.

Bramo, Steel Ball & Seat, 1½ x 1¾", V1p193-4, $10.00.

Brandle Smith $.10, Butter Scotch Waffers, 1⅛ x 2¼ x 3¾", V2p167-3, $25.00.

Brandreth's, Pills 36, ½ x ⅞ x 2", V1p78-5, $18.00.

Brandreth's, Vegetable Pills, ⅝ x 1 x 1⅝", V1p78-6, $18.00.

Brasso sample, Metal Polish, 1⅛ x 1⅞", V1p217-6, $30.00.

Brater's, Asthma Powder, ⅞ x 1¾ x 2⅞", no photo, $35.00.

Brater's sample, Asthma Powder, ⅞ x 1¾ x 2⅞", V1p78-7, $40.00.

Brater's sample, Asthma Powder, ⅞ x 1¾ x 3", V2p50-5, $40.00.

Brawntawns $.50, Tonic Tablets, ½ x 1¾ x 3", V2p50-7, $80.00.

Breakfast Cheer sample, Coffee, 2¼ x 2¾", V2p123-4, $130.00.

Breethem, Breath Mints, ¼ x 1⅝ x 2⅛", V1p286-2, $30.00.

Breethem, Breath Mints, ¼ x 1⅝ x 2⅛", V1p286-3, $30.00.

Breethem $.05, Breath Mints, ¼ x 1½ x 2⅛", V1p286-4, $20.00.

Breivogel P.J., Watch Dial, ⅜ x 1⅝ x 1⅝", V1p335-1, $30.00.

Breivogel P.J., Watch Dial, ⅜ x 1⅝ x 1⅝", V1p335-2, $25.00.

Bremond John sample, Coffee, 2½ x 2½", V1p226-4, $215.00.

Brewer's, Chocolate Cathartics, ⅜ x 1⅞ x 2½", V2p51-1, $25.00.

Bright's $.50, Kidney Beans, ½ x 1½ x 2½", V1p78-8, $150.00.

Brilliantone 300, Needles, ½ x 1¼ x 1¾", V2p111-6, $30.00.

Brimfull Brand, Mustard, 3⅞ x 2⅜ x 1", V2p140-4, $15.00.

Bristol Meyers, Sal Hepatica Laxative, 1¾ x 2¾", no photo, $25.00.

Britain's Best, Gramophone Needles, ¼ x 1¼ x 1½", V1p203-10, $30.00.

Britain's Best, Gramophone Needles, ¼ x 1¼ x 1¾", V1p203-11, $30.00.

Britain's Best, Talking Machine Needles, ½ x 1¼ x 1½", V1p203-12, $35.00.

Britain's Best Nita, Needles Phonographic, ¼ x 1¼ x 1¾", V1p204-1, $40.00.

Britians Best Loud, Needles, no photo, $35.00.

Britians Best sample, Needles, ⅝ x 2", V2p111-2, $50.00.

Britians Masterpiece, Needles 200, no photo, $35.00.

Brittens Royal Nip, Gum, no photo, $90.00.

Broadcast Loud Tone, Needles Gramaphone, ½ x 1¼ x 1½", V1p204-2, $35.00.

Broadway, Needles Gramaphone, no photo, $35.00.

Bromo $.25, Laxine, ⅜ x 1½ x 2½", no photo, $45.00.

Bronco Brand, Type Ribbon, ¾ x 2¼ x 2¼", no photo, $15.00.

Bronk-lets, Throches, ¾ x 2 x 2¾", no photo, $22.00.

Bronzeforall, Paint Shade 29, ⅜ x 2⅛ x 3¼", V1p181-8, $35.00.

Brooklyn Bridge, unknown, no photo, $90.00.

Brookside Carnation sample, Talcum Powder, 1 x 2", V1p256-6, $125.00.

Brown, Herb Tablets, ⅞ x 2⅛ x 3¼", V1p78-10, $20.00.

Brown, Herb Tablets, ⅞ x 2⅛ x 3¼", V1p78-9, $20.00.

Brown $1.00, Herb Tablets, ⅞ x 2¼ x 3¼", V1p78-11, $20.00.

Brown B.F., Shoe Polish Russet, ⅝ x 1½", V1p277-6, $20.00.

Brown Beauty, Boot Polish, ⅝ x 2⅝", V1p277-7, $25.00.

Brown Tonic, Stomach & Liver Tablets, ½ x 1¾", V1p78-12, $55.00.

Brownie, Ointment, no photo, $22.00.

Brown's, Bronchial Troches, 1 x 2 x 2½", V1p291–2, $15.00.

Brown's Pharmacy, Medicine, ⅜ x 1¼", V1p79–1, $5.00.

Bruguiers sample, Antiseptic Tooth Powder, no photo, $30.00.

Brunswick, Needles, no photo, $35.00.

Brunswick 12 yards, Dental Floss Silk, 1⅛ x 1¾", no photo, $15.00.

Brunswick 30 yards, Dental Floss, 1⅛ x 1½", V2p40–7, $20.00.

Brunswick-Balke, Court Plaster, ⅞ x ⅞ x 3", V1p193–5, $10.00.

Bruton's, Scotch Snuff, 1½ x 2⅛", V1p191–2, $30.00.

Bruton's, Scotch Snuff, 1¼ x 1¾", V2p204–7, $22.00.

Bryan, Aspirin, ¼ x 1¼ x 1¾", V1p79–2, $10.00.

Bryant and Mays, Match Safe, ⅜ x 1¼ x 1¾", V2p205–1, $60.00.

Buch A.M., Cold Cream, ⅞ x 1⅞", V1p28–6, $35.00.

Buck Cleaner, Buckskin Shoe Cleaner, 1¾ x 1½", V1p277–8, $40.00.

Buckard's, Aspirin 30, ⅜ x 1⅞ x 2⅜", V2p51–4, $8.00.

Buckeye Brand, Type Ribbon, 1⅝ x 1⅝ x 2", V1p303–6, $45.00.

Bucki Supreme, Type Ribbon, ¾ x 2½ x 2½", V1p303–7, $18.00.

Bucki Supreme, Type Ribbon, ⅞ x 2½", V2p175–7, $15.00.

Bucki Supreme, Type Ribbon, ⅞ x 2½ x 2½", V2p176–1, $12.00.

Buckingham Sample, Smoking Tobacco, ¾ x 2¼ x 3", V2p205–3, $90.00.

Bucklen's, Arnica Salve, ¾ x 2⅜", V1p79–3, $8.00.

Bucklen's, Salve, ⅞ x 2½", V1p79–4, $6.00.

Bucklen's sample, Arnica Salve, ¼ x 1", V1p79–5, $20.00.

Bucklen's sample, Salve, ⅜ x ⅞", V1p79–6, $15.00.

Buckley's $.35, Cinnamated Capsules, ⅜ x 1½ x 2⅜", V2p51–6, $15.00.

Buckley's sample, White Rub Ointment, ¼ x 1⅛", V1p79–7, $20.00.

Buckskin, Type Ribbon, 1¾ x 1¾ x 2", V1p303–9, $65.00.

Buckskin, Type Ribbon, ¾ x 2½ x 2½", V1p303–8, $25.00.

Buddies $.25, Aspirin, ¼ x 1¼ x1½", V1p79–8, $20.00.

Buddy Brooks sample, Talcum Powder for Men, 1 x 2⅜", V1p256–7, $40.00.

Buddy Universal Prod., Headache Wafers, 1⅜ x 3½", V1p162–2, $12.00.

Budge's, Type Ribbon, ¾ x 2½ x 2½", V1p303–10, $18.00.

Budget, Flint, ¼ x ⅞ x 1⅜", V2p205–6, $8.00.

Buescher sample, True Tone, ¼ x ⅞", V1p79–9, $10.00.

Buffalo sample, Peanut Butter, no photo, $165.00.

Builtmore, Auto Fuses, no photo, $10.00.

Bukets, Diuretic, ¼ x 1⅝ x 1¾", V1p79–10, $6.00.

Bull Dog, Type Ribbon, ¾ x 2½ x 2½", no photo, $75.00.

Bull John, Tire Repair Outfit, ⅝ x 1¼ x 4½", V1p12–10, $30.00.

Bundy, Type Ribbon, no photo, $18.00.

Bundy, Type Ribbon, ¾ x 2½", V1p303–11, $18.00.

Bundy, Type Ribbon, ¾ x 2½ x 2½", no photo, $10.00.

Bundy, Type Ribbon, ⅝ x 2¼", V2p176–4, $18.00.

Bunsen's sample, Catarrh Cure, ¼ x 1", V1p79–11, $30.00.

Bunsen's sample, Catarrhal Cream, ¼ x 1", V1p79–12, $35.00.

Bur-Mack $.25, Headache Pills, ¼ x 1¼ x 1¾", V2p51–2, $12.00.

Burchard's Salon, Needles, ⅜ x 1¼ x 1¾", V2p111–4, $40.00.

Burckard, Patent Leather Polish, ¾ x 1¾", V1p277–9, $35.00.

Burdox 6, Torch Lighter, ¼ x 1 x 1⅜", V1p193–6, $6.00.

Burford's Wm. B., Type Ribbon, ¾ x 2½ x 2½", no photo, $20.00.

Burham, Shaving Stick, 1½ x 3¼", V1p274–2, $75.00.

Burham $.10, Safety Razor, ¾ x 1¾ x 3⅜", V1p270–3, $90.00.

Burkhalter & Co., Spices, 1¼ x 3", no photo, $35.00.

Burma, Allspice, 1¼ x 2¼ x 3¾", no photo, $45.00.

Burma, Cinnamon, 3 x 2¼ x 1", V2p140–7, $30.00.

Burnham's E. sample, Skin Food, ¼ x 1⅛", V1p50–3, $22.00.

Burnishine sample, Nickel\Chromium Polish, ⅝ x 1½", V2p37–5, $15.00.

Burnley, Soldering Paste, 1½ x 2", V1p285–3, $12.00.

Burnley, Soldering Paste, ¾ x 2½", V1p285–2, $15.00.

Burrough's, Adding Machine Ribbon, 1⅝ x 1⅝ x 3⅜", V1p303–12, $12.00.

Burroughs, Adding Machine Ribbon, 1⅝ x 1⅝ x 2⅜", V2p176–6, $20.00.

Burroughs, Adding Machine Ribbon, ⅞ x 2⅛ x 2⅛", V1p304–1, $15.00.

Burroughs, Adding Machine Tape, ½ x 2 x 2", no photo, $8.00.

Burrough's, Moon-Hopkins Special, 2⅝ x 1⅝ x 2", no photo, $50.00.

Burroughs Wellcome, Amyl Nitrite, ⅝ x 1¾ x 2⅜", V1p80–1, $2.00.

Bursa sample, Coffee, no photo, $55.00.

Busch Mills, Nutmeg, 4 x 2½ x 1¾", V2p141–1, $22.00.

Business Brand, Type Ribbon, ¾ x 2½ x 2½", no photo, $18.00.

Buss, Auto Fuses, ¼ x 1¼ x 1¾", V1p7–8, $5.00*.

Buss, Auto Fuses, ¼ x 1¼ x 1¾", V1p7–9, $10.00.

Buss Adapters, Auto Fuses, ⅜ x 1⅜ x 1½", no photo, $8.00.

Buster Brown, Mace, 1⅜ x 1⅜ x 2⅝", V2p141–4, $45.00.

Buster Brown, Paprika, 2¾ x 2¼ x 1¼", V2p141–6, $60.00.

Buster Brown, Sage, 3¼ x 2¼ x 1¼", no photo, $50.00.

Busy Biddy, Mustard, 3¾ x 2¼ x 1¼", V2p141–2, $75.00.

Busy Biddy, Turmeric, 1¼ x 2¼ x 3", V2p141–3, $75.00.

Buttercup sample, Snuff, 1⅜ x 1¾", V1p191–3, $40.00.

ButterNut sample, Coffee, 1½ x 2½", V1p226–5, $45.00.

Buy-Roz, Gum, ¾ x 1½", V2p172–1, $25.00.

Buy-Roz, Gum Rose, ⅜ x 1½ x 2", no photo, $30.00.

C & T, Chain Lubricant, ½ x 1⅝ x 2⅝", V1p174–3, $70.00.

C R, Mainsprings, ¾ x 2½ x 2½", V1p335–3, $35.00.

C R, Watch Mainspring, ¾ x 2½ x 2½", V1p335–4, $35.00.

C-B Drug, Aspirin, ¼ x 1¼ x 1¾", V2p51–3, $8.00.

C.W.S. E&S sample, Tea, 1½ x 1½ x 1¾", V1p267–2, $35.00.

Ca-bi-na, Stomach Powder, 1½ x 1½ x 1½", V1p80–2, $20.00.

Cachoo $.10, Sneeze Powder, ¼ x ⅞", V1p193–7, $4.00.

Cachou, Aromatise, ⅜ x 1⅛ x 1¾", V2p167–5, $45.00.

Cactus, Tire Repair Outfit, ½ x 1½ x 2½", V1p13–1, $65.00.

Cadets Three, Condom, ⅝ x 1½", V1p23–3, $45.00.

Cadets Three $.35, Condoms, ⅜ x 1⅝ x 2⅛", V2p17–2, $75.00.

Cadillac, Type Ribbon, ¾ x 2½ x 2½", V2p176–2, $18.00.

Cadum, Ointment, ¼ x 2⅜", V2p51–5, $12.00.

Cadum sample, Ointment, ¼ x 1¼", V1p81–3, $20.00.

Cafe Puerto Rico sample, Coffee, no photo, $110.00.

Cafe Savoy sample, Coffee, 2¼ x 1½ x 2", V1p226–6, $160.00.

Cafotan, Pain Tablets, ¼ x 1¼ x 1¾", V1p80–3, $10.00.

Cain's, Bouillon Cubes, 1 x 3½", V1p19–8, $6.00.

Cain's, Bouillon Cubes, 1 x 3⅜", V1p19–7, $8.00.

Calder's $.10, Saponageous Dentine, 1⅜ x 2⅞", V1p61–1, $90.00.

Cali, Needles, ⅜ x 1¼ x 1¾", V1p204–3, $35.00.

California Crystal, Soap, no photo, $20.00.

Caligraph, Type Ribbon, no photo, $20.00.

Calumet, Mainsprings, no photo, $40.00.

Calumet, Valve Cores, ¼ x 1 x 1⅜", V1p16–8, $12.00.

Calumet sample, Baking Powder, 2 x 3", V1p243–4, $40.00.

CAM sample, Ointment Colds, ¼ x 1⅛", V1p80–4, $15.00.

Camel, Ink Pad, ⅜ x 1⅞ x 1⅞", V1p179–1, $35.00.

Camp Fire sample, Cocoa, no photo, $150.00.

Campbell's, Gall Cure, ½ x 1⅜", V1p330–12, $60.00.

Campbell's $.25, Gall Cure, ¾ x 2¾", no photo, $60.00.

Campho-Menthol sample, Lozenges, ¼ x 1¼", V2p169–3, $30.00.

Campho-Phenique sample, Powder, 1¼ x 1⅞", V1p248–8, $45.00.

Campho-Phenique sample, Powder, 1⅜ x 1⅞", V1p248–7, $40.00.

Campho-Phenique sample, Powder, ¾ x 1¼ x 2⅛", V1p248–6, $20.00.

Camphor Ice, Camphor Ice, ⅞ x 1¾ x 2⅞", V1p80–5, $15.00.

Camphor Ice, Camphor Ice, ⅞ x 1¾ x 2⅞", V2p51–7, $12.00.

Canada Motor Corp., Auto Fuses, ⅜ x 1¼ x 1¾", no photo, $12.00.

Canary 200, Needles, no photo, $40.00.

Cando sample, Polish Silver, ½ x 1½", V1p217–7, $25.00.

Candy Smokers, Candy Cigarette, ¼ x 3 x 3¼", V1p286–5, $25.00.

Canode Super Fine, Type Ribbon, ¾ x 2½ x 2½", V1p304–2, $18.00.

Canova Brand, Ginger, 3½ x 2¼ x 1¼", V2p141–5, $40.00.

Canton (Brauchler), Tire Repair Kit, ⅜ x 1½ x 2½", V1p13–2, $30.00.

Capri sample, Face Powder, ¼ x 1⅝", V1p250–8, $18.00.

Captain John, Orderlys, ¼ x 1¼ x 2½", V1p80–7, $50.00.

Captain John, Orderlys, ⅜ x 1½ x 2½", V1p80–6, $45.00.

Capt'n Hook, Fish Hook 50, ⅝ x 2", V1p175–5, $12.00.

Caravan, Condom, ¼ x 1½ x 2", V1p23–4, $75.00.

Caravel, Tea, ¾ x 2¼", V1p267–4, $15.00.

Caravel, Tea (Pan\fried), ¾ x 2⅜", V1p267–3, $12.00.

Caravel, Tea (Pan\fried), ¾ x 2⅜", V1p267–5, $12.00.

Carbolated Ointment, Salve, ¾ x 2", V1p80–8, $10.00.

Carbolic, Salve, ½ x 1½", V1p80–9, $8.00.

Carbolisalve sample, Salve, ¼ x 1⅛", V1p80–10, $35.00.

Carborundum, Abrasive Material, 2⅛ x 2⅛ x 2½", V1p11–5, $30.00.

Carborundum, Grind Salve, ⅜ x 1¼", V1p11–6, $8.00.

Carborundum, Valve Grind Compound, 1 x 2 x 3¾", V1p11–7, $35.00.

Carborundum sample, Valve Grind Compound, ¼ x 1⅛", V2p13–2, $15.00.

Cardinell, Ink\Stain Remover, 1¼ x 2¾", V1p21–4, $8.00.

Cardui $.50, Wash, ½ x 2 x 3⅛", V1p80–11, $75.00.

Carhart's, Scotch Snuff, 2⅜ x 1¾", V2p205–2, $22.00.

Carmen Brand, Latex Condom, ¾ x 1½", V1p23–5, $160.00.

Carnation, Corn Caps, ⅝ x 1 x 2⅜", V2p52–1, $30.00.

Carnation, Type Ribbon, no photo, $15.00.

Carnation, Type Ribbon, 1⅝ x 1⅝ x 1⅞", V2p176–3, $55.00.

Carnation, Type Ribbon, ¾ x 2½", V1p304–4, $20.00.

Carnation, Type Ribbon, ¾ x 2½", V1p304–5, $18.00.

Carnation, Type Ribbon, ¾ x 2½ x 2½", V1p304–3, $22.00.

Carnick's sample, Baby Food, no photo, $25.00.

Caroid, Dental Powder, ¾ x 1¼ x 2⅞", V1p57–1, $15.00.

Carter Superite, Type Ribbon, ¾ x 2¼ x 2¼", V1p304–6, $12.00.

Carter's, Indelible Outfit, ½ x 2 x 3¼", V1p179–2, $15.00.

Carter's, Iron Pills, ½ x 1¼ x 1½", V1p80–12, $18.00.

Carter's, Type Ribbon, 1 x 2½", no photo, $5.00.

Carter's $.10, Little Liver Pills, ½ x 1⅜", V2p52–4, $18.00.

Carter's $.50, Iron Pills, ½ x 1¼ x 1¾", V1p81–1, $15.00.

Carter's (Ideal), Type Ribbon, ¾ x 2¼ x 2¼", V1p304–7, $15.00.

Carter's Adanac, Type Ribbon, 1½ x 1½ x 2", no photo, $25.00.

Carter's Cavalier, Type Ribbon, ⅞ x 2¼ x 2¼", V2p176–5, $15.00.

Carter's Director, Type Ribbon, 1¾ x 1¾ x 1⅞", V2p177–1, $45.00.

Carters Director, Type Ribbon, 1 x 2¼ x 2¼", V1p304–8, $22.00.

Carter's Director, Type Ribbon, ¾ x 2¼ x 2¼", V2p176–7, $18.00.

Carter's Dragon, Type Ribbon, ¾ x 2¼", V1p304–9, $15.00.

Carter's Dragon, Type Ribbon, ¾ x 2¼ x 2¼", V1p304–10, $12.00.

Carter's Guardian, Type Ribbon, ⅞ x 2½", V1p305–1, $15.00.

Carter's Ideal, Type Ribbon, 1¾ x 1¾ x 2", V2p177–5, $45.00.

Carter's Ideal, Type Ribbon, ¾ x 2½", no photo, $6.00.

Carter's Ideal, Type Ribbon, ¾ x 2½", V2p177–3, $6.00.

Carter's Ideal Brand, Type Ribbon, 1¾ x 1¾ x 1¾", V1p304–11, $35.00.

Carter's Midnight, Type Ribbon, ¾ x 2½", V1p304,#12, 4.00.

Carter's Midnight, Type Ribbon, ⅝ x 2¼", no photo, $5.00.

Carters Nylon, Type Ribbon, ¾ x 2¼", V2p177–6, $12.00.

Carter's sample, Little Liver Pills, ½ x 1⅜", V1p81–2, $20.00.

Carter's Valiant, Type Ribbon, ¾ x 2½", V1p305–2, $6.00.

Cary's, Pills, ½ x 1½ x 3", no photo, $70.00.

Cascara-Elm $.10, Cure Constipation, ⅜ x 1⅝ x 2½", V1p81–4, $40.00.

Cascarets, Candy Cathartic Cure, ⅜ x 1½ x 2½", V2p52–6, $18.00.

Cascarets, Pill Box, ½ x ⅞ x 2", V1p81–5, $15.00.

Cascarets $.10, Candy Cathartic, ¼ x 1⅝ x 1⅞", V2p52–2, $8.00.

Cascarets $.10, Chocolate Laxative, ¼ x 1½ x 1¾", V1p81–6, $8.00.

Cascarets $.10, Chocolate Laxative, ¼ x 1¼ x 1¾", V1p81–7, $12.00.

Cascarets $.10, Laxative, ⅜ x 1¼ x 1¾", V2p52–3, $15.00.

Cascarets $.10, Laxative Candy, ¼ x 1⅝ x 1⅞", V1p81–8, $15.00.

Cascarets $.10, Laxative Candy Cathartic, ⅜ x 1¼ x 1¾", no photo, $12.00.

Cascarets $.25, Laxative, ½ x 1½ x 2½", V2p52–5, $10.00.

Cascarets $.25, Laxative Candy, ½ x 1⅝ x 2½", V1p81–9, $12.00.

Cascarets $.25, Laxative Candy Cathartic, ¼ x 1½ x 2½", V1p81–10, $35.00.

Cascarets $.50, Laxative Candy, ⅜ x 2¼ x 3¾", V1p81–11, $30.00.

Cascarets $.50, Laxative Tablets, ½ x 2¼ x 3¾", V1p81–12, $15.00.

Cascarets Free Sample, Laxative Candy, ⅜ x ¾ x 1⅞", V1p82–1, $12.00.

Cashmere Bouquet, Cleansing Pads, ½ x 2¼", V2p32–2, $8.00.

Castarlax $.10, Chocolate Laxative, ⅜ x 1⅝ x 1⅝", V2p52–7, $12.00.

Casterline Co., Cigarette Paper, ¼ x 1⅝ x 3", V2p205–4, $35.00.

Cat & Angel 200, Needles Phonographic, ½ x 1¼ x 1½", V1p204–4, $40.00.

Cathartic, Pills, ¼ x 1¼", V1p82–2, $20.00.

Causalins sample, Tablets, ¼ x 1¼ x 1¾", V2p53–1, $10.00.

Cavalier, Leather Soap, 1½ x 3⅜", V1p277–11, $8.00.

Cavalier, Leather Soap, 1⅜ x 3¾", V1p277–10, $8.00.

CCC, Lauxes Tablets, ⅜ x 1½ x 2¼", V2p53–3, $30.00.

Ce-Co Diamond Brand sample, Deodorant Powder, 1 x 2⅛", V2p201–2, $35.00.

Ce-pha-nol $.25, Tablets, ¼ x 1¼ x 1¾", V2p53–5, $8.00.

Cedesco (Acidex), Indigestion Tablets, ¼ x 1¾ x 2⅝", V1p68–10, $15.00.

Celestina sample, Talcum, no photo, $60.00.

Cenco, Type Ribbon, ¾ x 2½ x 2½", V2p177–2, $12.00.

Century, Spices, 3½ x 2¼ x 1¼", V2p141–7, $25.00.

Century (Sears), Safety Pins, ¾ x 1½ x 2½", V2p205–5, $20.00.

Century Dix #54, Needles Phonographic, ⅜ x 1¼ x 1¾", V1p204–5, $35.00.

Certified, Aspirin, ¼ x 1¼ x 1¾", V1p82–3, $8.00.

Certified, Aspirin, ¼ x 1¼ x 1¾", V1p82–4, $5.00*.

Certified, Aspirin, ¼ x 1¼ x 1¾", V1p82–5, $5.00*.

Certified, Aspirin, ¼ x 1¼ x 1¾", V1p82–6, $8.00.

Certified, Aspirin, ¼ x ⅞ x 1⅜", V1p82–8, $5.00.

Certified, Aspirin, ⅜ x 1⅞ x 2⅝", V2p53–7, $10.00.

Certified, Aspirin, ⅜ x 1 x 1½", V2p53–2, $5.00.

Certified, Aspirin 6 Tablets, ¼ x ⅞ x 1¼", V1p82–7, $8.00.

Certified Hospital, Aspirin, ¼ x 1¼ x 1¾", V2p53–4, $8.00.

Cest 20 AMP, Auto Fuses, ¼ x 1¼ x 1¾", V1p7–10, $15.00.

Challenge, Pens, no photo, $20.00.

Challenge, Type Ribbon, ¾ x 2½ x 2½", V1p305–4, $8.00.

Challenge, Type Ribbon, ¾ x 2 x 2", V1p305–3, $15.00.

Challenge $1.00, Safety Razor, ½ x 1⅜ x 2", V1p270–4, $250.00.

Challenge J., Pencil Case, no photo, $15.00.

Chamberlain's, Aspirin, ¼ x 1¼ x 1¾", V1p82–9, $15.00.

Chamberlain's, Stomach\Liver Tablets, ¼ x ⅞", V1p82–12, $45.00.

Chamberlain's $.25, Acetyl-Salicylic, ¼ x 1¼ x 1¾", V2p53–6, $15.00.

Chamberlain's $.25, Eye\Skin Ointment, ¾ x 1¾", V1p28–7, $20.00.

Chamberlain's $.25, Eye\Skin Ointment, ⅝ x 1¾", V1p83–1, $30.00.

Chamberlain's $.25, Stomach Liver Tablets, ¼ x 1⅛ x 2⅛", V1p82–11, $55.00.

Chamberlain's sample, Face Powder, ⅜ x1½", V1p250–9, $18.00.

Chamberlain's sample, Salve, ¼ x ⅞", V1p82–10, $45.00.

Champ, Pomade, no photo, $15.00.

Champion, Adhesive Tape, ¾ x 1", V2p53–8, $20.00.

Champion, Dental Floss, ¼ x 1⅛", V1p55–3, $20.00.

Chancellor, Type Ribbon, ⅞ x 2½", V1p305–5, $15.00.

Chandlers, Aspirin, ¼ x 1¼ x 1¾", no photo, $12.00.

Change, Laxative Tablets, ¼ x 1¼ x 1¾", V1p83–2, $8.00.

Chantecler 200, Needles, no photo, $45.00.

Chanty sample, Lavender Hair, ⅜ x 1¼", V2p35–3, $6.00.

Chap Stick sample, Salve, ¼ x ¾", V1p50–4, $5.00.

Chap Stick sample, Salve, ¼ x ⅞, 4.00*.

Chaperone $.10, Powder (dog repel), ¾ x 1¼ x 2⅜", V1p331–1, $80.00.

Chapoteaut's $.65, Phosphoglycerate, ⅜ x 1¼ x 2⅛", V1p83–3, $65.00.

Chariots, Condom, ¼ x 1¾ x 2", V1p23–6, $70.00.

Chartres, Type Ribbon, 1 x 2½ x 2½", V1p305–6, $50.00.

Chase & Sanborn sample, Coffee, 2½ x 2¼", V2p123–6, $65.00.

Chase & Sanborn sample, High Grade Coffee, 2½ x 2¼", V2p123–2, $60.00.

Chase & Sandborn sample, Coffee, 2½ x 2¼", V1p227–1, $60.00.

Chase & Sandborn sample, Coffee, 2½ x 2¼", V1p227–2, $75.00.

Chase & Sandborn sample, Coffee, 2½ x 2¼", V1p227–3, $70.00.

Chattanooga Medicine Co., see Cardui Wash, V1p80–11, $75.00.

Chef Boy-ar-dee sample, Grated Cheese, 2⅛ x 1⅝", V1p243–5, $30.00.

Chelsea, Clock (High Grade), ½ x 1½", no photo, $25.00.

Chem-Test Rx, Aspirin, ¼ x 1¼ x 1¾", V1p83–4, $12.00.

Chemico sample, Bath\House Cleaner, ¾ x 2", V2p37–2, $25.00.

Cheney's, Tooth Powder, no photo, $55.00.

Cherry Bloosom, Boot Polish, ½ x 2⅜", V1p277–12, $15.00.

Chesapeake, Type Ribbon, ¾ x 2½ x 2½", no photo, $12.00.

Cheseborough Mfg., Vaseline, ⅞ x 2⅝", V2p54–1, $12.00.

Chevrolet 3-A-15AMP, Auto Fuses, ¼ x 1¼ x 1¾", V1p7–11, $20.00.

Chieftain, Leather Polish, ⅝ x 1¾", V1p278–1, $18.00.

Chieftain, Shoe Paste, ½ x 1¾", V1p278–2, $18.00.

Chieftain, Type Ribbon, ¾ x 2½ x 2½", no photo, $70.00.

Chieftain, White Cake, 1 x 2¾", V1p278–3, $25.00.

Chieftan, Type Ribbon, no photo, $18.00.

China Balm, Salve, ⅜ x 1⅛", V1p83–5, $12.00.

Choclate Cream sample, Coffee, 2 x 3", V1p227–4, $115.00.

Chorister 200 Loud, Needles, no photo, $35.00.

Chorister 200 Medium, Needles, ½ x 2", no photo, $35.00.

Chorister 200 XLoud, Needles, no photo, $35.00.

Christy's 20, Aspirin, ¼ x 1¾ x 2⅛", V1p83–6, $10.00.

Chypre, Face Powder, no photo, $20.00.

Cigaret Loads, Novelty, ⅜ x ⅞", V1p193–8, $3.00*.

Cincho-Loid, Capsules (75), 1⅛ x 1⅝ x 2¼", V1p83–7, $20.00.

Citrox, Salve, ⅝ x 1½", V1p83–8, $4.00.

Citrox sample, Salve, ⅜ x 1¾", V2p54–4, $5.00.

Clark's Foster, Garden Peas, 1⅛ x 1½, $20.00.

Clary, Adding Ribbon, ¾ x 1¾ x 1¾", V2p177–4, $12.00.

Clean Point, Type Ribbon, no photo, $15.00.

Cleanzum sample, Hand Cleaner, ⅝ x 1½", V1p21–5, $275.00.

Clear-Again, Cold Tablets, ⅜ x ¾ x 1¾", V1p83–9, $20.00.

Clear-Again, Head Cold Tablets, ¼ x ¾ x 1¾", V2p54–6, $20.00.

Cleartone 200, Loud Needles, ⅜ x 1 x 1½", V1p204–6, $30.00.

Cleopatra, Needles, no photo, $30.00.

Click, Pain Pills, ⅜ x 1¼ x 1¾", V2p54–2, $15.00.

Cliffs, Siloam Tablets, ¼ x 1½ x 1⅞", V1p83–10, $50.00.

Clinic, Aspirin, ¼ x 1¼ x 1¾", V2p54–3, $12.00.

Clinic, Zinc Oxide, 1 x 1¼", V2p195–2, $35.00.

Clipper, Coffee, 4 x 3¼", V1p227–5, $180.00.

Cloister, Gramaphone Needles, no photo, $40.00.

Clover Brand, Valve Grind Compound, 1¼ x 2", V1p11–8, $10.00.

Clover Brand sample, Automotive Nickel Paste, ⅜ x 1¼", V2p13–3, $12.00.

Clover Farm, Mace, 3 x 2¼ x 1¼", V2p142–1, $22.00.

Clover Farm Brand, Aspirin, ¼ x 1¼ x 1¾", V2p54–5, $20.00.

Clover sample, Grinding Compound, ½ x 1¼", no photo, $6.00.

Cloverdale sample, Cocoa, 1¼ x 1¾ x 2", V1p220–8, $75.00.

Cloverine, Aspirin, ⅜ x 1¼ x 2⅛", V1p83–11, $4.00*.

Cloverine $.35, Lax Pills, ¼ x 1 x 1¾", V1p83,#12, 4.00*.

Cloverine $.50, Salve, ¾ x 2½", V2p54–7, $6.00.

Cloverine sample, Talcum Powder, no photo, $85.00.

CN $.25, Soap for the Skin, 2 x 3 x 1⅜", V1p50–5, $45.00.

Cock Fight, Needles, no photo, $55.00.

Cocoa sample, Coffee, no photo, 80.00.

Cocolatum $.15, Hair Tonic, ⅞ x 2½", V1p33–11, $25.00.

Cocomalt sample, Food Drink, 1⅞ x 1½", V1p243–6, $40.00.

Cocomalt sample, Food Drink, 2 x 1¾", V1p243–7, $40.00.

Cocomalt sample, Food Drink, 2 x 2¾", no photo, $35.00.

Cocorets $.10, Laxative, ⅜ x 1¼ x 2", V2p55–1, $12.00.

Codo Stenocraft, Type Ribbon, ¾ x 2½ x 2½", V2p177–7, $15.00.

Codo Typocraft, Type Ribbon, ¾ x 2½ x 2½", V1p305–7, $12.00.

Coffee Columbia sample, Coffee, 2¾ x 2¼", V1p227–6, $70.00.

Coffey's sample, Quick Relief Balm, ¼ x 1⅛", V1p84–1, $25.00.

Colburn's, Mace, 1¾ x 2⅞", V1p188–4, $45.00.

Colburn's, Paprika, 1⅝ x 2½", V2p142–4, $25.00.

Colchi-Sal, Tablets, no photo, $30.00.

Cold Cream, Cold Cream, 1 x 2⅜", V1p28–9, $15.00.

Cold Cream, Cold Cream, ¾ x 1½", V1p28–8, $18.00.

Cold Cream, Skin & Complexion, 1⅛ x 1¾", V1p28–10, $18.00.

Colgan's, Gum (Violet Chip), ¾ x 1½", V1p296–2, $25.00.

Colgan's, Gum Mint Chips, ¾ x 1½", no photo, $30.00.

Colgan's, Gum Mint Chips, ¾ x 1½", V1p296–3, $20.00.

Colgan's, Gum Violet Chips, ¾ x 1½", V2p172–5, $35.00.

Colgan's, Mint Chips, ⅝ x 1½", V2p172–3, $60.00.

Colgate, Compact Powder, ⅝ x 1½", V1p44–1, $20.00.

Colgate, Compact Powder, ⅝ x 1½", V1p44–2, $20.00.

Colgate, Shaving Stick, 1¼ x 1½", V1p274–4, $15.00.

Colgate, Shaving Stick, 1¼ x 2¼", no photo, $8.00.

Colgate Florient sample, Face Powder, ¼ x 1⅝", V2p23–3, $18.00.

Colgate Florient sample, Face Powder Flesh, ½ x 1½", V1p250–10, $18.00.

Colgate sample, Baby Powder, ¾ x 1¼ x 2", V2p127–2, $60.00.

Colgate sample, Baby Powder Talcum, ¾ x 1¼ x 2⅛", V1p256–8, $115.00.

Colgate sample, Cashmere Bouquet Talcum, ¾ x 1¼ x 2⅛, no photo, $40.00.

Colgate sample, Cashmere Bouquet Talcum, ¾ x 1¼ x 2⅛", V1p256–9, $50.00.

Colgate sample, Cashmere Bouquet Talcum, ¾ x 1⅛ x 3⅜", V1p256–10, $45.00.

Colgate sample, Cha Ming Talcum, ¾ x 1¼ x 2⅛", V1p256–11, $50.00.

Colgate sample, Dactylis Powder, ¾ x 1¼ x 2⅛", V1p256–12, $65.00.

Colgate sample, Dactylis Powder, ¾ x 1¼ x 2⅛", V1p257–1, $55.00.

Colgate sample, Dental Powder, 1 x 2¼", V2p40–2, $55.00.

Colgate sample, Eclat Talcum, ¾ x 1¼ x 2⅛", V1p257–2, $45.00.

Colgate sample, Exquisite Extracts, ½ x ¾ x 1½", V1p50–6, $20.00.

Colgate sample, Floriant Talcum Powder, ¾ x 1¼ x 2", no photo, $45.00.

Colgate sample, Florient Talcum, ¾ x 1¼ x 2⅛", V1p257–3, $40.00.

Colgate sample, La France Rose Talcum, ¾ x 1¼ x 2⅛", V1p257–4, $45.00.

Colgate sample, Monad Talcum, ¾ x 1¼ x 2", no photo, $35.00.

Colgate sample, Monad Talcum, ¾ x 1¼ x 2⅛", V1p257–6, $40.00.

Colgate sample, Monad Violet Talcum, ¾ x 1¼ x 2⅛", V1p257–5, $45.00.

Colgate sample, Rapid Shave Powder, ¾ x 1¼ x 2⅛", V1p274–3, $65.00.

Colgate sample, Shaving Stick, 1¼ x 1½", no photo, $20.00.

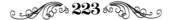

Colgate sample, Talc for Men, ¾ x 1⅛ x 3¼", V1p257–11, $15.00.

Colgate sample, Tooth Powder, ¾ x 1¼ x 2⅛", V1p57–2, $35.00.

Colgate sample, Violet Boric Anti.Talcum, ¾ x 1¼ x 2⅛", no photo, $40.00.

Colgate sample, Violet Talcum, ¾ x 1½ x 2", no photo, $35.00.

Colgate sample, Violet Talcum, ¾ x 1½ x 2", V1p257–8, $40.00.

Colgate sample, Violet Talcum, ¾ x 1¼ x 2⅛", V1p257–10, $35.00.

Colgate sample, Violet Talcum, ¾ x 1¼ x 2⅛", V1p257–7, $40.00.

Colgate sample, Violet Talcum, ¾ x 1¼ x 2⅛", V1p257–9, $40.00.

Colgate sample, Violet Talcum, ⅝ x ⅞ x 1⅞", V2p127–4, $100.00.

Colgate's, Rapid Shave Powder, 1¼ x 3¼", V2p134–3, $20.00.

Colonial Brand, Allspice, 3¾ x 2¼ x 1¼", V2p142–6, $45.00.

Columbia, Mainsprings, ¾ x 2¾ x 2¾", V2p194–5, $75.00.

Columbia, Type Ribbon, ¾ x 2½", no photo, $12.00.

Columbia, Type Ribbon, ¾ x 2½", no photo, $8.00.

Columbia, Type Ribbon, ¾ x 2½", V1p305–10, $12.00.

Columbia, Type Ribbon, ¾ x 2¼", V1p305–8, $10.00.

Columbia, Type Ribbon, ⅝ x 2¼", V2p178–1, $12.00.

Columbia 100, Needles (Duragold), ⅜ x 1¼ x 1½", V1p204–7, $35.00.

Columbia 200, Needles (Brilliant), ¼ x 1¼ x 1¾", V1p204–8, $35.00.

Columbia 200, Needles (DeLuxe), 14 x 1¼ x 1¾", V1p204–9, $40.00.

Columbia 200, Needles (Superbe), ½ x 1¼ x 1¾", V1p204–10, $35.00.

Columbia 200, Needles Talkie, ⅜ x 1¼ x 1¾", V1p204–11, $35.00.

Columbia 300, Highest Quality Needles, ⅜ x 1¼ x 1¾", V2p111–5, $40.00.

Columbia 300, Home-Light-Tone, ½ x 1¼ x 1½", V2p111–7, $40.00.

Columbia 300, Loud Tone Needles, ½ x 1¼ x 1½", V2p112–1, $35.00.

Columbia 300, Needles, ½ x 1¼ x 1½", V2p112–3, $30.00.

Columbia 300, Needles (loud tone), ½ x 1¼ x 1½", no photo, $30.00.

Columbia 300, Needles (med. tone), ½ x 1¼ x 1½", V1p205–2, $35.00.

Columbia 300, Needles Gramaphone, ½ x 1¼ x 1½", V1p205–3, $35.00.

Columbia 300, Needles Gramaphone, ½ x 1¼ x 1½", V2p112–5, $35.00.

Columbia 300, Needles Soft Tone, ½ x 1¼ x 1½", V1p205–4, $35.00.

Columbia 300, Soft Tone Needles, ¾ x 1¼ x 1½", no photo, $35.00.

Columbia Carbon, Twin Tex, ⅞ x 2½ x 2½", V2p178–3, $18.00.

Columbia Classic, Type Ribbon, ¾ x 2¼ x 2¼", V1p305–11, $18.00.

Columbia Economique, Type Ribbon, ⅞ x 2½", V2p178–6, $8.00.

Columbia Ideal, Soft Tone Needles, ¼ x 1⅜ x 1⅞", V2p112–7, $35.00.

Columbia Mineral Wax, Type Ribbon, ⅞ x 2½ x 2½", V1p305–12, $15.00.

Columbia sample, Antiseptic Powder, ¾ x 1¼ x 2⅛", V1p248–9, $45.00.

Columbia sample, Antiseptic Powder, ⅝ x 1⅜ x 2⅛", V2p201–4, $35.00.

Columbia sample, Gall Cure, ½ x 1⅜", V1p331–2, $70.00.

Columbia Superbe, Soft Tone Needles, ¼ x 1⅜ x 1⅞", V2p112–2, $35.00.

Columbus, Shoe Polish, ⅞ x 2¾", V1p278–4, $30.00.

Comet, Auto Fuses, ⅜ x 1¼ x 1¾", V2p13–4, $15.00.

Comfort, Foot Cooler, 1 x 1½ x 4½", V1p255–1, $30.00.

Comfort, Pain Tablets, ¼ x 1½ x 2½", no photo, $25.00.

Comfort (Sykes), Toilet Powder, 1 x 1⅜ x 4¼", no photo, $35.00.

Comfort (Sykes) sample, Baby Powder, 1 x 2", V1p264–5, $50.00.

Comfort (Sykes) sample, Baby Powder, ⅞ x 1¼ x 1⅝", V1p264–4, $215.00.

Commercial, Auto Fuses, ¼ x 1¼ x 1¾", V1p8–1, $15.00.

Commercial 20 AMP, Auto Fuses, ¼ x 1¼ x 1¾", no photo, $10.00.

Commercial Brand, Type Ribbon, ¾ x 2½ x 2½", no photo, $15.00.

Common Sense, Tire Repair Outfit, ½ x 2 x 3", V1p13–3, $70.00.

Common Sense sample, Baking Powder, 1¾ x 2½", V1p243–8, $45.00.

Commonwealth, Type Ribbon, ¾ x 2½ x 2½", no photo, $15.00.

Companion Pure Tone, Needles Gramaphone, ⅜ x 1¼ x 1¾", V1p205–6, $30.00.

Compound, Cathartic Pills, no photo, $18.00.

Compoz, Tablets, ¼ x 1¼ x 1¾", V1p84–2, $4.00.

Comtograph, Type Ribbon, ¾ x 2¼ x 2¼", V1p306–1, $15.00.

Concert Nadelyn, Needles, no photo, $30.00.

Concord, Needles Gramaphone, ¼ x 1¼ x 1¾", V1p205–7, $30.00.

Concord (Tayler), Needles Phono, ⅜ x 1¼ x 1¾", V1p205–8, $30.00.

Condor, Phonograph Needles, ½ x 1¼ x 1½", V2p112–4, $45.00.

Condor 50, Pins, ⅜ x 1¼ x 1⅞", V1p300–3, $40.00.

Confer's, Headache Tablets, ½ x 1½ x 2½", V2p55–3, $35.00.

Conqueror, Phonograph Needles, no photo, $40.00.

Conquest, Type Ribbon, ¾ x 2½ x 2½", V2p178–2, $8.00.

Consolidated Dental, Superior Dental Rubber, 1 x 3¼ x 6", no photo, $65.00.

Consolidated Fireworks, Fireworks Powder, 1⅜ x 3½", V2p205–7, $200.00.

Continental, 1 x 2 x 3", no photo, $115.00.

Cook\Old Reliable, Type Ribbon, ¾ x 2½ x 2½", V2p178–4, $20.00.

Cook's, Laxative Quinine Cold Tablets, ¼ x 1¼ x 1¾", no photo, $8.00.

Cooks Friend sample, Baking Powder, 1⅛ x 1⅝ x 1", V2p125–1, $30.00.

Coote's, Carbolic Salve, ¾ x 2¾", V2p55–5, $12.00.

Copco, Type Ribbon, ½ x 2½ x 2½", V1p306–2, $6.00.

Copper Chief, Type Ribbon, ¾ x 2½", V1p306–3, $15.00.

Copy Craft, Type Ribbon, ¾ x 2½", V1p306–4, $8.00.

Copy-Right Brand, Type Ribbon, ⅞ x 2¼ x 2¼", V2p178–5, $45.00.

Corax, Analgesic Laxative, ¼ x 2 x 2¾", V1p84–3, $15.00.

Corega sample, Dental Powder, ¾ x 1¼ x 2", V2p40–4, $40.00.

Corn Fix sample, Salve, ⅜ x ⅞", V1p84–4, $15.00.

Cornease $.25, Corn Salve, ½ x 1¼", V1p84–5, $15.00.

Cornease sample, Salve, ⅜ x 1⅜", V1p84–6, $18.00.

Corona Athletic, Gum Wintergreen, ⅜ x 1 x 3¼", V1p296–4, $200.00.

Corona Brand, Type Ribbon, ¾ x 2½ x 2½", V1p306–5, $20.00.

Corona sample, Ointment, ⅝ x 1⅝", V1p84–7, $10.00.

Corona sample, Wool Fat Compound, ⅝ x 1½", V1p193–9, $15.00.

Corsage Bouquet sample, Toilet Powder, ¾ x 1¼ x 2⅛", no photo, $65.00.

Corsage sample, Bouquet Talcum, ¾ x 1¼ x 2⅛", V2p127–6, $140.00.

Corticelli, Dental Floss, ¼ x 1⅜", V2p40–6, $40.00.

Corylopsis of Japan sample, Talcum Powder, ¾ x 1⅛ x 2", V1p257–12, $90.00.

Cosmo sample, Coffee, 1¼ x 2¼ x 3⅛", V1p228–1, $65.00.

Cossack Tablets $1.00, Horse Medicine, ¾ x 2⅛ x 3⅛", V2p192–3, $80.00.

Cotton King, Type Ribbon, ¾ x 2½ x 2½", V1p306–6, $25.00.

Countess Brouetelle, French Pansy Female Pills, no photo, $45.00.

Counting House F\H, Paper Fastners #2, 1 x 1½", V1p62–3, $20.00.

Counting House R\H, Paper Fastners #2, 1½ x 1¼", V1p62–4, $18.00.

Country Store, Candle Adhesive, ⅝ x 2⅛", V1p193–10, $6.00.

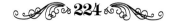

Courtland 333, Fly Line Cleaner, ⅜ x 2", V1p175–6, $10.00.
Cowan E.A. Co., Jewelers Material, ½ x 1⅛", no photo, $12.00.
Cowan's sample, Cocoa, 1 x 1⅜ x 1⅝", V1p220–9, $145.00.
Cowan's sample, Instant Cocoa, 1 x 1⅜ x 1⅝", V2p122–1, $175.00.
Cox's, Tire Repair Outfit, ⅞ x 1¾ x 4¼", V1p13–4, $85.00.
CPC, Nail Cream, ½ x 1½", V1p42–2, $10.00.
CPC, Radiant Nail Powder, 1⅜ x 3¼", V1p42–3, $35.00.
CPC, Radiant Nail Powder, ¾ x 1½ x 3", V1p42–4, $20.00.
CPC, Tooth Powder, 1 x 2¼", V2p40–8, $45.00.
CPC sample, Talcum Powder, no photo, $55.00.
CPC Trailing Arbutus, Cold Cream, ⅝ x 1½", V2p27–2, $45.00.
CPC White Nail, Stain Remover, ½ x 1⅝", V1p42–5, $8.00.
Craig's $.10, Pure Aspirin, ¼ x 1¼ x 1½", V2p55–7, $15.00.
Crane Brand, Type Ribbon, ¾ x 2½ x 2½", V1p306–7, $25.00.
Crane John, Metalic Packing, 1⅛ x 1", V1p193–11, $8.00.
Crane John, Water Pump Packing, 1⅛ x 1⅛", V1p193–12, $8.00.
Crane John, Water Pump Packing, 1⅛ x 1⅞", V1p194–1, $10.00.
Crane's, Aspirin, ¼ x 1¼ x 1¾", V1p84–8, $20.00.
Cream Dove sample, Peanut Butter, 1¾ x 2⅜", V1p243–9, $125.00.
Creamalin, Tablets, ¼ x 1½ x 2", V1p84–9, $8.00.
Crescent, Adhesive Plaster, 1 x 1", V1p345–6, $18.00.
Crescent, Needle Mill, ½ x 2¼", V1p185–7, $35.00.
Crescent, Safety Razor, ½ x 1 x 2⅛", V1p270–5, $175.00.
Crescent, Watch Mainspring, ⅝ x 2¾ x 5", V1p335–5, $40.00.
Crescent $.25, Healing Ointment, 1 x 2½", V1p84–10, $10.00.
Cressy, Family Remedies, ⅜ x 1½ x 2½", V2p55–2, $15.00.
Crest, Condom, no photo, $45.00.
Crest, Type Ribbon, ¾ x 2¼ x 2¼", V1p306–8, $12.00.
Criterion, Type Ribbon, ¾ x 2½", V1p306–9, $5.00.
Criterion McDonovan, Type Ribbon, 1⅝ x 1⅝ x 2", V2p178–7, $55.00.
Crittenden, Headache Tablets, ¼ x 1¼ x 1¾", V2p55–4, $10.00.
Crocker H.S. Co., Railroad Pins #219, ¾ x 1¾ x 2⅞", V2p206–1, $35.00.
Cross Country, Valve Caps, ½ x 1 x 1½", V1p16–1, $8.00.
Croupline, Cough Drops, no photo, $75.00.
Crow Jim, Corn Salve, ½ x 1", V2p5–6, $18.00.
Crow Jim $.10, Corn Salve, ½ x 1", V1p84–11, $18.00.
Crow Jim $.10, Salve, ⅜ x 1", V2p55–8, $20.00.
Crowfoot, Type Ribbon, ¾ x 2½ x 2½", V1p306–10, $15.00.
Crowfoot, Type Ribbon, ⅞ x 2¼ x 2¼", V2p179–1, $20.00.
Crowley 300, Needles, no photo, $30.00.
Crown, Type Ribbon, ¾ x 2½", V2p179–3, $12.00*.
Crown, Type Ribbon, ¾ x 2¼", no photo, 12.00*.
Crown, Type Ribbon, ¾ x 2¼ x 2¼", V1p306–11, $18.00.
Crown 200, Needles Phonograph, ½ x 1¼ x 1½", V1p205–9, $35.00.
Crown Brand, Allspice, 3½ x 2 x 1", V2p142–2, $25.00.
Crown Brand, Aspirin, ¼ x 1¼ x 1¾", V1p84–12, 8.00*.
Crown Brand, Type Ribbon, 1⅝ x 1⅝ x 2", V1p306–12, $60.00.
Crown Brand, Type Ribbon, ¾ x 2½ x 2½", no photo, 12.00*.
Crown Brand, Type Ribbon, ¾ x 2½ x 2½", V1p307–1, $15.00.
Crystal Beaver, Type Ribbon, ¾ x 2½ x 2½", V1p307–2, $35.00.
Cupid, unknown, 1 x 2", V1p286–6, $50.00.
Curity, Dental Floss, ⅜ x 1⅛", V1p55–4, $20.00.
Cushman & Denison sample, Pinch Fastners, ¼ x ⅞", V2p206–3, $15.00.
Cutex, Powder Polish, ½ x 1⅛", V1p42–6, $8.00.
Cutex, Powder Polish, ⅞ x 1½", V1p42–7, $8.00.
Cutex (pink), Polishing Paste, ⅜ x ⅞", V1p47–6, $5.00.
Cutex sample, Nail Brilliance, ¼ x ⅞", V1p42–8, $5.00.
Cutex sample, Nail White, ¼ x ⅞", V1p42–9, $8.00.
Cuticura, Ointment, ⅝ x 1⅞", V1p85–1, $6.00.
Cuticura, Ointment, ⅝ x 2", V1p85–2, $8.00.
Cuticura, Salve, ¾ x 2", V1p85–4, $8.00.
Cuticura sample, Ointment, ⅜ x 1⅜", V1p85–3, $12.00.
Cuticura sample, Talcum Powder, 1¼ x 2¼ x 3⅝", no photo, $50.00.
Cuticura sample, Talcum Powder, ¾ x 1¼ x 2", V2p128–1, $65.00.
Cuticura sample, Talcum Powder, ¾ x 1¼ x 2⅛", V1p258–1, $75.00.
Cuticura Soap, Shaving Stick, 1½ x 3⅛", V1p274–5, $18.00.
Cutigien, Night Cream, no photo, $18.00.
Cutigien, Toilet Cream, no photo, $18.00.
CW, Ground Mustard, 3⅝ x 2⅜ x 1⅛", V2p142–3, $15.00.
Cypridol, Capsules, ⅜ x 1¼ x 2⅛", V1p85–5, $35.00.
Cystitis #645, Tablets, ¼ x 1⅜", V1p85–6, $8.00.
Czarina, Tea Afternoon, sample 1 x 4 x 2", $8.00.
D & C Diaphram, Diaphram, 1 x 3½", no photo, $10.00.
Daisy, Gun Cleaning Kit, ½ x 1 x 13⅝", V1p66–9, $50.00.
Daisy, Russet Polish, ⅜ x 1¾", V2p118–6, $18.00.
Daisy BB's, Target Shot, ¾ x 2", V1p66–7, $20.00.
Daisy Brand, Type Ribbon, 1½ x 1½ x 2", no photo, $35.00.
Daisy Brand sample, Coffee, no photo, $70.00.
Dalton, Adding Ribbon, no photo, $12.00.
Dalton's sample, Coffee, 1¼ x 2½", V1p228–2, $65.00.
Damascus, Watch Mainspring, ½ x 2½ x 2½", V1p335–6, $60.00.
Damtana sample, Waffers, no photo, $35.00.
Dan Patch, Gall Salve, no photo, $45.00.
Dandy Pepsin, Gum, no photo, $110.00.
Dandy Pepsin, Gum, no photo, $165.00.
Dandy-Line, Type Ribbon, ¾ x 2½ x 2½", no photo, $35.00.
Dandy-Line, Type Ribbon, ¾ x 2½ x 2½", V1p307–3, $40.00.
Darby's, Toothache Plaster, ¼ x 1⅛ x 2⅛", V2p41–1, $35.00.
Darby's S\J, Tooth Plaster, ¼ x 1¼ x 2⅛", V1p61–2, $90.00.
Darby's S\J, Toothache Plaster, ¼ x 1¼ x 2⅛", V1p61–3, $90.00.
Darkie, Tooth Paste, no photo, $160.00.
Davidson & Son, Jewelry Ring, ⅝ x 1½", V1p180–2, $10.00.
Davis, Menthol Salve, ¾ x 2", V1p85–7, $18.00.
Davis sample, Baking Powder, 2 x 1¾", V1p243–10, $50.00.
Davis Tryme Brand, Black Pepper, 4½ x 2¼ x 1¼", no photo, $15.00.
Dawn, Type Ribbon, no photo, $12.00.
Dawn, Type Ribbon, no photo, $18.00.
Daxalan sample, Ointment, ⅜ x 1¼", V1p85–8, $10.00.
Daxalan sample, Pediatric Ointment, ⅜ x 1¼", V1p85–9, $10.00.
Day & Martin's, Boot Polish, ½ x 2½", V1p278–5, $6.00.
Dayton, Type Ribbon, no photo, $10.00.
Dazzle, Cloth, no photo, $15.00.
Dazzle sample, Nail Polish, ¼ x 1⅝", V1p42–10, $18.00.
De Loste's, Aspirin, ¼ x 1¼ x 1¾", V1p85–10, $15.00.
De Luxe, Saffron, ⅜ x 1½ x 2½", V2p203–1, $15.00.
De Luxe $.10, Saffron Spanish, ⅜ x 1⅝ x 2½", V1p187–5, $18.00.
De-Fi, Type Ribbon, 1 x 2½ x 2½", V2p179–5, $18.00.
De-Fi, Type Ribbon, ¾ x 2½ x 2½", V1p307–1, $20.00.
Dean ½ oz., Snuff, 2 x 2½ x ⅜", V2p206–5, $20.00.
Deane Ready-Real, Adhesive Plaster, 1 x 1¼", V2p195–4, $25.00.
Deane's, Adhesive Plaster, 1¼ x 2¼", V1p345–7, $18.00.
Deane's, Zinc Oxide, 1 x 1¼", V1p345–8, $25.00.
Dean's, Zinc Plaster, ¾ x 1", V2p195–6, $25.00.
Dean's Peacock, Condoms, ½ x 1⅝", V1p23–7, $50.00.
Dean's Peacock, Condoms, ¼ x 1⅝ x 2⅛", V1p23–8, $65.00.
Dearkis, Gum Violet Sweetheart, no photo, $35.00.
Deb's Delux, Condoms, no photo, $70.00.
Decca Loud, Needles, ¼ x 1 x 2⅛", V1p205–10, $20.00.
Deer, Type Ribbon, no photo, $10.00.
Deere, Eye Brows\Lashes, ¼ x 1⅛ x 3", V2p32–4, $12.00.
Deere, Mascara, ⅜ x 1⅛ x 3", V1p50–7, $20.00.
Deere, Powder, ¼ x 2½", V1p44–4, $6.00.
Deere, Powder Compact, ¼ x 2", V1p50–8, $15.00.
Defiance, Spice, 3 x 2¼ x 1¼", V2p142–5, $30.00.
Degan, Type Ribbon, ¾ x 2½ x 2½", no photo, $15.00.
Delfa, Licorice Pellets, ½ x 1½ x 2", V1p291–3, $8.00.
DeLong Twin Grip #5, Fastners, 1⅛ x 1⅞", V1p63–7, $15.00.

Delux Clean Type, Type Ribbon, ¾ x 2½ x 2½", V1p307–5, $20.00.
DeLuxe, Type Ribbon, ¾ x 2½ x 2½", V1p307–6, $8.00.
Den Theku, Needles Gramaphone, ¼ x 1¼ x 1¾", V1p205–11, $30.00.
Denault's, French Pills, no photo, $35.00.
Denneys sample, Myana Face Powder, ¼ x 1⅝", V1p250–11, $18.00.
Dennison No.1, Mending Tape, 1 x 1", V1p194–2, $5.00.
Dennison's #22, Paper Fasteners, 1½ x 1⅛", V1p62–5, $12.00.
Dennison's #24, Paper Fasteners, 1¼ x 2", V1p62–6, $15.00.
Dennison's #31, Paper Fasteners, ½ x 2", V1p62–7, $15.00.
Dennison's #32, Fasteners RH, ¾ x 2", V1p62–8, $15.00.
Dental Aid sample, Tooth Powder, 1 x 1¼ x 2½", V2p41–3, $20.00.
Dental Plate Kleen, Powder sample, ¾ x 1¼ x 2¼", V1p61–4, $75.00.
Dentlock, Denture Powder, ⅞ x 2 x 2⅞", V1p57–3, $20.00.
Dentlock, Denture Powder, ⅞ x 2 x 3", V1p57–4, $20.00.
Dentogen, Tooth Powder, 1⅝ x 3⅝", V1p57–5, $40.00.
Denton's, Famous Salve, 1¾" rd., no photo, $18.00.
Denty Silk, Silk Dental Floss, ⅛ x 1½", no photo, $20.00.
Deodo sample, Deodorant Powder, ¾ x 1¼ x 2¾", V2p201–6, $30.00.
Derbies Rolled, Condom, ¼ x 1⅝ x 2⅛", V2p17–4, $70.00.
Derbies Three, Condom, ¼ x 1¼ x 2", V2p17–6, $75.00.
Derby sample, Peanut Butter, 2½ x 2⅝", V1p243–11, $110.00.
Derma Medicone sample, Anesthetic Ointment, ⅜ x 1⅝", V1p85–11, $5.00.
Derma Medicone sample, Ointment, ⅜ x 1⅛", V1p85–12, $5.00.
Dermacilia, Skin Food, ⅞ x 2½", V1p50–9, $75.00.
Dermatol, Medicine, 1¼ x 1¼ x 1½", $15.00.
Dermis Cura $.35, Hair Grower, ⅞ x 2¼", V1p33–12, $18.00.
Dermis-Cura $.75, Scalp Food, ⅞ x 2⅜", V1p34–1, $22.00.
DerSangerkrieg Auf, Gramaphone Needles, no photo, $40.00.
Derwood, Type Ribbon, ⅞ x 2½", V2p179–7, $6.00.
Desitin sample, Med. Nursery Powder, ¾ x ¼ x 2", V1p266–2, $15.00.
Desitin sample, Med. Nursery Powder, ¾ x 1¼ x 2⅛", V1p266–1, $18.00.
Desitin sample, Medical\Nursery Powder, 1 x 1¼ x 2½", V1p266–2, $15.00.
Desitin sample, Suppositories, ½ x 1⅛ x 1⅝", V1p86–1, $6.00.
Detoxyl, Medicine, ⅝ x 2 x 2⅞", V2p56–1, $18.00.
Detoxyl, Powder sample, no photo, $18.00.
Devoe #2, Water Colors, ⅜ x 2 x 4½", V1p181–9, $22.00.
Devonshire, Type Ribbon, ¾ x 2½ x 2½", V2p179–2, $20.00.
DeWitt's, Cold Tablets, ¼ x 1⅝ x 2⅜", V1p86–4, $10.00.
DeWitt's, see Kodol Antacid.
DeWitt's, Kodol Tablets, V1p114–2, $10.00.
DeWitt's, see Man-Zan sample, V1p119–8, $10.00*.
DeWitt's, Witch Hazel Salve, ¼ x 1⅛", V1p86–8, $15.00.
DeWitt's, Witch Hazel Salve, ¼ x ⅞", V1p86–7, $12.00.
DeWitt's $.25, Antacid Tablets, ½ x 1⅞ x 2⅜", V1p86–2, $10.00.
DeWitt's $.25, Cocomint Laxative, ½ x 2 x 2⅜", V1p86–3, $10.00.
DeWitt's $.25, Cocomint Lozenges, ⅜ x 2 x 2⅜", V1p291–4, $15.00.
DeWitt's $.25, Creosant Tablets, ⅜ x 2½ x 3⅛", V1p86–5, $10.00.
DeWitts $.25, Headache Tablets, no photo, $10.00.
DeWitt's $.25, Throat Lozenges, ⅜ x 2½ x 3⅛", V1p291–5, $12.00.
DeWitt's 1 oz., Witch Hazel Salve, ⅞ x 2⅛", V1p86–9, $8.00.
DeWitt's Man-Zan, Pile Ointment, ¼ x ⅞", V1p86–6, $5.00.
DeWitt's sample, Vapor Balm, ¼ x ⅞", V1p86–10, $15.00.
Diamond, Gramaphone Needles, no photo, $30.00.
Diamond, Type Ribbon, no photo, $8.00.
Diamond Brand, Chi Ches Ters Pills, 1⅜ x 2⅜ x 1", V1p86–11, $20.00.
Diamond Brand, Chi Ches Ters Pills, 1⅝ x 2⅞ x 1", V2p56–4, $25.00.
Diamond King, Razor Hone, ½ x 2 x 5½", V1p274–6, $85.00.
Diamond Match, Match Holder, ⅞ x 1¾ x 6¼", V1p180–8, $70.00.
Diamond Match, Matches, ½ x 1½ x 2¼", V1p180–5, $60.00.
Diamond Match, Matches, ½ x 1½ x 2¼", V1p180–6, $100.00.
Diamond Match Co, Match Holder, ⅝ x 1½ x 2¼", V1p180–7, $115.00.
Diana, Air Gun Slugs, ⅝ x 3", V1p66–8, $10.00.
Dic-a-Doo sample, Type Cleaner, ⅞ x 2¼", no photo, $12.00.
Dietzgen, Stake Tacks 1 lb., 1 x 3½ x 3⅝", V1p194–3, $35.00.
Dietzgen, Thumb Tacks, ⅜ x 1 x 1½", V1p194–4, $3.00.
Dietzgen, Thumbtacks, ⅜ x 1⅛ x 1¾", $6.00.
Dietzgen, VanDyke Salt, 2⅜ x 1¾", V2p206–6, $15.00.
Digestoids, Lax-Tonic-Digest., ½ x 1⅝ x 2⅝", V1p87–1, $25.00.
Digestoids, Laxative, ½ x 1½ x 2⅝", V1p86–12, $30.00.
Digestoids New, Laxative, ⅝ x 1½ x 2⅝", V2p56–6, $25.00.
Dik, Phonogragh Needles, ⅜ x 1⅛ x 2¼", V1p205–12, $20.00.
Dike's $.10, Laxative, ⅜ x 1¼ x 1¾", V1p87–2, $18.00.
Dil-Lax, Laxative, ¼ x 1⅝ x 1⅝", V1p87–3, $6.00.
Dil-Lax, Laxative, ⅜ x 1⅝ x 1⅝", V1p87–4, $18.00.
Dill, Tire Valve Caps, ½ x ⅜ x 2⅛", V1p16–2, $8.00.
Dill, Tire Valve Caps, ⅜ x ¾ x 1⅝", V1p16–3, $8.00.
Dill, Tire Valve Insiders, ¼ x 1 x 1⅛", V1p16–9, $12.00.
Dill, Valve Stems, ¼ x 1 x 1¼", V1p16–10, $10.00.
Dill's, Adhesive Plaster, 1 x 1¼", V1p345–9, $18.00.
Dill's, Aspirin, ¼ x 1¼ x 1¾", V1p87–5, $15.00.
Dill's, Aspirin, ¼ x 1¼ x 1¾", V2p56–2, $15.00.
Dill's, Aspirin, ¼ x 1 x 1¼", V1p87–6, $12.00.
Dill's, Salve, 1 x 2¾", no photo, $18.00.
Dill's sample, Ez-A-Cold, ⅜ x ⅞", V1p87–7, $25.00.
Dilworth's sample, Golden Urn Coffee, 2 x 2½", V1p228–3, $120.00.
Dime, Safety Razor, no photo, $65.00.
Dime, Safety Razor, 1 x 3⅛", no photo, $30.00.
Dime, Safety Razor, 1 x 3⅛", V1p270–6, $35.00.
Dime-Lax $.10, Laxative, ¼ x 1¼ x 1¾", V1p87–8, $12.00.
Dims, Aspirin, ¼ x 1¼ x 1½", V1p87–9, $12.00.
Diotex sample, Anti-gas, ¼ x 1 x 1¼", V2p56–3, $6.00.
Disston Henry & Son, Silver Solder 1oz., ⅞ x 1", V1p285–4, $20.00.
Distinctive Silk, Type Ribbon, ¾ x 2½", no photo, $6.00.
Ditmars', Type Ribbon, 1¾ x 1¾ x 2", no photo, $55.00.
Ditto, Type Ribbon, ¾ x 2½ x 2½", V2p179–6, $8.00.
Ditto, Type Ribbon, ⅞ x 2½", V2p179–4, $8.00.
Diurbital sample, Tablets, ¼ x 1¼ x 1¾", V1p87–10, $20.00.
Dixie Maid, Hair Dressing, 1 x 2⅜ x 2¾", V1p34–2, $20.00.
Dixiebelle $.50, Salve Skin, ⅞ x 2⅜", V1p28–11, $20.00.
Dixon's $.10, Aspirin, ¼ x 1¾ x 2⅝", V1p87–11, $15.00.
Dixon's sample, Axel Greese, ¾ x 2¼", V2p13–5, $25.00.
Dixon's sample, Silica Graphite, ¾ x 1¼", V2p206–2, $25.00.
Djer-Kiss sample, Cream, ⅜ x 1⅝", V2p27–4, $12.00.
Do-X, Needles, no photo, $45.00.
Doan's, Diuretic Pills 85, 1¼ x 3¼", V1p87–12, $5.00.
Doan's, Ointment, ⅝ x 1⅞", V1p88–3, $55.00.
Doan's, Pills Tablets, 1 x 2½", V1p88–1, $4.00*.
Doan's $.60, Ointment, ⅝ x 1⅞", V1p88–2, $50.00.
Doan's $.60, Ointment, ⅝ x 1⅞", V2p56–5, $50.00.
Doan's sample, Ointment, ¼ x 1⅛", V2p57–1, $30.00.
Doan's sample, Ointment, ⅝ x 1⅞", V2p56–7, $30.00.
Doc Bim sample, Pile Remedy, ¾ x 1⅞", no photo, $5.00.
Doc Bim sample, Rub-On-Salve, ½ x 1¼", V1p88–4, $5.00.
Dock & Robbins $.10, Excel Troches, ⅜ x 1⅜ x 2½", V1p291–6, $75.00.
Dockson, Torch Lighter, ¼ x ¾ x 1¼", V1p194–5, $5.00.
Doctor & Nurse, Baby Cream, ⅜ x 1½", V2p27–6, $18.00.
Doctor & Nurse, Vitamin Candy Pills, ¼ x 1¼ x 1½", V1p286–7, $15.00.
Doctor & Nurse sample, Baby Powder, ⅜ x 1⅜", V1p264–6, $18.00.

Dodge's, Sure Cure, no photo, $35.00.

Dodson, Seed Store, no photo, $10.00.

Dog & Angel 200, Loud Needles Phono, ¼ x 1¼ x 1¾", V1p206–1, $35.00.

Dog & Baby, Needles, ½ x 1¼ x 1⅝", V1p206–2, $40.00.

Dog and Boy, Needles, ½ x 1¼ x 1½", V2p112–6, $30.00.

Dog with Needle, Needle, no photo, $30.00.

Doggies Little Friend, Needle, no photo, $40.00.

Doherty Eugene, Dental Rubber, 1 x 3¼ x 6", no photo, $65.00.

Dolphs, Rectal Ointment, ½ x 1½", V1p88–5, $6.00.

Dominican, Healing Salve, ⅞ x 2½", V1p88–6, $55.00.

Dominion $.05, Headache Tablets, ¼ x ⅞ x 1⅜", V2p57–3, $10.00.

Dominion Half Tone, Needles, ½ x 2", no photo, $35.00.

Dominion Loud Tone, Needles, no photo, $35.00.

Domitor, Type Ribbon, ¾ x 2½ x 2½", V1p307–7, $15.00.

Donald Duck (bank), Coffee, 3 x 2¼", V1p228–4, $400.00.

Dormaphen, Capsules, ¼ x 1 x 1⅜", V1p88–7, $5.00.

Dot sample, Coffee, 2 x 2½", V1p228–5, $50.00.

Double-Pepsin, Tablets, ⅜ x 1¼ x 1¾", V2p57–5, $12.00.

Douglas B.H.& Son, Cough Drops, 1¼ x 2½ x 4", V1p291–7, $75.00.

Dove, Pumpkin Spice, 2 x 2¼ x 1¼", V2p142–7, $22.00.

Dove, Spanish Saffron, ¼ x 1¼ x 1¾", V1p187–6, $10.00.

Dove Brand, Allspice, 1⅜ x 1¾ x 3½", V2p143–1, $40.00.

Dove Brand, Allspice, 2½ x 2 x 1¼", V2p143–4, $35.00.

Dove Brand, Paprika, 2 x 4", V2p143–6, $60.00.

Dove Brand, Tumeric, 3⅛ x 2¼ x 1¼", V2p143–2, $40.00.

Dove Brand, Whole Cinnamon, 2 x 4", V2p143–3, $60.00.

Dr. & Nurse, Vitamin Candy, ¼ x 1¼ x 1¾", V1p286–7, $15.00.

Dr. Aldrich $1.00, Lung Salve, 1⅜ x 3½", V2p57–2, $18.00.

Dr. Allen's, Corn Cure, ½ x 1½", V1p88–8, $20.00.

Dr. Anderson's sample, Carbolic Talcum, no photo, $55.00.

Dr. Barken's $.50, Hair Grower, 1⅛ x 2¾", V1p34–3, $35.00.

Dr. Baxter's $.25, Mandrake Bitters, no photo, $95.00.

Dr. Bell sample, Anti-septic Salve, ¼ x ⅞", V2p57–3, $40.00.

Dr. Bell's, Anti-Septic Salve, ⅞ x 2½", V1p88–9, $30.00.

Dr. Bell's, Unguento, ¾ x 1⅞", V2p57–6, $25.00.

Dr. Bell's, V.C. Tooth Powder, no photo, $30.00.

Dr. Bengue's, French Laxative, ¼ x 1 x 2¾", V1p88–10, $10.00.

Dr. Blair's Snow White, Bleaching Cream, ¾ x 2¾", V1p29–1, $25.00.

Dr. Blair's Snow White, Hair Beautifier, 1 x 3½", V1p34–5, $25.00.

Dr. Blair's Snow White, Hair Beautifier, 3" tall, no photo, $25.00.

Dr. Blosser's, Catarrh Remedy, ¼ x 1⅝ x 3⅛", V1p88–11, $30.00.

Dr. Bobo's sample, Ointment, ½ x 1⅝", no photo, $25.00.

Dr. Bovel's $.25, Rose Bud Tooth Soap, ⅝ x 1⅞ x 2½", V2p41–5, $65.00.

Dr. Brigadell's sample, Camphorole Cold Rub, ¼ x 1⅛", V2p58–1, $12.00.

Dr. Brinkley's, Stomach Tablets, ⅜ x 2½ x 3⅛", V1p88–12, $12.00.

Dr. Brown's, Fruit Tablets, no photo, $25.00.

Dr. Buker's, Kidney Pills Cure, ½ x 1⅝ x 2⅞", V1p89–1, $125.00.

Dr. Butler's $.10, Buckthorn Splits Lax, ¼ x 1½ x 2", V2p58–3, $25.00.

Dr. Butler's $.25, Buckthorn Splits Lax, ¼ x 2 x 2¾", V1p89–2, $25.00.

Dr. Cadwell's, Laxative, no photo, $25.00.

Dr. Cadwell's $.25, Vegetable Tonic Liver Pills, ½ x 1½ x 2⅝", no photo, $55.00.

Dr. Caldwell's $.25, Pine Balm, ¼ x 1⅝", V1p89–3, $20.00.

Dr. Camp's, Tooth Soap, ½ x 2 x 3⅛", V1p60–3, $70.00.

Dr. Cannon J., Salve, 1 x 2⅜", V1p89–4, $22.00.

Dr. Casey's, Bromo Aspirin, ¼ x 1¼ x 1¾", V2p58–5, $12.00.

Dr. Charcott, Kola Nervine Tablets, ½ x 1¾ x 2½", V2p58–6, $90.00.

Dr. Charles, Flesh Food, 1 x 2½", V1p50–10, $30.00.

Dr. Charles $.50, Face Powder, 1¼ x 2¾", V2p23–5, $45.00.

Dr. Chase A.W., Ointment, ¾ x 1¾", V1p89–5, $8.00.

Dr. Chase's, Catarrh Powder, ¾ x 2½", no photo, $30.00.

Dr. Chase's, Ointment, ¾ x 1¾", V1p89–6, $20.00.

Dr. Chase's sample, Ointment, ¼ x 1⅛", V1p89–7, $35.00.

Dr. Chevallier's, Gum Paste, ¾ x 3¼ x 2¼", no photo, $60.00.

Dr. Coffee W.O., Massage Ointment #4, ¼ x 1⅛", V2p58–2, $15.00.

Dr. Coffee W.O., Prescription #48, ¼ x 1⅛", V2p58–4, $15.00.

Dr. Constans, Nerve Pills, no photo, $30.00.

Dr. Daniel's, Hoof Grower, no photo, $65.00.

Dr. Daniel's, Linament Powder, no photo, $50.00.

Dr. Daniels' $.25, Gallcura, ⅞ x 2⅞", V1p331–3, $60.00.

Dr. Daniels' $.50, Absorbent Blister, 1⅛ x 1⅞", V1p89–8, $50.00.

Dr. Davis, Rumagon, ⅜ x 2⅛ x 2⅝", V1p89–9, $12.00.

Dr. Du Bois $2.00, Specific Pills, ⅝ x 1⅝ x 3", V2p58–7, $50.00.

Dr. Ducor's, French Pennyroyal, no photo, $30.00.

Dr. Dunlop's $.25, Quick Relief, ⅜ x 1½ x 2½", V1p89–10, $55.00.

Dr. Edward's, Olive Tablets, ½ x ¾ x 1¾", V1p90–2, $5.00*.

Dr. Edward's, Olive Tablets, ¼ x 1¼ x 1½", V1p90–5, $6.00.

Dr. Edward's, Olive Tablets, ⅞ x 1⅛ x 2⅜", V1p89–11, $10.00.

Dr. Edward's $.15, Olive Tablets, ½ x ⅞ x 1½", V1p90–1, $8.00.

Dr. Edward's $.15, Olive Tablets, ½ x ⅞ x 1¾", V2p59–1, $8.00.

Dr. Edward's $.25, Dandelion Pills, ½ x 1⅝ x 2½", V2p59–3, $50.00.

Dr. Edward's $.30, Olive Tablets, ⅝ x ⅞ x 2½", V1p90–3, $10.00.

Dr. Edward's $.30, Olive Tablets, ⅝ x ⅞ x 2⅛", V1p90–4, $10.00.

Dr. Edward's $.60, Olive Tablets, ¾ x 1⅛ x 2½", V1p89–12, $6.00.

Dr. Edward's $.60, Olive Tablets, ⅞ x 1⅛ x 2⅜", V2p59–5, $12.00.

Dr. Emerick's $.25, White Salve, ⅞ x 2⅝", V1p90–6, $40.00.

Dr. Foote's $.35, Magnetic Pills, ¾ x 2½", V1p90–7, $40.00.

Dr. Franchoise, Female Pills, no photo, $45.00.

Dr. Gordshell's, All-Healing Salve, 1⅝ x 1½", V1p90–8, $20.00.

Dr. Grave's, Tooth Powder, no photo, $35.00.

Dr. Graves sample, Talcum Powder, ⅝ x 1¾", V1p258–2, $140.00.

Dr. Guertin's $.25, Laxative Tablets, ½ x 1⅜ x 2⅛", V1p90–10, $25.00.

Dr. Guertin's $.25, Laxative Tablets, ¼ x 1⅜ x 2⅛", V1p90–9, $30.00.

Dr. Guertin's $.25, Laxative Tablets, ⅜ x 1½ x 2", V2p59–2, $30.00.

Dr. Guild's $.25, Asthmatic Compound, ⅜ x 1⅝ x 3⅛", V1p90–11, $8.00.

Dr. Hale's $.25, Ointment, ¾ x 2⅛", V1p90–12, $20.00.

Dr. Hale's sample, Household Ointment, ¼ x 1", V1p91–1, $40.00.

Dr. Hall's sample, Catarrh Remedy, ⅜ x 1", no photo, $35.00.

Dr. Hamilton's $.25, Pills, ½ x 1½", V2p59–4, $15.00.

Dr. Hamilton's $.25, Pilules, ½ x 1⅝", V1p91–2, $18.00.

Dr. Hammonds, Nerve Brain Pills, ½ x 1⅝ x 2⅞", V2p59–6, $95.00.

Dr. Hand's, Chafing Powder, 1¼ x 3", V2p60–1, $75.00.

Dr. Hess sample, Healing Powder, 1¼ x 2½", no photo, $60.00.

Dr. Hildebrand's, Gall Stone Capsules, 1⅜ x 3¼ x 2¼", V1p91–4, $25.00.

Dr. Hildebrand's sample, Gall Stone Capsules, ¼ x ¾ x 1⅝", V1p91–3, $25.00.

Dr. Hitchcock's, Laxative Powder, 1 x 2⅜ x 2¾", V1p91–8, $25.00.

Dr. Hitchcock's, Laxative Powder, 2¼ x 1⅛ x 2¾", V1p91–9, $25.00.

Dr. Hitchcock's $.10, Laxative Powder, 1 x 1⅝ x 2⅜", V1p91–6, $20.00.

Dr. Hitchcock's $.25, Laxative Powder, 1⅛ x 2⅛ x 2¾", V1p91–7, $22.00.

Dr. Hitchcocks $.25, Liver, Kidney, Blood, 1⅛ x 2⅛ x 2¾", V2p60–4, $25.00.

Dr. Hitchcock's sample, Laxative Powder, 1 x 1½ x 2⅜", V1p91-5, $30.00.
Dr. Hitchcock's W.L., Laxative Powder, 1 x 2¼ x 2¾", V1p91-10, $25.00.
Dr. Hobb's $.50, Sparagus Kidney Pills, ½ x 1½ x 2½", V2p60-6, $60.00.
Dr. Hobb's $.50, Sparagus Pills, ½ x 1½ x 2½", V1p91-11, $65.00.
Dr. Hobb's $.50, Sparagus\Kidney Pills, ⅜ x 1½ x 2½", no photo, $60.00.
Dr. Hobson's, Blister Spavin, no photo, $30.00.
Dr. Hobson's, Laxative Cascara, ½ x 1½ x 1⅞", V1p91-12, $15.00.
Dr. Hobson's #121, Carbolic Salve, ¾ x 2¾", V1p92-1, $25.00.
Dr. Hobson's #123, Arnica Salve, ¾ x 2¾", V1p92-2, $35.00.
Dr. Hobson's #125, Itch Ointment, ¾ x 2", V1p92-3, $25.00.
Dr. Hobson's #127, Derma Zema Ointment, ¾ x 2¾", V1p92-4, $30.00.
Dr. Hobson's #127, Eczema Ointment, ¾ x 2¾", V1p92-5, $30.00.
Dr. Hobson's #301, Witch Hazel Salve, ¾ x 2⅝", V1p92-6, $30.00.
Dr. Hobson's $.10, Corn Salve, ⅝ x 1", V1p92-7, $25.00.
Dr. Hobson's $.25, Eye Salve, ¼ x 1⅛", V1p92-8, $22.00.
Dr. Hobson's $.25, Eye Salve, ¼ x 1⅛", V1p92-9, $22.00.
Dr. Hobson's $.25, Laxative Cascara Tablets, ⅜ x 2¼ x 3½", V2p60-2, $40.00.
Dr. Hobson's $.25, Tooth Soap, ½ x 2 x 3¼", V1p57-6, $65.00.
Dr. Hobson's $.25, Witch Hazel Arnica Glyc., ¾ x 2½", V1p92-10, $30.00.
Dr. Hough's $.10, White Ointment, ⅜ x 1¼", V2p60-3, $20.00.
Dr. Hugo's, Health Tablets (Women), ½ x 1½ x 2½", V2p60-5, $80.00.
Dr. Hunter's $.25, Sure Relief, ⅜ x 1½ x 2½", V1p92-11, $65.00.
Dr. Hunt's, Domestic Sweatine, no photo, $40.00.
Dr. Jayne's, see Jayne's.
Dr. Jayne's, Laxative, ¾ x 1¾", V2p60-7, $25.00.
Dr. Jayne's, Expectorant Opium, ⅜ x 1¾ x 2¾", V2p61-1, $150.00.
Dr. Jayne's, Laxative Pills, no photo, $35.00.
Dr. Jayne's, Sanative Pills, ¾ x 1¾", V1p93-1, $25.00.
Dr. Jayne's, Sanative Pills, ¾ x 1¾", V1p93-2, $22.00.
Dr. Jayne's, Sanative Pills, ⅞ x 1¾", V1p92-12, $30.00.
Dr. Jayne's $.10, Sanative Pills, ¼ x ¾ x 1¼", V1p93-3, $30.00.
Dr. Jayne's $.25, Expectorant Tablets, ⅜ x 1¾ x 2¾", V1p112-3, $150.00.
Dr. Jayne's sample, Laxative Pills 5, ⅜ x ¾", V1p112-2, $22.00.
Dr. Jayne's sample, Pildoras Sanative, ¼ x ¾", V2p61-3, $35.00.
Dr. John's, Pile Cure Pills, ⅝ x 1¾", V1p93-4, $30.00.
Dr. Johns $.25, Cascara Tablets, ⅜ x 1½ x 2½", V1p93-5, $60.00.
Dr. Johnson's sample, Anti-Flu-Rub, ½ x 1½", V1p93-6, $25.00.
Dr. Kay's $.10, Lung Balm, ⅜ x 1½ x 2½", V1p93-7, $45.00.
Dr. Kellogg's J.D., Asthma Remedy, 1¾ x 2⅝ x 4 ⅞", V1p93-8, $65.00.
Dr. Kellogg's J.D., Asthma Remedy, 1¾ x 2⅝ x 5", V1p93-9, $60.00.
Dr. Kilmer's sample, U & O Anointment, ⅜ x 1", V1p93-10, $22.00.
Dr. King's, Heel-all Ointment, ½ x 1½", no photo, $30.00.
Dr. King's Star Crown, PennyRoyal Pills, ¾ x 1¾ x 3", V1p93-11, $75.00.
Dr. Koch's, Allspice, 3¼ x 2¼ x 1⅜", V2p143-5, $55.00.
Dr. Koch's, Corn Salve, ½ x 1¼", V2p61-5, $25.00.
Dr. Koch's, Dyspepsia Tablets, 1½ x 2 x 3", no photo, $35.00.
Dr. Koch's $.25, Vegetable Tea Tablets, ¾ x 1¾ x 3", V1p93-12, $45.00.
Dr. Koch's sample, Rolatum Healing Salve, ½ x 1⅛", V2p61-6, $30.00.
Dr. Lawrence, Sure Corn Cure, no photo, $40.00.
Dr. LeGear's, A-A Poultry Tabs, 1½ x 2", no photo, $45.00.
Dr. LeGear's, Dog Prescription, ⅝ x 1⅝ x 2⅛", V1p331-5, $30.00.
Dr. LeGear's, Nicotine Pills, 1⅝ x 2¾", V1p331-4, $45.00.
Dr. LeGear's, Pepsin Compound, ¾ x 1⅝ x 2⅛", V2p192-5, $45.00.
Dr. LeGear's, Special Tablets, ⅝ x 1⅝ x 2⅛", V1p331-7, $40.00.
Dr. LeGears $.25, Gall Remedy, 1 x 2⅝, no photo, $75.00.
Dr. LeGear's $.25, Gall Salve, ⅞ x 2⅝", V1p331-9, $22.00.
Dr. LeGear's $.25, Head Lice Remedy, 1 x 2¾", V2p192-6, $70.00.
Dr. LeGear's $.30, Gall Salve, ⅞ x 2¾", V1p331-6, $50.00.
Dr. LeGear's 1¾ oz, Gall Salve, ⅞ x 2⅝", V1p331-10, $35.00.
Dr. LeGear's sample, Antiseptic Powder, 1¼ x 2", V1p331-11, $60.00.
Dr. LeGear's sample, Healing Powder, 1⅜ x 1¾", V1p331-12, $70.00.
Dr. LeGear's sample, Lice Powder, 1⅝ x 2⅝", no photo, $45.00.
Dr. Long's W.H. $1.00, Prairie Blossom, 1 x 2¼ x 3½", V1p94-1, $125.00.
Dr. Luke's, Sarsaparilla, 2¼ x 3½ x 1¼", V2p61-2, $70.00.
Dr. Lyon's, Tooth Powder, 1 x 2⅛", V1p57-7, $90.00.
Dr. Lyon's, Tooth Powder, ⅞ x 1½ x 3", V2p41-7, $30.00.
Dr. Lyon's L.W., Tooth Powder Tablets, ⅞ x 2 x 3½", V1p57-8, $70.00.
Dr. Lyons sample, Tooth Powder, 1¼ x 2¾", V1p57-9, $40.00.
Dr. Martel's $2.00, French Female Pills, 1¾ x 2½ x 1¼", V1p94-2, $65.00.
Dr. Martel's $2.00, Female Pills, 1¼ x 1⅝ x 2½", V2p61-4, $55.00.
Dr. Martin's, Tooth Powder sample, no photo, $45.00.
Dr. McBain's $.50, Famous Blood Pills, ½ x 1⅝ x 2¾", V1p94-3, $45.00.
Dr. McLean's $.25, Pepsanels, ⅜ x 1¼ x 2⅛", V1p94-4, $45.00.
Dr. McLean's sample, Volco Salve, ¼ x 1", V1p94-5, $25.00.
Dr. Merriam's, Female Herbal Pastilies, ½ x 1⅞ x 3", no photo, $55.00.
Dr. Miles, Anti Pain Pills, ¼ x 1 x 1¼", V1p94-8, $15.00.
Dr. Miles, Anti Pain Pills, ¾ x 2¾", V1p94-6, $12.00.
Dr. Miles, Anti Pain Pills, ¾ x 2¾", V1p94-7, $12.00.
Dr. Miles, Anti-Pain Pills, 1½ x 3¼", V2p61-7, $25.00.
Dr. Miles, Anti-Pain Pills, ¼ x ¾ x 1¼", V1p94-10, $18.00.
Dr. Miles, Anti-Pain Pills, ¼ x ¾ x 1¼", V1p94-11, $15.00.
Dr. Miles, Anti-Pain Pills, ¼ x ¾ x 1¼", V1p94-9, $15.00.
Dr. Miles, Lax Tablets, ¼ x ¾ x 1¼", V1p94-12, $15.00.
Dr. Miles, Laxative Tablets, ¼ x 1¼", V2p62-1, $15.00.
Dr. Miles, see Miles Anti-Pain.
Dr. Miles $.15, Aspir-Mint, ¼ x 1¼ x 1¾", V1p95-1, $15.00.
Dr. Miles $.15, Aspir-Mint, ¼ x 1¼ x 1¾", V2p62-3, $15.00.
Dr. Morse's, Indian Root Pills, ½ x 1 x 2", V1p95-2, $20.00.
Dr. Morse's, Indian Root Pills 33, ¼ x 1¼ x 1¾", V1p95-4, $18.00.
Dr. Morse's, Indian Root Pills 40, ¼ x 1⅜ x 1¾", V1p95-3, $18.00.
Dr. Myers' 24, Aspirin, ¼ x 1¾ x 2½", V1p95-5, $12.00.
Dr. Norwood's J.N., Gall Cure, 1 x 3", V1p332-1, $65.00.
Dr. Palmer's, Skin Whitner, ½ x 1⅞", V1p50-11, $6.00.
Dr. Palmer's Fred, Hair Dresser, 1⅜ x 2⅝ x 3", V1p34-6, $25.00.
Dr. Palmer's Fred, Skin Whitner, ⅝ x 1⅞", V1p51-1, $15.00.
Dr. Palmer's Fred, Skin Whitner, ⅝ x 2", V1p50-12, $12.00.
Dr. Palmer's sample, Alomeal Compound, 1¼ x 2⅜ x 2", V1p266-3, $65.00.
Dr. Palmer's sample, Hair Dresser, ¼ x 1", V1p34-7, $40.00.
Dr. Pettit's $.25, Tablets, ¼ x 1⅛", V1p95-6, $50.00.
Dr. Pettit's $.30, Eye Salve, ¼ x 1⅛", V2p62-5, $25.00.
Dr. Pettit's sample, Eye Salve, ¼ x 1⅛", V1p95-7, $25.00.
Dr. Pierce's, All Healing Salve, ⅞ x 2½", V1p95-8, $45.00.
Dr. Pierce's, Anodyne Pile Ointment, ⅞ x 2⅛", V1p95-9, $40.00.
Dr. Pierce's, Lotion Tablets, ½ x 2½", V1p95-10, $12.00.
Dr. Pierce's, Lotion Tablets, ¾ x 2⅜", V1p95-11, $40.00.
Dr. Pierce's, Lotion Tablets, ⅝ x 2⅜", V1p95-12, $35.00.

Dr. Pierce's, Lotion Tablets 28, ⅝ x 2½", V1p96–1, $45.00.

Dr. Pierce's, Pile Ointment, ⅞ x 2⅛", V1p96–2, $30.00.

Dr. Pierce's, Rectal Ointment, no photo, $25.00.

Dr. Pierce's, Salve, no photo, $30.00.

Dr. Pierce's, Suppositories, ¾ x 2¼", V1p96–3, $25.00.

Dr. Pierce's $.35, Favorite Prescription, ¼ x 2¼ x 2¾", V1p96–4, $12.00.

Dr. Pierce's $.50, GMD Tablets, ¼ x 2⅜ x 2¾", V1p96–5, $10.00.

Dr. Pierce's $.50, Payngon, ¼ x 1¼ x 1¾", V1p96–6, $15.00.

Dr. Pierce's Robert J., see Empress Brand, $45.00.

Dr. Pierce's Robert J., Empress Brand Tablets, 1⅝ x 2⅝ x 1", V2p62–6, $35.00.

Dr. Pierce's Robert J., Empress Pennyroyal Tabs, V1p134–7, $50.00.

Dr. Prince's $1.50, PennyRoyal Pills, 1 x 1⅝ x 2⅞", V1p96–7, $70.00.

Dr. Pusheck's $.25, Headache Dispeller #33, ½ x 1¼ x 2", V2p62–2, $35.00.

Dr. Rea's, Gall Salve, no photo, $40.00.

Dr. Roberts, Hard Milking Outfit, 1 x 2¼ x 3½", V2p192–2, $55.00.

Dr. Roberts David, Laxatonic, 2 x 3½", V1p96–8, $50.00.

Dr. Robert's David $.50, Dog Medicine, ¼ x 1¼ x 1¾", V1p332–2, $65.00.

Dr. Robinson 333, Condom, ¼ x 1⅝ x 2⅛", V1p23–9, $80.00.

Dr. Rumney's, Mentholyptus Snuff, ½ x 1¾ x 2⅜, no photo, $10.00.

Dr. Rumney's, Mentholypus Snuff, ⅜ x 1¼ x 1¾", V2p206–4, $15.00.

Dr. Ryan's $.25, Anti-Dyspeptic Pills, ⅜ x 1¼ x 2½", V1p96–9, $95.00.

Dr. Salsbury's sample, Phen-o-Sal Tablets, 1 x 1½", V1p96–10, $15.00.

Dr. Sauer's, Aspirin, ¼ x 1¼ x 1¾", V1p96–11, $15.00.

Dr. Sauer's, Stove Polish, 1 x 3½", no photo, $12.00.

Dr. Sauer's $.05, Aspirin 6, ¼ x ¾ x 1⅜", V1p96–12, $18.00.

Dr. Sayman sample, Salve, ¼ x ¾ x 1⅜", V1p97–1, $30.00.

Dr. Sayman's, Salve, ¼ x 1⅛", V2p62–7, $25.00.

Dr. Sayman's sample, Healing Salve, ¼ x 1¼ x ¾", V2p62–4, $18.00.

Dr. Sayman's sample, Salve, ¼ x 1⅛", V1p97–2, $18.00.

Dr. Sayman's sample, Salve Ointment, ¼ x 1⅛, no photo, $20.00.

Dr. Schiffmann's $.65, Asthmador, 1⅜ x 2¼ x 3½", V2p63–1, $20.00.

Dr. Schiffman's sample, Asthma Cure, ½ x 1¼ x 2", V1p97–3, $55.00.

Dr. Scholl's, Foot Powder, 1¼ x 3¾", V2p63–3, $15.00.

Dr. Scholl's, Foot Powder, 1¾ x 6", V1p97–6, $40.00.

Dr. Scholl's, Waterproof Adhesive, 1¼ x 2¼", V1p345–10, $12.00.

Dr. Scholl's sample, Foot Balm, ½ x 1⅛", V2p63–6, $18.00.

Dr. Scholl's sample, Foot Balm, ½ x 1⅜", V1p97–5, $18.00.

Dr. Scholl's sample, Foot Balm, ¼ x 1⅜", V1p97–4, $15.00.

Dr. Schoop's, Catarrh Remedy, no photo, $30.00.

Dr. Scott's, Safety Razor, 1¼ x 1⅞ x 3", V1p270–7, $245.00.

Dr. Scott's Electric, Razor Blades, ¼ x 1 x 2⅛", V1p269–1, $215.00.

Dr. Sharpsteen's, Hindo Salve, no photo, $40.00.

Dr. Shoops $.05, Lax-ets Laxative, ⅜ x 1⅛ x 2½", V2p63–2, $45.00.

Dr. Shoop's $.05, Preventics, ¼ x 1⅛ x 2⅜", V1p97–7, $40.00.

Dr. Shoop's sample, Catarrh Cure, ¼ x ⅞", V1p97–8, $60.00.

Dr. Shoop's sample, Green Salve, ⅜ x ⅞", V1p97–9, $45.00.

Dr. Simmons, see Simmons Laxative.

Dr. Simmon's $.25, Laxative Medicine, 1¾ x 1¾ x 2⅛", V1p97–10, $60.00.

Dr. Stanley's, Worm Candy, no photo, $55.00.

Dr. Stone's X.$.10, Throat Waffers, ¼ x 1½ x 1¾", V2p167–6, $15.00.

Dr. Stone's X.$.25, Throat Wafers, ½ x 2½ x 3⅛", V1p286–8, $12.00.

Dr. Swans $.25, Cascara Pills, ¼ x 1⅛ x 2⅛", V1p97–11, $65.00.

Dr. Tallerday's, Ointment, no photo, $30.00.

Dr. Taylor's, Torpedo Worm Capsule, ¾ x 2½", V1p332–3, $15.00.

Dr. Tepper's, Gumlyke, ½ x 3 x 6", no photo, $90.00.

Dr. Thacher's $.25, Liver Medicine, 1¾ x 2 x 2½", V1p97–12, $35.00.

Dr. Thacher's $.50, Uterina Pills, ½ x 2 x 3⅛", V2p63–4, $45.00.

Dr. Tucker's #59, Cough Drops, ½ x 2 x 3", V1p291–8, $115.00.

Dr. Tutt's $.25, Pills, ¼ x 1¼ x 1¾", V1p98–1, $15.00.

Dr. Tutt's $.25, Pills, ¼ x 1¼ x 1¾", V2p63–5, $15.00.

Dr. Welbourn's $.25, Anti-Bilious Pills, ¼ x 1½ x 1¾", V2p63–7, $15.00.

Dr. Wernet's, Tooth Powder, ¾ x 1¼ x 2¼", V1p59–4, $40.00.

Dr. Wernet's sample, Tooth Powder, ⅞ x 1¼ x 2⅛, no photo, $22.00.

Dr. Whetzel's sample, Asthma Relief Powder, ¾ x 1⅝ x 2⅛", V1p98–2, $25.00.

Dr. Whetzel's sample, Quick Relief Asthma, ¾ x 1½ x 2⅛", V1p98–3, $60.00.

Dr. Whites, Cough Drops, no photo, 185.00.

Dr. Whites, Whites Pink Tablets, Vol.2, $15.00.

Dr. Whites $.10, Pink Tablets, ¼ x 1¼ x 1¾", V1p98–4, $25.00.

Dr. William's $.05, Aspirin, ¼ x ¾ x 1⅜", V2p64–1, $12.00.

Dr. Winston's $.50, Pile Ointment, ⅝ x 2", V1p98–5, $18.00.

Dr. Wood's, Anti-Cold Remedy, ¾ x 1⅞", V1p98–6, $20.00.

Dr. Worden's $.50, Female Pills, ⅝ x 1⅝ x 2⅞", no photo, $50.00.

Dragon, Type Ribbon, no photo, $10.00.

Drake, Aspirin, ¼ x 1¼ x 1¾", V2p64–3, $12.00.

Drawing Room sample, Coffee, 1¾ x 3 x 2½", V1p228–6, $70.00.

Dreamlax $.10, Laxative, ⅜ x 1⅝ x 1⅝", V1p98–7, $12.00.

Dreco, Hi-Speed Laxative, ¼ x 1¼ x 1¾", no photo, $15.00.

Drefs, Gout & Rheumatism, ¾ x 1⅞", V1p98–9, $20.00*.

Drefs, Gout & Rheumatism, ¾ x 2", V1p98–8, $18.00*.

Drefs, Liver Pills (40), ¾ x 1⅞", V1p98–10, $20.00*.

Drefs sample, Corn Salve, ½ x 1⅛", V1p98–11, $35.00.

Drexel, Aspirin, ¼ x 1¼ x 1¾", V2p64–5, $12.00.

Droste's sample, Cocoa, 1⅛ x 1⅛ x 1⅞", V1p220–12, $150.00.

Droste's sample, Cocoa, 1¾ x 1¾ x 3¼", V1p220–11, $85.00.

Droste's sample, Cocoa, 1 x 1 x 1⅞", V2p122–4, $90.00.

Droste's sample, Cocoa (dining car), 1 x 1 x 1⅞", V1p220–10, $225.00.

Druckers, Teeth\Gum, no photo, $45.00.

Drucker's Revelation, Tooth Powder, 1 x 2½", V1p57–10, $30.00.

Drucker's sample, Revelation, 1 x 2¾", V1p57–11, $40.00.

Drucker's sample, Revelation Teeth Powder, 1 x 2½", V1p57–12, $35.00.

Drucker's sample, Revelation Tooth Powder, 1 x 2⅜", V2p41–2, $25.00.

Drucker's sample, Revelation Tooth Pwd, 1 x 2⅝", V2p41–4, $20.00.

Druco, Charcoal Tablets, ⅞ x 1¾ x 2⅞", V1p98–12, $25.00.

Drug-Pak (nutex), Condom, ¼ x 1½ x 2", no photo, $50.00.

Druggist, Tooth Soap, ½ x 2 x 3⅛", V2p41–6, $80.00.

Druggist Brand, Condom, no photo, $60.00.

Drury W.S. $1.00, Vinco Plasters, 1 x 2¼ x 3½", V2p64–6, $145.00.

DryBack, Waterproof, no photo, $18.00.

Du Barry RH sample, Face Powder, ⅜ x 1⅝ x 1⅞", V1p250–12, $45.00.

Du Bois $2.00, Pecific Pills, ⅞ x 1¾ x 3", V1p99–1, $75.00.

Du-Ra-Bul, Type Ribbon, 1⅝ x 2⅛ x 1¾", V2p179–8, $55.00.

Du-Ra-Bul, Type Ribbon, ¾ x 2¼ x 2¼", V1p307–8, $18.00.

DuBarry, Cachous Perfume, ⅝ x 1⅝", V1p51–2, $22.00.

DuBarry RH, Blackhead Prep., 1¼ x 2¾", V1p51–3, $40.00.

Duble Tip, Condom, ¼ x 1⅝ x 2⅛", V2p18–1, $200.00.

Duco, Wax, no photo, $18.00.

Duff's sample, Peanut Butter, no photo, $150.00.

Dulcephone 200, Needles, no photo, $30.00.

Dulcetto 100, Needles, no photo, $40.00.

DuMont, Red Pepper, 3½ x 2¼ x 1¼", V2p143–7, $15.00.

Dundee $.75, Type Ribbon, ¾ x 2½ x 2½", no photo, $15.00.

Dunham's sample, Cocoanut, ½ x 2¼ x 3½", V1p243–6, $85.00.

Dunhill's sample, Pipe Bowl Pres., ½ x 1⅛", V1p194–6, $18.00.

Dunlop, Repair Outfit, ⅝ x 1¼ x 4½", no photo, $70.00.

Dunlop sample, Tire Repair Kit, 1 x 1¼ x 2⅞", V1p13–5, $100.00.

Dunlop sample, Tire Repair Outfit, 1 x 1¼ x 2⅞", V1p13–6, $90.00.

DUO, Aspirin, ¾ x 2 x 2½", V2p64–2, $10.00.

Duo-Haler sample, Menthol Inhaler, ⅜ x ⅞", V1p99–2, $15.00.

Duplico Cotton King, Type Ribbon, ¾ x 2½ x 2½", V1p307–9, $25.00.

Dupont #6, Blasting Caps, ¾ x 1 x 1⅝", V1p64–3, $75.00.

DuPont No. 6, Blasting Caps, 1 x 1⅜ x 1½", V1p64–4, $30.00.

DuPont sample, Nickel 7 Polish, ⅜ x 1½", V1p217–8, $25.00.

Dupree Pills $2.00, Tablets, ¾ x 1¾ x 2⅞", V1p99–3, $35.00.

Durite, Type Ribbon, ¾ x 2½ x 2½", V1p307–10, $12.00.

Durkee's, Paprika, 2 x 3¾", V2p144–1, $20.00.

Durkee's, Spanish Saffron, ¼ x 1¼ x 1¾", V1p187–7, $6.00.

Duro-flex, Type Ribbon, ¾ x 2½", no photo, $10.00.

Duro-Tex, Type Ribbon, ¾ x 2½ x 2½", no photo, $15.00.

Durobuilt, Pump Packing, 1⅛ x 1", V1p194–7, $6.00.

Duroc Beaver, Type Ribbon, ⅞ x 2½ x 2½", V1p307–11, $35.00.

Durol, Type Ribbon, ¾ x 2½ x 2½", V1p307–12, $15.00.

Dustless New Life, Glass Cleaner, 1 x 2¾", V1p21–6, $8.00.

Dutch, Cleaner, ¼ x ⅞", V1p21–7, $15.00.

Dutch Boy, Soldering Paste, ⅞ x 2½", V1p285–5, $8.00.

Dutch Brand, Dec-O-Tape, ¼ x 1⅝", V1p194–8, $6.00.

Dymax 200, Needles Gramaphone, ¼ x 1¼ x 1¾", V1p206–4, $30.00.

E Pluribus Unum, Needles, no photo, $55.00.

E-Jay, Turmeric Spice, 1¼ x 2¼ x 2⅞", V2p144–3, $20.00.

E-Z, Shoe Polish (blk), ¾ x 2⅜", V1p278–6, $15.00.

E-Z, Throat Pastilles, ½ x 2 x 4", no photo, $6.00.

E.Z., Feet Corn Relief, ¾ x 1", no photo, $20.00.

E.Z. Tablets, Aspirin, ¼ x 1¼ x 1¾", V1p99–4, $12.00.

Eagle, Camphor Ice, ¾ x 1¾ x 2¾", V1p99–5, $12.00.

Eagle, Steel Pens, ⅜ x 1¼ x 1½", V1p183–1, $20.00.

Eagle Brand, Snuff, 1¼ x 2⅛ x 1½", V1p191–4, $60.00.

Eagle Brand, Suede Powder, 1⅜ x 2½ x 3⅜", V1p278–7, $20.00.

Eagle Brand $1.00, Type Ribbon, ¾ x 2½ x 2½", V2p180–1, $20.00.

Eagle Falcon E 10, Steel Pens, ½ x 1¼ x 1¾", V1p183–2, $18.00.

Eagle Loud Tone, Phono Needles, ½ x 1¼ x 1¾", V2p112–8, $35.00.

Earle's, Anti Gas, ½ x 1¾ x 3", no photo, $18.00.

Eastman #3 $.25, Flash Cartridge, 1¼ x 3", V2p206–7, $30.00.

Eastman Kodak # 1, Flash Cartridge, 1¾ x 3¾", V1p184–2, $35.00.

Eastman Kodak # 2, Flash Cartridge, 1½ x 3⅜", V1p184–3, $30.00.

Eastman Kodak # 3, Flash Cartridge, 1¼ x 3", V1p184–4, $30.00.

Eastman Kodak # 4, Flash Cartridge, 1¼ x 3", V1p184–5, $22.00.

Easybright, Shoe Polish Russet, ¾ x 1¾", V1p278–8, $20.00.

Easybright, Stove Polish No 5, 1 x 3¾", V1p217–9, $25.00.

Eaton, Needles, no photo, $30.00.

Eaton T. 200 Soft Tone, Gramophone Needles, ⅝ x 2", V2p113–1, $40.00.

Eaton T. Co 200, Needles, ¼ x 1¼ x 1¾", V2p113–3, $25.00.

Eaton T. X Loud Tone, Phono Needles, ⅝ x 2", V2p113–5, $35.00.

Eby's $.35, Flu Caps, ¼ x 1¾ x 2½", V2p64–4, $12.00.

Echo, Tea, 2½ x 2½ x 2⅜", V1p267–6, $65.00.

Eclectic $1.00, Herbs Bark\Roots, ¾ x 1¾ x 2⅝", V1p99–8, $70.00.

Eclipse, Polish Boot, ¾ x 1¾", V1p278–9, $20.00.

Eclipse, Safety Razor, no photo, 185.00.

Eclipse, Tire Repair Bicycle, ⅝ x 2¼ x 3⅝", V1p174–4, $75.00.

Eclipse, Tire Repair Bicycle, ⅝ x 2¼ x 3⅝", V1p174–5, $65.00.

Eclipse, Tire Repair Outfit, ½ x 2⅝ x 4½", V1p13–7, $90.00.

Economique, Type Ribbon, ¾ x 2½ x 2½", V1p308–1, $6.00.

Economo No.10, Wax Crayons, ⅜ x 2⅝ x 3¾", V1p181–10, $8.00.

Eczol sample, Salve, ⅜ x 1", V1p99–6, $20.00.

Eddy's, French Polish, ⅝ x 1¾", V1p217–10, $25.00.

Eden sample, Beauty Face Powder, ¼ x 1⅝", V1p251–1, $50.00.

Edison Bell, Needles, no photo, $25.00.

Edison Bell 100, Chromic Needles, ⅜ x 1¼ x 1¾", V2p113–7, $35.00.

Edison Bell 100, Needles, ⅜ x 1¼ x 1½", no photo, $35.00.

Edison Bell 100, Needles Chromic, ¼ x 1¼ x 1½", V1p206–5, $35.00.

Edison Bell 200, Needles, no photo, $35.00.

Edison Bell 200, Needles (spear point), ½ x 1¼ x 1½", V1p206–6, $35.00.

Edison Bell Chromic, Needles, no photo, $30.00.

Edjol, Cloves, 4½ x 2½ x 1½", V2p144–5, $25.00.

Educational Brand stock, Type Ribbon, ¾ x 2½ x 2½", V1p308–2, $4.00.

Edward's sample, Coffee, 2¾ x 2¾", V2p123–3, $60.00.

EFCO, Type Ribbon, ¾ x 2¼ x 2¼", V1p308–3, $8.00.

Egg, Candy, 2 x 2¾", V1p286–9, $80.00.

Egyptian, Face Powder, no photo, $25.00.

Eiffel $.25, Kid Cream Clnr., ⅞ x 2⅜", V1p21–8, $18.00.

Eight O'Clock sample, Coffee, 2¼ x 1½ x 4", V1p229–1, $25.00.

Einik's $1.00, Ointment, ¾ x 1⅞", V1p99–7, $25.00.

El Stado sample, Cleansing Cream, ¼ x 1½", V2p28–1, $18.00.

Elcaya, Complexion Cream, ⅜ x 1⅛", V1p29–2, $8.00.

Electric #52, Pens Steel 12, ⅜ x 1¼ x 1¾", no photo, $15.00.

Electric Co., Razor, 7" long, no photo, $95.00.

Electric Razor $2.50, Razor, ¾ x 1⅛ x 6½", V1p270–8, $90.00.

Electro Balm, Salve, ¼ x 1¼", no photo, $10.00.

Electro-Silicon sample, Polishing Cream, ½ x 1⅜", V1p217–12, $18.00.

Electro-Silicon sample, Polishing Cream, ⅜ x 1¼", V1p217–11, $18.00.

Elephant, Talking Needles, no photo, $50.00.

Elgin, Main Springs, 1 x 2¾ x ½", V2p194–6, $15.00.

Elgin Material, Setting Springs, ¼ x 2 x 2½", V1p335–9, $20.00.

Elgin Material, Timing Screws, ¼ x 1⅞ x 2½", V1p335–10, $25.00.

Elgin National, Watch Main Spring, ¾ x 2¾ x 5⅛", V1p335–8, $45.00.

Elgin National, Watch Mainsprings, ½ x 2¼ x 4⅝", V1p335–7, $50.00.

Elgin National #81, Watch Parts, ½ x 2", no photo, $25.00.

Elgin Premier, Watch Main Spring, ⅝ x 2⅞ x 3¼", V1p335–11, $45.00.

Eliassof Bros. Co., Watch Main Spring, ¾ x 2⅞ x 3⅜", V1p335–12, $40.00.

Elite, Type Ribbon, no photo, $20.00.

Elk Brand, Type Ribbon, 1½ x 1¾ x 1¾", V1p308–4, $50.00.

Elk Brand, Type Ribbon, ¾ x 2½", V1p308–5, $8.00.

Elk Brand, Type Ribbon, ¾ x 2½", V1p308–6, $18.00.

Elk Brand, Type Ribbon, ¾ x 2½ x 2½", V1p308–7, $20.00.

Elk Brand, Type Ribbon, ¾ x 2¼", V2p180–3, $20.00.

Elkah Special, Needles, ⅜ x 1¼ x 1¾", V2p113–2, $30.00.

Ellen's New Discovery, Horse Remedy, 1½ x 2", V1p332–4, $70.00.

Ellis, Chile Powder, 2¾ x 2¼ x 1¼", V2p144–6, $25.00.

Ellis P.W., Mainsprings, ½ x 2¾ x 5⅛", no photo, $35.00.

Ellwood, Type Ribbon, ¾ x 2¼", V1p308–8, $15.00.

Ellwood, Type Ribbon, ⅝ x 2¼ x 2¼", V1p308–9, $12.00.

Elmo RH sample, Face Powder, ¼ x 1⅝", no photo, $25.00.

Elvita $1.00, Pills, ¾ x 1½ x 3", no photo, $45.00.

Embassy, Gramaphone Needles, no photo, $30.00.

Embassy Extra Loud, Needles, ½ x 1¼ x 1¾", V1p206–7, $30.00.
Embassy Loud, Gramaphone Needles, no photo, $35.00.
Embassy Loud, Gramaphone Needles, no photo, $45.00.
Embassy Med. Tone, Needles Gramophone, ½ x 1¼ x 1¾", V1p206–8, $35.00.
Embassy Medium, Gramaphone Needles, no photo, $35.00.
Embassy Medium, Gramaphone Needles, no photo, $40.00.
Embassy Radiogram, Gilded Needles, no photo, $35.00.
Embassy Soft, Gramaphone Needles, no photo, $35.00.
Embassy X Loud, Gramaphone Needles, no photo, $35.00.
Embassy X Loud, Needles, no photo, $35.00.
Embasy Long Play, Radiogram Needles, ½ x 1¼ x 1½", V1p206–9, $30.00.
Emdee, Aspirin, ¼ x 1¼ x 1¾", V2p64–7, $12.00.
Emerald Brand, Type Ribbon, ¾ x 2½ x 2½", V1p308–10, $15.00.
Emergency, Adhesive Plaster, ¼ x 1⅛ x 2¼", V2p195–8, $35.00.
Empire, Tire Valves, ¼ x ⅞ x 1⅛", V1p16–11, $12.00.
Empire Brand, Type Ribbon, ¾ x 2½ x 2½", V1p308–11, $12.00.
Empire St. Drug, Cold Cream, no photo, $20.00.
Empress Brand, Nutmeg, 3¼ x 2¼ x 1¼", V2p144–2, $55.00.
Empress Brand, Paprika, 3¼ x 2¼ x 1", V2p144–4, $35.00.
Enameline, Stove Polish, ¾ x 3⅜", V1p218–1, $20.00.
Encharma (Luxor), Cold Cream Complex., ¼ x 1½ x 1⅞", V1p29–3, $25.00.
Encharma (Luxor) sample, Cold Cream Powder, ¼ x 1⅝ x 2", V1p251–3, $35.00.
Encharma sample, Face Powder, no photo, $20.00.
Encharma sample, Face Powder, ¼ x 1⅜", V1p251–2, $30.00.
English (Seroco), Pile Remedy, no photo, $45.00.
English Pharmal., Ointment, no photo, $25.00.
Ephedrine & Nembutal, Medicine, no photo, $12.00.
Erado, Ink & Stain Remover, 1 x 2⅞", V1p21–9, $10.00.
Erado, Ink Out, 1⅝ x 3", V1p21–10, $18.00.
Ergoapiol Smith, Capsules 20, ½ x 2 x 3¾", V1p99–9, $12.00.
Ergoapiol Smith, Menstral Disorder, ½ x 2 x 3¾", V1p99–10, $15.00.
Ermin #20, Boot Polish, 1 x 2½", V2p119–1, $15.00.
Ermino Canvas, Shoe Cleaner, no photo, $10.00.
Ero, Auto Fuses, ¼ x 1¼ x 1¾", V1p8–3, $12.00.
Ero 30 AMPS, Auto Fuses, ¼ x 1¼ x 1¾", V1p8–2, $10.00.
Eskay's, Oralator Inhaler, ½ x 2¾", V1p99–11, $6.00.
Eskay's sample, Albumenized Food, 1½ x 2⅜", V2p125–3, $40.00.
Essavie's, Complexion Powder, 1⅜ x 3 x 3", V1p44–5, $60.00.
Estabrook's sample, Coffee, 2¾ x 2½", V1p229–2, $80.00.
Esterbrook, Business Steel Pens, ½ x 1¼ x 1¾", V2p207–1, $25.00.
Esterbrook, Compass No.8, ¼ x 2½ x 3⅜", V1p190–4, $40.00.
Esterbrook's, Pens Steel 1 Doz., ¼ x 1¼ x 1⅞", V1p183–3, $25.00.
Eucathol sample, Colds, Burns, Fever, ¼ x ⅞", V1p99–12, $22.00.
Eupraxine $.30, Wound Salve, ¾ x 2", V2p65–1, $15.00.
Eureka, Knitting Pins, ½ x 9", V1p187–1, $65.00.
Eureka, Tape Repair, 1 x 2⅜", V1p185–8, $12.00.
Eureka, Type Ribbon, no photo, $18.00.
Eureka $1.00, Herbs, 1⅛ x 2¼ x 3¼", V1p100–1, $60.00.
Eureka Improved, Type Ribbon, ⅞ x 2¼", V1p308–12, $22.00.
Eureka Little Wonder, Tire Repair Kit, ½ x 1⅝ x 2¾", V1p13–8, $85.00.
Eureka S.F.W.& S. sample, Marshmallows, 1¼ x 4 x 6", no photo, $70.00.
Euthymol Park Davis sample, Violet Talcum, ¾ x 1¼ x 2⅛", V1p258–3, $65.00.
Euthymol sample, Talcum Powder, ⅝ x ⅞ x 1⅞", V1p258–4, $40.00.
Evans, Black Pepper, 3¼ x 2¼ x 1¼", V2p144–7, $30.00.
Evan's, Charcoal Tablets, ⅝ x 2¼ x 3½", V1p100–2, $65.00.
Evans's, Menthol & Glycerin, ⅞ x 1¾ x 2¾", V2p169–5, $12.00.
Evans, Pastilles, ¾ x 2⅛ x 3¼", V1p291–9, $8.00.
Evans C.C., Aspirin, ¼ x 1¼ x 1¾", V1p100–3, $12.00.

Evans's George B., Menthol & Glyc. Loz., ¾ x 1¾ x 2¾", V2p169–7, $20.00.
Evans's, Charcoal Tablets, ⅝ x 2⅛ x 3½", V2p65–3, $70.00.
Evans's, Tooth Powder, 1 x 1¾ x 2⅞", V2p41–8, $55.00.
Ever Clear $.10, Perfect Polish, ¼ x 1½ x 2⅛", V1p218–2, $25.00.
Ever-Ready, Blade Bank, 1 x 1⅞ x 1¾", V1p274–7, $25.00.
Ever-Ready, Blade Bank, 1 x 1⅞ x 1¾", V2p134–5, $25.00.
Ever-Ready, Blade Dispenser, 1 x 2 x 2", no photo, $20.00.
Everett & Barron, Ever Ready Suede Stick, 1 x 3¾", V2p119–3, $15.00.
Everfresh, Saccharin, ¼ x 1¼ x 1¾", V1p188–5, $12.00.
Evergreen City, Type Ribbon, ¾ x 2½ x 2½", V1p309–1, $15.00.
Everlasting, Ink Stamp Pad, ½ x 1¼ x 3¼", V1p179–3, $15.00.
Everlasting, Perfume, ¼ x 1⅛ x 1⅛", V1p183–8, $10.00*.
Everlasting, Type Ribbon, ¾ x 2½", V1p309–2, $18.00.
Everybodys, Safety Razor, no photo, 185.00.
Ex-Lax, Fig Flavor, 1 x 2½ x 3¾", no photo, $10.00.
Ex-Lax, Fig Flavor, 1 x 2½ x 3¾", V1p100–4, $10.00.
Ex-Lax $.10, Chocolate Laxative, ¼ x 1⅝ x 1⅝", V1p100–9, $5.00.
Ex-Lax $.10, Laxative, ¼ x 1⅝ x 1⅝", V2p65–4, $10.00.
Ex-Lax $.10, Laxative Chocolate, ⅜ x 1⅝ x 1⅝", V1p100–6, $12.00.
Ex-Lax $.10, Laxative Chocolate, ⅜ x 1⅝ x 1⅝", V1p100–7, $12.00.
Ex-Lax $.25, Chocolate Laxative, ¼ x 2⅜ x 3", V1p100–8, $10.00.
Ex-Lax $.25, Chocolate Laxative, ⅜ x 2¼ x 3", V2p65–6, $10.00.
Ex-Lax Figs, Laxative, 1 x 2½ x 3¾", V1p100–5, $15.00*.
Ex-Lax sample, Chocolate Laxative, ⅜ x 1⅝ x 1⅝", V2p65–4, $15.00.
Ex-Lax sample, Chocolate Laxative, ⅜ x 1⅝ x 1⅝", V2p65–5, $18.00.
Ex-Lax sample, Laxative, ¼ x 1½ x 1½", V2p65–7, $12.00.
Ex-Lax sample, Laxative, ¼ x 1⅝ x 1⅝", V1p100–10, $15.00.
Excedrin, Aspirin, ¼ x 1¼ x 1¾", V1p100–11, $3.00.
Excelento sample, Quinine Pomade, ¼ x1⅛", V1p34–8, $18.00.
Excellent, Self Inking Stamp Pad, ¼ x 1 x 2¼", V1p179–4, $12.00.
Excelsior, Indelible Outfit, ½ x 2 x 3¼", V1p179–5, $15.00.
Excelsior, Lube for Bicycles, ¾ x 2⅛", V1p174–6, $60.00.
Excelsior Jumbo, Stamp Pad, ½ x 2 x 3¾", V1p179–6, $15.00.
Exelento sample, Hair Pomade, ¼ x 1¼", V1p34–10, $25.00.
Exelento sample, Hair Pomade, ¼ x 1⅝", V1p34–9, $18.00.
Exello, Auto Fuses, ¼ x 1¼ x 1¾", V1p8–4, $15.00.
Exora sample, Cream, ¼ x ⅞", V1p29–4, $18.00.
Expello sample, Kills Moths, 2 x 2¾", V1p194–9, $12.00.
Expello sample, Moth Killer, 2¼ x 3½", no photo, $20.00.
F.F.F. sample, Coffee Roasted, 2 x 3½", V1p229–3, $85.00.
F.W. sample, Cough Drops, 1½ x 1½ x 2⅝", V1p291–10, $250.00.
Faber A.W., Pencil Case, ¾ x 2 x 7⅛", $12.00.
Fair-Plex, Ointment, ½ x 1½", no photo, $20.00.
Fairmont Brand, Turmeric, 3¼ x 2¼ x 1¼", V2p145–1, $40.00.
Fairway, Sodium Chloride Tabs, ¼ x 1¾ x 2⅝", V1p100–12, $12.00.
Fairway Brand, Allspice, 3¼ x 2¼ x 1½", V2p145–3, $75.00.
Fairway Brand, Red Pepper, 2½ x 1¾ x 1¼", V2p145–5, $30.00.
Fairy, Safety Razor, 1¼ x 2¼", V2p134–2, $375.00.
Fairy Cup sample, Tea, 2 x 2¾", V1p267–7, $35.00.
Famous, Mainsprings, ¾ x 3 x 3⅜", no photo, $70.00.
Famous Pride sample, Coffee, no photo, $75.00.
Fargotstein S., Watch Supply, ½ x 1⅞", V1p336–2, $3.00.
Fargotstein S., Watch Supply, ⅜ x 1⅛", V1p336–1, $3.00*.
Farmacia, Maisonave, ½ x 1⅜", V1p101–1, $6.00.
Farmers Pride, Ginger, 1¼ x 2¼ x 3¼", no photo, $45.00.
Farmers Pride sample, Coffee, no photo, $55.00.
Fasteeth sample, Denture holder, ¾ x 1⅜ x 2", no photo, $22.00.
Fasteeth sample, Denture Powder, ½ x 1½ x 2", V2p42–1, $20.00.
Fasteeth sample, Denture Powder, ¾ x 1¼ x 2⅛", V1p58–1, $35.00.
Fasteeth sample, Tooth Powder, ¾ x 1¼ x 2", no photo, $35.00.

Faultless, Type Ribbon, 1¾ x 1¾ x 2", V2p180–5, $45.00.
Faultless (Miller), Type Ribbon, ⅞ x 2½ x 2½", no photo, $18.00.
Favorite, Stamp Pad, ½ x 1⅝ x 2¾", V1p179–7, $18.00.
Favorite Brand, Cream Tartar, 1 x 2¼ x 4", V2p145–6, $20.00.
Favorite Record, Needles, no photo, $30.00.
Fawsco, Auto Fuses, no photo, $12.00.
Feasel's Noxal sample, Metal Polish, ⅜ x 1⅜", V2p37–4, $30.00.
Feather Touch, Type Ribbon, no photo, $10.00.
Federa sample, Pain Ointment, ¼ x 1¼", V2p66–1, $20.00.
Federal Brand, Type Ribbon, no photo, $20.00.
Federated Gardiner, Radio Solder, ¾ x 2½", V1p285–6, $4.00.
Feinste, Bonbons, ¾ x 1¾ x 2½", V1p286–10, $45.00.
Felco, Condom, no photo, $60.00.
Feminex, Analagesic Laxative, ¼ x 1¼ x 1¾", V2p66–3, $18.00.
Feminex, Tablets, ¼ x 1¼ x 1½", V2p66–5, $30.00.
Fencaps, Headache\Colds, ⅜ x 1¾ x 2⅝", V1p101–2, $15.00.
Feosol, Tablets, ¼ x 2⅞ x 2¾", V1p101–3, $10.00.
Fern, Red Pepper, 3 x 2¼ x 1¼", V2p145–2, $35.00.
Ferndell, Spice 2 oz., 1¼ x 1⅝ x 4 ⅜", V1p188–6, $40.00.
Ferratin, Tablets, ⅝ x 2¼ x 3½, $15.00.
Ferratin, Tablets, ⅝ x 2¼ x 3½", V1p101–4, $50.00.
Ferro Prussiate, Blue Print Paper, 1⅝ x 4½", V1p194–10, $20.00.
Festal Hall, Whole Cinnamon, 2 x 3¾", V2p145–4, $25.00.
Festival Brand, White Pepper, 3½ x 2¼ x 1¼", V2p145–7, $30.00.
Fett Puder #4711, Powder a la Rose, ⅞ x 2⅝", V1p44–6, $12.00.
Fi-na-st, Allspice, no photo, $30.00.
Fiancee sample, Face Powder, ¼ x 1½", V1p251–4, $18.00.
Fiebing's, Saddle Soap, 1⅛ x 3½", V1p278–10, $18.00.
Field's, Aspirin, ¼ x 1¼ x 1¾", V2p66–2, $10.00.
Fiesta Brand, Mustard, 3¾ x 2¼ x 1¼", V2p146–1, $35.00.
Figsen, Laxative, ⅝ x 2½ x 4¼", V1p101–5, $15.00.
Filmophone, Needles, no photo, $25.00.
Fine Service, Type Ribbon, ¾ x 2½ x 2½", V1p309–3, $18.00.
Fine Service Brand, Type Ribbon, ⅞ x 2½", V2p180–7, $10.00.
Finer Foods, Cinnamon, 4¼ x 2½ x 1½", V2p146–4, $15.00.
Fine's, Aspirin, ¼ x 1¼ x 1¾", V1p101–6, $12.00.
Finesse sample, Face Powder, ⅜ x 1½", V1p251–5, $20.00.
Finest Quality, Steel Pins, no photo, $15.00.
First Aid, Zinc Oxide, 1 x 2", no photo, $8.00.
First Texas Chem., Aspirin, ¼ x 1¼ x 1¾", V1p101–7, $15.00.
Firstaid, Adhesive Plaster, 1 x 2⅜", V1p345–11, $7.00.
Firstaid, Band-Aids, 1⅛ x 2⅜ x 3½", V1p101–8, $10.00.
Firstaid, Dental Floss, ⅛ x 1¼", V1p55–5, $25.00.
Firstaid, Readymade Bandage, ¼ x 3¼ x 3½", V1p101–9, $10.00.
Firstaid, Readymade Bandages, ½ x 3⅝ x 3⅝", V1p101–10, $10.00.
Firstaid, Surgical Plaster, 1 x 1¼", V1p346–12, $15.00.
Firstaid, Surgical Plaster, ⅞ x 1¾", V1p346–1, $18.00.
Firstaid, Zinc Oxide, 1 x 1¼", V1p346–2, $18.00.
Fisher, Type Ribbon, ¾ x 2½ x 2½", V2p180–2, $15.00.
Fisher's, Chocolate Laxative, ¼ x 1⅝ x 1⅝", V1p101–11, $12.00.
Fisher's, Ground Ginger, 4 ¾ x 2¼ x 1¼", V2p146–6, $35.00.
Fisher's, Indian Remedy, no photo, $35.00.
Fisher's $.10, Cold Tablets, ¼ x 1¼ x 1¾", V1p101–12, $12.00.
Fisher's $.15, Purple Laxative Pills, ⅝ x ⅞ x 1¾", V2p66–4, $18.00.
Fisk Rubber Co., Single Tube Repair Kit, ½ x 1¾ x 2¾", V2p14–1, $65.00.
Fixaco $.05, Cough Drops, ¼ x 1 x 1⅝", V1p291–11, $22.00.
Fixaco $.10, Cough Drops, ¼ x 1¼ x 1¾", V2p169–2, $15.00.
Flag, Needles, no photo, $35.00.
Flare sample, Rouge Vivant, ¼ x 1¼", V1p47–7, $10.00.
Flash Antiseptic, Hand Cleaner, no photo, $12.00.
Flax's, Type Ribbon, ¾ x 2½ x 2½", V1p309–4, $18.00.
Flax's High Grade, Type Ribbon, ¾ x 2½ x 2½", V1p309–5, $18.00.
Fleck J.J., see Jim Crow Salve, V1p84–11, $18.00.
Flemish Art, Absorb Material, 1¼ x 2¾", V1p194–11, $30.00.
Flents, Ear Plugs, ½ x 2 x 2¾", V2p207–3, $5.00.
Fletcher's, Z.B.T.Baby Powder, 1⅜ x 1⅜ x 3¾", no photo, $25.00.
Flex-O, Teat Dilators, 1¼ x 2⅜ x 2", V1p332–5, $4.00.
Flexa, Tire Repair Kit, ½ x 1½ x 2½", V1p13–9, $55.00.
Flexa, Tire Repair Kit, ½ x 1½ x 2½", V2p14–2, $55.00.
Flexible Match Co., Match Holder, ⅜ x 1¼", no photo, $35.00.
Flexo, Type Ribbon, ¾ x 2¼", V2p180–4, $12.00.
Flint Brand, Type Ribbon, no photo, $12.00.
Flint Brand, Type Ribbon, ½ x 2¼ x 2¼", V1p309–6, $5.00.
Flint Typewriter, Type Ribbon, 1¾ x 1⅞", V1p309–7, $50.00.
Floral Cluster sample, Talcum Powder, ⅞ x 1¼ x 2", no photo, $45.00.
Florence Nightingale, Paprika, 1¾ x 3½", V2p146–2, $15.00.
Florian sample, Face Powder, ¾ x 1¼ x 2⅛", V1p251–6, $50.00.
Flowery, Nail Polish Powder, ¾ x 1½", V1p42–11, $12.00.
Fluer DeGlorie, Talcum Puff, ¼ x 2½", V1p44–7, $10.00.
Foley's Banner, Pile Cure, ¼ x 1⅛", V1p102–1, $18.00.
Foley's Birch Flavor, Aspirin, ⅜ x 1¼ x 1¾", no photo, $15.00.
Folger's, Curry Powder, 3¼ x 2¼ x 1¼", V2p146–3, $30.00.
Folger's, Ginger, 1¼ x 2¼ x 3¼", V2p146–5, $35.00.
Folgers sample, Coffee, no photo, $30.00.
Folger's sample, Coffee, 2 x 2¼", V1p229–4, $15.00.
Folks, Cough Pastilles, 1 x 2½ x 3⅜", no photo, $6.00.
Forbes sample, Coffee, 2⅜ x 3", V1p229–6, $75.00.
Forbes sample, Coffee, 3 x 2¼", V1p229–5, $145.00.
Ford's sample, Hair Pomade, ⅜ x 1¼", V2p35–5, $15.00.
Formamint, Tablets, ¼ x 1⅜ x 1⅞", V1p102–3, $12.00.
Formamint, Tablets, ¾ x 2", V1p102–2, $8.00.
Fort Hamilton, Allspice, 3 x 2¼ x 1¼", V2p146–7, $55.00.
Fort Pitt, Blasting Caps, no photo, $35.00.
Foss Al, Dry Strip Pork Rind, ½ x 2 x 4", V1p175–8, $35.00.
Foss Al, Pork Rind Minnow, 1⅛ x 1¼ x 4", V1p175–9, $70.00.
Foss Al, Pork Rind Minnow, 1 x 1¼ x 4", no photo, $70.00.
Foss Al, Pork Rind Minnow, 1 x 1¼ x 4", V1p175–7, $70.00.
Foss Al, Pork Rind Minnow, ⅝ x ⅞ x 2½", V1p175–10, $70.00.
Foss Al., Fish Lure (No.8), ½ x ⅞ x 2½", V1p176–1, $90.00.
Foss Al., Pork Rind Minnow, 1 x 1¼ x 4", V1p176–2, $70.00.
Foss Al., Pork Rind Wiggler, 1 x 1¼ x 4", V2p198–1, $40.00.
Foster-Milburn, Ice Mint sample, V1p110–11, $25.00.
Foster-Milburn Co, see Doan's Ointment.
Fougera & Co., Glycogen Dr\De.Nittis, ⅜ x 1¼ x 2⅛", V2p66–6, $30.00.
Fougera & Co., see Kugloids sample, V1p115–2, $100.00.
Fougera Co., Cypridol Tablets, V1p85–5, $30.00.
Fougera's, Mustard Plaster, 1⅝ x 3⅞", V1p102–4, $25.00.
Fougera's, Mustard Plaster, ⅝ x 3¾ x 5", no photo, $35.00.
Four Fold sample, Salve, ⅜ x 1¼", V1p102–6, $18.00.
Fox, Paste, 2" high, no photo, $80.00.
Fox, Type Ribbon, ¾ x 2½ x 2½", no photo, $20.00.
Fox Hound, Aspirin box, ¼ x 1¼ x 1¾", V1p102–6, $30.00.
Fox Visible Writer, Type Ribbon, ¾ x 2½ x 2½", no photo, $35.00.
Foyer's Best, Type Ribbon, 1⅝ x 1⅝ x 2", V2p180–6, $55.00.
Foyer's Best, Type Ribbon, ¾ x 2¼ x 2¼", V1p309–8, $20.00.
Franco-American, Day Tint, no photo, $15.00.
Franco-American sample, Coffee, 3½ x 2 x 2½", V1p230–1, $85.00.
Frank Tea & Spice, Dove Brand, 2 x 3¾", no photo, $65.00.
Frank Tea & Spice, Spanish Saffron, ½ x 2⅛", V1p187–8, $22.00.
Frank Tea & Spice, Special Chilie, 1¾ x 3⅝", no photo, $40.00.
Franklin Brand, Type Ribbon, ⅞ x 2½", V1p309–9, $25.00.
Franklin Spearamint, Gum, ⅝ x 1¼ x 1¼", V1p296–5, $120.00.
Frank's, Aspirin, ¼ x 1¼ x 1¾", V1p102–7, $12.00.
Frank's, Aspirin, ¼ x 1¼ x 1¾", V2p67–1, $12.00.
Frank's, Saffron, ¼ x 1¼ x 1¾", V2p203–3, $4.00.
Frank's Nurse Brand, Zinc Oxide Plaster, 1 x 1⅜", V1p346–3, $40.00.
Frederick, Type Ribbon, ¾ x 2½ x 2½", V1p309–10, $25.00.
Frederick, Type Ribbon, ¾ x 2½ x 2½", V2p180–8, $20.00.

Freeman's sample, Face Powder, ⅝ x ¾ x 1⅛", V1p251–7, $18.00.
Freeman's sample, Face Powder Medicated, ½ x 1⅛ x 1⅛", V1p251–8, $20.00.
French,s, Insect Powder, ⅝ x 3", V1p194–12, $10.00.
French's, Adhesive Plaster, 1 x 1¼", V1p346–4, $30.00.
French's, Aspirin, ¼ x 1¼ x 1¾", V1p102–8, $12.00.
French's, Chileo Powder, 1½ x 3¼", V1p188–7, $40.00.
French's, Ketchup Spice, 1½ x 2¼ x 3¼", V2p147–1, $45.00.
French's, Nutmeg, 1¼ x 2⅞", V1p188–8, $40.00.
French's, Nutmeg, 1¾ x 4", V2p147–3, $35.00.
French's, Paprika, 1¼ x 3¼", V1p188–9, $40.00.
French's, Song Restorer, ¾ x 2 x 3", V1p195–1, $10.00.
Freshys $.25, Constipation, ⅜ x 1⅜ x 2", V1p102–9, $40.00.
Friedrich & Bros., Violin Rosin, 1⅝ x 1¼", V1p181–2, $30.00.
Friedrich John Bros., Violin Rosin, 1¼ x 1½", V1p181–3, $35.00.
Friedrich John Bros., Violin Rosin, 1¼ x 1⅝", V1p181–4, $30.00.
Fritch's, Salve, ⅞ x 2¼", V1p102–10, $5.00*.
Frog in Your Throat, Cough Drops, no photo, $95.00.
Frogletts, Cough Tablets, ⅞ x 3 x 2", V1p291–12, $110.00.
Frontier, Boot Polish, 1 x 3", no photo, $25.00.
Frozen Mints, Chewing Gum, 1⅜ x 2½ x 4", V2p167–2, $115.00.
Fru-A-tives $.25, Laxative, ⅝ x ⅞ x 2⅜", V1p102–11, $45.00.
Fruit-Bran, Laxative Compound, ⅜ x 1¾ x 2½", V2p67–3, $25.00.
Fruitatives $.25, Tablets, ⅜ x 1 x 1¾", V2p67–5, $18.00.
Frye Mfg., Type Ribbon, ¾ x 2½", V2p181–1, $18.00.
Fry's sample, Cocoa, no photo, $70.00.
Fry's sample, Cocoa, ½ x 2 x 2⅜", V1p221–1, $90.00.
Fuller sample, Furniture Polish, 1½ x 2⅜", V1p218–3, $25.00.
Fullotone Medium 200, Needles Phono, ½ x 2", V1p206–10, $55.00.
Fullotone sample, Needles Phono, ½ x 2", V1p206–11, $65.00.
Fulltone 200 Loud, Needles, no photo, $40.00.
Fulltone 200 Soft, Needles, no photo, $40.00.
Fulton, Ink Pad, ¼ x 1¼ x 2⅜", V1p179–8, $12.00.
Fulton, Type Ribbon, ¾ x 2½ x 2½", no photo, $20.00.
Fulton, Type Ribbon, ¾ x 2½ x 2½", V1p309–11, $15.00.
Fulton # 0, Stamp Pad, ⅜ x 2¼ x 3½", V2p200–3, $12.00.
Fulton No. XX, Ink Pad, ¼ x 1¼ x 2¼", V2p200–5, $8.00.
Fulton No. xx, Ink Pad, ⅜ x 1¼ x 2¼", V2p200–7, $8.00.
Furbish's M.I., Flexable Fly Line, ¾ x 2⅝ x 4", no photo, $25.00.
Fursten Spezial Pick Up, Needles, ⅜ x 1¼ x 2⅛", V1p206–12, $25.00.
Furstenbergs, Felsol, ¼ x 1½ x 2¾", V1p102–12, $10.00.
Fusetron, Auto Fuses, no photo, $12.00.
G & G Quality, Auto Fuses, ¼ x 1¼ x 1¾", V1p8–5, $15.00.
G & J, Tire Repair Kit, ½ x 1⅝ x 2½", V1p13–10, $50.00.
G-M-Co., Valve Caps, ½ x ⅞ x 1½", V1p16–4, $12.00.
G.A.Y., Split Shot BB's, no photo, $15.00.
G.M.Co, Valve Insiders, ¼ x 1 x 1⅜, no photo, $12.00.
Galena, Axel Grease Carriage, ⅞ x 2½", V1p11–2, $35.00.
Gallacin, Tablets, ¼ x 1¼ x 1¾", V1p103–1, $40.00.
Gallos Ruban, Machines, ¾ x 2½ x 2½", no photo, $18.00.
Gallotone 200, XLoud Needles, ⅜ x 1¼ x 1¾", V1p207–1, $30.00.
Gamage A.W. 200, Needles Phono, ½ x 1¼ x 1½", V1p207–2, $30.00.
Gamma, Needles, no photo, $25.00.
Gamulco, Type Ribbon, 1¾ x 1¾ x 2", V2p181–3, $45.00.
Gamulco, Type Ribbon, 1⅝ x 1⅝ x 2", V1p310–1, $50.00.
Gamulco, Type Ribbon, ¾ x 2½ x 2½", V1p309–12, $18.00.
Gamulco, Type Ribbon, ¾ x 2½ x 2½", V1p310–2, $18.00.
Garden Court sample, Face Powder, ¼ x 1⅝", V1p251–9, $22.00.
Gardenia RH sample, Face Powder, ¼ x 1½ x 1½", V1p251–10, $15.00.
Gardenia RH sample, Face Powder, ¼ x 1½ x 1½", V2p23–2, $18.00.
Gardenia RH sample, Talcum Powder, ¾ x 1¼ x 2⅛", V1p258–5, $50.00.
Garfield $.25, Digestive Tablets, ½ x 1½ x 3", V2p67–2, $75.00.
Garrett, Scotch Snuff, 1¾ x 2¼", V2p207–6, $20.00.
Garrett W.E., Snuff Mild\Sweet, 1¼ x 1¾", V1p191–5, $22.00.
Garwood's, Menthol Glycerine Waffers, ¾ x 1¾ x 3", V2p167–4, $18.00.
Garwood's, Peppermints 18, ½ x ⅞ x 2¾", V1p296–6, $75.00.
Garwood's, Rose Breath Hearts, ½ x 1½", V2p169–4, $20.00.
Garwood's, Spearmint Breath Gum, ½ x 1½ x 2", V1p296–7, $35.00.
Garwood's, Violet Breath Gum, ½ x 1⅜ x 2", V1p296–8, $40.00.
Garwood's, Violet Breath Hearts, ½ x 1⅝", V1p296–9, $40.00.
Garwood's, Violet Breath Hearts, ⅜ x 2", V1p286–11, $25.00.
Garwood's, Violet Breath Mints, ⅝ x 1⅝", V1p286–12, $30.00.
Garwood's #6569, Peppermint Breath Hearts, ½ x 1⅝", V2p169–6, $25.00.
Gas-Ker Co., Jewelers Supply, ½ x 1½", V1p336–3, $4.00.
Gasoda sample, Indigestion, ¼ x 1⅝", V1p103–2, $25.00.
Gastrogen $.20, Tablets, ¼ x 1½ x 2⅜", $8.00.
Gastrogen $.20, Tablets, ¼ x 1⅜ x 2¼", V1p103–3, $12.00.
Gate City, Type Ribbon, ¾ x 2½ x 2½", V2p181–5, $20.00.
Gauss', Catarrh Balm, ¾ x 1½", V1p103–4, $25.00.
Gauss sample, Catarrh Balm, ¼ x ⅞", no photo, $25.00.
Geha, Fish Food, 1⅜ x 2½", V1p195–2, $8.00.
Geisha, Needles, no photo, $45.00.
Gem, Blade Box, ¼ x 1⅛ x 2⅛", V2p134–4, $45.00.
Gem, Safety Razor, no photo, $85.00.
Gem $2.00, Safety Razor, 1⅜ x 2¼ x 1½", V1p270–9, $125.00.
Gem American, Razor Blades, ¼ x 1⅛ x 2⅛", V1p269–2, $65.00.
Gem Cutlery Co., Safety Razor, 1⅜ x 2⅜", V1p270–10, $115.00.
Gem New Safety Razor, Blade, ¼ x 1 x 2", V1p269–3, $50.00.
Gems, Condom, ¼ x 1⅝ x 2", V1p23–10, $60.00.
General, Auto Fuses, ¼ x 1¼ x 1¾", V1p8–6, $10.00.
General, Tire Valve Cores, ¼ x 1 x 1¼", V1p17–1, $12.00.
General, Type Ribbon, ¾ x 2½ x 2½", no photo, $15.00.
General Appliance, Gacor Products, ¼ x 1", V1p195–3, $8.00.
General Electric 50, Novalux Cutouts, 1 x 2⅛", V1p195–4, $6.00.
General Electric Co., Medicine, ⅜ x 1¼", V1p103–5, $5.00.
Gensco, Condom, ¼ x 1½ x 2", no photo, $50.00.
Gentner Carl, Mentholin, ½ x 1⅜", $15.00.
Genuaids, Constipation, ⅜ x 1¼ x 2", V1p103–6, $15.00.
Genuine Liquid Latex, Condom, no photo, $45.00.
Germolene sample, Skin Ointment, ½ x 1⅛", V2p67–3, $18.00.
Gibb's, Shaving Soap, no photo, $40.00.
Gibraltar, Type Ribbon, ¾ x 2½", V1p310–3, $15.00.
Gilbert, Needles, no photo, $30.00.
Gillette, Safety Razor, ½ x 1½ x 3⅝", V1p270–11, $25.00.
Gillett's, Cloves, 2¾ x 2¼ x 1¼", V2p147–5, $25.00.
Gillett's, Paprika, 1¾ x 3¾", V2p147–6, $35.00.
Gillett's, Saffron, 1¼ x 1¾ x 1⅞", V2p203–6, $20.00.
Gillett's, Saffron, ⅝ x 2½", V1p187–9, $30.00.
Gillott's J. 1160, Steel Pen Nibs, ¼ x 1¼ x 1¾", V2p207–2, $25.00.
Gillott's Joseph, Pens Steel #1155, ¼ x 1¼ x 1¾", V1p183–4, $25.00.
Gin, Kidney Pills, 1¼ x 2", V2p67–6, $20.00.
Gin, Pills, ⅞ x 1¾", no photo, $15.00.
Gino $.50, Pills 40, ¾ x 1¾", V1p103–7, $20.00.
Girl Scouts, Sewing Kit, 1 x 2½ x 3¾", V1p185–9, $18.00.
Gladding's, Line Tonic, ¾ x 2¾", V2p198–3, $8.00.
Gladiator, Dental Rubber, 1 x 3¼ x 6", no photo, $80.00.
Glassene $.25, Glass & Metal Cleaner, ¾ x 2⅝", V1p21–11, $25.00.
Glassoid $.25, Cleaner Glasses, ½ x 1½", V1p21–12, $25.00.
Glazo sample, Cuticle Massage, ⅜ x ⅞", V2p23–4, $45.00.
Glebeas sample, Adoration Face Powder, ¼ x 1½", V1p251–11, $18.00.
Glendora ½ Lb., Coffee, 3½ x 4", V1p230–3, $65.00.
Glendora sample, Coffee, 2 x 3¼", V1p230–2, $55.00.
Glendora sample, Coffee, 3¼ x 2", V1p230–3, $50.00.
Globe, Ava-Late, no photo, $35.00.

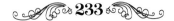

Globe, Horseshoe Nail, ⅝ x 1⅞ x 3", V2p207–4, $25.00.

Globe, Mainsprings, ¾ x 2¾ x 2¾", V2p194–2, $60.00.

Globe, Type Ribbon, ¾ x 2½", no photo, $18.00.

Globe, Type Ribbon, ¾ x 2½ x 2½", V1p310–4, $20.00.

Globe Brand, Type Ribbon, ¾ x 2½ x 2½", V1p310–5, $25.00.

Globe Labratory, Poultry Tablets, 1½ x 1½ x 2¼", V1p332–6, $25.00.

Glossantina, Straightner, no photo, $20.00.

Glove (Sears) sample, Powder, ⅝ x 3", V1p266–4, $35.00.

Glove sample, Powder, ⅝ x ⅞ x 1⅞", V1p266–5, $35.00.

Glover's, Condition Pills, no photo, $35.00.

Glover's, Condition Pills, ½ x 2 x 3⅛", V2p192–4, $35.00.

Glover's, Condition Pills, ½ x 2 x 3⅛", V2p192,$7, $55.00.

Glover's, Digestive Pills, ½ x 2 x 3", V2p193–1, $25.00.

Glover's, Digestive Pills, ⅝ x 2 x 3", V1p332–7, $75.00.

Glover's, Lax Pills Dogs, ½ x 2 x 3⅛", V1p332–8, $35.00.

Glover's, Sulphur Tablets, ½ x 2 x 3⅛", V1p332–9, $80.00.

Glover's 1543, Digestive Pills, ½ x 2 x 3", V1p332–10, $75.00.

Glover's Imperial, Worm Capsules, ¾ x 2 x 2", V1p332–11, $90.00.

Gold Bond, Red Pepper, 3½ x 2¼ x 1¼", V2p147–2, $25.00.

Gold Brand, Auto Fuses, no photo, $12.00.

Gold Camel Ceylon, India Tea, ¾ x 1⅞ x 2⅜", V1p267–8, $45.00.

Gold Camel sample, Tea, ¾ x 1⅞ x 2⅜", V1p267–9, $50.00.

Gold Coin, Gall Cure, ½ x 1¼", no photo, $45.00.

Gold Leaf sample, Baking Powder, 1⅜ x 1⅞", V2p125–5, $35.00.

Gold Medal, Aspirin, ¼ x 1¼ x 1¾", V2p68–1, $15.00.

Gold Medal, Aspirin, ¼ x 1¼ x 1¾", no photo, $10.00.

Gold Medal, Boil Salve, ¾ x 2", V1p103–8, $15.00.

Gold Medal, Boyol Salve, ¾ x 2", V2p68–3, $8.00.

Gold Medal, Gold Cross Primers, 1¼ x 2 x 2½", V2p207–5, $45.00.

Gold Medal, Salve, 1 x 2½", V1p103–9, $12.00.

Gold Medal, Type Ribbon, ¾ x 2½ x 2½", V1p310–6, $12.00.

Gold Medal $2.00, Compound Pills, 1 x 1¾ x 2⅞", V2p68–5, $15.00.

Gold Medal $2.00, Compound Pills, ⅞ x 1¾ x 2⅞", V1p103–10, $20.00.

Gold Medal Brand, Cloves, 3 x 2¼ x 1¼", V2p147–4, $20.00.

Gold Medal Brand, Type Ribbon, 1⅝ x 1⅝ x 2", V2p181–2, $45.00.

Gold Metal, Type Ribbon, ¾ x 2½ x 2½", no photo, $12.00.

Gold Seal, Aspirin, ¼ x 1¼ x 1¾", V1p103–11, $12.00.

Gold Shield, Tea, 2 x 2½", V2p133–1, $40.00.

Gold Tipped, Watch Mainsprings, ½ x 2¼ x 4⅝", V1p336–4, $45.00.

Gold Wing, Type Ribbon, ¾ x 2½ x 2½", no photo, $12.00.

Goldbeaters, Condom, ⅝ x 1⅝", V2p18–3, $50.00.

Golden, Eye Salve, ⅜ x 1⅝", V1p103–12, $10.00.

Golden Brown, Ointment, ¾ x 1¾", V1p104–1, $18.00.

Golden Brown sample, Hair Dressing, ½ x 1⅛ x 1⅛", V1p34–11, $25.00.

Golden Brown Sample, Ointment, ¼ x ⅞", V2p35–2, $18.00.

Golden Club sample, Coffee, no photo, $80.00.

Golden Days sample, Coffee, no photo, $125.00.

Golden Drip, Red Pepper, 3¾ x 2¼ x 1¼", V2p147–7, $30.00.

Golden Eagles, Condoms, ⅜ x 1⅝ x 2⅛, no photo.

Golden Gem, Hair Dressing, no photo, $15.00.

Golden Peacock, Powder Face, ¼ x 2", V1p44–8, $20.00.

Golden Pheasant, Condom, ¼ x 1½ x 2", V1p23–11, $60.00.

Golden Poppy, Type Ribbon, ¾ x 2½ x 2½", no photo, $20.00.

Golden Pyramid Talking, Machine Needles, no photo, $75.00.

Golden Sheaf, Ginger, 3 x 2¼ x 1¼", V1p148–1, $35.00.

Golden Sun, Cloves, 1¼ x 2¼ x 3", V2p148–4, $20.00.

Golden Sun sample, Coffee, 4 x 2½", V1p230–5, $80.00.

Golden Tex, Condom, no photo, $60.00.

Golden Urn sample, Coffee, no photo, $80.00.

Golden Voice x Loud, Needles, ½ x 1¼ x 1½", V1p207–3, $40.00.

Golden Wedding sample, Coffee, no photo, $175.00.

Golden Wedding sample, Coffee, 2 x 3", V1p230–1, $115.00.

Golden Wedding sample, Coffee, 2 x 3", V1p231–1, $90.00.

Golden West, Sage, 3¼ x 2¼ x 1¼", V2p148–6, $40.00.

Goldman's Mary T., Shampoo, 1 x 2⅜", V2p32–6, $70.00.

Goldmark's J., Perc. Caps, ½ x 2⅜", V1p64–6, $40.00.

Goldmark's J., Percussion Caps, ½ x 1½", V1p64–7, $40.00.

Goldmark's J., Precussion Caps, ½ x 1½", V1p64–5, $50.00.

Goldmark's J., U S Musket Caps, ½ x 2½", V1p64–8, $40.00.

Gollberg, Watch Parts, ½ x 1½", V1p336–5, $5.00.

Gonosan sample, Kava Santal, ¼ x 1¼ x 1¾", V1p104–2, $22.00.

Good Hope, Salve, ⅝ x 1⅞", V2p68–7, $15.00.

Good Samaritan, Aspirin, ¼ x 1¼ x 1¾", V1p104–3, $15.00.

Good Samaritan $.50, Ointment, 1 x 2½", V1p104–4, $25.00.

Goodrich, Repair Kit, no photo, $55.00.

Goodrich-Gamble, Aspirin, ¼ x 1¼ x 1¾", V1p104–5, $12.00.

Goodwinol sample, Follicular Mange, ¼ x 1⅝", V1p332–12, $70.00.

Goody Bank, Bank, ⅜ x 2⅛", V1p195–5, $35.00.

Gotham, Adhesive Plaster, 1 x 1¼", V2p196–1, $25.00.

Gotham, Adhesive Plaster, ¾ x 2⅜", V2p196–3, $8.00.

Gotham, Stickrite Advesive, 1 x ¾", no photo, $10.00.

Gotham "R" 8 $.10, Chocolate Laxative, ⅜ x 1⅝ x 1⅝", V2p68–2, $8.00.

Gould, Watch Material, ½ x 1¼", V1p336–6, $5.00.

Gould Barbara sample, Face Powder, ¼ x 1⅝", V1p251–12, $10.00.

Gould Barbara sample, Face Powder, ¼ x 1⅝", V2p23–4, $15.00.

Government, Type Ribbon, ¾ x 2½ x 2½", V1p310–7, $8.00.

Gowan's sample, Ointment, ½ x 1⅛", V1p104–6, $20.00.

Gra-Deer, Type Ribbon, ¾ x 2½", no photo, $10.00.

Graf's Hyglo sample, Nail Polish, ¼ x ⅞", V1p42–12, $15.00.

Graham, Haarlem Oil Caps., ⅜ x 1½ x 2⅜", V1p104–7, $12.00.

Gram-O-Phone, Needles, no photo, $35.00.

Grammophon-Nadeln LFC, Needles, ⅜ x 1¼ x 1¾", V1p207–4, $45.00.

Gramophone 200, Needles, ¼ x 1⅜ x 2⅛", V1p207–5, $25.00.

Granchel $.15, Magnesium Oxide, ⅝ x 2⅛", V1p104–8, $12.00.

Grand Duches, Tooth Powder, no photo, $55.00.

Grand Opera, Needles, no photo, $35.00.

Grand Prize, Type Ribbon, ¾ x 2½ x 2½", V1p310–8, $20.00.

Grand Prize, Type Ribbon, ⅞ x 2½ x 2½", no photo, $20.00.

Grand Prize Brand, Type Ribbon, ¾ x 2½ x 2½", no photo, $15.00.

Grand Prize Brand, Type Ribbon, ¾ x 2½ x 2½", V2p181–4, $20.00.

Grandma's, Carbolic Salve, ⅞ x 2⅛", V1p104–9, $15.00.

Grandma's sample, Absorbo, ¼ x 1⅛", V1p104–10, $20.00.

Grandma's sample, Absorbo Salve, ¼ x 1⅛", V1p104–11, $20.00.

Grandma's Wonder $.25, Healing Cream, 1¼ x 2", V2p28–3, $25.00.

Granger's $.25, Liver Regulator, 1¾ x 1¾ x 2⅝", V2p68–4, $35.00.

Grant U.S., Medal, no photo, $45.00.

Granzow's $1.00, Tonic Tablets, ½ x 2 x 2⅝", V1p104–12, $15.00.

Graphic Duplicator, Type Ribbon, ½ x 2¼ x 2¼", no photo, $12.00.

Grassyfork Fisheries, Aquarium Food, ⅞ x 2¾", V1p195–6, $15.00.

Gravely B.F., Superior Chewing Tobacco, ¼ x 2¼ x 3¼", V1p191–6, $20.00.

Gray's, Ointment, ⅝ x 1½", V1p105–1, $8.00.

Gre-Solvent sample, Cleaner, ⅝ x 2", V2p37–6, $12.00.

Gre-Solvent sample, Hand Cleaner, ½ x 2", V1p22–1, $10.00.

Gre-Solvent sample, Hand Cleaner, ¾ x 2", V1p22–2, $12.00.

Great American, Pepper, 1⅞ x 3¼", V2p148–2, $25.00.

Great Christopher $.35, Corn Cure, ½ x 1¼", V1p105–2, $40.00.

Great Christopher $.35, Corn Cure, ½ x 1¼", V2p68–6, $40.00.

Great Seal, Adhesive Plaster, 1 x 1¼", V1p346–5, $25.00.

Great Seal, Adhesive Plaster, 1 x 1¼", no photo, $15.00.

Great Seal, Adhesive Plaster, 1 x 1¼", V1p346–6, $22.00.
Great Seal, Aspirin, ¼ x 1¼ x 1¾", V1p105–3, $12.00.
Great Seal, Aspirin, ¼ x 1¼ x 1¾", V1p105–4, $10.00.
Great Seal, Aspirin, ¼ x 1¼ x 1¾", V2p68–8, $12.00.
Great Seal, Aspirin, ¼ x 1¼ x 1¾", V2p69–1, $12.00.
Great Seal, Chocolate Laxative, ¼ x 1¾ x 2⅛, no photo, $10.00.
Great Seal, Cold Tablets, ¼ x 1¼ x 1¾", V1p105–5, $12.00.
Great Seal, Laxative Cold Tablets, ½ x 1¼ x 2", V1p105–6, $15.00.
Great Seal, Quinine Cold Tabs, ⅜ x 1¼ x 2", V2p69–3, $12.00.
Green n Gold sample, Coffee, 2⅛ x 2⅞", V1p231–2, $45.00.
Greenfield's, Pepsin Mints, ¾ x ⅞ x 2½", V1p287–1, $50.00.
Green's Golden Salve $.25, Ointment, ¾ x 2", V1p105–8, $40.00.
Griffin, Fish Hooks, ⅝ x 2", V1p176–3, $5.00.
Griffin, Sterling Paste, 1 x 3½", V1p278–12, $12.00.
Griffin, Sterling Paste, ¾ x 1¾", V1p278–11, $20.00.
Griffin, Suede Powder, 1¼ x 2⅜ x 4", V1p279–1, $30.00.
Griffin Grifola, Shoe Polish, ⅝ x 1¾", V2p119–2, $20.00.
Griffon, Safety Blades, ¼ x 1⅛ x 2⅛", V1p269–4, $80.00.
Griffon, Safety Blades, ¼ x 1 x 2", no photo, $90.00.
Griffon, Safety Razor, 1⅛ x 1⅝ x 2¼", V1p270–12, $175.00.
Griffon $ 1.25, Safety Razor, 1¼ x 2¼", V1p271–3, $150.00.
Griffon $1.50, Safety Razor, 1⅜ x 2⅜", V1p271–4, $155.00.
Griffon $2.00, Safety Razor, 1¼ x 2¼", V1p271–2, $145.00.
Griffon ABC, Shoe Polish Blk, 1 x 2½", V2p119–4, $5.00.
Griffon ABC, Shoe Polish Blk, 1 x 2½", V2p119–5, $5.00.
Griffon ABC, Shoe Polish Tan, 1 x 2½", V2p120–1, $3.00.
Grisdale Brand, White Pepper, 4 x 2½ x 1", V2p148–3, $30.00.
Griswold's (Nelson), Tire Repair Tool, ⅝ x 1⅝ x 4⅛", V1p13–11, $95.00.
Grove E.W., Bro Mo Laxative, ¾ x 1¼ x 2", V1p105–9, $8.00.
Grove E.W., Bromo Quinine, ⅜ x 1⅝ x 2", V1p105–10, $8.00.
Grove's, Sanare Cutis for Eczima, ¾ x 2⅜", V2p69–5, $60.00.
Grove's $.35, O-Pen-Trate Salve, ⅞ x 2¾", no photo, $40.00.
Grove's sample, O-Pen-Trate Salve, ½ x 1½", V1p105–11, $20.00.
Guaranteed High, Fine Steel, no photo, $40.00.
Guards, Cold Tablets, ¼ x 1¼ x 1¾", V1p105–12, $8.00.
Guhabro, Type Ribbon, ¾ x 2¼ x 2¼", V1p310–9, $8.00.
Guild, Type Ribbon, ¾ x 2½", V1p310–10, $12.00.
Guild's, Green Mount. Asm. Rem., 1⅞ x 2½ x 4 ⅝", V1p106–1, $25.00.
Gum, Gum, ⅜ x 2 x 2", V1p296–10, $35.00.
Gunnell's sample, Catarrh Cream, ¼ x ⅞", V2p69–7, $20.00.
Gunther's, Cough Drops, ½ x 2¼ x 3½", V2p169–8, $95.00.
Guth $.05, Carmels, 1 x 1 x 5", V1p287–2, $75.00.
Gypsy, Foot Relief, ¾ x 2", V1p106–2, $25.00.
H & H, Type Ribbon, no photo, $10.00.
H & H $.25, Balm, ¾ x 2", V1p106–3, $25.00.
H & H Brand, Red Pepper, 3½ x 2¼ x 1¼", V2p148–5, $30.00.
H-C-S Brand, Type Ribbon, ¾ x 2½ x 2½", V1p310–11, $15.00.
H-L-F sample, Polish cars\furn., 1¼ x 2⅛ x 2", V2p38–1, $20.00.
Haan R.M., Candy Bonbons, 1 x 2⅝ x 4", V1p287–3, $35.00.
Habit, Type Ribbon, ¾ x 2½ x 2½", no photo, $10.00.
Haemoferrum sample, Iron Pills, ⅜ x 1¼", V2p69–2, $15.00.
Hairspring Vibrating, Watch Parts, ⅜ x 1⅛", V1p336–7, $8.00.
Hal-Balm, Ointment, ¾ x 2½", V1p106–4, $12.00.
Hall Frank B., Oct. Line & Level, ½ x ¾ x 3½", V1p190–5, $25.00.
Hallmark, Type Ribbon, ¾ x 2½ x 2½", V1p310–12, $6.00.
Hall's, Zinc Oxide, 1 x 1¼", V2p196–5, $18.00.
Hall's, Zinc Oxide, 1 x 1⅜", V1p346–7, $18.00.
Hall's, Zinc Oxide, ⅜ x 1¼ x 2⅜", V1p346–8, $35.00.
Hamilton, Watch Main Spring, ⅝ x 2¾ x 5⅛", V1p336–8, $50.00.
Hamilton Beach, Motor Oil, 1⅞ x 2", V2p207–7, $35.00.
Hamilton's, Gall Remedy, no photo, $25.00.
Hammond Brand, Type Ribbon, ⅞ x 2½ x 2½", V1p311–1, $65.00.
Hammond M M, Type Ribbon, no photo, $18.00.
Hammond Superior, Type Ribbon, ¾ x 2½ x 2½", V1p311–2, $45.00.
Hampden Watch Co., Jewels 11 Openface, ¾ x 2", no photo, $8.00.
Hance, Aspirin, ¼ x 1¼ x 1½", V2p69–4, $10.00.
Hance, Milk of Magnesia, ½ x 1⅝ x 2½", V1p106–5, $8.00.
Hance Bros. & White sample, Phenol Sodique Ointment, ¼ x ⅞", V2p69–6, $20.00.
Hancock's, Mutton Tallow, ⅞ x 1¾", V1p51–4, $12.00.
Hand Mate, Tobacco Sample, 1¾ x 1¼", V1p191–7, $35.00.
Handy & Reardon's sample, Coffee, 2½ x 2", V1p231–3, $90.00.
Handy Andy, Bolts and Screws, 1¼ x 3⅜ x 6¾", V1p195–7, $15.00.
Handy Andy, Goggles, ¼ x 1⅞", V1p177–9, $15.00.
Handy Roll, Air Mail Stamps, ½ x 2 x 3", V2p208–1, $5.00.
Handy Roll $.25, Mending Tape, ⅝ x 2 x 3", V1p186–1, $8.00.
Hanna's, Ointment, no photo, $15.00.
Hanson-Jenks sample, Violet Brut Talcum, ¾ x 1⅜ x 2⅛", V2p128–3, $50.00.
Hansons, Needles Gramaphone, ¼ x 1¼ x 1¾", V1p207–6, $25.00.
Happy Hour Brand, Pickling Spice, 2 x 4", V2p148–7, $30.00.
Happy Hour sample, Coffee, no photo, $115.00.
Harley Brand, Pepper, 2½ x 2½ x 4⅞", V2p149–1, $25.00.
Harmony, Cocoa Butter, 1 x 2⅞", V1p244–1, $25.00.
Harris, Bouillon Cubes, ⅝ x 1⅞ x 2⅝", V2p208–3, $10.00.
Hartford, Tire Repair Kit, ½ x 1⅞ x 2⅞", V1p13–12, $60.00.
Hartford, Tire Repair Kit, ½ x 2 x 2¼", V1p14–1, $65.00.
Hartline, Blotter Pen, ⅜ x 1¼", no photo, $6.00.
Hartney, Needles Phono, ¼ x 1¼ x 1¾", V1p207–7, $35.00.
Hartshorn, Carbolic Camphor Ointment, no photo, $15.00.
Hartz Mountain, Bird Song Food, 1⅛ x 2 x 2¾", V2p193–3, $15.00.
Hartz Mountain, Foot Balm, ⅜ x 1⅜", V2p69–8, $22.00.
Harva-Carbs sample, Indigestion Tablets, ⅜ x 1¼ x 1¾", V1p106–6, $8.00.
Hasen's Charles, Laboratory, no photo, $35.00.
Hassall John, Nails Brass & Copper, ¾ x 1¾ x 3", no photo, $5.00.
Hasty Maid sample, Coffee, 2½ x 3¼", V1p231–4, $50.00.
Hava-Lax, Laxative, ¼ x 1¼ x 1¾", V1p106–7, $12.00.
Hawes, Floor Wax, no photo, $25.00.
Hay R. & Son, Shoe Polish, ¾ x 2¼", V2p120–3, $25.00.
Hay-Fevin sample, Medicone, ¼ x 1½", V1p106–8, $12.00.
Haywood's, Poison Oak Salve, ¾ x 2¾", V1p106–9, $12.00.
Haywood's #378, Poison Oak Salve, ¾ x 2¾", V1p106–10, $30.00.
Hazard Indian, Rifle Powder, no photo, $85.00.
Hazard Smokeless, Gun Powder, no photo, $60.00.
Hazel Brand, Type Ribbon, ¾ x 2½ x 2½", no photo, $15.00.
Hazel Brand, Type Ribbon, ¾ x 2½ x 2½", V1p311–3, $20.00.
Hazel-Atlas Glass, Type Ribbon, ¾ x 2½", V2p181–6, $15.00.
Health Club sample, Baking Powder, 2⅜ x 2¾", V1p244–2, $45.00.
Health-O, Aspirin 24, ¼ x 1¾ x 2½", V2p70–1, $12.00.
Health-O, Carbolic Salve, ¾ x 2¾", V2p70–3, $20.00.
Heart, Needles, no photo, $40.00.
Heart, Needles, no photo, $65.00.
Heather, Rouge (Daytime), ¼ x 1⅝", V1p47–9, $8.00.
Heather, Rouge (Daytime), ⅜ x 1¾", V1p47–8, $10.00.
Heather, Rouge (Oramber), ¼ x 1⅝", V1p47–10, $8.00.
Heather, Rouge Medium, ⅝ x 1¾", V1p47–11, $6.00.
Heather, Rouge Or-Amber, ¾ x 1¾", V1p47,#12, 8.00*.
Heckler's $.50, Drawing\Healing Salve, ⅞ x 2⅜", V1p106–11, $30.00.
Hed-Aid, Tablets, ¼ x 1¼ x 1¾", V1p106–12, $15.00.
Heinrich's, Laxative Wafers, 3 x 5", no photo, $18.00.
Heiskell's, Ointment, ¾ x 2", V1p107–1, $10.00.
Helex, Healing Powder, 1 x 1⅞", V2p193–5, $45.00.
Helex sample, Healing Salve, ¼ x 1⅛", V2p70–6, $15.00.
Hellberg's, Kornlift, ½ x 1¼", V1p107–2, $8.00.
Hellebush C., Watch Materials, ¼ x 1¼", V1p336–9, $15.00.

Helps $.10, Throat Lozenges, ⅜ x 1¾ x 2⅛", V1p292–1, $18.00.

Hemo Sweets, Candy, 1¾", V1p287–4, $140.00.

Henderson,s Royal Blue, Needles, ⅞ x 1⅝", V1p207–8, $35.00.

Henderson's, Kid-nee Cure, ½ x 2 x 3⅛", V2p70–2, $70.00.

Heneph's, Aspirin High Test, ¼ x 1¼ x 1¾", V1p107–3, $18.00.

Heneph's, Kold Caps, 1 x 2", V1p107–4, $12.00.

Heneph's, Pills, ¾ x 2", V1p107–5, $18.00.

Heneph's $.25, Blue Flag Laxative, ¼ x 1¼ x 1¾", V2p70–4, $8.00.

Heneph's $.25, Laxative Cold Tablets, ¼ x 1¾ x 2½", V1p107–7, $10.00.

Heneph's $.25, Laxative Tablets, ¼ x 1¼ x 1¾", no photo, $10.00.

Heneph's $.50, Blue Flag Laxative, ¾ x 2", V2p70–5, $15.00.

Heneph's $.50, Pills, 1⅛ x 2½", V1p107–6, $15.00.

Henri, Bouillon Cubes, 1 x 3½", V1p19–9, $18.00.

Herald 200, Needles Phono, ½ x 1¼ x 1⅝", V1p207–9, $35.00.

Herald Square, Type Ribbon, ¾ x 2½ x 2½", V1p311–4, $8.00.

Herald Square, Type Ribbon, ¾ x 2½ x 2½", V2p182–1, $12.00.

Herb-Ox, Bouillon Chicken, 1 x 3½", V1p19–10, $6.00.

Herbies 7½, Pills, no photo, $30.00.

Hercules, Type Ribbon, ¾ x 2½ x 2½", V1p311–5, $15.00.

Hercules, Valve Insiders, ¼ x 1 x 1½", V1p17–2, $12.00.

Hercules, Watch Mainsprings, ¾ x 3 x 3⅜", V1p336–10, $65.00.

Herold, Needles, no photo, $30.00.

Herold Electro, Tonmeister Needles, ¼ x 1¼ x 1¾", no photo.

Herold Nadeln 200, Needles, no photo, $35.00.

Herold Wengelin, Phonograph Needles, ⅜ x 1½ x 3", V2p113–8, $65.00.

Herold-Doppelton, Needles, ⅜ x 1¼ x 1¾", V2p113–4, $30.00.

Herold-Nadeln, Needles, ⅜ x 1½ x 1½", no photo, $30.00.

Herold-Nadeln, Needles, ⅜ x 1½ x 1½", V2p113–6, $30.00.

Herold-Sortiment, Needles Phono, ⅜ x 1⅝ x 3", V1p207–10, $30.00.

Herold-Zukunft, Needles, ⅜ x 1¼ x 1¾", V2p114–1, $30.00.

Herolin sample, Pomade Hair Dressing, ¼ x 1⅛", V1p34–12, $30.00.

Hershey sample, Chocolate, no photo, $80.00.

Herz, Spark Plugs, 1¼ x 1½ x 2½", V1p12–3, $50.00.

Hess, Clown White, ⅞ x 2½", V1p51–5, $15.00.

Hess C.D., Clown White, ⅞ x 2½", V2p33–1, $15.00.

Hess Co., Indianola, ¾ x 2⅜", V1p107–8, $20.00.

Hess Hawkins, Type Ribbon, ¾ x 2½ x 2½", V2p182–3, $18.00.

Hexin, Tablets, ¼ x 1¼ x 1¾", V1p107–9, $12.00.

Hexin, Tablets, ¼ x 1¾ x 2", V1p107–10, $10.00.

Hexin sample, Tablets, ¼ x ¾ x 1¼", V1p107–11, $12.00.

Hexylresorcinol, Sucrets, ¾ x 2⅜ x 3", V1p292–2, $4.00*.

Heyer's Special, Type Ribbon, 2¼ x 2¼ x 2", no photo, $15.00.

Hi-Hat, Type Ribbon, ¾ x 2½", V1p311–6, $15.00.

Hi-Hat $.25, Scalp Treatment, ¾ x 2½", V1p35–1, $20.00.

Hi-Hat sample, Hair Dressing, ¼ x 1¼", V1p35–2, $25.00.

Hi-Ja sample, Quinine Hair Dressing, ⅜ x 1⅜", V1p35–3, $22.00.

Hi-Test, Aspirin, ¼ x 1¼ x 1¾", V1p107–12, $15.00.

Hi-Volt, Synthetic Crystal, ⅜ x ⅞", V2p208–5, $15.00.

Hickman's, Purifina Salve, ¾ x 2⅛", V2p70–7, $30.00.

Hicks, Central Fire Caps, 1 x 1½", V1p64–9, $25.00.

Hick's, Percussion Caps, ½ x 1½", no photo, $40.00.

Hicks' #12, Percussion Caps, ¾ x 2", V1p64–10, $45.00.

Hick's No. 11, Percussion Caps, ⅝ x 1½", V2p208–6, $30.00.

Hicks No. 12, Percussion Caps, ½ x 1½", V2p208–2, $40.00.

Hick's No. 12, Percussion Caps, ⅝ x 1½", V1p64–12, $40.00.

Hicks No. 2, Primers 250, ⅞ x 1½", V1p66–1, $30.00.

Hick's No. 10, Percussion Caps, ½ x 1½", V1p64–11, $40.00.

Higgins, Aspirin, ¼ x 1¼ x 1¾", V2p71–1, $8.00.

High Flyers, Condom, ⅝ x 1⅝, no photo, $40.00.

High Grade, Type Ribbon, 1¾ x 1¾ x 2", V1p311–7, $22.00.

High Grade, Type Ribbon, 1¾ x 1¾ x 2", V1p311–9, $22.00.

High Grade, Type Ribbon, 1⅝ x 1⅝ x 2", V1p311–8, $22.00.

High Lindens sample, Coffee, 2 x 3⅝, no photo, $95.00.

High Pleasure, Tire Repair, no photo, $55.00.

High Point sample, Electric Perc Coffee, 3 x 2½", V2p123–5, $30.00.

Highland, Soldering Paste, 1⅛ x 2½", V1p285–7, $18.00.

Highlander, Type Ribbon, ¾ x 2½", V1p311–10, $8.00.

Hillman's, Spices, 1⅜ x 2⅜ x 3⅝", V2p149–3, $45.00.

Hill's, Cascara Laxative, ¼ x 1½ x 2¼", V1p108–1, $18.00.

Hill's, Cascara Quinine, ¼ x 1¼ x 1¾", V1p108–2, $12.00.

Hill's $.30, Cascara Quinine, ¼ x 1¾ x 1¼", V2p71–3, $15.00.

Hill's $.30, Cascara Quinine, ¼ x 1¾ x 2⅛", V1p108–3, $15.00.

Hill's $.30, Cold Tablets, ¼ x 1¾ x 2", V1p108–4, $12.00.

Hills Bros., Coffee, 3 x 4", V1p231–5, $50.00.

Himrod's, Asthma Powder, 1⅜ x 2¼ x 3½", V1p108–5, $65.00.

Himrod's Cure, Asthma, ½ x 1½ x 2", V1p108–6, $90.00.

Hinds Cre-mis sample, Talc Powder, ¾ x 1¼ x 2⅛", V1p258–3, $70.00.

Hinds Cre-mis sample, Talcum Powder, ¾ x 1¼ x 2⅛", V1p258–7, $70.00.

Hinds Cre-mis sample, Talcum Powder, ¾ x 1⅜ x", V2p128–5, $75.00.

His Favorite Song, Needles, no photo, $35.00.

Ho-Ro-Co $.25, Salve, ⅞ x 2¾", V1p108–7, $30.00.

Ho-Ro-Co. $.50, Laxative Tablets, ½ x 1½ x 2½", V1p108–8, $20.00.

Hoadley's $.05, Tolu Chewing Gum, ¾ x 1 x 2⅛", no photo, $175.00.

Hobart's, Aspirin, ¼ x 1¼ x 1¾", V1p108–10, $12.00.

Hobart's, Aspirin, ¼ x 1¼ x 1¾", V1p108–9, $15.00.

Hobbs', Kidney Pills, ½ x 1½ x 2½", V1p108–11, $40.00.

Hobbs $.50, Sparagus Kidney Pills, ⅜ x 1½ x 2½", V1p108–12, $85.00.

Hobbs $.50, Sparagus Kidney Pills, ⅜ x 1½ x 2½", V2p71–5, $70.00.

Hobson's, Antiseptic Salve, ¾ x 2¾", V1p109–3, $12.00.

Hobson's, Aspirin Tablets, ½ x ⅞ x 3", V2p71–7, $12.00.

Hobson's, Camphor Ice, ⅞ x 1¾ x 2⅞", V1p109–1, $18.00.

Hobson's, Cold Cream Cam Ice, 1 x 1¾ x 2⅞", V1p29–5, $22.00.

Hobson's, Cold Cream Camphor, 1 x 3¾", V1p29–6, $15.00.

Hobson's, Dermazema Ointment, ¾ x 2¾", V1p109–2, $12.00.

Hobson's, see Dr. Hobson's.

Hoffman & Lauer, Res. Mainsprings, ½ x 2¾ x 5⅛", V1p336–11, $40.00.

Hoffman W., Metal Polish, ¼ x 1¼", V1p218–4, $18.00.

Hoffman-La Roche Inc., see Allonal Roche, V1p69–5, $15.00.

Hoffman-La Roche Inc., see Larodon, V1p115–11, $8.00*.

Hoffman-La Roche Inc., see Syntrogel, V1p157–6, $8.00.

Hoffman-La Roche Inc., see Syntrogel, V1p157–7, $6.00.

Hoff's, Goodlax Tablets, ⅝ x ⅞ x 2⅜", V1p109–4, $35.00.

Hoff's Johann $.10, Malt Bonbons, ½ x 2 x 3⅛", V1p287–8, $65.00.

Hoff's Johann $.10, Malt BonBons, ⅝ x 2 x 3⅛", V1p287–6, $65.00.

Hogan James, Type Ribbon, ¾ x 2½ x 2½", no photo, $15.00.

Hold Fast, Chain Lubricant, ⅞ x 3⅜", V2p208–4, $35.00.

Hole Proof, Type Ribbon, 2¼ x 2¼ x 2", no photo, $18.00.

Holland Roasted Java sample, Coffee, 2½ x 3¼", V1p231–6, $75.00.

Hollister's $.35, Golden Nugget Tablets, ¼ x 2 x 2½", V1p109–5, $40.00.

Hollister's $.35, Rocky Mountain Tea, ¼ x 2 x 2⅝", V1p109–6, $40.00.

Hollyhock, Type Ribbon, ¾ x 2½ x 2½", V1p311–11, $25.00.

Hollyhock Brand, Type Ribbon, ¾ x 2½", no photo, $15.00.

Holmes, Booth, Hayden #1, Rivets FH, ⅝ x 1⅞", V1p62–9, $15.00.

Holt's Bowel Manna, Laxative, ⅜ x 2½", V1p109–7, $75.00.

Home $2.00, Safety Razor, 1⅞ x 3 x 1⅝", V2p134–6, $275.00.

Home Brand, Red Pepper, 3 x 2¼ x 1¼", V2p149–5, $35.00.

Home Remedy, Hazine Healing Ointment, 1 x 2⅜", V2p71–2, $30.00.
Home-Need, Adhesive Plaster, 1 x 1¼", V2p196–7, $18.00.
Home-Need, Adhesive Tape, 1⅛ x 1¼", V2p71–4, $8.00.
Homokord, Needles, ¾ x 1¼ x 1⅞", V1p207–11, $50.00.
Hood & Reynolds, Dental Depot, no photo, $75.00.
Hood's, Olive Ointment, ½ x 1¾", V1p109–8, $35.00.
Hook's Elder, Healing Salve, no photo, $40.00.
Hoosier Boy, Coffee, 6 x 4", 400.00.
Hooton's Amazon sample, Cocoa, 1¼ x 1¾ x 2", V1p221–2, $90.00.
Hop, Ointment, no photo, $35.00.
Hope, Denture Powder, ¾ x 1¼ x 2⅛", V1p58–2, $40.00.
Hope $.25, Laxative, ⅜ x 3¼ x 3¼", V1p109–9, $10.00.
Horiman's sample, Cocoa, ½ x 1 x 1½", V1p221–3, $70.00.
Hornet Brand, Type Ribbon, ¾ x 2½", no photo, $12.00.
Horney & Wright #75, Triple Process, 1⅝ x 1⅝ x 2", V2p182–5, $65.00.
Horniman's sample, Boudoir Tea, 1¼ x 2⅛ x 1⅜", V2p133–3, $60.00.
Horniman's sample, Pure Tea, 1½ x 1½ x 1½", V2p133–5, $80.00.
Horniman's sample, Tea ⅛ lb., ½ x 1½ x 2½", V1p267–10, $55.00.
Horopart, Watch Parts, ½ x 1⅛", V1p336–12, $5.00.
Horrock's, Fishing Sinkers, ¼ x 1 x 1¼", V1p176–4, $10.00.
Horsey, Inner Tube Patch, 1 x 2½ x 3⅞", V2p14–3, $55.00.
Hospital, Adhesive Plaster, 1 x 1¼", V1p346–9, $20.00.
Hostess, Mustard, 4⅛ x 2¼ x 1¼", V2p149–6, $70.00.
Hot Scotch sample, Snuff, 1⅜ x 1⅞", V1p191–8, $40.00.
Hoxie, Aspirin, ¼ x 1¼ x 1¾", V1p109–10, $8.00.
Hoyt's, Carbolic Salve, ¾ x 2⅞", V1p109–12, $12.00.
Hoyt's, Corn Salve, ⅝ x 1¾", V1p110–1, $20.00.
Hoyt's, Poultry Seasoning, 2 x 3½", V2p149–4, $25.00.
Hoyt's, Pure Spice, 1 x 2¼ x 4⅛", V2p149–2, $22.00.
Hoyt's $.25, Blue Laxatabs, ¼ x 1¼ x 1¾", V1p109–11, $15.00.
Hub, Type Ribbon, ¾ x 2 x 2", V1p311–12, $20.00.
Hub Brand, Type Ribbon, ¾ x 2⅛ x 2⅛", V1p312–1, $10.00.
Hubbell's, Prepared Wheat, no photo, $25.00.
Hudson, Spanish Saffron, ⅜ x 1½ x 2½", V2p203–2, $12.00.
Hudson Brand, Cloves, 3 x 1¾ x 1¼", V2p149–7, $35.00.
Hugh George, Steel Pens, no photo, $20.00.
Hughes, Pens, no photo, $22.00.
Hun-e-Lax, Laxative, ⅝ x 2½ x 2½", V1p110–2, $45.00.
Hunt-Smith, Watch Parts, ½ x 1¼", V1p337–1, $8.00.
Huntley Palmer sample, Biscuits, 1½ x 1½ x 1¾", V1p244–3, $75.00.
Hunyadi Janos $.25, Stomach Pills, ⅜ x ¾ x 2", V1p110–3, $35.00.
Hush, Deodorant Cream, ¼ x 1⅞", V2p33–3, $10.00.
Hush, Ointment, ⅜ x 1½", V1p110–4, $3.00.
Hush, Sno Deodorant, ⅜ x 2⅛", V2p33–5, $12.00.
Hush sample, Deodorant Powder, ⅜ x ⅞", V1p44–9, $22.00.
Hutch $.35, Chocolate Tablets, ⅝ x 2", V1p110–5, $25.00.
Hutchline, Type Ribbon, 2¼ x 2¼ x ¾", no photo, $15.00.
Huyler's, Glycerine Tablets, ⅜ x 2⅛", V1p110–6, $35.00.
Huylers, Glycerine Tablets, ⅜ x 2⅛", V2p167–7, $40.00.
Huyler's, Glycerine Tablets, ⅞ x 1¾ x 3", V2p168–1, $40.00.
Huyler's, Gum (Spearmint), ½ x 1½ x 1½", V1p296–11, $115.00.
Huyler's, Gum (Spearmint), ½ x 1½ x 1½", V1p296–12, $125.00.
Huyler's, Gum Imperials, ½ x 2⅛", V2p172–7, $15.00.
Huyler's, Gum Sweatheart, ½ x 1½ x 1½", V1p297–1, $115.00.
Huyler's, Italian Pepps, ¼ x 1¼ x 1¼", V1p287–7, $18.00.
Huyler's, Italian Pepps, ¼ x 1⅜ x 1⅜", V1p287–8, $20.00.
Huyler's, Peppermint Dainties, ½ x 1⅞", V2p168–4, $15.00.
Huyler's, Pepsin Gum, ½ x 1⅛ x 2¼", V2p172–2, $25.00.
Huyler's, Pepsin Gun, ½ x 1½ x 1½", V1p297–2, $115.00.
Huyler's, Rose Danties, ½ x 1⅞", V2p168–5, $30.00.
Huyler's N.Y., Pepsin Gum, ½ x 1 x 2¼", V2p172–4, $25.00.
Huyler's sample, Cocoa, no photo, $70.00.
Huyler's sample, Cocoa ⅙ Lb., 1⅜ x 2¾ x 3¾", V1p221–4, $80.00.
Huyler's sample, Cocoa Butter, 1 x 2⅛", V1p244–4, $40.00.
Hy-Beaute $.35, Hair Dressing, 1 x 3⅜", V1p35–5, $20.00.
Hy-Beaute sample, Hair Dressing, ⅝ x 1½", V1p35–4, $15.00.
Hy-Grade, Tropical Fish Food, 1¼ x 2⅞", V2p208–7, $18.00.
Hy-Pure, Aspirin, ¼ x 1¼ x 1¾", V1p110–7, $15.00.
Hy-Pure, Condoms, ⅜ x 1⅛ x 2⅛, no photo, $40.00.
Hy-Pure, Peppets, ½ x 1⅝ x 3¼", V1p110–8, $8.00.
Hydrosal sample, Skin Cream, ¼ x 1⅛", V2p28–5, $10.00.
HyGee, VD Preventitive, ¼ x 1¾ x 2½", V2p71–6, $125.00.
HyGee, VD Preventitive, ⅜ x 1 2 x 2", V2p71–8, $175.00.
Hygenic Sponge, Condom, 1 x 1⅞", V1p27–1, $70.00.
Hygiana, Tablets, no photo, $35.00.
Hygienic, Complex Powder, no photo, $12.00.
Hygienic Cutigiene, Toilet Cream, 1 x 2½", V1p29–7, $20.00.
Hygienic Made, Adhesive Plaster, ⅞ x ¾", no photo, $20.00.
Hygienic sample, Cutigiene Toilet Cream, ¼ x ⅞", V2p28–2, $35.00.
Hygienic sample, Toilet Cream, ⅜ x ⅞", V1p29–8, $45.00.
Hygrade, Surg. Adhes. Plast., ⅞ x 2¼", V1p346–10, $12.00.
Hyman, Gum, 1 x 2¼", V2p172–6, $80.00.
Hyman's, Gum, 1 x 2⅜, no photo, $110.00.
Hymettus sample, Toilet Powder, no photo, $40.00.
Hypodermic sample, Tablets, ⅜ x 1⅛ x 2⅛", V1p110–9, $90.00.
I.D.L., Theatrical Cold Cream, no photo, $20.00.
I.X.L., Ointment, no photo, $25.00.
I.X.L., Tansy & Apiol Pills, ½ x 2 x 3", V1p110–10, $35.00.
Iatrol sample, Talcum Powder, ¾ x 1¼ x 2⅛", V1p258–8, $45.00.
Ice-mint sample, Ointment, ¼ x 1⅛", V1p110–11, $25.00.
ICR, Type Ribbon, ⅞ x 2½", V2p182–2, $15.00.
Ideal, Hinge for Stamps, ½ x 1⅝ x 2¼", V1p195–8, $10.00.
Ideal, Shoe Polish, ¾ x 2⅛", V1p279–2, $20.00.
Ideal, Sinkers (fish), ½ x 1½ x 2½", V1p176–5, $5.00.
Ideal, Split Shot Sinkers, ¼ x ¾ x 1¾", V1p176–6, $3.00.
Ideal (Powell), Polishing Paste, ¾ x 2⅛", no photo, $20.00.
Ideal 300, Needles, ¾ x 1¼ x 1½", V1p207–12, $30.00.
Ideal Deatal, Plate Powder sample, no photo, $55.00.
Ideal sample, Cocoa, 1¼ x 1⅝ x 2½", V2p122–6, $155.00.
Ideal sample, Talcum Powder, ¾ x 1¼ x 2⅛", V1p258–9, $40.00.
Idico, Cones, ½ x 1⅜", V2p72–1, $8.00.
Idico sample, Purifies the Air, ¼ x 1⅝", V1p195–9, $12.00.
IGA Brand, Allspice, 3¼ x 2¼ x 1¼", V2p150–1, $25.00.
Imperial, Cut Plug Tobacco, 1 x 2⅝", V2p209–1, $55.00.
Imperial, Phono Needles, ¼ x 1¼ x 1¾", V1p208–1, $25.00.
Imperial, Safety Razor, no photo, $145.00.
Imperial, Shaving Stick, 1½ x 3¼", V1p274–8, $55.00.
Imperial, Shaving Stick, 1½ x 3⅜", V1p274–9, $120.00.
Imperial, Tire Valve Cores, ¼ x 1 x 1½", V1p17–3, $12.00.
Imperial, Type Ribbon, 1⅝ x 1⅝ x 1⅞", V2p182–4, $60.00.
Imperial #5½, Metal Polish, 1 x 3⅛", V2p38–3, $15.00.
Imperial 200, Needles, no photo, $25.00.
Imperial Brand, Spice (ginger), 1¼ x 3⅞ x 6", V1p188–10, $25.00.
Imperial Crown, Soul Kiss Face Powder, ¾ x 2½ x 2½", no photo, $50.00.
Imperial Crown Perfumery, Cold Cream, 1 x 2", no photo, $50.00.
Imperial Granum sample, Food, 1¾ x 2⅜", V1p244–5, $25.00.
Impression, Type Ribbon, ¾ x 2½", no photo, $15.00.
Improve, Jet Black Polish, no photo, $25.00.
Improved, Pat Leather Polish, ⅞ x 2⅛", V1p279–3, $30.00.
Improved, Polish Shoe Paste, ½ x 1¾", V1p279–4, $35.00.
Imps, Licorice & Menthol, ½ x 1½ x 2⅛", V2p168–7, $20.00.
IMPS $.05, Throat Ease, ⅜ x 1½", V1p292–3, $125.00.
In-Step sample, Foot Ointment, ¼ x 1", V1p110–12, $10.00.
Indelible Outfit, Ink Pad, ⅝ x 2 x 3¼", V1p179–9, $18.00.
Independent Card Co., Playing Cards, ¾ x 2⅝ x 3⅝", V1p174–9, $65.00.
India Rubber Comb, Telescopic Cup, 1 x 2⅝", V1p195–10, $50.00.
Indian, Ointment, no photo, $45.00.

Indian, Tobacco Antidote, no photo, $75.00.

Indian Cerate, Pearl Ointment, ⅝ x 1⅞", V1p111–1, $70.00.

Indian Head, Type Ribbon, ¾ x 2½ x 2½", no photo, $65.00.

Indian Head sample, Marshmallow, no photo, $95.00.

Indian Mills, Ginger, 2 x 3¾", V2p150–3, $80.00.

Indian Tea, Tea, 2 x 3⅛ x 1⅜", V1p267–11, $22.00.

Indiana Carbon Co., Type Ribbon, ¾ x 2½ x 2½", no photo, $20.00.

Individuality, Type Ribbon, ¾ x 2½", V1p312.#2, $8.00.

Indo-Lacs, Laxative, ¼ x 1¾ x 2⅝", V1p111–2, $10.00.

Ingram's $.25, Witch Hazel Salve, ¾ x 2½", V1p111–3, $40.00.

Ingram's Elite, Cold Cream, ¾ x 2⅝", V2p28–4, $20.00.

Ingram's sample, Milkweed Cream, ¼ x 1⅛", V2p28–6, $45.00.

Ingram's sample, Shaving Cream, ¼ x 1¼", V1p274–10, $25.00.

Ingram's sample, Therapeutic Shave Cream, ¼ x ⅞", V1p274–11, $45.00.

Ingrim-Rutledge, Type Ribbon, ¾ x 2½ x 2½", V1p312–3, $20.00.

Inkeets, Ink Tablets, ½ x 1 x 1", V1p195–11, $15.00.

Inkspoon M.M., Ink Tips, ½ x 1 x 1½", V1p183–5, $25.00.

Insectolatum, Salve, ¼ x 1⅛", V2p72–3, $8.00.

Inspection Brand, Type Ribbon, 1½ x 1½ x 1¾", no photo, $25.00.

International, Antiseptic Healing, no photo, $25.00.

International, Gall Heal, 1 x 2⅝", V1p333–1, $50.00.

International Committee, Type Ribbon, ¾ x 2½ x 2½", V2p182–6, $18.00.

International Dial, Watch Parts, ⅜ x 1⅝ 1⅝", V1p337–2, $20.00.

Invincible, Type Cleaner, ¾ x 1½ x 2½", V2p183–1, $15.00.

Invincible, Type Ribbon, 1¾ x 2⅛ x 1⅝", V1p312–5, $40.00.

Invincible, Type Ribbon, ¾ x 2½", V1p312–4, $6.00.

Iodex sample, Methyl Salve, ⅜ x 1¾", V1p111–4, $10.00*.

Iodex sample, Ointment, ⅜ x 1¾", V1p111–5, $8.00*.

Iodoformal sample, Surgical Dressing, 1 x 1⅝", V1p266–6, $50.00.

Iris, Cloves, 2¼ x 2¼ x 1¼", V2p150–5, $15.00.

Iron Remedy Co.$1.00, General System Tonic, ⅜ x 1⅞ x 2⅝", V1p111–6, $6.00.

Isolax, Lax, ¼ x 1¾ x 2½", V1p111–7, $8.00.

Italina $.15, Laxative Prep., 2 x 3⅜", V2p72–6, $30.00.

J & T $.10, Aspirin, ¼ x 1¼ x 1¾", V1p111–8, $12.00.

J B, Cough Drops, no photo, $60.00.

J S B sample, Coffee Bank, 2¼ x 3", no photo, $60.00.

Jaciel, Talc, ⅞ x 1½ x 3¼", $30.00.

Jack Horner, Aspirin, no photo, $15.00.

Jack Sprat, Celery Salt, 3 x 2¼ x 1¼", V2p150–6, $25.00.

Jackie Coogan, Pencil Box, ¾ x 2 x 7¾", V1p182–6, $60.00.

Jackie Coogan, Pencil Box, ¾ x 2 x 7¾", V1p182–7, $65.00.

Jackie Coogan, Pencil Case, ¾ x 2 x 7¾", no photo, $55.00.

Jackie Coogan, Pencil Case, ¾ x 2 x 7¾", no photo, 182, $65.00.

Jackie Coogan, Pencil Case, ¾ x 2 x 7⅝", no photo, $60.00.

Jackson's, Line Level, ¾ x 1¾ x 2¼", no photo, $18.00.

James Drug Co., Temple of Allah, ⅜ x 2⅜ x 3⅛", V2p199–1, $18.00.

Jamieson, Milk of Magnesia, ¼ x 2⅜ x 2½", V1p111–9, $12.00.

Jap Honeysuckle sample, Talcum Powder, ⅝ x 1⅛ x 2", V1p258–10, $60.00.

Jap Rose (Kirk) sample, Talcum Powder, ¾ x 1½ x 2⅛", V1p258–11, $75.00.

Japanese Silk Wove, Type Ribbon, 1½ x 1½ x 1¾", no photo, $25.00.

Japol Ice $.25, Salve, ¾ x 2", V1p111–10, $20.00.

Jaques Capsules $.25, Digestion Tablets, ¼ x 1⅝ x 1¾", V1p111–11, $12.00.

Jarnac sample, Skin Clensing Crm., ¼ x 1⅜", V1p29–9, $18.00.

Jarnal, Skin Cream, no photo, $15.00.

Jaynes, Carbolic Healing Salve, ¾ x 2¼ x 2¼", V1p111–12, $25.00.

Jaynes, Dyspepsia Tablets, ¾ x 2½ x 4", no photo, $70.00.

Jaynes, Dyspepsia Tablets, ⅞ x 2½ x 4", V1p112–1, $75.00.

Jaynes', Nervo Pills, no photo, $75.00.

Jaynes 100, Kidney Pills, 1 x 1⅝ x 2¾", V1p112–4, $70.00.

JDZ, Thumb Tacks, 1 x 1", V1p195–12, $12.00.

Jefferson 20 AMP, Auto Fuses, ¼ x 1¼ x 1¾", V2p14–5, $20.00.

Jefferson Union, Auto Fuses, ½ x 1⅝ x 2⅝", V1p8–9, $25.00.

Jefferson Union, Auto Fuses, ¼ x 1¼ x 1¾", V1p8–10, $20.00.

Jefferson Union, Auto Fuses, ¼ x 1¼ x 1¾", V1p8–7, $20.00.

Jefferson Union, Auto Fuses, ¼ x 1¼ x 1¾", V1p8–8, $20.00.

Jenkin's & Son, Grand Opera Needles, ⅝ x 2", V2p114–3, $45.00.

Jergens Marie Antoinette, Cold Cream, 1 x 2", V2p29–1, $40.00.

Jergens sample, Eutaska Talcum Powder, ¾ x 1¼ x 2⅛", V2p128–2, $60.00.

Jerry Boy Guaranteed, Type Ribbon, ¾ x 2½", V1p312–6, $20.00.

Jerry Boy Guaranteed, Type Ribbon, ¾ x 2½ x 2½", no photo, $35.00.

Jewel, Phono Needles, ⅜ x 1¼ x 1¾", V1p208–2, $35.00.

Jewel Tea Co., Allspice, 2¼ x 2¼ x 2¾", V2p150–2, $25.00.

Jewel Tea Co., Black Pepper, 2¼ x 2¼ x 2¾", V2p150–4, $30.00.

Jewel Tea Co., Cinnamon, 2¼ x 2¼ x 2¾", V2p150–7, $30.00.

Jiffy, Type Cleaner, no photo, $10.00.

Jo Beth Co. Brand, Rubbed Sage, 2 x 4", V2p151–1, $50.00.

Jockey, Hoof Ointment, no photo, $45.00.

Jockey Club $.35, Hair Pomade, ½ x 1¼", V1p35–6, $10.00.

Johnny on the Spot, Dry Cleaner, 1 x 2¼", V1p22–3, $12.00.

Johnson & Johnson, Band Aids, 1¼ x 2½ x 3½", V1p112–6, $10.00.

Johnson & Johnson, Beauty Spots, ¼ x 1⅝", V2p33–2, $40.00.

Johnson & Johnson, Blue Cross Adhes Tape, ⅞ x 2¼", V1p346–11, $8.00.

Johnson & Johnson, Dental Floss, 1⅛ x 1½", V1p55–6, $25.00.

Johnson & Johnson, Dental Floss, 1⅛ x 1⅜", V1p55–7, $25.00.

Johnson & Johnson, Dental Floss, ¼ x 1¼", V1p55–8, $20.00.

Johnson & Johnson, Dental Floss, ¼ x 1¼", V1p55–9, $20.00.

Johnson & Johnson, Dental Floss Brunswick, 1⅛ x 1⅜", V1p55–10, $30.00.

Johnson & Johnson, Dental Tape (Medium), 1⅛ x 1½", V1p55–11, $25.00.

Johnson & Johnson, Dentotape floss, 1⅛ x 1½", V1p55–12, $25.00.

Johnson & Johnson, Kalms, ¼ x ⅞ x 2¾", V1p112–7, $8.00.

Johnson & Johnson, London Corn Plaster, ¾ x 1¾ x 2⅞", V1p112–8, $35.00.

Johnson & Johnson, Mustard Plaster, ⅝ x 3⅝ x 4¾", V1p112–9, $25.00.

Johnson & Johnson, Pocket Floss, ¼ x 1¼", V1p56–1, $20.00.

Johnson & Johnson, Pocket Floss Silk, ¼ x 1⅛", V1p56–2, $20.00.

Johnson & Johnson, Red Cross Tape, 1 x 1⅝", V1p112–10, $8.00.

Johnson & Johnson, Surgical Silk Isinglass, ¾ x 7⅜", no photo, $25.00.

Johnson & Johnson, Tea sample, no photo, $25.00.

Johnson & Johnson, Three Leaves Mustard Plast., 1⅛ x 3¾", V1p112–11, $8.00.

Johnson & Johnson, Vest Pocket 1st Aid, ½ x 1¼ x 2½", V1p112–12, $15.00.

Johnson & Johnson, Zonas Adhesive Plaster, 1 x ¾", V1p346–12, $15.00.

Johnson & Johnson, Zonas Adhesive Plaster, ¾ x 1", V1p347–1, $15.00.

Johnson & Johnson, Zonas Adhesive Plaster, 1 x 1¼", V1p347–2, $15.00.

Johnson & Johnson, Zonas Adhesive Plaster, 1 x ¾", no photo, $8.00.

Johnson & Johnson, Zonas Adhesive Plaster, 1 x 1¼", V2p196–4, $15.00.

Johnson & Johnson, Zonas Adhesive Plaster, 1 x 1¼", V2p196–6, $25.00.

Johnson & Johnson, Zonas Adhesive Plaster, 1 x 1¾", V1p347–4, $20.00.

Johnson & Johnson, Zonas Adhesive Plaster, 1 x ¾", V1p347–3, $15.00.
Johnson & Johnson, Zonas Adhesive Plaster, ¾ x 1⅝", V2p196–2, $25.00.
Johnson & Johnson $.10, Band-Aid, ⅜ x 1⅝ x 3⅛", V2p72–2, $8.00.
Johnson & Johnson sample, Baby\Toilet Powder, 1 x 2", V1p264–7, $25.00.
Johnson G.E., Polish, no photo, $30.00.
Johnson's, Anti Flu Rub, no photo, $20.00.
Johnson's, Automobile Wax, 1 x 2¾", V2p38–5, $18.00.
Johnson's, Prepared Wax, 1⅞ x 3½", no photo, $40.00.
Johnson's, Prepared Wax, ⅞ x 2⅜", V2p14–4, $75.00.
Johnson's, Stomach Tablets, 1 x 2 x 3", no photo, $35.00.
Johnson's $.25, Kidney Pills 70, ½ x 2 x 3⅛", V1p113–1, $75.00.
Johnson's S.C., Prepared Wax, ⅞ x 2⅜", V1p343–3, $100.00.
Johnson's S.C. sample, Prepared Wax, 1⅝ x 1⅛", V1p343–5, $60.00.
Johnson's S.C. sample, Powdered Wax, 1½ x 1¾", V1p343–4, $75.00.
Johnson's sample, Toilet\Baby Powder, 1 x 1 x 1⅞", V1p264–8, $40.00.
Johnston sample, Cocoa, ½ x 1⅝ x 2¼", V1p221–5, $115.00.
Johnny Bundy Child, Cough Drops, no photo, $65.00.
Jokes, Breath Mints, ¼ x 1 x 1⅜", V1p287–9, $45.00.
Jordan Standard, Auto Fuses, no photo, $10.00.
Joy-Walk $.25, Corn Plaster, ¾ x 2¼ x 4", V2p72–4, $70.00.
Judge & Dolph, Menthol & Glycerine, ⅝ x 2¼ x 3½", V1p113–2, $8.00.
Judge Brand 200, Needles, no photo, $35.00.
Junior XXX, Stamp Pad, ⅜ x 1 x 1¾", V2p200–2, $18.00.
Juno Brand, Allspice, 3¼ x 2¼ x 1¼", V2p151–4, $40.00.
Just Out, Shoe Polish, no photo, $45.00.
Justrite, Lice Powder, 1½ x 2½", V1p196–1, $8.00.
Justrite, Natural Fish Food, 1⅜ x 1¾ x 2½", V2p209–5, $10.00.
Justrite C, Ink Pad, ⅝ x 2¼ x 3½", V2p200–4, $12.00.
K, Cough Drops, 2⅛ x 2⅛ x 2⅝", V1p292–4, $90.00.
K & E, Thumb Tacks, ½ x 1 x 1⅝", V1p196–2, $5.00.
K M C, Cough Drops, no photo, $50.00.
K-E, Auto Fuses, ¼ x 1¼ x 1¾", V1p8–11, $8.00.
K-E, Auto Fuses Glass, ¼ x 1¼ x 1¾", V1p8–12, $8.00.
K-W, Aspirin Tablets, ¼ x 1¼ x 1¾", V1p113–3, $18.00.
Ka-Fen, Pain Relief Tablets, ¼ x 1¼ x 1¾", V1p113–4, $15.00.
Ka-Fen, Tablets, ¼ x 1¼ x 1½", V1p113–5, $18.00.
KaBell Brand, Type Ribbon, ¾ x 2½", V2p183–3, $15.00.
Kaffee Hag sample, Coffee, 2½ x 3¼", V1p232–1, $70.00.
Kalle, Antifebrin, 1 x 2⅛ x 2¾", V1p113–6, $25.00.
Kamels, Condom, ¼ x 1⅝ x 2⅛", V2p18–5, $65.00.
Kampfe's Star, Razor Strop, 1½ x 2 x 6 ⅛", V1p274–12, $140.00.
Kapaspirin, Aspirin, ½ x 1¼ x 1¾", V2p72–5, $16.00.
Kapseals, Digifortis, ¼ x 1½ x 2", V1p113–7, $15.00.
Karess sample, Powder Face, ⅜ x 1⅝", V1p252–1, $20.00.
Katz Sam, Oxygen Catarrh, 1¼ x 3½", no photo, $30.00.
Katz Sam, Oxygen Germicide, no photo, $30.00.
Katz Sam, Plumose Fibre, 1 x 3", V1p196–3, $30.00.
Katz Wm.R.Co., Watch Parts, ½ x 1¼", V1p337–3, $3.00.
Katz Wm.R.Co., Watch Parts, ½ x 1⅛", V1p337–4, $3.00.
Kaywoodie, Pipe Polish, ⅝ x 1⅜", V1p218–5, $10.00.
Kee-Lox, Black Record, ¾ x 2½ x 2½", no photo, 4.00.
Kee-Lox, Type Ribbon, 1⅝ x 1⅝ x 1½", V2p183–6, $25.00.
Kee-Lox, Type Ribbon, ¾ x 2½", V1p312–8, $12.00.
Kee-Lox, Type Ribbon, ¾ x 2½ x 2½", no photo, 4.00.
Kee-Lox, Type Ribbon, ¾ x 2½ x 2½", V1p312–11, $4.00.
Kee-Lox, Type Ribbon, ¾ x 2½ x 2½", V1p313–2, $4.00.
Kee-Lox, Type Ribbon, ¾ x 2¼ x 2¼", V1p312–12, 4.00.
Kee-Lox, Type Ribbon, ¾ x 2¼ x 2¼", V1p312–9, $12.00.
Kee-Lox, Type Ribbon, ¾ x 2¼ x 2¼", V1p313–4, $4.00.
Kee-Lox, Type Ribbon, ¾ x 2¼ x 2¼", V1p313–5, $4.00.
Kee-Lox, Wonder Brand, ¾ x 2½ x 2½", V1p312–10, $12.00.
Kee-Lox Silver Brand, Type Ribbon, ¾ x 2¼ x 2¼", no photo, 4.00.
Kee-Lox Silver Brand, Type Ribbon, ¾ x 2¼ x 2¼", V1p313–1, $4.00.
Keen Cutter, Razor Hone, ½ x 2 x 5½", V1p275–1, $60.00.
Keen-Rite, Type Ribbon, ¾ x 2¼", no photo, $12.00.
Keep M Cool, Chain Lubricant, no photo, $30.00.
Keller L.H., Watch Parts, ¼ x 1⅛", V1p337–6, $12.00.
Keller L.H., Watch Parts, ⅜ x 1¼", V1p337–5, $15.00.
Kellog's sample, Drinket, ¾ x 1½ x 2⅛", V1p244–6, $80.00.
Kellog's sample, Drinket, ¾ x 1½ x 2⅛", V1p244–7, $70.00.
Kellog's sample, Drinket, ¾ x 1½ x 2⅛", V1p244–8, $90.00.
Kellog's sample, Obesity Food, no photo, $25.00.
Kelly's, Slide Shoe Polish, 1 x 2⅞", V2p120–5, $150.00.
Kelwax, Polishing Wax, ⅝ x 1⅞", V2p38–7, $5.00.
Kemcolax, Peppermint Laxative, ¼ x 1½ x 2", V2p72–7, $15.00.
Kenny C.D., Unknown, ⅝ x 1½ x 1¾", V2p172–8, $75.00.
Kenny C.D. Co., Candy, 1 x 2⅜", V1p297–4, $95.00.
Kester, Aluminum Solder, ⅞ x 2¼", V2p209–7, $8.00.
Kester, Radio Solder, ⅞ x 2⅞", V1p285–8, $8.00.
Key sample, Graphic Paste, 1⅛ x 2⅛", V2p209–2, $10.00.
Key-Bright $.25, Piano Key Polish, ¾ x 2⅜", V1p218–6, $8.00*.
Keystone $.25, Hair Groom, ⅞ x 3", V1p35–7, $18.00.
Keystone 4x5, Blue Print Paper, 1½ x 5½", V1p196–4, $30.00.
Keystone 5x7, Blue Print Paper, 1⅝ x 5½", V1p196–5, $35.00.
Kickapoo, Salve, ⅝ x 1⅞", V1p113–8, $110.00.
Kickapoo $.25, Indian Salve, ⅝ x 1⅞", V2p73–1, $90.00.
Kiddie's, Stamp Pad, ¼ x 2¼ x 3", V1p179–10, $30.00.
Kilb-Beck, Watch Material, ½ x 1½", V1p337–7, $2.00.
Kilb-Beck, Watch Material, ½ x 1¾", V1p337–8, $4.00.
Killakes $.50, Relieves Headaches, ⅝ x 1⅝ x 2⅝", V2p73–3, $15.00.
Killark, Auto Fuses, ¼ x 1¼ x 1¾", V2p15–1, $12.00.
Killark, Auto Fuses 30 Amp, ¼ x 1¼ x 1¾", V1p9–2, $8.00.
Killark 20 SFE, Auto Fuses, ¼ x 1¼ x 1¾", V1p9–1, $8.00.
Killark 3AG, Auto Fuses, ¼ x 1¼ x 1¾", V1p9–3, $8.00.
Killgore's Chas. sample, Cascara Tablets, ¼ x 1⅜ x 1⅜", V1p113–9, $12.00.
Kimhar No.1, Eyelets, ¾ x 2", V1p196–6, $5.00.
Kindel's $.25, Liver Regulator, 1¾ x 1¾ x 2⅝", V2p73–5, $45.00.
King, Cinnamon, 4¼ x 2½ x 1¾", V2p151–6, $45.00.
King, Laxative Cold & Grippe, ⅜ x 2¾ x 3½", V2p73–7, $25.00.
King, Needles, no photo, $30.00.
King $.25, Salve, ⅝ x 2", no photo, $35.00.
King Crop Brand, Allspice, 3¾ x 2¼ x 1¼", V2p151–2, $55.00.
King of Salve, Salve, no photo, $35.00.
King's Antiseptic, Catarrh Cream, no photo, $40.00.
King's Medicated, Cooling Cream, ⅝ x 2", V1p113–10, $40.00.
Kirk Dial, Watch Parts, ⅜ x 1⅝ x 1⅝", V1p337–9, $15.00.
Kirk-Rich, Watch Parts, ½ x 1¾", V1p337–10, $10.00.
Kis-Me, Gum, ⅝ x 1½ x 1½", V1p297–5, $200.00.
Kismet, Incense, 1¾ x 2 x 2¼", V1p178–2, $35.00.
Kissproof, Face Powder, ½ x 2", no photo, $10.00.
Kissproof sample, Clinging Powder, ¼ x 1⅜", V1p252–3, $18.00.
Kissproof sample, Face Powder, ¼ x 1½", V1p252–2, $18.00.
Klean Write, Type Ribbon, ¾ x 2½ x 2½", V1p313–6, $15.00.
Klean-Write, Type Ribbon, 1 x 2½", V2p183–2, $18.00.
Klean-Write, Type Ribbon, ⅞ x 2½", V1p313–7, $15.00.
Kleckner's, Saffron, ⅜ x 1½ x 2½", V2p203–4, $30.00.
Kleckner's, Spanish Saffron, ⅜ x 1½ x 2½", V1p187–10, $30.00.
Kleen, Foot Balm, ¾ x 1¾", V1p113–11, $20.00.
Kleen sample, Foot Balm, ¾ x 1¾", V2p73–2, $20.00.
Kleenertype, Type Ribbon, ¾ x 2½ x 2½", V1p313–8, $8.00.
Kleinert, Dental Rubber, no photo, $60.00.
Kleinert, Dress Shields, no photo, $30.00.
Klein's Japanese $.15, Cough Drops, ⅞ x 3 x 3", V2p170–1, $40.00.
Klein's sample, Cocoa, 1¼ x 1½ x 1¾", V1p221–6, $130.00.

Kleiser Albert, Watch Main Spring, ⅞ x 2¾ x 2¾", V1p337–11, $50.00.

Klind sample, Dental Adhesive, no photo, $40.00.

Kling sample, Dental Paste Adhesive, ¾ x 1¼ x 2⅛", V2p42–3, $25.00.

Klingsor, Loud Needels, no photo, $35.00.

Klingsor-Nadeln, Needles, ⅜ x 1⅛ x 2¼", V2p114–5, $25.00.

Klix, Styptic Powder, ¾ x 1¼ x 3¼", V1p255–7, $12.00.

Klok-Lax $.35, Laxative 18, ¼ x 1¾ x 2⅝", V1p113–12, $12.00.

Klutch $.10, Dental Adhesive Powder, ⅝ x 1¼ x 2⅜", V2p42–5, $25.00.

Klutch sample, Adhesive Powder, ¾ x 1¼ x 2⅛", V1p248–10, $35.00.

Klutch sample, Dental Powder, ¾ x 1¼ x 2⅜", V1p58–4, $30.00.

Klutch sample, Dental Powder, ¾ x 1⅝ x 2⅛", V2p42–7, $30.00.

Knapp's, Throat Cure, ½ x 2 x 3⅛", V1p292–5, $110.00.

Knickerbocker, Ginger, 3⅜ x 2⅜ x 1⅜", V2p151–3, $35.00.

Knicks, Auto Fuses, no photo, $15.00.

Knight Campbell, Steel Needles, no photo, $45.00.

Knights C.H. Co., Watch Mainsprings, ¾ x 2¾ x 2¾", V1p337–12, $45.00.

Knights Thearle, Watch Parts, ¼ x 1⅛", V1p338–1, $15.00.

Knoebels Sundry, Type Ribbon, ¾ x 2½ x 2½", no photo, $15.00.

Knorr's, Bouillon Cubes, 1 x 3½", V1p19–11, $18.00.

Knox Tarnish, Rust Remover, ⅝ x 1¾", V1p181–11, $25.00.

Ko-we-ba Brand, Caraway Seed, 3½ x 2¼ x 1¼", V2p151–5, $30.00.

Ko-we-ba Brand, Mustard, 3½ x 2¼ x 1¼", V2p151–7, $30.00.

Kochs, Pomatum, 1⅝ x 2⅛ x 2¾", V1p35–8, $22.00.

Kodak, Ribbon Holder Mag, ¼ x 1¾ x 4¾", V1p184–6, $25.00.

Kodak #0, Portrait Attachment, ½ x 1⅛", V1p184–7, $4.00.

Kodak #3, Portrait Attachment, ½ x 1¼", V1p184–8, $5.00.

Kodak #8, Portrait Attachment, ½ x 1⅛", V1p184–9, $4.00.

Kodak Filter, Color 17, ½ x 1¾", V1p184–10, $5.00.

Kodol $.25, Antacid Tablets, ½ x 1⅞ x 3⅛", V1p114–1, $18.00.

Kodol Tablets $.25, Acid Stomach, ½ x 1⅞ x 3⅛", V1p114–2, $12.00.

Koh-i-noor, Dress Fastner, ½ x 2 x 3⅛", V1p186–2, $12.00.

Kohinsoor, Type Ribbon, ¾ x 2½ x 2½", no photo, $12.00.

Kohler, One Night Corn Cure, ½ x 1⅛", V1p114–3, $22.00.

Kohler, One Night Corn Cure, ⅜ x 1⅛", V2p73–4, $22.00.

Kohler, One Night Corn Salve, ¼ x 1⅛", V1p114–4, $15.00.

Kohler $.10, One Night Corn Cure, ½ x 1⅛", V1p114–5, $25.00.

Kohler Antidote $.40, Headache Tablets, ¼ x 1½ x 2⅛", V2p73–6, $20.00.

Kohler-Antidote $.25, Pain Pills, ⅜ x 1¼ x 1¾", V2p73–8, $15.00.

Kohler's $.10, Corn Cure, ½ x 1⅛", V2p74–1, $25.00.

Koin-Pack, Condom, ⅛ x 1⅝, no photo, $20.00.

Kolapyrine, Headache Cure, ¾ x 1⅛ x 3¼", V1p114–6, $40.00.

Kolok, Type Ribbon, ⅞ x 2½", V2p183–3, $18.00.

Kolona sample, Tea, ¾ x 1⅞ x 2½", V2p133–6, $35.00.

Komo Indian, Ointment, no photo, $45.00.

Kondon's, Kidney\Backache Remedy, ¼ x 1½ x 2½", V2p74–4, $25.00.

Kondon's, Kidney\Backache Tablets, ½ x 1½ x 2½", V1p114–7, $25.00.

Kondon's, Pilease Pile Salve, ¾ x 2", V1p114–9, $45.00.

Kondon's Pilease sample, Pile Salve, ⅜ x ⅞", no photo, $60.00.

Kondon's sample, Catarrhal Jelly, ¼ x ⅞", V1p114–10, $45.00.

Kondon's sample, Catarrhal Jelly, ¼ x ⅞", V2p74–2, $40.00.

Kondon's sample, Catarrhal Jelly, ¼ x ⅞", V2p74–3, $45.00.

Kondon's sample, Catarrhal Jelly, ¼ x ⅞", V2p74–6, $18.00.

Kondon's sample, Nasal Jelly, ¼ x 1⅛", V1p114–8, $18.00.

Konjola $.30, Cold Compound, ¼ x 1⅜ x 2¼", V1p114–11, $10.00.

Kopper King, Spark Plugs, 1⅜ x 1⅜ x 4⅝", V1p12–4, $65.00.

Koskott sample, Hair Cream, ¼ x 1⅛", V2p35–4, $12.00.

Kotalko sample, Hair Grower, ¼ x ⅞", V1p35–9, $18.00.

Kraft $.25, Adhesive Tape, 1 x 2¼", V1p347–5, $8.00.

Krasny sample, Face Powder, ¼ x 1⅜", V1p29–10, $12.00.

Kreko, Type Ribbon, ¾ x 2½", V2p183–5, $18.00.

Kreko, Type Ribbon, ¾ x 2½ x 2½", V1p313–9, $15.00.

Kress Executive, Type Ribbon, ¾ x 2½ x 2½", V1p313–10, $15.00.

Krew-Pina sample, Cold Salve, ¼ x ⅞", V2p74–5, $15.00.

Kriptin, Cold, Hay Fever, ¼ x 1¼ x 1¾", V1p114–12, $8.00.

Kriptin, Cold, Hay Fever, ¼ x 1¼ x 1¾", V2p74–7, $8.00.

Kro-Raine, Pain Tablets, ¼ x 1¼ x 1¾", V1p115–1, $18.00.

Kropp, Razor Strop Paste, ¾ x 1", V2p135–1, $20.00.

Kruger Richard 200, Needles, no photo, $35.00.

Krystal, Soiloff, ½ x 1½", V1p22–4, $15.00.

Kuco No Chase sample, Powder, 1 x 2½", V1p252–4, $175.00.

Kugloids sample, Cure All, ⅜ x 1¼ x 2⅛", V1p115–2, $100.00.

Kuhn's $.25, Epsum Pills, ⅜ x 1½ x 1⅞", V1p115–3, $25.00.

Kutnows, Anti-Asthmatic, 1⅜ x 2¼ x 3⅛", V2p75–1, $30.00.

Kwatta sample, Cocoa, no photo, $95.00.

Kwik, Solder, ½ x 1½", V1p285–9, $8.00.

L A W (Seabury's), Pneumatic Mender, ⅞ x 1½", V1p18–8, $20.00.

La-Em-Strait sample, Hair Dressing, ¼ x 1⅛", V1p35–10, $18.00.

La-May, Compact Refill, ½ x 2½", V1p51–6, $25.00.

La-May, Face Powder, ½ x 2½", V2p23–6, $18.00.

Lactobacilline, Tablets, ½ x 1¾ x 3⅞", no photo, $30.00.

LaDainty $.10, Bleacing Oint., ½ x 1⅝", V1p29–11, $6.00*.

LaDainty $.10, Freckle Cream, ½ x 1⅝", V1p29–12, $10.00.

Lady Ester sample, Face Powder, ¼ x 1½", V1p252–5, $22.00.

Lady Lillian, Nail White, ⅜ x ⅞", V1p43–1, $15.00.

Lady Lillian sample, Nail White, ⅞ x 4", V1p43–2, $12.00.

Lady Smith, Knitting Needles, ¾ x 9", V1p187–2, $65.00.

Lady's Favorite, Hair Crimping, no photo, $30.00.

LaFrance, Type Ribbon, ¾ x 2½ x 2½", no photo, $12.00.

LaJac sample, Pink Cream, ¼ x 1½", V1p30–1, $25.00.

LaJaynees, Complexion Powder, ¼ x 1½", V2p24–1, $6.00.

LaJaynees sample, Powder, ⅜ x 1½", V1p252–6, $12.00.

LaJayness sample, Cold Cream, ¼ x 1", no photo, $15.00.

LaJean $.50, Temple/Scalp Dressing, ¾ x 3½", V1p35–11, $18.00.

Lake View, Whole Allspice, 2 x 3⅞", V2p152–1, $25.00.

Lake View, Whole Cinnamon, 2 x 3¾", V2p152–4, $25.00.

Lakeside, Strop Dressing, ⅝ x 1½", V2p135–3, $20.00.

LaKreem sample, Coffee, 2 x 2½", V1p232–2, $70.00.

LaMagique, Shoe Polish, 1⅛ x 2¾", V1p279–5, $30.00.

Lamo, Ointment, ⅝ x 1¾", V1p115–4, $30.00.

Lan-Tox, Witch Hazel Salve, ⅞ x 2¾", V2p75–3, $35.00.

Lancaster's English, Cascara Quinine Tablets, ½ x 1½ x 2½", V1p115–5, $45.00.

Lancaster's English $.25, Celery Caffeine, ½ x 1½ x 2½", V2p75–5, $40.00.

Landford $.10, Chocolate Laxative Tablets, ¼ x 1¾ x 2⅛", V1p115–6, $12.00.

Landford Nowland's, Laxative Quinine Tabs, ¼ x 1¼ x 1¾", V2p75–2, $8.00.

Landford sample, Petroleum Jelly, ¼ x 1¾", V1p115–7, $12.00.

Lange's, Lax Cold Tablets 65, ½ x 2¾ x 3⅝", V1p115–8, $12.00.

Langlois, Shaving Cream, 1⅜ x 2¼ x 2½", V2p135–5, $35.00.

Langspielnadein, Needles, no photo, $35.00.

Lanikol sample, Skin Ointment, ⅜ x 1¼", V2p75–4, $18.00.

LaPasticca DelReSole, Contro LaTosse, sample, 1 x 2 x 3", $8.00.

LaPerle sample, Creme Poudre, ¼ x 1½ x 1⅞", V1p252–7, $30.00.

Larkin, Camphor Ice, 1 x 3¾", V2p75–6, $12.00.

Larkin, Camphor Ice, 3¾" tall, no photo, $10.00.

Larkin, Corn Salve, ½ x 1⅛", V1p115–9, $10.00.

Larkin, Tooth Powder sample, no photo, $35.00.

Larkin $.10, Corn Salve, ½ x 1⅛", V1p115–10, $25.00.

Larkin & Morrill, Snuff Scotch, 1½ x 2¼", V1p191–9, $50.00.

Larkin sample, Nail White, ⅜ x ⅞", V1p43–3, $12.00.

Larkin sample, Orange Blossom Talcum, ¾ x 1¼ x 2⅛", V1p258–12, $40.00.

Larkin sample, Orange Blossom Talcum, ¾ x 1¼ x 2⅛", V1p259–1, $40.00.

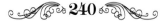

Larkin sample, Pink Polish Paste, ⅜ x ⅞", V1p48–1, $15.00.
Larkin sample, Pink Pollshing Paste, ⅜ x ⅞", V1p48–2, $15.00.
Larodon sample, Roche Tablets, ¼ x 1¼ x 1¾", V1p115–11, $8.00*.
LaRose S. Co., Tool Supplies, ½ x 1⅛", V1p348–2, $3.00.
Las-Stik, Tire Tube Patch, 1⅝ x 3½", V1p14–2, $25.00.
LaTosca, Complexion Cream, no photo, $25.00.
Laurel, Safety Razor, ½ x 1 x 1⅝", V1p271–5, $25.00.
Laurel Vest Pocket, Safety Razor, ½ x 1½ x 2", V2p135–2, $25.00.
LaValliere, Sub Rosa Cream, ⅞ x 1⅜", V2p29–3, $15.00.
LaValliere, Tooth Powder sample, no photo, $55.00.
LaValliere sample, Sub Rosa Cream, ⅜ x ⅞", V1p30–2, $18.00.
Lavender sample, Styptic Powder, ¾ x 1¼ x 2", V1p255–8, $35.00.
Lavex, Mineral Powder, 1¼ x 1¾ x 2½", V2p76–1, $20.00.
Lax-a-Fruit, Laxative, 1 x 3", no photo, $25.00.
Lax-ease $.10, Laxative, ⅜ x ⅞ x 2½", V2p76–3, $35.00.
Lax-ola $.25, Laxative, ⅜ x 1⅜ x 2⅛", V2p76–5, $15.00.
Lax-Root $.25, Laxative, ⅜ x 1⅝ x 2½", V2p76–2, $30.00.
Lax-Well, Laxative, ½ x 1¼ x 2", V1p116–5, $18.00.
Laxa-Dean, Wafers, no photo, $20.00.
Laxaco $.25, Laxative, ⅜ x 1⅞ x 2⅞", V1p115–12, $12.00.
Laxamints, Laxative, ½ x 1¼ x 2⅝", V1p116–1, $25.00.
Laxamints, Laxative, ⅜ x 1¼ x 1¼", V1p116–2, $20.00.
Laxatabs, Laxative, ¼ x 1¼ x 2", V1p116–3, $18.00.
Laxo Koto $.25, Liver, Kidney, Blood, Bowels, ⅝ x 1 x 2", V1p116–4, $35.00.
Laymon's, Asperline, ¼ x 1¼ x 1½", V2p76–4, $10.00.
Laymon's, Asperline, ¼ x 1¼ x 1¾", V1p116–6, $18.00.
Laymon's, Asperline, ¼ x 1¼ x 1¾", V1p116–7, $15.00.
Laymon's, Asperline, ¼ x 1¼ x 1¾", V2p76–6, $15.00.
Laymon's, Aspirin, ¼ x 1¼ x 1¾", V1p116–9, $12.00.
Laymon's, Aspirin, ¼ x 1¼ x 1¾", V2p77–1, $8.00.
Laymon's, Aspirin (Life), ⅜ x 1¼ x 1¾", V2p77–3, $10.00.
Laymon's, Face Powder, ⅝ x 2¼", V1p44–10, $10.00.
Laymon's #6, No-Sleep, ¼ x 1 x 1¼", V1p116–10, $12.00.
Laymon's $.05, Five-A-Lax Laxative, ¼ x ¾ x 1¾", V2p77–5, $8.00.
Laymon's $.10, Cascara Quinine, ¼ x 1¼ x 1¾", V1p117#5, $18.00.
Laymon's $.10, No-Sleep, ¼ x 1 x 1¼", V1p116–11, $10.00.
Laymon's 1½oz, Tooth Powder, 1¼ x 2¼ x 3⅛", V1p58–5, $20.00.
Laymon's 16's, Aspirin, ¼ x 1½ x 1⅞", V1p116–12, $8.00.
Laymon's 16's $.10, Aspirin Tablets, ¼ x 1¾ x 1¾", V1p117–1, $10.00.
Laymon's 6's, Aspirin, ¼ x 1 x 1¼", V1p117–2, $12.00.
Laymon's 6's $.05, Aspirin Tablets, ¼ x 1 x 1¼", V1p117–3, $12.00.
Laymon's Kwality, Aspirin, ¼ x 1¼ x 1¾", V1p117–4, $25.00.
Laymon's Pure $.10, Aspirin, ¼ x 1¼ x 1½", V2p77–7, $25.00.
Lazell Creme DeMeridor, Face Powder, ¼ x 1⅝", V1p252–8, $22.00.
Lazell DeMeridor sample, Complexion Cream Powder, ¼ x 1½", V1p252–9, $30.00.
Lazy Liver, Pills, ¼ x 1¼", V2p77–2, $60.00.
Le Transparent, Condoms, ⅜ x 1¾ x 2½", no photo, $65.00.
Leader, Shot Gun Sights, no photo, $50.00.
Lecroy's, Poultry Seasoning, 3 x 2¼ x 1¼", V2p152–6, $15.00.
Lederle, Aspirin, ¼ x 1⅜ x 2½", V1p117–6, $8.00.
Lee & Cady, Turmeric, 3 x 2½ x 1¼", V2p152–2, $30.00.
Lee's, Rubber Adhesive, 1 x 1⅝", V2p196–8, $25.00.
Lee's, Tooth Soap, ⅝ x 2 x 3⅛", V1p60–4, $70.00.
Lee's Elwood, Adhesive Plaster, no photo, $20.00.
Leete Robert S., Type Ribbon, ¾ x 2½ x 2½", V2p183–7, $15.00.
Leete's Leader, Type Ribbon, ¾ x 2½ x 2½", no photo, $15.00.
Lehn & Fink's, Black Pepper, 4 x 2½ x 1¼", V2p152–3, $45.00.
Leisespieler, Needles, ⅜ x 1½ x 1½", V2p114–7, $25.00.
Len-Oint $.50, Antiseptic Ointment, ¾ x 2", V2p77–4, $10.00.
Len-Oint sample, Antiseptic Dressing, ¼ x 1¼", V1p117–7, $8.00.
Len-Oint sample, Healing Cream, ¼ x 1⅛", V1p117–8, $12.00.

Lenk, Soldering Paste, ½ x 1⅜", V2p209–4, $6.00.
Leonard $.35, Laxative Cold Tablets, ¼ x 1¾ x 2⅝", V1p117–9, $10.00.
Leukoplast, Adhesive Plaster, ¾ x 1⅛, 4.00.
Lexoid $.30, Rheumatic Balm, ⅝ x 1½", V2p77–6, $18.00.
Libby sample, Histadyl, ¼ x 1 x 1¼", no photo, $10.00.
Libby, McNeill, Libby, Cooked Corn Beef, 1¼ x 2 x 1½", V1p244–9, $120.00.
Libby's, Asparagus (Calif), 1⅜ x 1⅝ x 2⅝", V1p244–10, $35.00.
Libby's, Kraut, 1¾ x 2", V1p244–11, $35.00.
Libby's, Red Salmon, 1⅜ x 2", V1p244–12, $70.00.
Libby's $.25, Painockers, ¼ x 1½ x 1¾", V1p117–10, $15.00.
Liberty Brand, Type Ribbon, 1¾ x 1¾ x 2", V2p184–1, $60.00.
Liberty Brand, Type Ribbon, ¾ x 2½ x 2½", no photo, $12.00.
Lifebuoy, First Aid, ⅝ x 1¼ x 1½", V2p209–6, $50.00.
Lifebuoy (sample), Soap, ⅝ x 1¼ x 1½", V1p284–1, $75.00.
Light 200, XLoud Gramaphone, ½ x 1¼ x 1¾", V1p208–3, $30.00.
Lightning, Tire Repair Kit, ⅜ x 1½ x 2½", V1p14–3, $65.00.
Lignol, Soap, ½ x 1⅝ x 2¾", V1p284–2, $100.00.
Lilas De France sample, Talcum Powder, ¾ x 1⅜ x 2⅛", V1p259–2, $55.00.
Lilly, see Ariphon Tablets, ¼ x 1¼ x 1¾", V1p71–10, $18.00.
Lilly, see Pulvule's Amytal Comp., V1p137–6, $18.00.
Lilly, Silver Nitrate, ¼ x 1⅜ x 1¾", V1p117–11, $12.00.
Lily, Black Pepper, 4 x 2¾ x 1¾", V2p152–5, $30.00.
Lily, Mace, 2¾ x 2 x 1", V2p152–7, $25.00.
Lily, Type Ribbon, ¾ x 2½ x 2½", no photo, $12.00.
Lindner, Reliable Fountain Brand, ⅜ x 1½", V1p348–3, $18.00.
Lindsay's $.15, Sure Cure, 1¼ x 1⅝ x 2¼", no photo, $65.00.
Lion, Valve Insiders, ¼ x 1 x 1½", V1p17–4, $20.00.
Lion Brand, Shoe Polish, ⅞ x 3", V1p279–6, $35.00.
Lion Brand, Silver Solder, 1 x 1", V1p285–10, $35.00.
Lion Brand, Type Ribbon, 1¼ x 2¼", no photo, $95.00.
Lion Brand, Type Ribbon, 2 x 2 x 2", no photo, $125.00.
Lion Brand E F, Type Ribbon, 1¾ x 1½", V2p184–3, $80.00.
Lion Tannery, Leather Samples, ⅜ x 1⅜ x 2½", V1p196–7, $140.00.
Lip-IVO, Lip Gloss, ½ x 1¾", V1p51–7, $5.00.
Liptons sample, Coffee, 2 x 3¼", V1p232–3, $55.00.
Liquozone, Laxative, ⅜ x 2⅜, no photo, $15.00.
Liquozone, Ointment, 1 x 2¼", V1p117–12, $30.00.
Listerine, Tooth Powder sample, 1 x 1¾", V1p58–6, $185.00.
Listerine sample, Talcum Powder, 1 x 2", V1p259–3, $110.00.
Little A.P., Type Ribbon, 1⅜ x 1¾ x 1¾", V1p314–1, $35.00.
Little A.P., Type Ribbon, ¾ x 2½ x 2½", no photo, $12.00.
Little A.P., Type Ribbon, ¾ x 2½ x 2½", no photo, $75.00.
Little A.P., Type Ribbon, ¾ x 2½ x 2½", V1p313–11, $85.00.
Little A.P., Type Ribbon, ¾ x 2½ x 2½", V1p313–12, $70.00.
Little Duke, Cards, Playing, ¾ x 2 x 2⅞", V1p174–10, $65.00.
Little Duke, Ginger, 1⅜ x 2⅜ x 3⅛", V1p188–11, $70.00.
Little Duke, Mace, 1⅜ x 1⅝ x 3⅛", V1p188,#12, 80.00.
Little Elf Brand, White Pepper, 3½ x 2¼ x 1¼", V2p153–1, $35.00.
Little Gem $.25, Tire Repair Outfit, ⅝ x 2¼ x 3½", no photo, $70.00.
Little Red Schoolhouse, Pen Points, no photo, $25.00.
Littlefuse, Auto Fuses Glass, ¼ x 1⅜ x 1½", V1p9–4, $5.00.
Little's, Type Ribbon, no photo, $15.00.
Little's A.P., Gold Seal Ribbon, ¾ x 2½ x 2½", V2p184–5, $15.00.
Little's Brilliant, Type Ribbon, ¾ x 2¼ x 2¼", V1p314–2, $22.00.
Little's Gold Seal, Type Ribbon, ⅞ x 2½", V1p314–3, $8.00.
Little's Indeliba, Type Ribbon, ¾ x 2½", V1p314–4, $8.00.
Llewellyn"s ⅝ oz., Spitta's Lozenges, ⅜ x 1½ x 2⅜", V1p292–6, $15.00.
Llewellyn's, Cough Lozenges, ⅜ x 1⅝ x 1⅜", V1p292–7, $12.00.
Llewellyn's, Spitta's Lozenges, ⅜ x 1½ x 2¼", V2p170–4, $10.00.
Llewellyn's, Wild Cherry Tablets, ⅜ x 2¼ x 3⅝", V1p292–8, $15.00.

Lloyd, Auto Fuses, ¼ x 1¼ x 1¾", V1p9–5, $18.00.
Lloyd's, Tablets, ⅝ x 1⅜ x 2⅝", V2p77–8, $25.00.
Loft, Gum (Peppermint), ¾ x ⅞ x 2⅞", V1p297–6, $80.00.
Loft Wintergreen, Gum, no photo, $80.00.
Log Cabin, see Towles.
Lollacapop, ⅝ x 1⅜ x 3", no photo, $35.00.
London, Balm, ½ x 2⅜, no photo, $30.00.
Long Aid, Scalp Ointment, ⅝ x 1½", V1p35–12, $5.00.
Long Aid sample, For the Hair, ⅝ x 1½", V1p36–1, $5.00*.
Long Aid sample, For the Hair\Scalp, ⅝ x 1½", no photo, $8.00*.
Long Aid sample, Sulphur, ⅝ x 1½", no photo, $8.00*.
Longines & Agassiz, Watch Material, ⅜ x 1⅛", V1p338–4, $20.00.
Loomis A.P. $.25, Anti-Phlogistic Salve, ¾ x 2", V2p78–1, $20.00.
Lord Needles, Needles Phono, ½ x 1½ x 2¾", V1p208–4, $55.00.
Lord's, House Plant Fertilizer, ⅝ x 1¼ x 2", V1p196–8, $12.00.
Loriot, Violette Pastilles, ⅜ x 1¾ x 2", V1p292–9, $35.00.
Loshar, Type Ribbon, ¾ x 2½ x 2½", no photo, $12.00.
Louis Joe, Hair Pomade, no photo, $25.00.
Louis Sherry', Tea, 1¾ x 2½ x 1¼", V1p267–12, $45.00.
Lovell & Colvel, Candy, 3 x 3", V1p288–2, $220.00.
Lovell & Covel, Candy, 3 x 3", V1p287–11, $185.00.
Lovell & Covel, Candy, 3 x 3", V1p287,#12, 400.00.
Lovell & Covel, Candy, 3 x 3", V1p288–1, $245.00.
Lovell & Covel, Candy, 3x3", V1p287–10, $230.00.
Lowney's sample, Cocoa, 1 x 1⅜ x 1⅝", V1p221–7, $145.00.
Lowney's sample, Cocoa Butter, ⅞ x 2¾", V2p125–2, $15.00.
Lucilline, Petroleum Jelly, 1¾ x 2¼ x 2½", V1p118–1, $70.00.
Lucky Brown, Hair Dressing, ⅜ x 1⅛, no photo, $18.00.
Lucky Brown, Pressing Oil, ¾ x 2⅝", V1p36–2, $18.00*.
Lucky Heart $.10, Wonder Skin Ointment, ¼ x 1½", V1p30–3, $25.00.
Lucky Heart $.25, Frozen Perfume, ¼ x 1½", V1p51–8, $20.00.
Lucky Heart $.25, Wonder Skin Ointment, ¾ x 2", V1p51–9, $18.00.
Lucky Heart sample, Hair Pomade, ⅜ x 1⅛, no photo, $18.00.
Lucky Heart sample, New White Pomade, ⅜ x 1⅛", V1p36–3, $25.00.
Lucky Magic, Hair Glow, ⅞ x 3½", V1p36–4, $15.00.
Ludens, Cough Drops, ⅜ x 2 x 3½", no photo, $145.00.
Luken's Peggy, Gum Holder, 1¼", V2p173–1, $110.00.
Lung Top, Salve, ½ x 1¾", V1p118–2, $100.00.
Lupex sample, Dysmenorrhea, ¼ x 1¼ x 1¾", V1p118–3, $10.00.
Lustr-ite, Nail Paste, ¼ x 1⅛", V1p43–4, $12.00.
Lustrite sample, Cuticle Ice, ¼ x ⅞", V1p43–5, $12.00.
Lutona sample, Cocoa (natural), ½ x 1¼ x 2", V1p221–8, $85.00.
Lux, Needles, ¼ x 1¼ x 1¾", V1p208–5, $35.00.
Luxor, Complexion Powder, ⅜ x 1¾ x 1¾", V1p44–11, $15.00.
Luxor, Cream Rogue, ¼ x 1⅛", V1p48–3, $15.00.
Luxor, Nail Polish Stone, ¾ x 1½", V1p43–6, $18.00.
Luxurie, Rubbed Sage, 3¾ x 2¼ x 1¼", V2p153–3, $25.00.
Luzianne sample, Coffee, 2½ x 3", V1p232–4, $165.00.
Luzianne sample, Coffee, 2½ x 3", V1p232–5, $95.00.
Luzier's sample, Deodorant Powder, no photo, $45.00.
Luziers sample, Talcum Powder, ¾ x 1¼ x 2⅛", V1p259–4, $35.00.
Lyon's Swansdown sample, Marshmallows, no photo, $65.00.
M & B, Hook and Eye, no photo, $8.00.
M & M, Type Ribbon, ¾ x 2½", no photo, $15.00.
M & M, Type Ribbon, ⅝ x 2", V1p314–5, $22.00.
M & M (Oliver), Type Ribbon, ⅞ x 2¼", V1p314–6, $25.00.
M & M Improved, Type Ribbon, ¾ x 2¼", V1p314–7, $80.00.
M & R, Wafers, ⅝ x 1⅝ x 2⅛, no photo, $15.00.
M & V Paragon, Type Ribbon, 1 x 2⅜", V1p314–8, $25.00.
M J B sample, Regular Grind Coffee, 2 x 3", V1p233–1, $40.00.
M-S-A, First Aid, ⅝ x 1½ x 2½", V1p118–4, $10.00.
M.B.P., Type Ribbon, ¾ x 2½ x 2½", V1p314–9, $10.00.
M.J.B. (bank), Coffee, 3 x 2¾", V1p232–6, $50.00.
Ma-la-na $.10, Cough Tablets, ⅜ x 2⅛ x 2⅝", V1p292–10, $75.00.
Ma-Le-Na, Ointment, ⅞ x 2⅜", V1p118–5, $6.00.
Ma-le-na $.10, Cough Tablets, ⅜ x 2⅛ x 2½", V1p292–11, $50.00.
Ma-le-na sample, Blood Tablets, ⅜ x 2⅛ x 2⅝", V1p118–7, $65.00.
Ma-le-na sample, Salve, ¼ x 1⅛", V1p118–6, $15.00.
MacDonalds, As-Co Tablets, 1 x 2½", V1p118–8, $30.00.
Macey, Hook and Eye, ⅞ x 2¼", V1p186–3, $12.00.
Mack's Foot Life sample, Salve, ¼ x 1½", V1p118–9, $50.00.
Mack's sample, Camphor Rub, ⅜ x 1⅜", no photo, $15.00.
MaClean Brand, Stomach Tablets, ¼ x 2⅜ x 2¾", V2p78–4, $10.00.
Macy's Reliable, Type Ribbon, ¾ x 2½ x 2½", no photo, $15.00.
Mad Cap, Rouge, ¼ x ⅞, no photo, $18.00.
Mad Cap sample, Cream Rouge, ¼ x ⅞, no photo, $15.00.
Mad-Ox, Herb Tablets, ¾ x 1¾ x 2⅞", V2p78–6, $25.00.
Madam Pivet's, Complexion Beautifier, ½ x 1⅜", V1p51–10, $20.00.
Madame Butterfly, Type Ribbon, ¾ x 2½", no photo, $6.00.
Madame Lily's, Marcellene Hair, 1 x 2¾", V1p36–8, $25.00.
Madison, Adhesive Tape, ¾ x 1", no photo, $5.00.
Magic, Aspirin, ¼ x 1¼ x 1¾", V2p78–2, $10.00.
Magic, Hair Pin Cabinet, 1½ x 2¾", V1p36–9, $25.00.
Magic, Song Restorer, 1¼ x 1¾ x 3", V2p209–8, $15.00.
Magic Pocket Lamp, Cigar Lighter, ⅜ x 1⅜", V1p196–9, $22.00.
Magic Regulator, Foot Draft, ¼ x ¾ x 1⅝", V1p118–11, $35.00.
Magic Regulator, Foot Draft, ¼ x ¾ x 2", V1p118–12, $45.00.
Magic Regulator Trial, Foot Remedy, ¼ x ¾ x 2", V1p118–10, $45.00.
Magic sample, Baking Powder, 1⅜ x 2", V1p245–1, $35.00.
Magic Wand, Hair Dressing, 1 x 3⅜", V1p36–10, $15.00.
Magic-Lax $.10, Laxative, ⅜ x 1⅞ x 1⅞", V2p78–3, $15.00.
Magic-Lax $.10, Laxative Nuggets, ⅜ x 1⅝ x 2⅛", V1p119–1, $18.00.
Magic-Lax $.25, Laxative, ⅜ x 2⅛ x 4¾", V2p78–5, $12.00.
Magna, Razor Blade Case, ⅜ x 1⅛ x 2⅛", V2p135–4, $90.00.
Magnetic, Nervine Pills, no photo, $40.00.
Magnetic Nervine $1.00, Nerve Tonic\Restorer, ½ x 1½ x 2½", V2p78–7, $75.00.
Magnolia, Hair Dressing, no photo, $20.00.
Mahar & Engstrom, Watch Supply, ½ x 1¼", V1p338–5, $5.00.
Maiden Herbs $2.00, Laxative, ⅞ x 2⅛ x 3¼", V2p79–1, $30.00.
Maid's sample, Vaporizing Rub, ½ x 1¼", V1p119–2, $12.00.
Maillard's sample, Cocoa, no photo, $75.00.
Maine Spring, Watch Main Spring, ¾ x 3 x 3⅜", V1p338–6, $75.00.
Majesty, Type Ribbon, ¾ x 2½ x 2½", no photo, $12.00.
Make Man 1902, Brain, Blood, Nerve, ½ x 2 x 2¾", V1p119–3, $70.00.
Make Man 1915, Tablets, ½ x 2 x 2½", V1p119–5, $45.00.
Make Man 1920, Tablets, ½ x 2 x 2¾", V1p119–4, $40.00.
Malco, Pickling Spice, 2 x 3¾", V2p153–5, $25.00.
Malmstrom, Wool Fat Lanolin, 1 x 2¾", V1p196–10, $3.00.
Malt Extract, Candy Bonbons 1.5oz., ¾ x 1¾ x 2⅞", V1p288–3, $60.00.
Maltbie sample, Mercene Powder, 1 x 2¼", V2p202–1, $20.00.
Maltese Cross, Allspice, 3 x 2¼ x 1¼", V2p153–6, $50.00.
Maltine $.20, Cod Liver Oil Concentrate, ¼ x 1¼ x 1¾", V1p119–6, $15.00.
Man-a-lin $.25, Laxative Tablets, ¾ x 1¾ x 3", V1p119–7, $15.00.
Man-Zan sample, Rectal Discomfort, ¼ x ⅞", V1p119–8, $10.00*.
Manhattan, Allspice, 3¼ x 2¼ x 1¼", V2p153–2, $30.00.
Manifold Supplies, Type Ribbon, ¾ x 2½ x 2½", V1p314–10, $12.00.
Manischewitz's, Ginger, 3¼ x 2 x 1", V2p153–4, $15.00.
Manischewitz's, White Pepper, 3½ x 2 x 1", V2p153–7, $35.00.
Manru sample, Coffee, 2 x 2½", V1p233–2, $70.00.
Mansfield's, Pepsin Gum, ½ x ⅞ x 2⅜", V1p297–7, $30.00.
Maple Leaf $1.00, Type Ribbon, ¾ x 2¼ x 2¼", V1p314–11, $15.00.

Maquinas Parlantes 200, Needles, no photo, $55.00.
Mar-Vel, Teething Balm, ½ x 2", V1p196–11, $8.00.
Marathon, Dryline Dope, ¾ x 2¾", V2p198–5, $8.00.
Marathon Loud, Needles, no photo, $60.00.
Marathon sample, Foot Powder, 1 x 1¼ x 2¼", V1p255–2, $15.00.
Marathon sample, Foot Powder, 1 x 1¼ x 2¼", V1p255–3, $15.00.
Margo, Healing Salve, ¾ x 2⅜", V1p119–9, $6.00.
Marinello Girl sample, Powder, ⅝ x 1½", V1p252–10, $20.00.
Marinello sample, Astringent Cream, ¼ x 1⅛", V1p30–4, $8.00.
Marinello sample, Combination Cream, ¼ x 1⅛", V1p30–5, $8.00.
Marinello sample, Lettuce Cream, ¼ x 1⅝", V1p30–6, $5.00.
Marinello sample, Motor Cream, ¼ x 1⅝", V1p30–7, $5.00.
Marinello sample, Tissue Cream, ⅜ x 1⅜", V1p30–8, $5.00.
Marque Perfectaphone, Deposee Needles, no photo, $75.00.
Mars, Pencil Box, ¾ x 2 x 7", no photo, $18.00.
Marschall, Forte Needles Piano, ½ x 1¼ x 1⅝", V1p208–10, $30.00.
Marschall, Needles, ½ x 1¼ x 1½", V2p114–2, $35.00.
Marschall, Pianissimo Needles, ½ x 1¼ x 1½", V1p208–7, $30.00.
Marschall, Piano Needles, ½ x 1¼ x 1⅝", V1p208–11, $25.00.
Marschall (dog\boy), Needles Phono, ½ x 1¼ x 1½", V1p208–6, $35.00.
Marschall 100, Needles Pick Up, ¼ x 1¼ x 1¾", V1p208–8, $30.00.
Marschall 200, Needles, ¼ x 1¼ x 1¾", V1p208–9, $25.00.
Marschall Extra, Salon Needles, ⅜ x 1⅝ x 1⅝", V1p208–12, $30.00.
Marschall xLoud, Needles, no photo, $65.00.
Marshall Co., Jewelers Material, ¼ x 1⅛", V2p210–1, $5.00.
Marshall Co., Jewelers Supply, ¼ x 1¼", V1p338–7, $8.00.
Marshall Field, Type Ribbon, ¾ x 2½ x 2½", no photo, $8.00.
Marshall Wells, Split Shot, ⅜ x 1½", V2p198–2, $20.00.
Martin's, Laxative Cold Breakers, ⅜ x 1⅜ x 1⅞", V1p119–10, $15.00.
Martin's $.25, Ko-Ko-Tar Hair Prep., ¾ x 2⅝", V1p36–11, $18.00.
Martin's Bruno, Med. Snuff, ⅝ x 2", V1p191–10, $12.00.
Martin's Capsules, Aspirin, ¼ x 1¼ x 1¾", no photo, $10.00.
Martinson's, Tea Bags, 1¾ x 2¼ x 3", V2p133–2, $25.00.
Marvello, Type Ribbon, ¾ x 2½", V1p314–12, $6.00.
Marvine, Aspirin, no photo, $12.00.
Maryland Club sample, Coffee, 1½ x 2½", no photo, $45.00.
Maryland Club sample, Coffee, 2 x 2¼", no photo, $40.00.
Mascot, Headache Cure, ½ x 1¼ x 1¾", V1p119–11, $60.00.
Mason & Risch 200, Opera Medium Needles, ⅜ x 1¼ x 1¾", no photo, $25.00.
Mason Jas. S., Betun Para Zapatos, ⅝ x 2½", V1p279–7, $40.00.
Mason's, Blacking (original), ⅝ x 2⅞", V1p279–8, $50.00.
Mason's, Challenge Polish, ¾ x 1¾", V1p279–9, $30.00.
Mason's, Cord Shoe Polish, ½ x 1¾", V1p279–10, $30.00.
Mason's, Dressing & Polish, ½ x 1 x 1¾", no photo, $25.00.
Mason's, Plumber's Soil, ⅝ x 3½", V1p279–11, $75.00.
Mason's, Rug Dressing, no photo, $30.00.
Mason's, Shoe Polish, 1 x 2⅞", V1p279–12, $10.00.
Mason's, Shoe Polish (blk), 1⅛ x 3¼", V1p280–1, $10.00.
Mason's $.30, Cream of Olives, ¾ x 2", V1p119–12, $40.00.
Mason's sample, Stove Polish, ¾ x 1⅞", V1p218–7, $55.00.
Massatta sample, Talcum, ¾ x 1⅛ x 2", V1p259–5, $70.00.
Massatta sample, Talcum Powder, ¾ x 1⅛ x 2", V1p259–6, $80.00.
Matador, Insect Powder, 1⅝ x 3½", no photo, $20.00.
Mathews Guaranteed, Type Ribbon, 1 x 1 x 1½", no photo, $40.00.
Mavis, Cold Cream Vivaudou, ¾ x 1", V2p29–5, $10.00.
Mavis Sweet Violet, Candy, ¼ x 1⅝ x 2⅛", V1p288–4, $20.00.
Max Factor, Cleansing Cream, ⅞ x 2½", V1p30–9, $15.00.
Max Factor, Face Powder, ¼ x 1⅝", V2p24–3, $8.00.
Max Factor, Lining, ½ x 1½", V1p51–11, $8.00.
Max Factor, Moist Rouge, ½ x 1", V2p26–5, $15.00.
Max Factor sample, Rouge Supreme, ⅝ x 1⅛", V1p48–4, $25.00.
Max-I-um sample, Coffee, no photo, $55.00.
Maxro, Type Ribbon, ¾ x 2½ x 2½", no photo, $12.00.
May Bloom\Queen, Tea, no photo, $20.00.
May Breath, Breath Mints, ¼ x 1⅝ x 2⅛, no photo, $18.00.
May Breath, Breath Mints, ⅝ x 1⅝ x 2⅛", V1p288–5, $12.00.
Maybell $.50, Lash-Brow-ing, ½ x 2⅛", V2p33–4, $12.00.
Mayets, Laxative, ¼ x 1¼ x 1¾", V1p120–1, $8.00.
Mayr's sample, Catarrh Balm, ¼ x ⅞", no photo, $25.00.
May's, Cold Tablets, ½ x 1⅝ x 2½", V2p79–3, $18.00.
May's, Glycerine Menthol Loz., ¾ x 2½ x 4⅛", V1p292–12, $20.00.
Mazawattee sample, Latariba Cocoa, ⅝ x 1½ x 2¼", V2p122–2, $120.00.
Mazda, Auto Lamps, 1½ x 3½ x 1½", V1p18–9, $10.00.
McAleers sample, Quick Cleaner (paste), ⅝ x 1½", V1p22–5, $20.00.
McAleer's sample, Quick Cleaner Paste, ⅝ x 1½", V2p38–2, $25.00.
McAleer's sample, Quick Wax, ⅝ x 1½", V2p38–4, $20.00.
McAlister, Ointment, ⅞ x 1½", V1p120–2, $12.00.
McAller's, Quick Wax, no photo, $40.00.
McAm Thom $.10, Big 4 Shoe Oil Paste, 1 x 3", V1p280–2, $15.00.
McCall, Indigestion Capsules, ¼ x 1¼ x 1¾", V2p79–5, $8.00.
McClinton's, Hibernia Stick, 1½ x 3½", V2p75–2, $25.00.
McConnon, Pepper, 4½ x 2½ x 1½", V2p154–1, $20.00.
McCormick, see Reliable Aspirin, V1p143–3, $12.00.
McCormick, Spanish Saffron, ¼ x 1¼ x 1¾", V1p188–1, $6.00.
McCormick & Co., see Bee Brand Tablets, ¼ x 1¼ x 1¾", V1p74, $35.00.
McCormick Banquet, Tea, 1¾ x 2¼ x 2½", V2p133–4, $30.00.
McCormick's Bee Brand, Tumeric, 3½ x 2¼ x 1¼", V2p154–4, $35.00.
McDonald's sample, Cocoa, 1⅛ x 1¾", V1p221–9, $130.00.
McGill's # 1, Fasteners, ½ x 1⅜", V1p62–10, $15.00.
McGill's #1 RH, Fasteners, ⅝ x 1¾", V1p62–11, $15.00.
McGill's #2, Fasteners, 1⅛ x 1½", V1p62–12, $25.00.
McGill's #2 FH, Fasteners, 1¼ x 1½", V1p63–1, $18.00.
McGill's #3, Fasteners, 1½ x 1¾", V1p63–2, $20.00.
McGregor, Type Ribbon, ⅞ x 2½", V2p184–6, $12.00.
McKay's $.10, Aspirin, ¼ x 1¼ x 1¾", no photo, $8.00.
McKesson, see AxAr Tablets, ¼ x 1¼ x 1¾", V1p73–3, $6.00.
McKesson, see Corax Analgesic Laxative, ¼ x 2 x 2¼", V1p84–3, $15.00.
McKesson & Robbins, see Analax Laxative, ¼ x 1¼ x 1¾", V1p120–3, $12.00.
McKesson & Robbins, Analax Laxative, ⅜ x 2⅛ x 4", V1p120–4, $8.00.
McKesson & Robbins, Antacid Powder, 1⅜ x 1⅝ x 2", V1p120–6, $15.00.
McKesson & Robbins, Aspirin, ¼ x 1¼ x 1¾", V1p120–7, $8.00.
McKesson & Robbins, Aspirin, ¼ x 1¼ x 1¾", V2p75–4, $8.00.
McKesson & Robbins, see Calox Tooth Powder, 1 x 1½", V1p56–9, $40.00.
McKesson & Robbins, Kidney Pills, ⅝ x 1½ x 2½", V1p120–10, $18.00.
McKesson & Robbins, Milk of Magnesia Tablets, ¼ x 1¾ x 3⅞", V1p120–8, $8.00.
McKesson & Robbins, Surin Laxative, 1 x 1¾", V2p75–6, $12.00.
McKesson & Robbins, Tablets #99, ¼ x 1¼ x 1¾", V1p120–9, $10.00.
McKesson & Robbins 25, see Analax Laxative, ⅜ x 2⅛ x 3⅞", V1p120–5, $18.00.
McKesson's, Copper-Iron, ⅜ x 1½ x 2¼", V2p80–1, $15.00.
McKesson's, Talkies for Throat, ⅞ x 2⅛ x 3⅛", V1p293–1, $8.00.
McLaughlin's sample, Coffee 4 oz., 2½ x 3½", V1p233–3, $40.00.
McNess, Krestol Salve, no photo, $25.00.
McNess, Throat Lozenges, ⅜ x 1⅞ x 3", V1p293–2, $6.00.

McNess F.W., Laxative Candy, ½ x 2¾ x 4¼", V1p120–11, $20.00.
McNess F.W., Vaperol, ⅜ x 1¼", V1p120–12, $12.00.
McNess G.W. sample, Cocoa, 1¼ x 1¾ x 2¼", V1p221–10, $50.00.
McQueen Viola, Mutton Tallow, ⅝ x 2", V1p51–12, $12.00.
Mead Johnson & Co., Viosterol, ¼ x 1¼ x 1⅞", V2p80–4, $15.00.
Meadow Brook, Split Shot Sinkers, ¼ x ¾ x 1¾", V1p176–7, $3.00.
Mead's No. 1 sample, Dextri-Maltose, 2 x 2½", no photo, $25.00.
Mead's No. 3 sample, Dextri-Maltose, 2 x 2½", no photo, $25.00.
Mecca Compound, Ointment Burns, 1 x 2¾", V1p121–1, $25.00.
Mecca Compound sample, Soothing Ointment, ⅜ x 1⅛", V2p80–6, $20.00.
Mecca sample, Home Remedy, ¾ x 2", V1p121–2, $20.00.
Mecca sample, Ointment, ¼ x ⅞", V2p80–2, $15.00.
Meccano, Erector Parts, ⅝ x 2½ x 2½", V1p196–12, $40.00.
Mechanical Servants, Aspirin, ¼ x 1¼ x 1¾", V1p121–3, $8.00.
Medicone, see Derma Medicone, V1p85–11, $5.00.
Medicone, Douche Tablets, ¼ x 1⅜, no photo, $40.00.
Medicone, Foot Cream, ⅜ x 1⅝", V1p121–4, $6.00.
Medicone, see Rectal Suppository, V1p142–2, $8.00.
Medicone Co. sample, Evacuant Pill Cathartic, ¼ x 1¼ x 1⅝", V2p80–3, $8.00.
Medicone sample, Dressing, ¼ x 1¾", V1p121–5, $8.00*.
Medicone sample, see Hay-Fever sample, L. (wht\blue), V1p106–8, $12.00.
Medicone sample, Hemorhoidal Suppository, V1p142–1, $8.00.
Medicone Suppos sample, Vaginal Jelly, ¾ x 1¾", V2p80–5, $55.00.
Mehmert Joseph, Watch Material, ⅜ x 1⅛", V1p338–8, $8.00.
Meiskey, Watch Material, ½ x 1⅛", V1p338–9, $8.00.
Melba, Nail Finish Paste, ½ x 2", V1p43–7, $18.00.
Melba Bouquet, Face Powder, ⅝ x 1⅜ x 1⅜", V2p24–5, $15.00.
Melba Fleurs, Face Powder, ¼ x 1⅝", V1p252–11, $25.00.
Melba Fluers, Face Powder, ¾ x 1½", V1p252–12, $30.00.
Melba sample, Cuticle Salve, ¼ x 1⅛", V2p26–2, $10.00.
Melba sample, Lov'me Face Powder, ¾ x 1¼ x 2⅛", V1p44–12, $40.00.
Mello-glo, Facial Tone Powder, ¼ x 1½ x 1½", V1p45–1, $10.00.
Mellomints sample, Candy, 2 x 1½", V1p288–6, $50.00.
Meloids, Candy (licorice), ⅜ x 1½ x 2⅞", $8.00.
Meloids, Candy Licorice, ⅜ x 1½ x 2⅜", $6.00.
Melorose sample, Powder, ¼ x ⅞", V2p24–2, $15.00.
Men-tho-eze sample, Burn Salve, ⅜ x ⅞", no photo, $20.00.
Mender, Metal Mending, ⅞ x 2⅜", V1p197–1, $8.00.
Mennen, Baby Powder, 1⅜ x 1⅜ x 4", no photo, $8.00.
Mennen Baby sample, Talcum Powder, no photo, $110.00.
Mennen sample, Antiseptic Borated Pwr., 1 x 2", V1p248–11, $45.00.
Mennen sample, Borated Talcum, 1 x 1⅞", V1p259–8, $150.00.
Mennen sample, Borated Talcum, 1 x 2", no photo, $15.00.
Mennen sample, Borated Talcum, ¾ x 1¼ x 2¼", V1p259–7, $125.00.
Mennen sample, Flesh Tint Talcum, ¾ x 1¼ x 2⅛", V1p259–10, $45.00.
Mennen sample, Flesh Tint Talcum, ¾ x 1¼ x 2⅛", V1p259–9, $45.00.
Mennen sample, Flesh Tint Talcum, ¾ x 1¼ x 2⅛", V2p128–4, $40.00.
Mennen sample, Kora Konia Talcum, 1 x 1 x 2", V1p259–11, $30.00.
Mennen sample, Kora-Konia Powder, ¾ x 1⅛ x 2", V2p128–6, $30.00.
Mennen sample, Narangia Talcum Powder, ¾ x 1¼ x 2", V2p129–1, $60.00.
Mennen sample, Narangia Talcum Powder, ¾ x 1¼ x 2⅛", V1p259–12, $60.00.
Mennen sample, Sen Yang Talcum Powder, ¾ x 1¼ x 2⅛", V2p129–3, $125.00.
Mennen sample, Sen Yang Toilet Powder, ¾ x 1¼ x 2⅛", V2p129–5, $110.00.
Mennen sample, Talc for Men, 1 x 2", no photo, $15.00.
Mennen sample, Talc for Men, 1 x 2", V1p260–5, $15.00.
Mennen sample, Talc for Men, 1 x 2", V1p260–3, $18.00.
Mennen sample, Talc for Men, ½ x 1 x 2½", V1p260–2, $12.00.
Mennen sample, Talc for Men, ¾ x 1¼ x 2⅛", V1p260–1, $45.00.
Mennen sample, Toilet Powder, no photo, $65.00.
Mennen sample, Violet Talcum, ¾ x 1½ x 2⅛", V1p260–6, $140.00.
Mennen sample, Violet Talcum, ⅞ x 1¼ x 2", V1p260–7, $40.00.
Mentho-Nova, Salve, ⅞ x 2¼", V2p80–7, $20.00.
Mentho-Nova $.25, Ointment, ¾ x 2⅜", V1p121–6, $18.00.
Mentho-Nova $.25, Ointment, ¾ x 2⅜", V2p81–1, $15.00.
Menthol $.10, Corn Plaster, ⅝ x 2¼ x 3½", no photo, $25.00.
Menthol Quinol, ¾ x 2½ x 2½", no photo, $12.00.
Menthol Quinol $.75, Developer, ¾ x 3 x 3", V2p210–3, $30.00.
Menthol Wafer, Novelty Plaster, no photo, $25.00.
Mentholatum, Ointment, ⅜ x ⅞", V1p121–8, $8.00.
Mentholatum, Salve, ¼ x 1⅛", V1p121–7, $8.00.
Mentholatum, Salve, ¼ x 1⅛", V1p122–3, $10.00.
Mentholatum, Salve, ¼ x 1⅛", V1p122–4, $10.00.
Mentholatum, Salve, ¼ x 1⅜", V1p121–12, $10.00.
Mentholatum, Salve, ⅜ x 1½", V1p122–11, $20.00.
Mentholatum, Salve (skin), ⅜ x 1½", V1p122–1, $20.00.
Mentholatum, Vapor Rub, ¼ x 1⅜", V1p121–11, $15.00.
Mentholatum sample, Ointment, ¼ x 1⅜", V1p122–6, $10.00.
Mentholatum sample, Ointment, ⅜ x 1½", V1p122–8, $50.00.
Mentholatum sample, Ointment, ⅜ x 1¾", V1p122–5, $8.00.
Mentholatum sample, Salve, ¼ x 1⅛", V1p121–9, $12.00.
Mentholatum sample, Salve in Spanish, ¼ x 1½", V2p81–4, $12.00.
Mentholoids, Cough Drops, ½ x 1⅜ x 2⅛", V1p293–3, $25.00.
Mercirex sample, Ointment, ⅜ x 1", V1p122–9, $15.00.
Merck Co., see Kalle Antifebrim, V1p113–6, $25.00.
Meredith's, Pile Driver, ½ x 1½", V1p122–10, $30.00.
Merican, Salve, ¾ x 2⅛", V1p122–11, $40.00.
Merit, Auto Fuses, ¼ x 1¼ x 1¾", V1p9–6, $8.00.
Meritoe, Corn Salve, ⅝ x 1½", V1p122–12, $15.00.
Meritone 100, Needles, no photo, $30.00.
Meritone 200, Needles, no photo, $30.00.
Meritone 200, XLoud Needles, ⅜ x 1¼ x 1¾", V1p209–1, $30.00.
Meritt ½ oz., Powder, ⅞ x 1½ x 3½", $15.00.
Merke, Hair Tonic, 1 x 3⅜", V1p36–12, $30.00.
Merles, Aspirin, ¼ x 1¼ x 1¾", V1p123–1, $18.00.
Merrell, see Analgia Tablets, ¼ x 1¼ x 1¾", V1p70–3, $15.00.
Merrell, Aspirin, ¼ x 1¼ x 1½", V1p123–2, $12.00.
Merriam's #9, Rivets, ⅝ x 1⅝ x 3¼", V1p63–3, $22.00.
Merrill's $.25, Liver\Kidney Pills, ¾ x 1¼ x 3¼", V1p123–3, $45.00.
Merrit sample, Hair Pomade, ¼ x 1", V1p37–1, $25.00.
Merritt's sample, Super-Plate Powder, ½ x ⅞ x 2", V2p42–2, $30.00.
Merry Widow $1.00, Condom Perfecto, ½ x 1½", V1p23–12, $30.00.
Merry Widows, Steam Cured Condoms, ⅝ x 1⅝", V2p18–2, $30.00.
Merry Widows $1.00, Condom, ⅝ x 1⅝", V2p18–4, $30.00.
Merry Widows 3, Condoms, ⅝ x 1⅝", V1p24–1, $25.00.
Merry Widows 3 $1.00, Condom, ⅝ x 1½", V1p24–2, $25.00.
Messer's $.05, Gum Charcoal, ½ x ⅞ x 2½", V1p297–8, $125.00.
Messer's $.05, Gum Spearmint, ½ x ⅞ x 2½", V1p297–9, $80.00.
Messer's $.05, Gum Violet, ½ x ⅞ x 2½", V1p297–10, $75.00.
Metcalf's, Coca Tablets, 2¼ x 3½ x 1½", V2p81–6, $60.00.
Metol Quinol, Developer, ⅝ x 3 x 3", V1p184–11, $40.00.
Metol Quinol, Developer, V2p210–3, $30.00.
Mexene, Seasoning, 1⅜ x 3⅜", V1p189–1, $25.00.
Mexene sample, Chile Powder, 1 x 1¼", V1p245–2, $45.00.
Mexican $.15, Corn Salve, ¼ x 1¼", V2p81–2, $25.00.

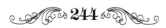

Mexican Java sample, Coffee, 2½ x 2½", V1p233–4, $155.00.

Meyer, Aspirin, ¼ x 1¼ x 1¾", V1p123–4, $10.00.

Meyer Charles, Grease Paint, 1 x 3¾", V1p52–1, $8.00.

Meyer Red Diamond, Adhesive Plaster, 1 x 1¼", V1p347–6, $22.00.

Meyer's Putz sample, Metal Polish, 1 x 1¾", V1p218–8, $70.00.

Miami Brand, Type Ribbon, ¾ x 2½ x 2½", V1p315–1, $4.00.

Micro, Cork Grease, ⅜ x 1⅜", V1p197–2, $3.00.

Micro-Audiphones, Hearing Aid, 1½ x 2¼ x 3½", V1p197–3, $90.00.

Middelton John, Pipe Polish, ¾ x 1⅝", V1p218–9, $8.00.

Midland Drugs, see Barrick's Lazy Liver.

Midol, ¼ x 1⅛, no photo, $6.00.

Midol $.40, Discomfort Tablets, ¼ x 1⅛ x 3⅛", V1p123–5, $5.00.

Midwest, Aspirin, ¼ x 1⅝ x 2", V1p123–6, $10.00.

Milburne's $.35, Cold Capsules, ⅜ x 1⅝ x 2⅜", V2p81–5, $5.00.

Miles, Anti Pain Pills, 1½ x 3⅛", V1p123–7, $12.00.

Miles, Anti-Pain Pills, ¾ x 2¾", V1p123–8, $10.00.

Miles, see Dr. Miles.

Miles $.25, Anti-Pain Pills, ¼ x 1⅜ x 2¼", V1p123–9, $12.00.

Milkweed Cream sample, Sunburn, Redness, ¼ x ⅞", V2p81–3, $40.00.

Millar L.B. sample, Coffee, 2 x 2½", V1p233–5, $50.00.

Millar's, Chili Powder, 3¼ x 2¼ x 1¾", V2p154–6, $30.00.

Millar's, Poultry Seasoning, 3¼ x 2¼ x 1¼", V2p154–2, $55.00.

Millar's sample, Magnet Coffee, 2⅜ x 3", V2p123–7, $110.00.

Miller, Type Ribbon, ¾ x 2½", V1p315–2, $6.00.

Miller, Type Ribbon, ¾ x 2½ x 2½", V1p315–4, $5.00.

Miller Bros. U S, Steel Pens, ½ x 1¼ x 1½", V2p210–5, $22.00.

Miller Geo. A, Aspirin 24, ⅜ x 1¾ x 2⅝", V2p81–7, $8.00.

Miller Geo. A $.25, Cold Laxative Tablets, ½ x 1⅝ x 2½", no photo, $10.00.

Miller Geo. S., Type Ribbon, ⅞ x 2⅝", V1p315–3, $25.00.

Miller Line, Type Ribbon, 1⅝ x 1⅝ x 2¼", V2p184–2, $45.00.

Miller Line, Type Ribbon, ¾ x 2½ x 2½", no photo, $5.00.

Miller Line Carnation, Type Ribbon, ¾ x 2½ x 2½", V1p315–5, $10.00.

Miller Line Elk, Type Ribbon, ¾ x 2½ x 2½", V1p315–6, $8.00.

Miller Line M.B.P., Type Ribbon, ¾ x 2½ x 2½", V2p184–2, $8.00.

Miller Line M.B.P., Type Ribbon, ¾ x 2½ x 2½", V2p184–7, $10.00.

Miller's Frank #2, Brake Waffers, 1¼ x 2⅛", V1p7–1, $50.00.

Miller's sample, Breakfast Cocoa, 1⅛ x 1¾ x 2", V1p221–11, $175.00.

Miller's sample, Cocoa, 1⅝ x 1⅛ x 2", no photo, $135.00.

Milliken, Wintergreens (mints), ⅜ x 1⅞ x 1⅞", V1p288–7, $18.00.

Milnesia, Anti-Acid Wafers, ¼ x 1⅜ x 2", V1p123–10, $15.00.

Milnesia Wafers, Milk of Magnesia, ¼ x 1⅜ x 2", V1p123–11, $10.00.

Milo, Type Ribbon, ¾ x 2½ x 2½", V1p315–7, $25.00.

Milo, Type Ribbon, ¾ x 2½ x 2½", V1p315–8, $15.00.

Mineral Wax, Type Ribbon, ¾ x 2½ x 2½", no photo, $18.00.

Mineral Wax-Twins, see Columbia.

Mineral Waxtwins, Type Ribbon, ¾ x 2½ x 2½", V1p315–9, $18.00.

Miner's, Cold Cream, ⅞ x 2⅜", V2p29–2, $12.00.

Miner's, Make-up, ¼ x 1¼", V1p52–2, $12.00.

Miner's, Natural Blush Rouge, ¾ x 2¾", V2p26–6, $10.00.

Miner's, Theatrical Powder, ⅞ x 2⅜", V2p24–4, $12.00.

Miner's sample, Theatrical Face Powder, ½ x 1⅜", V2p24–6, $25.00.

Minifus, Auto Fuses, ⅜ x 1⅜ x 1½", no photo, $8.00.

Mir a cle $1.00, Motor Gas, ¾ x 1¾ x 3¼", V2p15–2, $75.00.

Miraglo, Nail Bleach, ⅜ x ¾", V2p26–3, $8.00.

Miraglo, Nail Polish Powder, ¾ x 1½", V1p43–8, $10.00.

Mirelle sample, Toilet Powder, ¾ x 1½ x 2⅛", V1p264–9, $55.00.

Mitchell, Auto Fuses, ¼ x 1¼ x 1¾", V1p9–7, $18.00.

Mitchell-Rand, Soldering Paste, 1¼ x 2", V1p285–11, $18.00.

Mitre Brand Medium, Shefields Needles, ⅜ x 1¼ x 1¾", V1p205–2, $35.00.

Mity-Mags, Milk of Magnesia, ¼ x 1¾ x 2½", V1p123–12, $15.00.

Mizpah, Gum Peppermint, ⅜ x 1½ x 2", V1p297–11, $40.00.

Mizpah, Mints Peppermint, ⅜ x 1 x 3", V1p288–8, $70.00.

Mizpah, Spearmint Pepsin, ¼ x 1½ x 2", V1p297–12, $40.00.

Mizpah, Spearmint Gum, ⅜ x 1½ x 2", V1p298–1, $50.00.

Mizpah, Teaberry Pepsin, ¼ x 1½ x 2", V1p298–2, $35.00.

Mizpah, Type Ribbon, ¾ x 2½", V1p315–10, $18.00.

Mizpah (Zion Office), Type Ribbon, ¾ x 2½ x 2½", V1p315–11, $25.00.

Mobo, Paste Polish, ½ x 1½", V1p218–10, $22.00.

Modern, Type Ribbon, ¾ x 2¼ x 2¼", V1p315–12, $15.00.

Modern Tex, Condom, no photo, $60.00.

Mohawk, Tire Repair Kit, no photo, $110.00.

Mohican, Pure Spices, 3¾ x 2¼ x 1¼", no photo, $40.00.

Mohican, Pure Spices, 3¾ x 2¼ x 1¼", V2p154–3, $40.00.

Mohican, Safety Razor, 1¼ x 1⅝ x 2⅜, no photo, 320.00.

Mohr G.W., Shoe Polish (red), ¾ x 2⅛", V1p280–3, $20.00.

Moist, Colors, no photo, $25.00.

Momasa sample, Coffee, no photo, $140.00.

Momenta, Pain Tablets, ¼ x 1¼ x 1¾", V1p124–1, $15.00.

Mona Lisa, Pill Box, ⅜ x 1½ x 2", V1p288–9, $80.00.

Monarch, Healing Salve, 1 x 2¾", no photo, $35.00.

Monarch, Mending Kit, ⅝ x 2⅛ x 2⅞", V2p210–6, $20.00.

Monarch, Paint, 2⅛ x 2⅛", V1p181–12, $25.00.

Monarch, Type Ribbon, ¾ x 2¼ x 2¼", V2p185–1, $15.00.

Monarch Cycle Co, Tire Repair Kit, no photo, $70.00.

Monarch sample, Cocoa, 1¾ x 1¾ x 3", V1p221–12, $90.00.

Monark, Shoe Powder, 1⅝ x 3⅛", V1p280–4, $40.00.

Monday's, Allspice, 4½ x 2¼ x 1½", V2p154–5, $22.00.

Monell C.E., Compound Extract, 1½ x 1⅝ x 2¾", V1p124–2, $90.00.

Monitor Brand, Mace, 2⅞ x 2½", V2p154–7, $35.00.

Monogram, Type Ribbon, ¾ x 2½ x 2½", V2p185–3, $20.00.

Monsoon, Allspice, 1¼ x 2¼ x 3⅜", V2p155–1, $25.00.

Montague, Varnish for Rods, 2 x 2", V1p176–8, $20.00.

Montauk Star Brand, Female Pills, no photo, $50.00.

Montclair Brand, Bouillion Cubes, ¾ x 2 x 2¾", V2p210–2, $15.00.

Montclair Brand, Bouillon Cubes, ⅞ x 1¾ x 3", V2p210–4, $15.00.

Montgomery Ward, Cecilian Needles, ½ x 1½ x 2½", V1p209–3, $35.00.

Montgomery Wards sample, Peerless Corn Wax, ½ x 1⅛", V2p82–1, $15.00.

Montgomery's, Spice, 1⅜ x 2¼ x 3¼", no photo, $35.00.

Monument, Mainsprings, no photo, $35.00.

Mooney's Best sample, Baking Powder, no photo, $40.00.

Moore, Thumbtacks, ⅜ x 1¼ x 2", V2p210–7, $8.00.

Moore Brothers, Tea, no photo, $20.00.

Moore-Push-Pin, Thumb Tacks, ⅝ x 1 x 1⅝", V1p197–4, $5.00.

Moore's, Flat Lunch Box, ½ x 4 x 6¾", V1p197–5, $65.00.

Moore's, Throat & Lung Loz., ½ x 2 x 3⅛", V2p170–6, $75.00.

Mopar Chrysler, Auto Fuses 3AMP, ¼ x 1¼ x 1¾", V1p9–8, $12.00.

Morgan & Wright, Quick Repair Outfit, ½ x 1⅝ x 2½", V1p14–5, $35.00.

Morgan & Wright, Quick Repair Outfit, ½ x 1⅝ x 2½", V1p14–7, $35.00.

Morgan & Wright, Quick Repair Outfit, ½ x 1⅝ x 2⅝", V1p14–4, $40.00.

Morgan & Wright, Quick Repair Outfit, ½ x 1⅝ x 2⅝", V1p14–6, $35.00.

Morgan & Wright, Soapstone, 1⅝ x 3", no photo, $15.00.

Morgan & Wright, Tire Repair Outfit, ½ x 1½ x 2½", V1p14–8, $30.00.

Morgan & Wright Double, Tire Repair Kit, ½ x 1½ x 2½", V1p14–9, $55.00.

Morgan & Wright Single, Tire Repair Kit, ½ x 1½ x 2½", V1p14–10, $50.00.

Morgan's, Aspirin, no photo, $12.00.

Morgan's $.25, Vegetable Tablets, ¼ x 1¼ x 1¾", V1p124–3, $35.00.

Mormon Elders, Damiana Wafers, ½ x 2 x 3", no photo, 250.00.

Morning Sip, Coffee, 5 x 4", $65.00.

Morning Sip sample, Coffee, no photo, $75.00.

Morrison Lew, Dry-Pak Pork Rind, ½ x 2½ x 3⅝", V2p198–4, $18.00.

Mosco sample, Corn Salve, ⅜ x 1¼", V1p124–4, $12.00.

Moscos $.25, Catarrh Cure, ½ x 1½", V1p124–5, $110.00.

Moscos $.25, Great Peruvian Catarrh Cure, ½ x 1½", V2p82–4, $100.00.

Moscos $.25, Peruvia Catarrh Cure, ½ x 1½", V2p82–6, $110.00.

Moseman's sample, Peanut Butter, 1 x 2", V1p245–3, $130.00.

Moses Try, Cough Drops, no photo, 190.00.

Moses Try, Cough Drops, 1⅛ x 1¾ x 2½", V1p293–4, $155.00.

Moses Try, Cough Drops, 1⅝ x 2½ x 2⅜", V1p293–5, $170.00.

Moss Geo. A., Stove Polish, 1 x 3¼ x 4⅛", V1p218–11, $65.00.

Moth-ene, Moth Crystals, ¾ x 2¼ x 2¼", V1p197–6, $10.00*.

Mother Goose, Pencil Holder, ¾ x 2 x 7¾", V1p182–8, $60.00.

Mother's, Complexion Powder, 1¼ x 2½", V1p45–2, $35.00.

Mother's, Complexion Powder, 1¼ x 2¾", V1p45–3, $30.00.

Mother's (B&B), Mustard Plaster, 1½ x 3¾", V1p124–7, $40.00.

Mother's (B&B), Mustard Plaster, ½ x 3¾ x 4⅞", V1p124–6, $35.00.

Motif, Pencil Holder, ⅝ x 2 x 7½", V1p182–9, $20.00.

Mount Everest, Needles, ⅜ x 1¼ x 1¾", V1p209–4, $35.00.

Mouquin, Bouillon Cubes, ½ x 1⅞ x 2¼", V1p19–12, $15.00.

Moxie $.05, Candy, ⅝ x 1⅝ x 2¾", V1p288–10, $65.00.

Moyer J. Bird sample, Dental Powder, ¾ x 1½ x 2", V2p42–4, $25.00.

Mrs. Dietsch's, Salve, ¾ x 2¼", V1p124–8, $40.00.

Mrs. Dolph Road's, Superior Quality Salve, ¼ x 1⅛", V1p124–9, $8.00.

Mrs. Halfin's, Bird Balm, ⅜ x 1⅜", V1p197–7, $4.00.

Mrs. McGregor's, Nail Box, ½ x 2⅛ x 3⅜", V1p197–8, $8.00.

Mrs. Rodeback's $.50, Eczema Salve, 1½ x 2¼", V1p124–10, $40.00.

Mrs. Roulston Jessie, Rouge Color, ⅝ x 1¾", V2p26–7, $25.00.

Mrs. Van Cott's $.10, Excelsior Throat Loz., ½ x 1⅛ x 2⅛", V1p293–6, $140.00.

Mrs. VanCotts, Throat Lozenges, no photo, $120.00.

Mrs. Webb's $.30, Family Ointment, ⅞ x 2", V1p124–11, $25.00.

Mu-Col sample, Hygienic Powder, 1 x 1½", V1p266–7, $25.00.

Mucilin, Ointment fishing, ⅝ x 2", V1p176–9, $3.00.

Muco sample, Solvent, ⅜ x ⅞", V1p22–6, $15.00.

Mudlavia, Medicine, no photo, $40.00.

Mueller's, Vegetable Tablets, ½ x 1⅜ x 2½", V1p124–12, $35.00.

Mulford, Anti-Acidity 25, ½ x 1⅞ x 2⅞", V1p125–1, $18.00.

Mulford, Aromatics, ¾ x ¾ x 2¾", V2p168–2, $40.00.

Mulford, Crystal Pastilles, ½ x 2 x 3⅛", V1p293–7, $15.00.

Mulford, Mints, ¾ x ¾ x 2¾", V1p289–1, $45.00.

Mulford H.K., Dyspepsia Fermentative, ½ x 1¾ x 2⅞", V1p125–2, $40.00.

Mulford No.2, Thyrocalx Tablets, ¼ x 1¼ x 1¾", V2p82–2, $15.00.

Mulford Wintergreens, Breath Mints, ¾ x ¾ x 2¾", V1p288–12, $40.00.

Mulford's sample, Toilet Talcum, ¾ x 1¼ x 2", V2p129–2, $70.00.

Mulford's sample, Toilet Talcum, ¾ x 1¼ x 2⅛", V1p264–10, $70.00.

Multi Kopy, Ink Stamp Pad, ⅞ x 1½ x 2¾", V1p179–11, $30.00.

Mum, Deodorant, ⅜ x 1⅝", V2p33–6, $4.00.

Mum $.10, Deodorant, ⅜ x 1⅝", V1p45–4, $6.00.

Mumsell's, Mineral Tablets, ½ x 1½ x 2½", no photo, $6.00.

Munyon's, Paw-Paw Pills, ⅜ x 1¼ x 1¼", V2p82–3, $35.00.

Munyon's sample, Corn Cure, ¼ x 1⅛", V2p82–5, $35.00.

Murphy's sample, Oil Soap, ¾ x 2", V1p284–3, $30.00.

Murphy's sample, Oil Soap, ⅞ x 2⅛", V2p34–1, $25.00.

Murray Hill sample, Java Coffee, 1⅜ x 1⅞ x 2", V2p124–1, $90.00.

Murray's, Charcoal Tablets, 1¼ x 1¾ x 2⅝", V1p125–3, $40.00.

Murray's, Hair Dress Pomade, 1¼ x 2", V1p37–2, $8.00*.

Murray's, Hair Dressing, ⅝ x 2", V1p37–3, $12.00.

Murray's $.25, Hair Dressing Pomade, ¼ x 1⅝", V1p37–5, $20.00.

Murray's Edgar, Fly Killer, 1 x 2⅞", V1p197–9, $10.00.

Murray's sample, Hair Dressing Pom, ⅝ x 1¾", V1p37–4, $25.00.

Murray's sample, Scalp\Pressing Oil, ⅝ x 2", V1p37–6, $22.00.

Mustad Pocket Pack, Fish Hooks #101, ⅜ x 1½ x 2⅛", V1p176–10, $5.00.

Mustad-Kirby, Fish Hooks #101, ⅜ x 1½ x 2⅛", V1p176–11, $5.00.

Musterole, Laxative Cold Tablets, ⅜ x 1½ x 2", V1p125–4, $12.00.

Muza, Needles, ⅜ x 1¼ x 1¾", V2p114–4, $30.00.

My Roy sample, Coffee, 2¾ x 2½", V1p233–6, $150.00.

Myers M., Watch Main Spring, ⅝ x 2¾ x 5⅛", V1p338–10, $30.00.

Myer's M. Co., Hub Mainsprings, ½ x 2¾ x 5⅛", V1p338–11, $40.00.

Myer's M.Co., Hub Mainsprings, ½ x 2¾ x 5⅛", V1p338–12, $30.00.

Myer's University, Pen Points, ⅜ x ⅝ x 1¾", V1p183–6, $18.00.

Mystic, Foot Powder, 1¾ x 1¾ x 3¼", V1p255–4, $25.00.

Mystic Cream, Skin Cream, ¼ x 1⅛", V1p30–10, $18.00.

Na tur Tone, Needles, no photo, $30.00.

Na-Dru sample, Royal Rose Talcum, ½ x 1 x 2", no photo, $95.00.

Naa Galena, Crystal, 1 x 1", V1p197–10, $5.00.

Nabob, Mint, 3¼ x 2¼ x 1", V2p155–4, $45.00.

Nabob sample, Coffee, no photo, $100.00.

Nadine, Face Powder Flesh, ⅜ x 1¼ x 1¾", V2p25–1, $12.00.

Nadine sample, Face Powder, ¼ x 1⅜", V1p253–2, $18.00.

Nadine sample, Face Powder, ¼ x 1⅜", V1p253–1, $15.00.

Nagle's Anthracite, Type Ribbon, ¾ x 2½", V1p316–1, $12.00.

Nail White, Polish, ¼ x ¾", V2p26–4, $5.00.

Nannette, Face Powder, ¾ x 1⅛ x 2½", V1p45–5, $55.00.

Napoleans, Condom, no photo, $65.00.

Nara, Fish Food, ¾ x 2½", V1p197–11, $15.00.

Nasal Filter, Hayfever, 1¼" rd., no photo, $10.00.

Nash Coffee sample, Coffee, 2 x 3¼", V1p234–1, $75.00.

Nash's, Aspirin, ¼ x 1¼ x 1¾", V2p82–7, $10.00.

Nash's $.25, Cold Capsules, ⅜ x 1¾ x 1¾", V1p125–5, $10.00.

Nash's sample, Coffee, 2¾ x 3⅜", V2p124–3, $80.00.

Nash's sample, Coffee, 2 x 3¼", no photo, $100.00.

Nash's sample, Croup & Pneumonia, ⅜ x 1⅛", V1p125–6, $20.00.

Nasco, Saccharin Tablets, ¼ x 1¼ x 1¾", V1p125–7, $12.00.

National, Coffee (essence), 2 x 2½", V1p245–4, $35.00.

National, Safety Razor, 1¼ x 2¼", V1p271–6, $75.00.

National, Tumeric, 1⅝ x 3¼", no photo, $60.00.

National, Type Ribbon, ¾ x 2½ x 2½", V1p316–2, $20.00.

National (Borden) sample, Beta Lactose, 2½ x 3", V1p245–5, $30.00.

National Dairy sample, Malted Milk, no photo, $25.00.

National Drug Co., see Nature's Cure.

National Drug Co., see Wells' Tablets.

National Healer $.25, Salve, ¾ x 2⅜", V1p125–8, $30.00.

National Lead, Pure White Lead, ⅝ x 2⅛ x 3¼", V1p197–12, $15.00.

National Silk Spun, Type Ribbon, 1½ x 2 x 1¾", no photo, $30.00.

Natoma sample, Talcum Powder, ¾ x 1¼ x 2⅛", V1p260–9, $175.00.

Natural Bridge, Type Ribbon, ¾ x 2½ x 2½", V2p185–5, $35.00.

Natural Voice 200, Needles Gramaphone, ½ x 1¼ x 1½", V1p209–5, $35.00.

Natural Voice 200, Needles Phono, ½ x 1¼ x 1½", V2p114–6, $35.00.

Nature's Cure $.50, Blood Purifier, ½ x 2 x 3⅛", V1p125–9, $45.00.

Nature's Remedy, Laxative, ⅜ x 1¼ x 1¾", V1p125–12, $8.00.

Nature's Remedy, Laxative (Jrs.), ⅜ x 1¼ x 1½", V1p125–11, $12.00.

Nature's Remedy, Laxative Tablets, ¼ x 1 x 1¾", V1p125–10, $6.00*.

Nature's Remedy, NR Tablets, 1 x 3 x 4", no photo, $8.00.

Nature's Remedy $1.00, Laxative Tablets, 1 x 2¾ x 3⅜", V1p126–5, $8.00.

Nature's Remedy $.10, Vegetable Laxative, ¼ x 1 x 1¾", V1p126–6, $10.00.

Nature's Remedy $.25, Laxative, ½ x 1¼ x 1⅝", V1p126–7, $10.00.

Nature's Remedy $.25, Laxative, ½ x 1¼ x 1⅝", V1p126–8, $8.00.

Nature's Remedy $.25, Laxative, ⅜ x 1¼ x 1½", V1p126–4, $8.00.

Nature's Remedy $.29, Laxative, ¼ x 1¾ x 2½", V1p126–1, $8.00.

Nature's Remedy $.29, Laxative Tablets, ¼ x 1¾ x 2⅝", V1p126–2, $8.00.

Nature's Remedy $.50, Laxative, 1 x 2 x 2⅞", V2p83–1, $12.00.

Nature's Remedy $.50, Laxative (Jrs), 1 x 2⅛ x 1½", V2p83–4, $6.00.

Nature's Remedy $.50, Laxative 60 Tablets, 1 x 2 x 1¾", V1p126–3, $8.00.

Nature's Remedy $.50, Tablets 60, 1 x 2 x 2⅞", V1p126–10, $8.00.

Nature's Remedy $1.00, Jr. Laxative, 1 x 2⅛ x 2¾", V1p126–11, $8.00.

Nature's Remedy $1.00, Laxative, 1 x 2¾ x 4⅜", V1p126–9, $8.00.

Naturkist, Powder, ⅝ x 1½", V1p45–6, $8.00.

Navy Arms Co., Percussion Caps, ½ x 1½", V1p65–1, $40.00.

Neal, Tire Repair Kit, ½ x 1⅞ x 3", V1p14–11, $60.00.

Neal's, Gas Tablets, ½ x 2 x 3", no photo, $25.00.

Nebia, Turmeric, 3½ x 2¼ x 1¼", V2p155–6, $40.00.

Nebs, Tablets, ¼ x 1¼ x 1¾", V1p126–12, $8.00.

Neco Brand, Type Ribbon, ¾ x 2½ x 2½", V1p316–3, $18.00.

Neco-Brand, Type Ribbon, ¾ x 2½ x 2½", V1p316–4, $15.00.

Needle of Quality, Needles, no photo, $25.00.

Neilson's sample, Cocoa, 1⅜ x 2", V2p122–3, $30.00.

Neilson's sample, Cocoa (Jersey), 1¾ x 2½", V1p222–1, $30.00.

Nelson Baker, Santonin Chocolates, ⅞ x 1⅝ x 3", V2p83–6, $45.00.

Nelson Baker, Seidlitz Powders, 1⅜ x 2⅞ x 4⅛, no photo, $40.00.

Nelson Baker, Witch Hazel Ointment, ⅞ x 2⅝", V1p127–1, $30.00.

Nelson's $.10, Hair Dressing, 1½ x 1¾ x 2", V1p37–7, $18.00.

Nelson's $.25, Hair Dressing, 1¾ x 2¼ x 2¾", V1p37–8, $20.00.

Nelson's sample, Hair Dressing, ⅜ x 1 x 2", V1p37–10, $70.00.

Nelson's sample, Hair Dressing, ⅜ x 1 x 2", V1p37–9, $75.00.

Nelson's sample, Hairdressing, ⅜ x 1 x 2", V1p37–11, $70.00.

Nembutal, Capsules, ¼ x 1 x 1½", no photo, 4.00.

Nembutal, Methyl-Butyl, ⅜ x ⅞ x 1½", no photo, 4.00.

Neo-Syn, Tablets, ¼ x 1¼ x 1¾", no photo, $12.00.

Nepera $.50, Developer, 1⅛ x 1½ x 2⅛", V2p211–1, $30.00.

Nerve Berries, Pills, ⅜ x 1½ x 2½", V1p127–2, $90.00.

Nerve Seeds, Nerve Seeds, ½ x 1½ x 2½", V1p127–3, $55.00.

Nervo $.25, Vital Tablets, no photo, $65.00.

Nescafe 4 oz., Coffee, 2½ x 3¼", V1p234–2, $35.00.

Nescafe sample, Coffee, 1½ x 2¼", no photo, $35.00.

Nescafe sample, Coffee, 1½ x 2¼", V1p234–3, $35.00.

Nescafe sample, Coffee, 1¾ x 2⅛", V1p234–4, $35.00.

Nestles, Bouillon Cubes, 1 x 3½", V1p20–1, $6.00.

Nestle's sample, Food, 1¼ x 1¾", V2p125–6, $30.00.

Nestles sample, Lactogen, 2⅞ x 2½", V2p125–4, $30.00.

Neu Carb, Stomach Antacid Pills, ¼ x 1¼ x 1¾", V1p127–4, $12.00.

Neuman, Tooth Powder, 1⅝ x 3¾", V1p58–7, $45.00.

Never-Dull sample, Polish, ¾ x 1⅞, no photo, $10.00.

Nevralgol $.25, Faguet, ¼ x 1⅜ x 1⅞", V1p127–5, $15.00.

New Brunswick, Tire Repair Kit, ½ x 2 x 3⅛", V2p15–3, $80.00.

New Brunswick, Stamp Holder, ¼ x 1¼ x 1¾", V2p211–3, $100.00.

New Discovery $.50, Salve, ¾ x 2⅛", V1p127–6, $18.00.

New England Brand, Type Ribbon, no photo, $12.00.

New Haven, Steel Ball Bearings, ⅝ x 1¼", no photo, $5.00.

New Skin, Liquid Court Plaster, ¾ x 1 x 2⅛, no photo, $15.00.

New Skin, Liquid Court Plaster, ⅝ x ⅞ x 2¼", V2p83–2, $20.00.

New York Standard, Watch 35 Jewelsng, ¾ x 2", V1p339–1, $60.00.

New York\London Drug, see Nyal Drug Co.

Newarks, Velvet Cream (shoe), ¾ x 2⅛", V1p280–5, $20.00.

Newly Wed sample, Marshmallows, no photo, $120.00.

Newman-Stern, Microphone Bottom, 1⅝ x 1¾", V1p198–1, $15.00.

Newton's, Allspice, 3¼ x 2¼ x 1½", V2p155–2, $35.00.

Newton's, Fly Line Dressing, ¾ x 2¾", no photo, $8.00.

Newton's, Vaporine Ointment, ½ x 2⅛", V2p83–3, $10.00.

Ngoma, Needles, ½ x 1¼ x 1⅝", V1p209–6, $25.00.

Nicholas, Carbolic Dentifrice, no photo, $35.00.

Nickel Brand $.05, Antacid Tablets, ¼ x ⅞ x 1½", V1p127–7, $12.00.

Nickel Brand $.05, Head Cold Tablets, ¼ x 1 x 1⅜", V2p83–5, $12.00.

Nickel Brand $.05, Laxative, ¼ x 1 x 1⅜", V2p83–7, $12.00.

Nickel Brand $.05, Laxative Tablets, ¼ x 1 x 1⅜, no photo, $12.00.

Nigger Head, Stove Polish, 1 x 2¾", V1p218–12, $150.00.

Night Before XMas, Candy Pail, 2½ x 4½ x 2⅜", $175.00.

Nightingale, Softone Neednles, no photo, $25.00.

Nigroids, Throat and Voise Loz., ¼ x 1¼ x 1¾", V2p170–2, $20.00.

Nigroids, Throat Loz., ⅜ x 1¼ x 1¾", V2p170–3, $15.00.

Nigroids, Throat Loz., ⅜ x 1¼ x 1¾", V2p170–5, $18.00.

Nigroids, Throat Lozenger, ½ x 1¼ x 1¾", V1p293–8, $15.00.

Nil-Mist, Glass Protector, ¾ x 3", V1p198–2, $10.00.

Nit, Pomade, no photo, $22.00.

No-Bluf, Metal Polish, 1⅝ x 2¾", V1p219–1, $40.00.

No-Cola Yankee, Shoe Polish, no photo, $30.00.

No-To-Bac, Cure for Tobacco Habit, ½ x 2⅜ x 3¾", V1p127–8, $85.00.

No-To-Bac, Positive\Permanent Cure, ⅝ x 2¼ x 3¾", no photo, $75.00.

No-To-Bac $1.00, Intended to Assist, ½ x 2¼ x 3½", V2p84–1, $85.00.

No-To-Bac $1.00, Positive\Permanent Cure, ½ x 2¼ x 3¼", V2p84–3, $80.00.

No-To-Bac $1.00, Positive\Permanent Cure, ½ x 2¼ x 3¾", V2p84–5, $75.00.

No-To-Bac $1.00, Quit Tobacco Remedy, ½ x 2¼ x 3¾", V2p84–2, $95.00.

No-To-Bac $1.00, Quit Tobacco Remedy, ⅝ x 2⅜ x 3¾", V2p84–4, $95.00.

No-To-Bac $2.00, Quit Tobacco Habit, ⅝ x 2¼ x 3¾", V1p127–9, $70.00.

Nokorode, Soldering Paste, 1¼ x 2", no photo, $12.00.

Nokorode, Soldering Paste, ½ x 1⅜", V1p285–12, $12.00.

Noma, Auto Fuses, ¼ x 1⅜ x 1½", V1p9–9, $8.00.

Noma, Auto Fuses, ⅜ x 1⅜ x 1½", no photo, $8.00.

Nomodust, Sweeping Powder, no photo, $15.00.

Non-Smut, Type Ribbon, ¾ x 2½", no photo, 3.00.

None-Such, Paprika, 1⅝ x 3⅝", V2p155–3, $30.00.

Nonsuch Black Cat, Shoe Polish, ¾ x 1¼", V1p280–6, $40.00.

Noonan's sample, Lemon Cream, ¼ x 1½", V1p30–11, $18.00.

Norcroft, Type Ribbon, ¾ x 2½ x 2½", V1p316–5, $15.00.

Norida sample, Fleur Sauvage Powder, ¼ x 1⅝", V1p253–3, $25.00.

Noris, Needles, no photo, $45.00.

Norman Merle sample, Skin Salve, ¼ x ¾", V1p30-12, 5.00*.
Norta, Type Cleaner, ¾ x 1½ x 2⅜", V1p316-9, $15.00.
Norta, Type Cleaner, ⅝ x 1¾ x 2⅞", V1p316-6, $8.00.
Norta, Typewriter Cleaner, ¾ x1½ x 2⅜", V1p316-10, $18.00.
North Star sample, WoolFat, ¾ x 1½", V2p193-7, $18.00.
Northeastern sample, Nail White, ⅜ x ¾", V1p43-9, $10.00.
Northrop & Lyman, Klearoids Throat Loz., ⅜ x 1½ x 2½", V2p170-7, $15.00.
Norton, Cough Drops, no photo, $75.00.
Norwesco Sample, Grinding Compound, ¼ x 1⅛", V2p15-4, $30.00.
Norwich, Aspirin, ¼ x 1¼ x 1¾", V1p127-10, $10.00.
Norwich, Aspirin, ¼ x 1¼ x 1¾", V1p127-11, $8.00.
Norwich, Laxative Cold Tablets, ¼ x 1¾ x 2½", V1p127-12, $10.00.
Norwich, Thaloin Laxative, ¼ x 1¼ x 1¾", V2p84-6, $10.00.
Norwich Pharmacal, see Unguentine Salve, V1p161-12, $6.00.
Norwood's Pharmacy, C.C. Capsules, ⅜ x 1¼", no photo, $8.00.
Nosena sample, Catarrh Ointment, ¼ x 1", no photo, $20.00.
Nottingham Rexall, Cough Drops, ¾ x 2⅛ x 3⅛", V1p293-9, $20.00.
Nova Eagle Brand, White Leather Polish, ¾ x 2⅜, no photo, $22.00.
Nowland's, see Landford, V1p115-7, $12.00.
Nowland's, Petroleum Jelly, V1p115-7, $12.00.
Noyes', Dyspepsia Tablets, ⅜ x 1½ x 2½", V1p128-1, $55.00.
Noyes', Dyspepsia Tablets, ⅜ x 1⅛ x 2⅛", V2p85-1, $60.00.
Noyes, Pulv. Antipyretic, 1½ x 1½ x 2¼", V1p128-2, $75.00.
Nu-Enamel sample, Enamel Paint, 2 x 1⅞", V2p211-5, $6.00.
Nu-Glo $.10, Pomade for Men, 1⅛ x 1⅞", V1p37-12, $20.00.
Nu-Glo sample, Hair Dressing, ⅜ x 1⅛", V1p38-1, $25.00.
Nu-Lax $.10, Laxative, ⅜ x 1½ x 1½", V1p128-3, $15.00.
Nu-Tips, Condom, no photo, $65.00.
Nu-Way Cod, Cod Oil Tablets, ⅝ x 2½ x 4 ⅜", V1p128-4, $40.00.
Nugget sample, Shoe Polish, ½ x 1½", V1p280-7, $22.00.
Nun-Better, Cay. Pepper, 3⅛ x 2¼ x 1⅜", V2p155-5, $45.00.
Nunbetter, Condom, no photo, $65.00.
Nurse Brand, Aspirin, no photo, $15.00.
Nut House of Lynn, Peanuts 2 oz., 1½ x 2¼ x 2½", V1p245-6, $70.00.
Nutex, Condom, no photo, $45.00.
Nutex, Condom, ⅝ x 1⅝", V2p18-6, $210.00+.
Nutex Radium, Condom, ¼ x 1⅝ x 2⅛", V2p19-1, $70.00.
Nutex Rolled, Nu-Tips Condom, ¼ x 1⅝ x 2⅛", V2p19-3, $70.00.
Nutex Transparent, Condom, no photo, $45.00.
Nutrio, Turtle Food, 1¼ x 1¾ x 2¼", V1p198-3, $25.00.
Nutriola, Blood\Nerve Food, no photo, $45.00.
Nutriola, Granules, no photo, $45.00.
Nyal, Antacid Tablets D-431, ¼ x 1½ x 2", V1p128-5, $15.00.
Nyal, Aspirin, ¼ x 1¼ x 1¾", V1p128-6, $18.00.
Nyal, Aspirin 36 D-274, ¼ x 1¾ x 3⅞", V1p128-8, $15.00.
Nyal, Aspirin D-229, ¼ x 1¼ x 1¾", V1p128-7, $12.00.
Nyal, Aspirin D-230, ⅜ x 1¾ x 2½", V2p85-3, $18.00.
Nyal, Carbolic Salve RD-14, 1 x 2⅜", V2p85-5, $10.00.
Nyal, Cascara Compound, 1 x 1¾", V1p128-9, $22.00.
Nyal, Figsen, ½ x 2 x 4", V1p129-2, $12.00.
Nyal, Hinkle Tablets D-155, 1 x 1½", V2p85-6, $18.00.
Nyal, Hinkle Tablets D-155, 1 x 1½", V2p85-8, $20.00.
Nyal, Itch Ointment, ⅞ x 2⅜", V1p129-5, $10.00.
Nyal, Laxaco Tablets D-248, ⅜ x 1½ x 2⅜", V2p85-7, $15.00.
Nyal, Laxacold D-248, ⅜ x 1⅝ x 2⅜", V1p129-6, $10.00.
Nyal, Lullit, ¼ x 1¼ x 1¾", no photo, $10.00.
Nyal, Manacea Laxative D-10, ⅜ x 1¼ x 1¾", V1p129-7, $10.00.
Nyal, Nyaloids Cough, ⅜ x 1½ x 2⅞", V2p171-1, $15.00.
Nyal, Nyaloids Throat D-152, ⅜ x 1½ x 2½", V2p171-3, $15.00.
Nyal, Nyderma Ointment, ⅞ x 2⅜", V1p129-8, $10.00.
Nyal, Tansy Pennyroyal Cottonroot, ¾ x 2⅛ x 3½", V2p85-2, $65.00.
Nyal $.10, Figsen Laxative D-49, ⅜ x 1¼ x 1¾", V1p129-3, $15.00.
Nyal $.25, Chocolax, ¼ x 1¾ x3¼", V1p128-10, $12.00.
Nyal $.25, Eye Salve, ¾ x 1⅜", V1p128-12, $18.00.
Nyal $.25, Figsen Laxative, ½ x 1⅞ x 2½", V1p129-1, $20.00.
Nyal $.25, see Laxaco Capsules D-247, V1p115-12, $12.00.
Nyal $.50, Cold Capsules, ⅜ x 1⅞ x 2¾", V1p128-11, $12.00.
Nyal $.50, Kidney Pills, ⅞ x 2¼", V2p85-4, $15.00.
Nyal $.50, Pilo Ointment, ⅞ x 2⅜", V1p129-9, $12.00.
Nyal A-51, Dandruff Shampoo, 1 x 2¼ x 3⅛", V2p34-3, $35.00.
Nyal's $.10, Headache Tablets, ¼ x 1⅛ x 1⅝", V1p129-4, $22.00.
Nyal's $.25, Eye Salve, ⅝ x 1¾", V2p86-1, $25.00.
Nylotis, Face Powder, no photo, $20.00.
Nymfaun, Finish Cream, no photo, $15.00.
O Cedar sample, Wax, ⅝ x 1½", V1p343-7, $35.00.
O-D $.25, Laxative Pills, ¼ x 1¼ x 1¾", V1p129-10, $20.00.
O-Hi-O, Salve, 1½ rd., no photo, $15.00.
O-Zo-Nol sample, Antiseptic Salve, ¼ x ⅞", V2p86-3, $18.00.
O.K., Hair Dressing, ¾ x 2½", V1p38-2, $12.00.
Oak Hill, Nutmeg, 1½ x 4½", V2p155-7, $60.00.
Oakley's sample, Talcum Powder, ⅞ x 1⅛ x 2⅛", V1p260-10, $90.00.
Oasis, Type Ribbon, ¾ x 2½", no photo, $18.00.
Oatey No. 5, Soldering Paste, ½ x 1½", no photo, $4.00.
Ocean Spray (bank), Cranberry Sauce, 2⅜ x 2⅝", V2p126-1, $40.00.
Odorono sample, Deodorant Powder, ¾ x 1⅛ x 1⅞", V2p202-4, $30.00.
Office Outfitters, Type Ribbon, ¾ x 2½ x 2½", no photo, $6.00.
Ohashi Co., Type Ribbon, ¾ x 2¼ x 2¼", no photo, $15.00.
Ohashi Standard, Type Ribbon, ¾ x 2½ x 2½", no photo, $15.00.
Oil-Eze Arnica, Salve, ⅞ x 2¾", V1p129-11, $20.00.
Oil-Glow, Shoe Polish (tan), 1 x 3", V1p280-8, $12.00.
Ointol, Pile Dressing, 1 x 2⅜", V1p129-12, $18.00.
Oka-San, Breath Perfume, ¾ x 1½", V1p289-2, $40.00.
Okade, Turmeric, 1⅛ x 2⅛ x 3⅛", V2p156-1, $35.00.
Old Colony, Type Ribbon, ¾ x 2½ x 2½", V1p316-12, $12.00.
Old Doc Turner's sample, Inflammacine, ¼ x 1⅝", no photo, $20.00.
Old Dutch, Type Ribbon, ¾ x 2", V1p316-9, $8.00.
Old Dutch Line, Type Ribbon, ¾ x 2½ x 2½", V1p316-10, $20.00.
Old Dutch Line, Type Ribbon, ¾ x 2½ x 2½", V2p185-2, $25.00.
Old Dutch Line, Type Ribbon, ¾ x 2¼ x 2¼", no photo, $15.00.
Old Dutch Line W&W, Type Ribbon, ¾ x 2½ x 2½", V1p316-11, $25.00.
Old Dutch Super Qual., Type Ribbon, ¾ x 2¼", V1p317-1, $10.00.
Old English, Type Ribbon, ¾ x 2½", V2p185-4, $15.00.
Old Fire Side sample, Tea, ⅝ x 1½ x 2¼", V1p268-1, $75.00.
Old Hickory, Type Ribbon, ⅞ x 2½ x 2½", V1p317-2, $18.00.
Old Hickory Brand, Type Ribbon, ¾ x 2½ x 2½", V1p317-3, $100.00.
Old Hi's, Line Cleaner & Dres., ⅜ x 1¼", V1p176-12, $10.00.
Old Indian sample, Java Moca, no photo, $125.00.
Old Judge sample, Coffee, 2⅜ x 4", V1p234-5, $125.00.
Old King Cole, Crayon Case #93, ⅜ x 3¾ x 6¼", V1p182-1, $35.00.
Old Mariner sample, Smooth Tabacco, 1½ x 2¼ x 1¾", V2p211-6, $25.00.
Old Reliable, Liver Regulators, 1½ x 2⅛ x 3", V1p130-1, $40.00.
Old Reliable, Type Ribbon, ¾ x 2½ x 2½", V1p317-4, $30.00.
Old Reliable (Ft.Pitt), Type Ribbon, ¾ x 2½ x 2½", V1p317-5, $22.00.
Old Reliable 12oz., Peanut Butter, 3 x 3", $70.00.
Old Sauls, Pile Ointment, ⅞ x 1⅜", no photo, $45.00.
Old Town, Type Ribbon, 1¾ x 2½", V2p185-6, $15.00.
Old Town, Type Ribbon, ⅞ x 2½ x 2½", V1p317-6, $20.00.
Old Town, Type Ribbon, ⅞ x 2½ x 2½", V1p317-7, $15.00.
Old Town Dawn, Type Ribbon, ¾ x 2½ x 2½", V1p317-8, $18.00.
Old Town Hermetic, Type Ribbon, 1 x 2⅝", V1p317-9, $12.00.

Old Town Typal, Type Ribbon, ¾ x 2½ x 2½", no photo, $12.00.
Old Woman, unknown, 3 x 5", V2p211–2, $120.00.
Olivenharz $.25, Pomade, 1⅜ x 2¾", V1p38–3, $12.00.
Oliver, Type Ribbon, 1⅝ x 1⅝ x 2", V1p317–11, $30.00.
Oliver, Type Ribbon, ¾ x 2¼ x 2¼", V1p317–10, $30.00.
Oliver, Type Ribbon, ¾ x 2¼ x 2¼", V2p186–1, $20.00.
Oliver, Type Ribbon, ¾ x 2¼ x 2¼", V2p186–3, $12.00.
Oltyco Brand, Type Ribbon, ¾ x 2¼ x 2¼", no photo, $15.00.
Oman, Auto Fuses, ¼ x 1¼ x 1¾", V1p9–10, $12.00.
Omega Chemical Co, see Cadum Ointment, ¼ x 1¼", V1p81–3, $20.00.
Omin, Tonic Tablets, ¾ x 2⅛", V1p130–2, $25.00.
Omin Gland Product, Tablets, ¾ x 2⅜", V1p130–3, $25.00.
On the Square, Tool, no photo, $30.00.
O'Neill's $.25, Vegetable Remedy, ⅜ x 1¼ x 1¾", V1p130–4, $25.00.
O'Neils sample, Vegetable Remedy, ⅜ x 1½ x 1⅞", V2p86–5, $20.00.
On's Corega, Denture Powder, ¾ x 1¼ x 2¼", V1p59–8, $40.00.
Onyx, Type Ribbon, ¾ x 2½ x 2½", no photo, $12.00.
Opal, Red Pepper, 3¼ x 2¼ x 1¼", V2p156–3, $25.00.
Opera, Pencil Box, ⅞ x 1½ x 6½", no photo, $8.00.
Opera Stars $.10, Throat Lozenges, ¼ x 1¾ x 2¾", V2p171–5, $75.00.
Opler Brothers sample, Cocoa, 1⅜ x 2¼ x 3¼", V1p222–2, $80.00.
Optimus, Condom, ¼ x 1⅝ x 2⅛", V1p24–3, $80.00.
Orangeine 12, Tablets, ⅜ x 1¼ x 1¾", V2p86–6, $15.00.
Ordway's $.25, Pi-Le-O, ¾ x 1¾", V1p130–5, $80.00.
Ordway's $.25, Pi-Le-O, ¾ x 1¾", V1p130–6, $90.00.
Oriental, Condom, ⅜ x 1¼ x 1¾", no photo, $150.00.
Oriental (Leigh) sample, Sandal Face Powder, ½ x 1⅛ x 1⅛", V1p253–4, $25.00.
Oriole, Type Ribbon, 1⅝ x 1⅝ x 2", no photo, $25.00.
Orissa, Condom, ¼ x 1¾ x 2⅝", V2p19–5, $190.00.
Orium sample, ⅜ x 1⅜", no photo, $8.00.
Orlis, Throat Lozenges, ½ x 2½ x 3¼", V2p171–7, $5.00.
Ormont's sample, Camphor Ice, ¼ x 1¾ x 2", V2p86–2, $15.00.
Orr, Brown & Price, Carbolic Salve, 1 x 2⅞", no photo, $18.00.
Ortal, Sodium, ¼ x 1¼ x 1¾", V1p130–7, $15.00.
Osage, Pills, no photo, $70.00.
Osgood, Tooth Powder, no photo, $60.00.
Otab, Minnow Servival, ¾ x 1¼", V1p177–1, $5.00.
Otto, Cold Cream, ¾ x 1¾", V2p29–4, $12.00.
Our Own, Corn Salve, ⅜ x 1", no photo, $15.00.
Outdoor Girl sample, Eye Show, ¼ x ⅞", no photo, $20.00.
Outdoor Girl sample, Face Powder, ¼ x 1⅝", V1p253–6, $18.00.
Outdoor Girl sample, Face Powder, ¼ x 1⅝", V1p253–5, $22.00.
Ovaltine sample, Food Drink, 2 x 2", V2p126–3, $45.00.
Ovalyn Bullets, Piles, 1 x 2¼ x 3", no photo, $45.00.
Ovelmo, Blood Purifier, ⅜ x 1⅝ x 2½", V2p86–4, $20.00.
Ovelmo, Cream, ⅜ x 1⅛", V1p31–1, $6.00.
Ovelmo, Digestive Tablets, ⅜ x 1⅝ x 2½", no photo, $20.00.
Ovelmo, Skin Balm Cream, 1 x 2⅜", V2p29–6, $15.00.
Ovelmo, Skin Cream, ⅞ x 2⅜", no photo, $6.00.
Ovelmo sample, Skin Balm Cream, ¼ x 1⅛", V2p30–1, $15.00.
Overland, Mainsprings, ⅝ x 2¾ x 5⅛", V2p194–4, $125.00.
Overton High-Brown, Hair Dressing, 1 x 2½ x 2½", V1p38–4, $30.00.
Owl, Throat Pastilles, ½ x 2¾ x 3⅝", no photo, $30.00.
Owl Brand, Spice (paprika), 1⅝ x 3½", V1p189–2, $30.00.
Owl Drug $.25, Purletts Laxative, ¾ x 2¼ x 2¼", V2p86–7, $15.00.
Owl Drug $.50, Scott Vegetable Tablets, ½ x 1⅝ x 2½", V2p87–1, $40.00.
Owl Drug Co., see Capt. John Orderleys.
Owl Drug Co., Medicine, ½ x 1⅝", V2p87–4, $8.00.
Owl Drug Co., Seidlitz Powder, 1½ x 2 x 3", V2p87–6, $35.00.
Owls (Improved), Condom, ¼ x 1¾ x 2⅝", V2p19–2, $65.00.
Owzthat, Game, ½ x 1 x 1¼", V1p174–11, $25.00.

Oxien Nazone $.25, Salve, ⅝ x 1¾", V1p130–8, $65.00.
Oxien Nazone $.35, Salve, ⅝ x 1¾", V1p130–9, $55.00.
Oxiphen, Laxative, ¼ x 1¼ x 1½", V1p130–10, $10.00.
Oxo, Bouillon Cubes, ¾ x 1 x 2¾", V1p20–2, $6.00.
Oxweld, Lighter Renewal, ¼ x 1 x 1¼", V1p198–4, $8.00.
Ozalid, Type Ribbon, ¾ x 2½ x 2½", V1p317–12, $18.00.
Ozark, Healing Plaster, ¾ x 1½", no photo, $30.00.
Ozone Co., Violin Rosin #16, 1¼ x 1½", V1p181–5, $35.00.
P-Kay Dental Plate, Cleaner sample, ¾ x 1¼ x 2", V2p42–6, $60.00.
P.C.W sample, Cough Drops, 1¾ x 1¾ x 2¼", V1p293–11, $90.00.
P.C.W. sample, Cough Drops, 1⅞ x 1⅞ x 2¼", V1p293–10, $90.00.
P.D.C., Dypepsia Cure, no photo, $40.00.
P.S., Auto Wax, ¾ x 2½", V1p343–8, $25.00.
Pa-pay-ans Bell sample, Indigestion, ¼ x 1⅜ x 2⅝", V1p130–11, $12.00.
PAAC, Tablets, ¼ x 1¼ x 2", V1p130–12, $10.00.
Packard's, Shoe Polish, ¾ x 2⅛", V1p280–9, $25.00.
Packard's, Shoe Polish Black, ⅞ x 2⅛", V1p280–10, $25.00.
Packer's, Tar Soap, 1 x 2½ x 3½", V1p284–4, $10.00.
Packer's sample, Tar Soap, ⅝ x 1¾ x 2⅝", V1p284–5, $25.00.
Pagal Balm sample, Ointment, ¼ x ⅞", no photo, $20.00.
Page's sample, Ointment, ⅛ x 1⅛", V2p87–2, $12.00.
Page's sample, Pile Ointment, ¼ x 1⅛", V1p131–1, $15.00.
Page's sample, Ready Relief Ointment, ¼ x ⅞", V1p131–2, $35.00.
Page's sample, Ready Relief Ointment, ¼ x ⅞", V2p87–3, $40.00.
Paislay's sample, Lavender Styptic Powder, ¾ x 1¼ x 2", V2p202–2, $25.00.
Palladium, Needles, no photo, $45.00.
Palmer Garland Violets sample, Talcum Powder, ¾ x 1¼ x 2⅛", V1p260–11, $60.00.
Palmer Sandelwood sample, Talcum Powder, ½ x 1¾ x 2⅛, no photo, $70.00.
Palmer's, Bleaching Cream, ½ x 1¾", V1p31–2, $10.00.
Palmer's, Ointment Skin, ½ x 1¾", V1p52–4, $8.00.
Palmer's, Skin Success, ½ x 2", V1p52–3, $5.00.
Palmer's, Skin Success, ⅝ x 1¾", V1p31–3, $10.00.
Palmer's $.35, Hair Success, 1¾ x 2¼ x 2⅜", V1p38–6, $25.00.
Palmer's .50 Oz., Skin Success Oint., ½ x 1¾", no photo, $6.00.
Palmer's Mentholyce, Menthol Salve, ½ x 1⅜", V1p131–3, $15.00.
Palmer's sample, Gardenglo Face Powder, ¼ x 1⅝", V2p25–3, $18.00.
Palmer's sample, Hair Success Dressing, ⅝ x 1⅝", V1p38–5, $30.00.
Palmer's sample, Skin Success Ointment, ¼ x ⅞", no photo, $25.00.
Palmer's sample, Skin Success Ointment, ¼ x ⅞", V2p25–5, $25.00.
Palmolive sample, Talcum (After Shave), ⅞ x 1½ x 3⅜", V1p260–12, $25.00.
Panama, Type Ribbon, ¾ x 2½", no photo, $15.00.
Panama, Type Ribbon, ¾ x 2¼ x 2¼", V1p318–3, $18.00.
Panama Bronze, Type Ribbon, ¾ x 2½ x 2½", V1p318–4, $18.00.
Panama Bronze, Type Ribbon, ¾ x 2½ x 2½", V1p318–5, $20.00.
Panama Commercial, Type Ribbon, ¾ x 2½ x 2½", V1p318–6, $15.00.
Panama Ink Control, Type Ribbon, ¾ x 2½ x 2½", V1p318–7, $18.00.
Panama Lustra, Type Ribbon, ¾ x 2½ x 2½", V1p318–8, $12.00.
Panama Popular, Type Ribbon, ¾ x 2½ x 2½", V1p318–2, $15.00.
Panama Standard, Type Ribbon, ¾ x 2½ x 2½", V1p318–1, $12.00.
Pancrobilin, Tablets, V1p131–4, $20.00.
Panodynes, Aspirin 12, ¼ x 1 x 2⅞", V1p131–5, $8.00.
Papa Bros., Polish Shoe Russet, ¾ x 1¾", V1p280–11, $30.00.
Papa Brothers, Polish Shoe, ⅝ x 1¾", no photo, $20.00.
Pape's, Diapepsin 14, ⅜ x 1⅜ x 3", V1p131–6, $8.00.

Papsomax sample, Medicinal Powder, 1½ x 1½ x 2¼", V1p248–12, $18.00.

Paquette, Type Ribbon, ¾ x 2½", V1p318–9, $5.00.

Paquin, Hand Cream, no photo, $20.00.

Para-Flux $.50, Tire Repair Kit, 1½ x 2½ x 3½", V1p14–12, $25.00.

Paradise Brand, Pepper, 3¼ x 2¼ x 1¼", V2p156–6, $25.00.

Paragon, Type Ribbon, 1¾ x 1¾ x 2", V2p186–5, $50.00.

Paragon, Zinc Oxide Adhesive, 1 x 1¼", V2p197–1, $25.00.

Paragon Remington, Type Ribbon, ½ x 1½ x 3½", V1p321–9, $125.00.

Paragon\Remington, Type Ribbon, no photo, $22.00.

Paragum Darner, Mending Paste, 2 x 4⅜", V1p186–4, $35.00.

Paramount, Auto Fuses, ¼ x 1¼ x 1¾", V1p9–11, $18.00.

Paramount, Type Ribbon, ¾ x 2½", V2p186–7, $15.00.

Paramount, Type Ribbon, ¾ x 2½ x 2½", no photo, $15.00.

Paramount Deluxe, Condom, no photo, $60.00.

Paramount sample, Cleansing Cream, ⅜ x 1½", V2p30–3, $12.00.

Paratroop, Boot Polish, 1 x 3", V1p280–12, $18.00.

Parisian Beauty sample, Face Powder, ⅛ x 1½", V2p25–2, $25.00.

Park Laboratory, see Grandma's Absorbo, V1p104.

Park Newport, Allspice, 1¾ x 4", V2p156–2, $45.00.

Parke L.H. sample, Coffee, 2 x 2 x 2½", V1p234–6, $95.00.

Parke, Davis & Co., Euthymol Tablets, ½ x 2¼", V2p168–4, $15.00.

Parke, Davis Co., Adhesive Plaster, ¾ x 1⅞", no photo, $8.00.

Parke, Davis Co., Amyl Nitrite, ½ x 2 x 3¾", V1p131–7, $18.00.

Parke, Davis Co., Amyl Nitrite, ½ x 2 x 4", V1p131–8, $5.00.

Parke, Davis Co., see Hypodermic Samples, V1p110–9, $100.00.

Parke, Davis Co., see Kapseals Digifortis, V1p113–7, $15.00.

Parke, Davis Co., Ortal Sodium, ¼ x 1¼ x 1¾", V1p131–9, $6.00.

Parke, Davis Co., Pepsinum Purum, 1 x 1¾ x 2½", V2p87–5, $90.00.

Parke, Davis Co., Pharmaceuticals, 1¼ x 1¾ x 2⅜", V1p131–11, $55.00.

Parke, Davis Co., Pharmaceuticals, 1¾ x 2⅜ x 1⅞", no photo, $55.00.

Parke, Davis Co., Sal-Ethyl Tablets, V1p148–8, $15.00.

Parke, Davis Co., see Taka-Diastase, ¼ x 1¼ x 2⅛", V2p87–7, $12.00.

Parke, Davis Co., Taka-Diastase sample, V1p157–11, $20.00.

Parke, Davis Co. sample, see Euthymol Powder, 1 x 2½", V1p266–8, $55.00.

Parke, Davis Co.sample, Thyroid Gland Emplets, ¼ x 1¼ x 1¾", V1p131–10, $15.00.

Parke, Davis sample, Euthymol Talcum Powder, ⅝ x ⅞ x 2", V2p129–4, $30.00.

Parker's $.25, Hair Dressing, 1 x 3⅝", V1p38–7, $20.00.

Parker's S., Kidney Pills, 3¼" tall, no photo, $30.00.

Parker's sample, Hair Dressing, ¼ x 1⅛", V2p35–6, $35.00.

Parke's sample, Dry Roast Coffee, 1 x 2 x 2⅜", V1p235–1, $70.00.

Parkinson, Blood\Stomach Pills, ½ x ¾", V1p77–9, $55.00.

Parmelee Pills, Laxative, ⅝ x 2⅛", V1p131–12, $35.00.

Parrot Loud 200, Gramophone Needles, ¼ x 1¼ x 1¾", V1p209–7, $45.00.

Parrot Loud 200, Gramophone Needles, ¼ x 1¼ x 1¾", V1p209–8, $40.00.

Parrot Loud 200, Gramophone Needles, ¼ x 1¼ x 1¾", V1p209–9, $40.00.

Parson's Alex, Petroleum Jelly, ⅝ x 2⅛", V1p132–1, $22.00.

Partola $.15, Laxative Candy Mint, ½ x 1 x 1¾", no photo, $10.00.

Partola $.50, Laxative Candy, ¾ x 2⅛ x 2¾", V1p132–2, $15.00.

Partola $1.00, Laxative Blood Purifier, 1⅜ x 2⅛ x 3½", no photo, $15.00.

Partola sample, Mint Candy Laxative, ¼ x ⅞ x 1⅜", V1p132–3, $18.00.

Pasta Superior sample, Shoe Polish #2, ⅝ x 1¾", V2p120–2, $20.00.

Patent Superior, Condom, no photo, $55.00.

Pathe, Needles, ¼ x 1¼ x 1¾", no photo, $40.00.

Patton's, Sun Proof Paint, 1 x 1" w/handle, no photo, $70.00.

Patton's, Sun Proof Paints, 1⅝ x 2¼ x 2", V2p211–4, $30.00.

Paul A.Co. Resiliant, Watch Mainspring, ¾ x 2¾ x 5", V1p339–2, $35.00.

Paulette's $2.00, Tablets, 1 x 1⅝ x 2¾", V1p132–4, $20.00.

Paulson, Jewelers Prod., ⅝ x 1¾", V1p339–3, $8.00*.

Paulson, Jewelers Prod., ½ x 1⅞", V1p339–5, $4.00.

Paulson, Jewelers Prod., ⅜ x 1⅛", V1p339–4, $5.00.

Payson's, Ink Indeliable, 1 x 2⅜", no photo, $10.00.

Pazo, Pile Ointment, ¾ x 2", V1p132–5, $8.00.

Pe-ru-na $.50, Tablets, ¾ x 2¼ x 3⅝", V1p132–6, $12.00.

Peaches Double Test, Condom, ¼ x 1½ x 2", no photo, $90.00.

Peaches Improved, Condom, ¼ x 1½ x 2", no photo, $95.00.

Peacock Silk, Type Ribbon, ¾ x 2½ x 2½", no photo, $12.00.

Peacock Soft Tone, Needles 200, no photo, $35.00.

Peacocks, Air Tested Condom, ¼ x 1⅝ x 2⅛", V2p19–4, $70.00.

Pearl Brand, Type Ribbon, ¾ x 2½ x 2½", no photo, $15.00.

Pearson's, Snuff Red Top, 1⅜ x 2⅛", V1p191–11, $40.00.

Peaslee-Gaulbery-Corp., Aspirin, ¼ x 1¼ x 1¾", V2p888–1, $8.00.

Peau-Doux sample, Styptic Powder, no photo, $40.00.

Pebeco, Tooth Powder sample, no photo, $70.00.

Pecards, Shoe Dressing, 1½ x 3½", no photo, $8.00.

Peck's, Valve Insiders, ¼ x 1 x 1½", V1p17–5, $10.00.

Peck's, Valve Insiders, ¼ x 1 x 1½", V1p17–6, $10.00.

Pedacura, Pliable Plaster, no photo, $22.00.

Peerless, Tooth Powder sample, no photo, $45.00.

Peerless, Type Ribbon, 1½ x 1½ x 2", no photo, $25.00.

Peerless, Watch Main Spring, ¾ x 2½ x 2½", V1p339–6, $65.00.

Peerless #0, Ink Pad, ½ x 2¼ x 3¾", V2p200–6, $8.00.

Peerless Chips, Gum, ¾ x 1⅜", V1p298–3, $30.00.

Peerless sample, Piles Panacea, ⅜ x 1⅜", no photo, $10.00.

Pegasus, Needles, ⅜ x 1¼ x 1¾", V1p209–10, $30.00.

Pegasus BB Zukunft, Needles, no photo, $35.00.

Pegasus Sichel, Needles, no photo, $30.00.

Penetro, Cold Capsules, ¼ x 1½ x 2", V1p132–7, $10.00.

Penetro (Plough), Cold Capsules, ¼ x 1½ x 1¼", V1p132–8, $12.00.

Penetro sample, Salve, ⅜ x 1¼", V2p88–3, $15.00.

Penetro sample, Salve Cold, ⅜ x 1⅜", V1p132–9, $18.00.

Pennant Brand, Type Ribbon, ¾ x 2½", no photo, $12.00.

Pennant sample, Syrup, 1¾ x 2⅜", V1p245–7, $75.00.

Pennsylvania Heeren Bros., Watch Main Spring, ⅝ x 2¾ x 5⅛", V1p339–7, $40.00.

Penrose, Type Ribbon, ¾ x 2½ x 2½", no photo, $12.00.

Penslar, Aspirin, ¼ x 1¼ x 1¾", V1p132–10, $12.00.

Penslar, Corn Salve, ¾ x 1½", V2p88–5, $18.00.

Penslar, Laxative Cold Breakers, ⅜ x 1¾ x 2⅝", V1p132–11, $12.00.

Penslar, Throat Dragees, ⅜ x 2¾ x 3½", V1p293–12, $18.00.

Penslar, Witch Hazel Salve, no photo, $20.00.

Penslar $.10, Pen-Lax-Tablets, ⅜ x 1¼ x 1¾", V2p88–6, $8.00.

Penslar $.10, Regulax, ½ x 1½ x 2½", V1p132–12, $15.00.

Penslar $.25, Laxative, ½ x 1½ x 2½", V1p133–1, $15.00.

Penslar $.25, Laxative Cold Breaker, ½ x 1⅝ x 2½", V1p133–2, $18.00.

Peoples, Aspirin, ¼ x 1¼ x 1¾", V2p88–2, $8.00.

Peoples, Saccharin, ¼ x 1¼ x 1½", V2p211–7, $12.00.

Peppets $.30, Family Laxative 24, ⅜ x 1½ x 2½", V1p133–3, $8.00.

Peppets .25, Laxative, ½ x 1¾ x 3¼", V2p88–4, $10.00.

Peppets 8, Laxative, ¼ x 1¼ x 1¾", V1p133–4, $8.00.

Peps, Cough Pastille, ⅝ x 1¾ x 3½", V1p294–1, $18.00.

Pepsikola, Digestant Tablets, ⅝ x 2⅞ x 4", no photo, $25.00.

Pepsodent, Tooth Powder 23gms., ⅞ x 1⅝ 3¼", V2p42–8, $18.00.

Peptenzyme, Medicine, ½ x 1⅜ x 1⅞", no photo, $18.00.

Per A Lga, Tablets 12, ¼ x 1¼ x 1½", V1p133–5, $10.00.

Percival, Watch Main Spring, ¾ x 3 x 3⅜", V1p339–8, $40.00.
Perfect, Allspice, 3¼ x 2¼ x 1¼", V2p156–4, $55.00.
Perfect, Mustard Plaster, no photo, $20.00.
Perfect Matched Line, Type Ribbon, ¾ x 2½", no photo, $25.00.
Perfection, Condom, ¼ x 1½ x 2⅛", V2p19–6, $55.00.
Perfection, Needles, no photo, $30.00.
Perfection, Tire Repair Kit, ½ x 4 x 2½", V2p15–5, $70.00.
Perfection, Tire Repair Kit, ⅝ x 2⅜ x 3¾", V1p15–1, $80.00.
Perfection $.50, Tire Repair Kit, ⅝ x 2¼ x 3¾", V1p15–2, $70.00.
Perfekto 100, Needles, ⅜ x 1¼ x 1½", V1p209–11, $30.00.
Perkins, Onor-Maid Carbolic Salve, ⅞ x 2¾", V2p88–6, $35.00.
Perkins Dorothy, Face Powder, ¼ x 1½", V1p253–7, $10.00.
Perkins Dorothy sample, Face Powder, ¼ x 1½", V1p253–8, $10.00.
Perlmed sample, Health Drink, no photo, $25.00.
Perm-o-Rite, Type Ribbon, ¾ x 2½", V1p318–11, $10.00.
Perm-O-Rite, Type Ribbon, ¾ x 2½ x 2½", V1p318–10, $20.00.
Perm-o-Rite, Type Ribbon, ¾ x 2¼", no photo, $8.00.
Perma Grip sample, Dental Powder, ¾ x 1⅜ x 2¼", V1p58–8, $30.00.
Perophone, Needles (phono), ½ x 1¼ x 1½", V1p209–12, $35.00.
Perrigo's, Adhesive Plaster, 1⅛ x 1⅛", V1p347–6, $20.00.
Perrigo's, Adhesive Plaster, 1⅛ x 1⅛", V2p197–4, $15.00.
Perry & Co. sample, Pens, ¼ x 1¼ x 1½", V1p183–7, $60.00.
Persian, Perfume & Charm, ⅛ x 1⅛ x 1⅛", V1p183–9, $30.00.
Persian, Perfume\Charm, ¼ x 1⅛ x 1⅛", V1p183–10, $40.00.
Peruvian Remedy, Elixir Pills, no photo, $60.00.
Peruvian Remedy, Vegetable Liver Pills, no photo, $40.00.
Peter Pan, Type Ribbon, ¾ x 2½ x 2½", V1p318–12, $40.00.
Peter Pan sample, Peanut Butter, 1¾ x 2¼", V1p245–8, $115.00.
Peter Paul's $.10, Cream Mints, 1¾ x 2½ x 3", V1p289–3, $20.00.
Peter Rabbit, Candy Pail, 2½ x 4½ x 2⅜, 200.00.
Peterman's, Moth Food, 1⅜ x 2¼ x 3½", V1p198–5, $20.00.
Peter's, Vegetable Pills, no photo, $30.00.
Peter's #1½, Primers, ½ x 1¼", V1p66–2, $60.00.
Peter's No.2, Primers 250, ⅞ x 1½", V1p66–3, $55.00.
Peterson's $.60, Ointment, ¾ x 1⅞", V1p133–6, $15.00.
Peterson's $.75, Ointment, ¾ x 2⅝", V2p89–1, $10.00.
Peterson's &.35, Ointment, ⅝ x 1⅞", V1p133–7, $8.00*.
Peterson's sample, Ointment, ¼ x 1", V1p133–8, $30.00.
Peterson's sample, Ointment, ¼ x ⅞", V1p133–9, $30.00.
Peterson's sample, Ointment, ¼ x ⅞", V2p89–4, $35.00.
Petrojel, Petroleum Jelly, ½ x 2¼", V1p133–10, $8.00.
Petry, Retainers, ¾ x 2½ x 2½", V2p43–1, $45.00.
Pettibone P.F., Election Specialists, ½ x 1½ x 2½", no photo, $6.00.
Pettit's, Eye Salve, ¼ x 1⅛", V2p89–6, $8.00.
Pettit's, Pile Salve, ½ x 1⅝", V1p133–11, $15.00.
Pettit's, see Dr. Pettit's, V1p95–7, $18.00.
Peyton Palmer, Pure Spices, 2½ x 2¼ x 1¼", V2p156–5, $15.00.
Pfeiffer Chemical, see Allan's Star Brand Pills.
Pfeiffer Chemical, see Dr. Hobsons Lax Cascara.
Pfeiffer Chemical Co., Haywood's Poison Oak, V1p106–10, $30.00.
Pfeiffer Chemical Co., Hobson's Camphor Ice, V1p109–1, $18.00.
Pfeiffer Mfg., see Quinarets Tablets, V1p138–4, $10.00.
Pfeiffer Mfg., see Rid-A-Pain Tablets, V1p146–8, $20.00.
Pflueger, Fish Hooks, ⅞ x 2", V1p177–2, $3.00.
Pflueger, Sinkers, ¼ x ⅞ x 1¾", V1p177–3, $2.00.
Phelp's $.25, Night Caps, ½ x 1½ x 2½", V2p89–3, $80.00.
Phen-amy-Caps $.25, Capsules, ½ x 1¼ x 1¾", V2p89–5, $15.00.
Pheny O-Caffein, Headache Pills, ¼ x 1¼ x 1¾", V1p133–12, $15.00.
Philco, Type Ribbon, ¾ x 2½ x 2½", V1p319–1, $18.00.
Philco Standard, Type Ribbon, ¾ x 2½", V1p319–2, $8.00.
Phillip's, Milk of Magnesia, ¼ x 2⅜ x 2¾", V1p134–1, $6.00.
Phillip's $.10, Milk of Magnesia, ¼ x 1¾ x 1⅞", V2p89–7, $8.00.
Phillips $.25, Milk of Magnesia, ¼ x 2⅜ x 2¾", V1p134–2, $8.00.
Phillips sample, Cocoa, 1⅛ x 1¾ x 2⅝", V1p222–3, $65.00.
Phillips sample, see Corona Ointment, V1p84–7, $10.00.
Phillip's sample, Corona Ointment, ⅝ x 1½", V1p134–3, $15.00.
Phillips sample, Milk of Magnesia, ¼ x 2⅜ x 2¾", V1p134–4, $12.00.
Philmore, X Loud Crystal, ½ x 1¼", V2p212–1, $15.00.
Phipps', Catarrh Cure, ¼ x 1", no photo, $45.00.
Phoenix, Rubber Adhesive Plaster, 1 x 1¼", V2p197–6, $30.00.
Phoenix, Type Ribbon, 1¾ x 1¾ x 2", no photo, $70.00.
Physician's Beef sample, Peptonoids, ½ x 1⅝ x 2¾", V1p134–5, $75.00.
Pickle's J., Foot Ointment, ½ x 1½", V1p134–6, $8.00.
Picnic sample, Coffee, 3½ x 3", V1p235–2, $90.00.
Pier-Bro, Type Ribbon, ⅞ x 2½ x 2½", V1p319–3, $4.00.
Pierce Co., Canton Ginger, ⅞ x 2½ x 4", V1p189–3, $30.00.
Pierce's, Dr. Pierce's Salve, ¾ x 2½", no photo, $30.00.
Pierce's $1.50, Empress Brand, 1¼ x 2¼ x 1¼", V2p90–1, $45.00.
Pierce's Payngon, Dr. Pierces Tablets, ⅜ x 1½ x 1¾", no photo, $35.00.
Pierce's R.J. $1.50, Empress Pennyroyal Tabs, 1¼ x 2¼ x 1⅜", V1p134–7, $50.00.
Pierce's R.J.$2.00, Empress Brand Tablets, 1 x 1⅝ x 2¾", V1p134–8, $45.00.
Pigeon, Type Ribbon, ¾ x 1¾ x 1¾", no photo, $25.00.
Pigeon, Type Ribbon, ¾ x 1¾ x 1¾", V1p319–6, $30.00.
Pigeon, Type Ribbon, ¾ x 2½ x 2½", no photo, $15.00.
Pigeon, Type Ribbon, ¾ x 2⅛ x 2⅛", V1p319–5, $15.00.
Pigeon Brand, Type Ribbon, ¾ x 1⅝", V2p186–1, $12.00.
Pigeon Brand, Type Ribbon, ¾ x 2 x 2", V2p186–4, $15.00.
Pildoras, Zehenas, ½ x 1", $8.00.
Pildoras, Zehenas, ¾ x 1½", $10.00.
Pilgrim, Aspirin Tablets, ¼ x 1¼ x 1¾", V2p90–3, $15.00.
Pill Alophen, Aspirin, no photo, $12.00.
Pilot, Type Ribbon, ¾ x 2½", V2p186–6, $18.00.
Pilot Brand, Type Ribbon, ¾ x 2½ x 2½", V1p319–8, $55.00.
Pine Tree, Ribbons, ½ x 1⅛ x 1⅝", V2p212–3, $15.00.
Pineoleum $.25, Laxative Tablets, ¼ x 1¼ x 1¾", V2p90–5, $8.00.
Pineule, Pine Salve, ¼ x ⅞", V1p134–9, $8.00.
Pinex $.15, Cold Tablets, ¼ x 1¼ x 1¾", V2p90–6, $16.00*.
Pinex $.25, Laxative, ⅜ x 1¾ x 3¼", V2p90–2, $18.00*.
Pinkham's Lydia, Vegetable Compound, ¾ x 2⅛", V1p134–10, $6.00.
Pinko-Laxin $1.00, Laxative, ⅝ x 2⅛ x 2¾", V2p90–3, $25.00.
Pinnacle, Type Ribbon, 1⅝ x 1⅝ x 2", V2p186–8, $55.00.
Pinnacle, Type Ribbon, ¾ x 2¼", V1p319–9, $12.00.
Pinxav sample, Pink Salve, ⅜ x 1⅜", V1p134–11, $15.00.
Pioneer, Red Pepper, 3¾ x 2½ x 1¾", V2p156–7, $22.00.
Pioneer, Type Ribbon, ¾ x 2½", V1p319–10, $12.00.
Pioneer Brand, Type Ribbon, ¾ x 2¼ x 2¼", V2p187–1, $18.00.
Piper Heidsieck, Chew Tabacco, ⅜ x 2¾ x 2¾", V2p212–5, $10.00.
Pipestiks $.10, Keeps Pipe Lit, ½ x 1½ x 2½", V1p198–6, $18.00.
Piquante Colgate sample, Face Powder, ¼ x 1⅝", V1p253–9, $40.00.
Pirates, Condom, no photo, $150.00.
Pitkin's Old Home, Paprika, 3¾ x 2⅛ x 1¼", V2p157–1, $30.00.
Pixine $.25, Veterinary Ointment, 1 x 2⅜", V1p333–2, $25.00.
Plantation Java, Coffee, 7 x 5 x 5", 195.00.
Planters Nubian Tea $.25, Liver Regulators, 1¾ x 1¾ x 2½", V1p134–12, $65.00.
Playrite, Needles, ½ x 1¼ x 2⅛", V1p210–1, $30.00.
Plenty Copy, Type Ribbon, ¾ x 2½", V1p319–11, $6.00.
Plenty-Copy, Type Ribbon, ¾ x 2½ x 2½", V2p187–3, $8.00.
Plex sample, Catarrh & Cold Salve, ¼ x ⅞", V1p135–1, $20.00.
Plough Inc., Aspeco Pain Tablets, ¼ x 1¼ x 1¾", V1p72–2, $12.00.
Plough Inc., Black & White Ointment, ½ x 1¾", V1p76–1, $8.00.
Plough Inc., see Penetro, V1p132, $8.00.
Plough Inc., see St. Joseph Aspirin, V1p154.
Plough Inc., Black & White Salve, ¼ x 1⅝", V1p135–2, $8.00.

Plough Mexican $.10, Powder, 1¼ x 2⅜", V2p90–7, $18.00.

Ploughs, Black & White, ⅝ x 1¾", V1p31–4, $6.00.

Plough's, Black & White Hair Dressing, 2⅛ x 2⅛ x 1½", no photo, $10.00.

Plough's sample, Mon Secret, ⅜ x 1⅝", V1p52–5, $15.00.

Ply Para Patch, Tire Repair Kit, 1½ x 2½ x 3½", V1p15–3, $35.00.

Po-Do sample, Styptic Powder, ¾ x 1¼ x 2⅛", V1p255–10, $40.00.

Po-Do sample, Styptic Powder, ¾ x 1¼ x 2⅛", V1p255–9, $35.00.

Police & Fireman's, Corn Salve, ⅜ x 1¼", V1p135–3, $6.00.

Policeman, Piles Cure, no photo, $35.00.

Pollantin, Hay Fever Powder, ⅝ x 1½ x 4", $30.00.

Polly Peachtree, Hair Dressing, 1 x 2 x 2½", V1p38–8, $12.00.

Polly Peachtree, Hair Dressing, 1 x 2 x 2⅜", V1p38–7, $12.00.

Poloris, Tablets 12, ¼ x 1¼ x 1¾", V1p135–4, $6.00.

Poloris $.25, Tablets, ¼ x 1¼ x 1¾", V1p135–5, $8.00.

Poltock, Watch Materials, ½ x 1½", no photo, $4.00.

Poltock, Watch Materials, ⅝ x 1¾", no photo, $4.00.

Polygrapgh, Designs, no photo, $40.00.

Polyshine, Shoe Polish, 1 x 2¾", V1p281–1, $25.00.

Polyshine, Shoe Polish (blk), ⅞ x 2⅝", V1p281–2, $25.00.

Pomatex sample, Hair Cream, ⅜ x 1½", V2p36–1, $6.00.

Pomezio, Cleaner, no photo, $20.00.

Pompeian, Bloom, ¼ x 1⅜", V1p48–5, $12.00.

Pompeian, Day Cream, ⅜ x 1⅜", V2p30–5, $5.00.

Pompeian sample, Day Cream, ½ x ⅞", V1p31–5, $5.00.

Pompeian sample, Night Cream, ½ x ⅞", V1p31–6, $10.00.

Pompeian sample, Talcum Powder, ¾ x 1¼ x 2¾", V1p261–1, $30.00.

Ponca $1.00, Compound Uterine, 1¼ x 1⅝ x 2¼", V2p91–1, $35.00.

Pond's $.10, Digestans Tablets, ⅜ x 1⅝ x 2½", V1p135–8, $18.00.

Pond's $.15, Tablets, ⅜ x 1½ x 2½", V2p91–4, $18.00.

Pond's $.25, Laxative Pills, ¼ x 1⅝ x 2⅛", V1p135–6, $10.00.

Pond's sample, Digestans Tablets, ⅜ x 1⅜ x 2⅛", V1p135–7, $20.00.

Popular, Cough Drops, no photo, $65.00.

Popular, Type Ribbon, ¾ x 2½ x 2½", V1p319–12, $18.00.

Popular Quality, Type Ribbon, ¾ x 2½ x 2½", V1p320–1, $18.00.

Porter-Seal, Block Sealer, 1¼ x 2¼ x 3⅜", V1p198–7, $12.00.

Porter's, Laxative, ⅜ x 1½ x 1⅞", V1p135–12, $18.00.

Porter's, Liniment Salve, 1 x 3½", V1p135–10, $22.00.

Porter's, Liniment Salve, ½ x 1¾", V1p135–11, $25.00.

Porter's $.25, Laxative, ¼ x 1½ x 1⅞", V1p136–1, $12.00.

Porter's $.25, Laxative, ¼ x 1½ x 2", V1p136–2, $15.00.

Porter's $.25, Laxative, ⅜ x 1½ x 1⅞", V2p91–6, $12.00.

Porter's $.25, Pain King Salve, 1⅛ x 3½", V1p135–9, $20.00.

Poslam, Salve, ½ x 1⅞", V1p136–3, $6.00.

Poslam $.10, Salve, ¼ x 1", V2p91–2, $8.00.

Poslam $.50, Salve, ½ x 1⅝", V1p136–4, $8.00.

Poslam $.50, Salve (skin), ½ x 1⅝", V1p136–5, $6.00.

Poslam sample, Ointment, ¼ x 1", V1p136–6, $10.00.

Post F. Co., Ring Box, ½ x 1", V1p180–3, $30.00.

Postal Telegraph, Type Ribbon, 1⅝ x 1⅝ x 2", V1p320–3, $70.00.

Postum sample, Cereal, ¾ x 1⅝ x 1¾", V1p245–9, $45.00.

Postum sample, Cereal, ⅞ x 1¾ x 2⅛", V1p245–10, $65.00.

Potmend, Mend w\Heat, 1¼ x 1⅝", V1p198–8, $12.00.

Potter Drug & Chem., see Cuticura Ointment, V1p85.

Potter's, White Hands, 1½ x 3¾", no photo, $45.00.

Power's sample, Asthma Specific, ½ x 1½ x 3⅛", V1p136–7, $80.00.

Powow sample, Household Cleaner, 2 x 3⅜", V1p22–7, $50.00.

Prang, Crayons, ⅜ x 2¾ x 3¾", V1p182–2, $12.00.

Pratt's, White Diarrhea Rem, 1⅝ x 2½", no photo, $15.00.

Pratt's sample, Healing Powder, no photo, $45.00.

Preferred, Auto Fuses, ¼ x 1¼ x 1¾", V1p9–12, $15.00.

Premier, Allspice, 2¾ x 2¼ x 1¼", V2p157–3, $18.00.

Premier, Mainsprings, no photo, $35.00.

Premier, Tea, 1½ x 2½ x 2⅞", V2p133–7, $30.00.

Premier Brand Smith, Type Ribbon, ¾ x 2¼ x 2¼", V2p187–5, $30.00.

Premier Golden, Snuff, ½ x 1¾ x 2⅜", V2p212–6, $20.00.

Premier Smith, Type Ribbon, 1⅝ x 2 x 1⅝", V1p320–4, $25.00.

Premo, Aspirin, ¼ x 1¼ x 1¾", V1p136–8, $12.00.

Prentils $.25, Aches & Pains, ¼ x 1⅝", V1p136–9, $10.00.

Prentils $.25, Aches & Pains Tabs, ¼ x 1⅝", V1p136–10, $8.00.

Prentils $.25, Pain Relief, ¼ x 1⅝", V2p91–3, $8.00.

Pres-ope, Toilet Soap, ¾ x 3 x 3", V1p284–6, $18.00.

Prescription, Aspirin, ¼ x 1¼ x 1¾", V1p136–11, $12.00.

President, Thumb Tacks, ½ x 1", V1p198–9, $10.00.

President's, Cloves, 1½ x 2¼ x 3¼", no photo, $45.00.

Prestite, Crayons, ⅜ x 2¾ x 3¾", V1p182–3, $18.00.

Presto, Stove Polish, 1 x 3½", V2p38–7, $10.00.

Preventa, Salve, ¼ x ⅞", V2p91–5, $8.00.

Prevento Hole, Sewing, no photo, $18.00.

Price's Spices, Ginger, 3¾ x 2 x 1¼", V2p157–5, $45.00.

Prid Smile, Salve, ¾ x 1⅞", V1p136–12, $8.00.

Prid Smile, Salve, ¾ x 1⅞", V2p91–7, $10.00.

Princess, Spice, no photo, $25.00.

Princess $2.00, Pennyroyal Tansy Pills, ⅞ x 1¾ x 2⅞", V1p137–1, $65.00.

Princess Brand, Type Ribbon, ¾ x 2½", V1p320–5, $15.00.

Princess Pat, Almond Base Face Powder, ⅜ x 1½ x 2", no photo, $12.00.

Princess Pat, Compact, ½ x 1½", V1p52–6, $20.00.

Princess Pat, Eye Shadow, ¼ x 1¼", V1p52–7, $15.00.

Princess Pat, Light Lips\Cheeks, ¼ x 1⅛", $10.00.

Princess Pat, Lip Rouge, ¼ x 1⅛", V2p26–8, $10.00.

Princess Pat, Lip\Cheek, ¼ x 1¼", V2p34–2, $15.00.

Princess Pat, Powder Face, ⅜ x 2⅝", V1p45–7, $12.00.

Princess Pat, Rouge, ¼ x 1⅛", V1p48–6, $10.00.

Princess Pat, Rouge, ¼ x 1⅝", V1p48–7, $10.00.

Princess Pat sample, Face Powder, ¼ x 1⅝", V1p253–10, $10.00.

Princess Pat sample, Lips & Cheeks, ¼ x ⅞", V1p52–8, $8.00.

Princess Pat sample, Powder, Face, ¼ x 1½", V1p253–11, $12.00.

Princess sample, Talcum Powder, no photo, $65.00.

Printz & French, Pure Spices, 1¼ x 3⅝", V2p157–2, $20.00.

Priory Brand, Rubber Adhesive Plaster, 1¼ x 2", V1p347–8, $12.00.

Priscilla, Stamping Paste, ¾ x 3⅛", V2p212–2, $15.00.

Prize Medal, Ginger, 4¼ x 2¼ x 1¼", V2p157–4, $18.00.

Pro-co-Pax $.10, Laxative Cold Tablets, ¼ x 1¼ x 1¾", no photo, $8.00.

Prof. Dykes $.25, Hair & Beard Elixer, ½ x 1½ x 2½", V2p36–3, $35.00.

Prof. Warnesson J., Electric Lip Rogue, ½ x 1⅛", V1p48–8, $15.00.

Prof. Warnesson's, Theatre Rouge, ¾ x 2¾", V1p48–9, $15.00.

Professor Newton's, Healing Balm, no photo, $35.00.

Professors $.15, Laxative Tablets, ¼ x 1¼ x 2⅛", V2p92–1, $5.00.

Progress Corp., Aspirin, ¼ x 1 x 1¾", V1p137–2, $8.00.

Progress of Dandruff, Hair, no photo, $40.00.

Propert's, Saddle Soap, 1 x 3", V1p281–3, $5.00.

Prostacones sample, Suppositories, ½ x 1 x 1½", V2p92–3, $10.00.

Protects, Condom, ⅝ x 1⅝, no photo, $55.00.

Protonuclein, Prophylactic Viles, V1p142–7, $80.00.

Prototype, Type Ribbon, ¾ x 2½ x 2½", no photo, $15.00.

Protype Phillip's, Type Ribbon, ¾ x 2½ x 2½", V2p187–6, $15.00.

Prunets $.10, Tonic Lax\Liver Pellets, ¼ x ½ x 1½", V2p92–5, $18.00.

Prurito Sample, Salve, ¼ x 1⅜", V1p137–3, $45.00.

Prym 555, Needles (phono), ½ x 1¼ x 1½", V1p210–2, $30.00.

Publix, Emergency Kit, ⅜ x 2¾ x 3¾", V1p137–4, $10.00.

Pugsley's $.35, Utor Ointment, ⅜ x 1½ x 2⅜", V1p137–5, $18.00.

Pulver's $.05, Kola Pepsin Gum, ⅜ x 3 x ⅞", no photo, $175.00.

Pulvule's (Lilly), Amytal Compound, ¼ x 1¼ x 1¾", V1p137–6, $18.00.

Pure Quill, Curry Powder, 3½ x 2¼ x 1¼", V2p157-6, $45.00.
Pure Test, Quinine Pills, ⅝ x 1 x 1⅞", no photo, $10.00.
Pure Test, Zinc Sterate, no photo, $15.00.
Pure-Herb $1.00, Tablets, ½ x 2 x 3⅛", V1p137-7, $45.00.
Purepac 24, Laxative Cold Tabs, ¼ x 1¾ x 2⅝", no photo, $9.00.
Puretest, A.S.A Aspirin, ⅜ x 1¾ x 2½", V2p92-7, $10.00.
Puretest, Aspirin, ¼ x 1¾ x 2⅝", V1p137-8, $8.00.
Puretest, Aspirin, ⅜ x 1¾ x 2½", V2p92-2, $8.00.
Puretest Rexall, Aspirin, ⅜ x 1¾ x 2⅝", V1p137-9, $12.00.
Puretest US 901, Aspirin, ⅜ x 1¾ x 2½", V2p92-4, $12.00.
Purgaret $1.00, Laxative, 1½ x 2⅛ x 3½", V1p137-10, $12.00.
Purila $.25, Tooth Powder, 1¾ x 2⅞ x 1", V2p43-3, $80.00.
Purita, Dental, no photo, $30.00.
Puritan $1.00, Celery Tablets, ½ x 2 x 3", no photo, $65.00.
Puritana, Type Ribbon, ¾ x 2½ x 2½", no photo, $12.00.
Purity Tested, Aspirin, ¼ x 1¼ x 1¾", V1p137-11, $12.00.
Pussy Scat $.25, Powder, ⅞ x 2 x 2⅞", V2p193-2, $80.00.
Putnam's Fisheries, Fish Food, ¾ x 2⅜", V1p198-10, $12.00.
Pyramid, Ointment, ¾ x 2", no photo, $15.00.
Pyramid, Ointment, ¾ x 2", V1p138-1, $15.00.
Pyramid (O'Bryon), Watch Main Spring, ½ x 2¾ x 5⅛", V1p339-9, $45.00.
Pyramid Brand, Type Ribbon, ¾ x 2½", V1p320-6, $20.00.
Pyramid sample, Ointment, ¼ x ⅞", V1p137-12, $35.00.
Pyramid sample, Ointment, ¼ x ⅞", V1p138-2, $35.00.
Pyramid sample, Ointment, ¼ x ⅞", V2p92-6, $35.00.
Quaker, Spice, no photo, $22.00.
Quality, Type Ribbon, ¾ x 2½ x 2½", V1p320-7, $8.00.
Quality, Type Ribbon, ¾ x 2½ x 2½", V1p320-8, $15.00.
Quality (Guertin), Type Ribbon, ½ x 2½ x 2½", V1p320-9, $15.00.
Quayle & Son, Medicine, ½ x 1", V2p92-8, $15.00.
Quayle sample, Salve, ¼ x ⅞", V1p138-3, $12.00.
Queen, Hair Dressing, 1 x 1¾ x 1⅝", V1p38-11, $15.00.
Queen, Hair Dressing, 1 x 2 x 2⅜", V1p38-10, $15.00*.
Queen, Needles, no photo, $45.00.
Queen, Pressing Compound, ⅞ x 3⅜", V1p39-3, $15.00.
Queen, Sarcoptic Mange, ½ x 1½", V1p39-2, $18.00.
Queen, Type Ribbon, ¾ x 2½", V2p187-2, $15.00.
Queen Brand, Type Ribbon, ¾ x 2½ x 2½", V2p187-4, $25.00.
Queen City, Shoe Polish, ¾ x 1¾", V1p281-4, $25.00.
Queen of Hearts, Type Ribbon, ¾ x 2½ x 2½", no photo, $40.00.
Queen of Hearts, Type Ribbon, ¾ x 2½ x 2½", V1p320-11, $75.00.
Queen Ointment $.25, Skin Bleach, ⅝ x 2", V1p52-9, $8.00.
Queen sample, Hair Dressing, ½ x 1¼ x 1¾", no photo, $22.00.
Queen sample, Pine Tar, ½ x 1½", V1p39-1, $20.00.
Quentin's, Breath Mints, no photo, $60.00.
Quest, Deodorant Powder, 1 x 3¼", V1p45-8, $22.00.
Quick Seal, Tire Repair Kit, 1 x 3⅜", V2p16-1, $50.00.
Quick-O sample, Hair Dressing, ⅜ x 1⅛", V1p39-4, $25.00.
Quickway, Socket Set A, 1¼ x 1¼ x 4½", V1p190-6, $25.00.
Quinarets, Analgesic\Laxative, ⅜ x 1¾ x 2⅛", V1p138-4, $10.00.
Quinarets, Laxative, ¼ x 1¾ x 2⅜", V2p93-1, $10.00.
Quinine, Pills, ⅜ x 1¼", V1p138-5, $18.00.
Quinine, Pills, ⅜ x 1¼", V1p138-6, $18.00.
Quinine, Pills, ⅜ x 1⅛ x 1⅝", V2p93-4, $15.00.
Quinine 2 grains, Capsules, ½ x 1⅛ x 1⅝", V1p138-7, $20.00.
Quinine 5 grains, Capsules, ½ x 1⅛ x 1⅝", V1p138-8, $20.00.
Quinn's, Ointment, no photo, $15.00.
Quinn's sample, Rub-in-Hale, ¼ x 1⅛", no photo, $18.00.
Quinolan Powder, Surgical Dressing, 1⅜ x 2¾", V2p93-6, $25.00.
Quinsana sample, Athletes Foot, no photo, $25.00.
Quintaline sample, Ointment, ¼ x 1", V1p138-9, $30.00.
R & R, Aspirin Tablets, ¼ x 1¼ x 1¾", V1p138-10, $15.00.
R & R, Pink Marvel Pills, ⅝ x ⅞ x 2", V1p138-11, $22.00.
R & R $.25, Pink Marvel Pills, ½ x ¾ x 2⅛", V1p138-12, $25.00.
R & S, Crys. Ginger, ⅞ x 2⅝ x 4½", V1p189-4, $30.00.
R 6, Aspirin, ¼ x 1 x 1¼", V1p139-1, $10.00.
R. 96, Condom, no photo, $50.00.
Rabelais, Spice for Pork, 1⅛ x 2¾", no photo, $10.00.
Radiant, Polish, ¾ x 2¼", V1p281-6, $20.00.
Radiator, Menthol Licorice, ½ x 1¼ x 1¾", V2p168-6, $20.00.
Radio Girl sample, Face Powder, ¼ x 1⅝", V1p253-12, $30.00.
Radiol Ointment, Pimples Salve, ⅞ x 2 x 2", V1p139-2, $30.00.
Radium, Condom, no photo, $50.00.
Radway's R R R $.35, Regulators Pills 30, ⅝ x 1 x 2", V1p139-3, $30.00.
Rail-Road 3R, Type Ribbon, 1¾ x 1¾ x 2", V2p187-7, $65.00.
Rainbow, Type Ribbon, ¾ x 2½ x 2½", V1p320-12, $8.00.
Rainbow, Type Ribbon, ¾ x 2½ x 2½", V1p321-1, $8.00.
Rainbow Silkworm, Gut Leader Fishing, 1 x 3⅜", V2p198-6, $60.00.
Ral-U-G, Liniment, ¾ x 2", V2p93-2, $30.00.
Raleigh's sample, Catarrh Pills, ¼ x 1¼", no photo, $15.00.
Raleigh's sample, Shaving Cream, ¼ x 1⅛", V2p135-6, $6.00.
Ralston (Tom Mix), Make-up, ⅜ x 1⅜", V1p52-10, $8.00.
Ralston Robt., Beauty Paste Polish, ¾ x 2⅛", V2p120-4, $15.00.
Ram Lal's sample, Indian Tea, ⅝ x 1¾ x 2⅜", V1p268-2, $35.00.
Ramar, Type Ribbon, ¾ x 2½ x 2½", no photo, $15.00.
Ramon's, Aspirin, ¼ x 1¼ x 1¾", V1p139-4, $15.00.
Ramon's, Brownie Pills, 1 x 2", no photo, $20.00.
Ramon's, Brownie Pills, 1 x 2", V1p139-5, $22.00.
Ramon's, Eczema Cure, ¾ x 2", V1p139-7, $50.00.
Ramon's, Headache Pills, ¼ x 1¼ x 1¾", V1p139-8, $15.00.
Ramon's, Laxative Cold Tablets, ⅜ x 1¼ x 2", V2p93-3, $12.00.
Ramon's, Pink Pills, ¾ x 2", V1p139-10, $18.00.
Ramon's, Pink Pills, ¾ x 2", V1p139-9, $18.00.
Ramon's, Tabs Aches & Pains, 1 x 2", V1p139-11, $25.00.
Ramon's $.10, Co-Tabs, ⅜ x 1¼ x 1¾", V2p93-5, $15.00.
Ramon's $.10, Relief Aspirin, ¼ x 1¼ x 1¾", V2p93-7, $15.00.
Ramon's $.25, Cold Tabs, ¼ x 1⅞ x 2¾", V1p139-6, $12.00.
Ramon's $.25, Laxative Mild, 1 x 2", V1p139-12, $18.00.
Ramon's $.25, Liver\Tonic Pills, ½ x 1¼", V1p140-1, $60.00.
Ramon's $.25, Tonic Regulator, 1⅝ x 2 x 2½", V1p140-2, $30.00.
Ramon's $.60, Brownie Pills, 1 x 2", V1p140-3, $20.00.
Ramses, Condom, ¼ x 1¾ x 2⅝", V1p24-4, $60.00.
Ramses, Condom, ¼ x 1¾ x 2⅝", V2p20-1, $70.00.
Ramses, Condom, ¼ x 1¾ x 2½", V1p24-5, $60.00.
Ramses, Diaphragm, ⅝ x 2⅜, no photo, $75.00.
Ramses, Diaphram, ¾ x 2⅞", V2p94-1, $70.00.
Rankin Alfred J., Ammunia Lozenges, ½ x 2 x 3⅛", V1p294-2, $80.00.
Rantos, Powder, 1½ x 1½ x 4½", V1p140-4, $25.00.
Raphae's, Type Ribbon, ⅞ x 2½ x 2½", no photo, $10.00.
Rapid, Harness Mender, ⅝ x 3⅝", V1p198-11, $70.00.
Raven, Type Ribbon, ¾ x 2½", V1p321-2, $12.00.
Raven $.25, Laxative Tablets, ⅝ x ⅞ x 2⅜", V1p140-5, $40.00.
Rawleigh $.25, Headache Tablets, ½ x 1½ x 2½", V2p94-3, $30.00.
Rawleigh's, Antiseptic Salve, 1¼ x 3⅝", V1p140-6, $8.00.
Rawleigh's, Asafen Tablets, ¼ x 2⅛ x 2⅛", V1p140-8, $12.00.
Rawleigh's, Asafen Tablets, ¼ x 3 x 3½", V1p140-7, $8.00.
Rawleigh's, Cold Tablets, ½ x 2¾ x 3½", V1p140-12, $8.00.
Rawleigh's, Cold Tablets 35, ½ x 1½ x 2½", V2p94-6, $10.00.
Rawleigh's, Cream of Tartar, 1¼ x 1¾ x 2⅝", V1p189-5, $22.00.
Rawleigh's, Laxative Tablets, ½ x 2½ x 4¼", V1p141-2, $18.00.
Rawleigh's, Shave Soap Stick, 1½ x 3⅜", V1p275-2, $15.00.
Rawleigh's $.25, Aspirin 30, ¼ x 2 x 2⅜", no photo, $12.00.
Rawleigh's $.50, Laxative Wafers, ⅝ x 2⅝ x 3⅞", V1p141-3, $10.00.
Rawleigh's 100, Cathartic Pills, ⅜ x 2½ x 3⅛", V1p140-11, $12.00.
Rawleigh's' 30, Aspirin Tablets, ¼ x 1⅞ x 2⅜", V1p140-9, $12.00.
Rawleigh's 35, Cathartic Pills, ¼ x 1¼ x 1¾", V1p140-10, $12.00.
Rawleigh's 50th, Tooth Powder sample, no photo, $35.00.
Rawleigh's 64, Headache Tablets, ⅜ x 3⅛ x 3⅛", V2p94-2, $10.00.

Rawleigh's sample, Baking Powder, 1 x 1½", V1p245–11, $40.00.

Rawleigh's sample, Cocoa, 1¼ x 1¾ x 2¼", V1p222–5, $60.00.

Rawleigh's sample, Cocoa, ¾ x 1⅛ x 1¾", V1p222–4, $70.00.

Rawleigh's sample, LaJayness Powder, ¼ x 1⅜", V1p254–1, $18.00.

Rawleigh's sample, Ointment, ¼ x 1⅛", V1p141–4, $15.00.

Rawleigh's sample, Vapor Balm, ¼ x ⅞", V1p141–1, $25.00.

Rawlplugs, Screw Fast Anchors, ⅜ x 2½ x 4⅜", V1p198–12, $18.00.

Raymond, Auto Fuses, no photo, $10.00.

Raymond sample, Floral Sachet Talcum, no photo, $40.00.

Raymond's, Wonderoil Ointment, ⅞ x 2⅛", V1p141–5, $8.00.

Raymond's sample, Wonderoil, ¼ x ⅞", V2p94–5, $30.00.

Raymond's sample, Wonderoil Antiseptic, ¼ x ⅞", V2p94–4, $30.00.

Ray's, Salve, ¼ x 1¼", V1p141–6, $10.00.

Razorette, Razor, ¼ x 1¼ x 2", V1p271–7, $25.00.

Razorkeen $.10, Sharpens Razors, ¼ x 1¼", V2p136–1, $20.00.

Re-Bild, Tonic Tablets, ⅜ x 1⅜ x 2", V1p141–7, $25.00.

Re-joyce, Pepper, no photo, $20.00.

Re-Ma, Tire Repair Kit, ⅝ x 2¼ x 3½", V1p15–4, $20.00.

Ready Light, Portable Light, ⅜ x 2¼ x 2¼", V2p212–4, $35.00.

Real Relief, Aspirin 6, ¼ x ⅞ x 1⅜", V1p141–8, $12.00.

Real Worth $.50, Antiseptic Salve, 1⅞ x 3 x 1⅞", V1p141–9, $75.00.

Real-Lax, Chocolate Laxative, ⅜ x 1⅝ x 1⅝", V1p141–10, $10,00.

Real-Lax $.10, Laxative, ¼ x 1½ x 1½", V2p94–7, $10.00.

Realeef $.05, Aspirin, ¼ x ⅞ x 1½", V1p141–11, $8.00.

Rectal Medicone, Suppository, ¼ x 1¼ x 1½", V1p141–12, 8.00*.

Rectal Medicone sample, Hemoroid Suppository, ⅜ x 1¼ x 1¾", V1p142–1, $8.00*.

Rectal Medicone sample, Suppositories, ⅜ x 1¼ x 1½", V1p142–2, $8.00.

Red, Tire Repair Outfit, ½ x 2¼ x 3½", V1p15–5, $65.00.

Red & White, Allspice, 3¾ x 2¼ x 1¼", V2p158–1, $15.00.

Red Arrow, Mustard, 5⅛ x 2⅜ x 1⅜", V2p158–4, $20.00.

Red Circle, Coffee, 2¼ x 1½ x 4", V1p235–3, $20.00.

Red Cloverine $.15, Salve, ¾ x 2½", V2p95–1, $15.00.

Red Cross, Headache Plaster, no photo, $12.00.

Red Cross, Lemon Flavor Powder, 1¼ x 2½", V1p189–6, $50.00.

Red Cross $.25, Salve, 1 x 2½", V2p95–4, $25.00.

Red Cross sample, Coffee, 2 x 3", V1p235–4, $360.00.

Red Cross sample, Foot Powder, ⅞ x 1½ x 2⅜", V1p255–5, $60.00.

Red Cross sample, Salve, ¼ x 1¼", no photo, $35.00.

Red Front sample, Cocoa, no photo, $80.00.

Red Goose, Football, 1½ x 2¼", V1p199–1, $20.00.

Red Goose, Pencil Case, no photo, $45.00.

Red Indian, Germ Ointment, ½ x 2⅜", V1p142–3, $20.00.

Red Label, Arrowroot, 4 x 2½ x 1¾", no photo, $25.00.

Red Line Standard, Auto Fuses, no photo, $15.00.

Red Monogram, Ginger, 3¼ x 2¼ x 1¼", V2p158–6, $25.00.

Red Ribbon, Pure Spices, 3¾ x 2¼ x 1¼", V2p158–2, $25.00.

Red Seal, Sweet Snuff, 2⅜ x 1¾", V2p212–7, $25.00.

Red Seal $.50, Hair Dressing, 1 x 3⅜", V1p39–5, $25.00.

Red Star, Mace, 3⅝ x 2⅜ x 1⅛", V2p158–3, $25.00.

Red-Cloverine $.10, Salve, ⅞ x 2½", V1p142–5, $25.00.

Red-Cloverine $.10, Salve, ⅞ x 2⅝", V1p142–4, $18.00.

Red-Cloverine sample, Salve, ¼ x 1⅛", V2p96–6, $25.00.

Red-Cloverine sample, Salve, ¼ x ⅞", V2p95–2, $20.00.

Red-Line, Auto Fuses, ¼ x 1¼ x 1¾", V1p10–1, $15.00.

Redding's Russia, Salve, ⅝ x 2", V1p142–6, $25.00.

Reed & Carnrick, see Pancrobilin Tablets, V1p131–4, $18.00.

Reed & Carnrick, Protonuclein, ⅜ x 1⅛ x 2⅛", V1p142–7, $80.00.

Reed & Carnrick sample, Pancrobilin Laxative, ¼ x 1¼ x 1¾", no photo, $10.00.

Reed & Carnrick sample, Pancrobilin Tablets, ¼ x 1¼ x 1¾", V2p95–3, $15.00.

Reed's, Antacid Tablets, no photo, $15.00.

Reed's, Aspirin, ¼ x 1¼ x 1¾", V1p142–8, $8.00.

Reed's, Aspirin, ¼ x 1¼ x 1¾", V2p95–5, $5.00.

Reed's, Aspirin 6 Tablets, ¼ x ⅞ x 1¼", V1p142–9, $12.00.

Reed's, Butter Scotch Patties, 1 x 4", no photo, $18.00.

Reed's, Butterscotch Patties, 1⅛ x 3", V1p294–3, $18.00.

Reel Ola, Adhesive Plaster, 1 x 1⅜", V1p347–9, $20.00.

Reese's, Blu-Tabs, ⅜ x 1¼ x 1¾", V1p142–10, $12.00.

Regal, Type Ribbon, 1¾ x 2 x 1¾", V1p321–7, $40.00.

Regal, Type Ribbon, ¾ x 2⅝ x 2⅝", V2p188–1, $20.00.

Regal 200, Needles Loud Tonee, ¼ x 1¼ x 1¾", V1p210–3, $30.00.

Regal sample, Talcum Powder, ¾ x 1¼ x 2", V2p129–6, $65.00.

Regina, Type Ribbon, ¾ x 2½", V1p321–3, $6.00.

Regoes, Aspirin, ¼ x 1¼ x 1¾", V1p142–11, $12.00.

Regoes, Rubbed Sage, 3½ x 4¼", V2p158–5, $35.00.

Regs, Laxative, ⅜ x 1⅝ x 2⅛", V2p95–7, $8.00.

Regs, Laxative Chocolate 48, ¾ x 3⅛ x 3¼", V1p142–12, $8.00.

Regs, Regular Laxative, ¼ x 1¾ x 1¾", V1p143–1, $8.00.

Regs sample, Laxative, ¼ x 1⅝ x 1⅝", V2p96–1, $15.00.

Reid's $1.00, Nometa Tab Ladies, ½ x 2 x 3⅛", V1p143–2, $110.00.

ReJoyce, Black Pepper, 5 ¼ x 2¼ x 1¼", V2p158–7, $75.00.

Reliable, Lighter Wicks, ¼ x ⅞ x 2⅝", V1p199–2, $30.00.

Reliable Brand, Aspirin, ¼ x 1¼ x 1¾", V1p143–3, $12.00.

Reliance Ribbon\Carbon, Type Ribbon, ¾ x 2½ x 2½", V1p321–4, $40.00.

Reliant, Type Ribbon, ¾ x 2½ x 2½", V1p321–5, $10.00.

Relpaw, Fish Food, ⅞ x 2½", V1p199–3, $8.00.

Remick's sample, Eczema Remedy, ¼ x ⅞", no photo, $30.00.

Remiller Co. $.10, Purletts Laxative, ½ x 1½ x 1½", V2p96–4, $18.00.

Remiller Co. $.25, Purletts Laxative, ¾ x 2⅛ x 2¼", V2p96–6, $18.00.

Remington (Letter Book), Type Ribbon, 1⅝ x 2 x 1¾", no photo, $25.00.

Remington (Letter), Type Ribbon, 1¾ x 2 x 1⅞", V1p321–6, $25.00.

Remington (Paragon), Type Ribbon, ¾ x 2¼ x 2¼", V1p321–10, $25.00.

Remington Standard, Type Ribbon, ¾ x 2½ x 2½", V1p321–11, $10.00.

Remmington 100, Precission Caps, ⅝ x 1½", V1p65–2, $30.00.

Remrandco, Type Ribbon, ⅞ x 2½", V1p321–12, $10.00.

Remtito (Paragon), Type Ribbon, ¾ x 2½ x 2½", V1p322–1, $15.00.

Rennene $.20, Whey Sweetner, 1⅝ x 2 x 3", V1p177–7, $70.00.

Renner's Rose Jelly, Hair and Skin Salve, ⅝ x 1⅞", V2p36–5, $30.00.

Renner's Rose Jelly, Hair and Skin Salve, ⅝ x 2", V2p36–2, $28.00.

Renner's Rose Jelly, Hair Skin\Salve, ¾ x 1⅞", V1p39–6, $30.00.

Repetti sample, Cocoa, 1¼ x 1¼ x 2", V1p222–6, $140.00.

Reppenhagen, Razor Paste, no photo, $120.00.

Requaid, Adhesive Plaster, 1 x 1", no photo, $20.00.

Requa's #9, Charcoal Tablets, ⅞ x 2⅝ x 2⅞", V1p143–4, $15.00.

Resillent, Watch Mainsprings, ⅜ x 2¼ x 4 ⅝", V1p339–10, $35.00.

Resinol sample, Ointment, ¼ x 1⅛", V1p143–5, $15.00.

Resinol sample, Ointment, ¼ x 1⅛", V1p143–6, $15.00.

Resinol sample, Ointment, ⅝ x 1¾", V1p143–7, $20.00.

Restaco, Type Ribbon, ¾ x 2½", no photo, $10.00.

Results $.10, Laxative, ¼ x 1½ x 1¾", V1p143–8, $12.00.

Results $.10, Laxative, ¼ x 1¼ x 1¾", V2p96–2, $12.00.

Retlaw $.25, Quick-Healing Salve, ⅞ x 2⅛", V2p96–3, $18.00.

Revelation, Nail Polish, 1¼ x 2¼ x 1¾", V1p43–10, $20.00.

Revere Java sample, Coffee, 1½ x 2½ x 4", V1p235–5, $250.00.

Revilo, Type Ribbon, ¾ x 2¾ x 2¾", V1p322–2, $80.00.

Revilo (Oliver), Type Ribbon, ¾ x 2½ x 2½", V1p322–3, $18.00.

Revilo No.5, Type Ribbon, ¾ x 2½ x 2½", V1p322–5, $15.00.

Revivo, Remedy, ½ x 1½ x 2½", V1p143–9, $35.00.

Rex, Ant Bait, ¾ x 2¼", no photo, $6.00.

Rex, Ant Bait, ¾ x 2¼", V1p199–4, $8.00.

Rex, Brake Waffers, 1¼ x 2⅛", V1p7–2, $70.00.

Rex Brand, Type Ribbon, ¾ x 2¼ x 2¼", V2p188–3, $20.00.

Rex O, Cleaner, no photo, $20.00.

Rex Quality, Type Ribbon, ¾ x 2½ x 2½", V1p322–6, $12.00.

Rex sample, Ointrex, ⅜ x 1¼", V2p96–5, $18.00.

Rexall, Antiseptic Surgical Powder, 1¾ x 3¼", no photo, $30.00.

Rexall, Carbolic Salve, ¾ x 2¼ x 2¼", no photo, $15.00.

Rexall, Cold Tablets, ⅜ x 1¼ x 1¾", no photo, $12.00.

Rexall, Orderlies, ½ x 1¾ x 3¼", V1p143–11, $25.00.

Rexall, Orderlies Laxative, ¼ x 1½ x 2⅜", V1p144–10, $30.00.

Rexall, Pro Cap Adhesive Tape, ⅞ x 2½", no photo, $5.00.

Rexall, Skin-Fix, ½ x 1⅜ x 2½", V2p96–7, $35.00.

Rexall, Tooth Powder, ⅞ x 1⅛ x 1⅞", V1p58–9, $90.00.

Rexall 100, Little Liver Pills, ¾ x 1¾", V1p144–8, $15.00.

Rexall A-15, Orderlies, ⅜ x 1½ x 2⅜", V1p143–12, $18.00.

Rexall A-16, Orderlies Laxative, ½ x 1¾ x 3¼", V1p144–1, $15.00.

Rexall A-16, Orderlies Laxative, ½ x 1¾ x 3¼", V1p144–2, $15.00.

Rexall A-17, Orderlies 60, ½ x 2 x 4", V2p97–1, $15.00.

Rexall A-17, Orderlies Laxative, ½ x 2 x 4", V1p144–3, $15.00.

Rexall A-21, Dyspepsia Tablets, ½ x 1¾ x 3¼", V1p145–2, $12.00.

Rexall D-141, Corn Salve, ½ x 1¼", V1p145–1, $18.00.

Rexall D-16, Orderlies, ¼ x 2¼ x 3¼", V1p144–4, $12.00.

Rexall D-16, Orderlies Chocolate Lax, ½ x 1¾ x 3¼", no photo, $12.00.

Rexall D-17, Orderlies Laxative, ½ x 2 x 4", V1p144–5, $12.00.

Rexall D-17, Orderlies Laxative, ½ x 2 x 4", V1p144–6, $8.00.

Rexall D-174, KoKoKasKets Laxative, ⅜ x 1⅝ x 2⅜", V1p145–5, $12.00.

Rexall D-2, see Regs Choc Laxative.

Rexall D-22, Acid-Dyspepsia, ½ x 2 x 4", V1p145–3, $15.00.

Rexall D-251, Witch Hazel Ointment, ¾ x 2¼ x 2¼", V1p145–12, $30.00.

Rexall D-260, Milk of Magnesia 26, ¼ x 1¾ x 3¼", V1p145–9, $10.00.

Rexall D-260, Milk of Magnesia Tablets, ½ x 1½ x 1⅞", V2p97–6, $15.00.

Rexall D-260, Milk of Magnesia Tablets, ¼ x 1⅝ x 3⅛", V1p145–8, $10.00.

Rexall D-269, Rexpirin, ¼ x 1¼ x 1¾", V1p145–10, $8.00.

Rexall D-284, Cold Tablets, ⅜ x 1½ x 2¼", no photo, $12.00.

Rexall D-285, Throat Pastilles, ¾ x ⅜ x 2", V1p294–4, $18.00.

Rexall D-286, Throat Pastilles, ¾ x 2⅜ x 3⅞", V1p294–5, $22.00.

Rexall D-286, Throat Pastilles, ¾ x 2⅞ x 3⅞", no photo, $15.00.

Rexall D-308, Little Liver Pills, 1 x 1¾", V2p97–1, $15.00.

Rexall D-308, Little Liver Pills, ¾ x 1¾", V1p144–9, $20.00.

Rexall D-308, Little Pills, ¾ x 1¾", V1p144–10, $20.00.

Rexall D-326, Cold Tablets, ¼ x 1⅝ x 2⅜", V1p144–11, $10.00.

Rexall D-326, Cold Tablets Spec., ¼ x 1⅞ x 2½", V1p144–12, $8.00.

Rexall D-326, Cold Tablets Spec., ⅜ x 1½ x 2¼", V2p97–3, $10.00.

Rexall D-367, Cold Tablets, ¼ x 1⅞ x 2⅝", V1p145–7, $8.00.

Rexall D-367, Lax Cold Tablets, ⅜ x 1½ x 2¼", V1p145–6, $12.00.

Rexall D-367, Laxative Cold Tablets, ½ x 1½ x 2¼", V2p97–5, $12.00.

Rexall D-384, Pain Tablets, ⅜ x 1¼ x 1¾", no photo, $12.00.

Rexall D-411, Headache Tablets, ¼ x 1¾ x 2½", V1p145–4, $15.00.

Rexall D-411, One Minute Headache, ¼ x 1¾ x 2⅜", V2p97–4, $12.00.

Rexall D-489, Bismarex Laxative, ¼ x 1¼ x 2½", V1p146–1, $8.00.

Rexall D-545, Itch Ointment, ½ x 2¾", V1p146–2, $5.00.

Rexall D-545, Itch Ointment, ½ x 2¾", V1p146–3, $12.00.

Rexall D-840, Monacet Compound, ¼ x 1¼ x 1¾", V2p97–7, $6.00.

Rexall D-933, Aspirin, ¼ x 1¾ x 3¾", V1p146–4, $7.00.

Rexall sample, Violet Talcum Powder, ¾ x 1⅜ x 2⅛", V2p130–1, $60.00.

Rexall U-902, Aspirin, ¼ x 1¾ x 2½", V1p146–5, $6.00.

Rexall U-903, Aspirin, ¼ x 1¾ x 3⅞", V1p146–6, $6.00.

Rexall W-4103, Pro Cap Adhesive Tape, 1 x 2½", no photo, $5.00.

Rexpirin D 269, Tablets, ¼ x 1¼ x 1½", no photo, $8.00.

Rhodes, Dandruff Remedy, ½ x 2½", no photo, $20.00.

Rhu-Laxo, Laxative, ⅜ x 1⅞ x 2¾", no photo, $15.00.

Ricco sample, Hair Croquignole Oil, ⅜ x 1¼", V1p39–7, $10.00.

Richard Hudnut, Nail Polish, 1 x 2½ x ⅞", V1p43–11, $8.00.

Richard Hudnut sample, Creme Sec, ½ x 1½", V1p31–7, $15.00.

Richards, Type Ribbon, 1½ x 1½ x 2", no photo, $55.00.

Richards $.25, Carbolic Salve, ⅞ x 2¾", V1p146–7, $35.00.

Richards Frank, Triangle Dominos, 2¼ x 3½ x 1⅝", V1p175–1, $220.00.

Richardsons, Cough Drops sample, no photo, $25.00.

Richardson's U-All-No, After Diner Mint, 1 x 2½ x 2½", no photo, $12.00.

Richelieu, Bouillon Cubes, 1 x 3½", V1p20–3, $8.00.

Richelieu sample, Java & Mocha, 2⅜ x 2", V2p124–5, $115.00.

Richelieu sample, Tea, 2 x 2 x 2⅞", V1p268–3, $45.00.

Richford, Grinding Compound, 1⅜ x 2⅜", V1p11–9, $22.00.

Rich's, Canton Ginger, 1 x 2⅝ x 4½", V1p189–7, $30.00.

Rid-a-Pain, Tablets, ¼ x 1⅜ x 1¾", no photo, $20.00.

Rid-A-Pain, Tablets 12, ¼ x 1¼ x 1⅞", V1p146–8, $20.00.

Riddle's $.25, Herb Tablets, ⅜ x 1¼ x 2", V1p146–9, $35.00.

Ridgway's, Her Majesty's Blend, 1¾ x 2⅜ x 1¼", V1p268–4, $18.00.

Ries & Porter, Red Pepper, 3¼ x 2¼ x 1¼", V2p159–1, $25.00.

Rigaud Chapoteaut, Phosphoglycerate of Lime, ⅜ x 1⅞ x 1⅞", V1p146–10, $35.00.

Riker Labs., Camphor Ice, 1 x 3½", V1p146–11, $8.00.

Riker Labs., see Jaynes Dyspepsia Tablets, V1p112–1, $75.00.

Riker Labs., see Jaynes Healing Salve, V1p111–12, $30.00.

Riker Labs., see Jaynes Kidney Pills, V1p112–4, $60.00.

Riker sample, Tooth Powder, 1 x 2⅝", V1p43–5, $80.00.

Riker-Janes, Dental Floss, ⅛ x 1⅜", V2p43–7, $45.00.

Riker's sample, Violet Excelsis Talcum, ¾ x 1¼ x 2", V2p130–3, $45.00.

Riker's sample, Violet Excelsis Talcum, ¾ x 1¼ x 2⅛, no photo, $65.00.

Rimer's, Liver Pills, ½ x ¾ x 2½", V1p146–12, $20.00.

Rimer's $.10, Liver Tablets, ⅝ x ⅞ x 1¾", V1p147–1, $25.00.

Ring's $.10, Witch Hazel Ointment, ¾ x 1½", $18.00.

Ring's $.10, Witch Hazel Ointment, ¾ x 1½", V2p98–1, $25.00.

Ring's $.10, Witch Hazel Salve, no photo, $20.00.

Ring's $.25, Witch Hazel Ointment, 1 x 2⅜", V1p147–2, $15.00.

Ripans $.35, Tabules, ¾ x 2", V1p147–3, $18.00.

Rite Rite, Type Ribbon, ¾ x 2½ x 2½", V1p322–7, $18.00.

Rite-Right, Type Ribbon, ¾ x 2½ x 2½", V1p327–12, $15.00.

Rival $1.00, Herb Tablets, 1¼ x 2⅛ x 3¼", no photo, $15.00.

Rival $1.00, Herb Tablets, 1¼ x 2⅛ x 3¼", V2p98–3, $15.00.

Rival $1.00, Herb Tablets, ⅞ x 2⅛ x 3¼", V1p147–4, $22.00.

Riveris sample, Talcum Powder, no photo, $70.00.

Riverside, Carpet Tacks, 1⅝ x 1⅝ x 2⅞", V1p199–5, $40.00.

Ro-Zol $.25, Complexion Clarifier, ¾ x 1¾", V2p30–2, $15.00.

Rob-Roy, Mace, 3¼ x 2¼ x 1¼", V2p159–3, $35.00.

Robert's, Sulfur Tablets, no photo, $40.00.

Robinson Bill $.10, Hair Dressing, 1 x 2¾ x 1¾", V1p39–8, $25.00.

Robinson's sample, Nail White Cream, ¼ x ⅞", V1p43–12, $18.00.

Roger & Gallet, Pomade, ½ x 1⅞", $8.00.

Rolan sample, Baking Powder, 1½ x 2¼", V1p245–12, $50.00.

Rolon No. 1, Clip, ¾ x 1½", V2p213–1, $25.00.

Romay Products $.10, Aspirin, ¼ x 1½ x 1¾", V1p147–5, $10.00.

Romeos, Condom, ¼ x 1½ x 1¾", V2p20–3, $90.00.

Romeos, Condom, ¼ x 1⅝ x 2⅛", V2p20–6, $80.00.

Romeos, Condom, ¼ x 1⅝ x 2⅝", V1p24–6, $80.00.

Romets, Bouillon Cubes, 1 x 3¾", V1p20–4, $15.00.

Roocroft's T.I.C.'s, Throat\Chest Relief, ½ x 1¼", $5.00.

Roosa & Ratliff, Red Pepper, 3 x 2⅛ x 1⅛", V2p159–5, $20.00.

Rooster, Snuff, 1¼ x 2", V2p213–3, $35.00.

Roreen $.25, Oint. Brightner, ⅝ x 2", V1p39–9, $15.00*.

Roreen $.25, Ointment\Brightner, ¾ x 2", V1p39–9, $15.00*.

Roreen sample, Ointment, ⅜ x 1½", no photo, $25.00.

Rosa & Ratliff, Adhesive Plaster, 1 x 1⅜", V1p347–10, $15.00.

Rosa & Ratliff sample, Mutton Tallow, ⅞ x 1⅝ x 2⅞", V1p52–11, $20.00.

Rosa & Ratliff $.35, Mutton Tallow, ⅞ x 1¾ x 3", V1p52–12, $12.00.

Rose, Corn Salve, ½ x 1", V2p98–5, $6.00.

Rose, Leaf Pourri, no photo, $15.00.

Rose Bud, Ginger, 1⅛ x 2¼ x 3⅝", V2p159–6, $20.00.

Rose Bud sample, Coffee, 2 x 2 x 3", V1p235–6, $450.00.

Rose King $.10, Salve, ½ x 1½", V1p147–6, $20.00.

Rose King $.10, Salve, ⅝ x 1½", V1p147–7, $20.00.

Rose-Vel, Great Healer, 1 x 2½", V2p98–7, $10.00.

Rose-Vel, Salve, ¼ x 1⅛", V2p98–2, $6.00.

Rose-Vel $.10, Balm, ⅞ x 1¾", no photo, $15.00.

Rose-Vel $.25, Salve, 1 x 2½", V1p147–8, $18.00.

Rose-Vel sample, Salve, ¼ x 1⅛", no photo, $22.00.

Rose-Vel sample, Salve, ¼ x 1⅛", V1p147–10, $6.00.

Rose-Vel sample, Salve, ⅜ x 1⅛", V1p147–9, $18.00.

Rosebud $.25, Regulators, ½ x 1½ x 1½", V2p98–4, $25.00.

Rosebud Perfume Co., see Smith's Rose Bud Salve, V1p153.

Rosebud Perfume Co., Tholene Salve, V1p159–2, $30.00.

Rosemary, Spices, 1¼ x 2¼ x 3", no photo, $20.00.

Rosemary, White Pepper, 3⅜ x 2⅜ x 1¼", V2p159–2, $15.00.

Rosemary Brand, Sage, 3 x 2¼ x 1¼", V2p159–4, $50.00.

Roseoline, Cream, ⅞ x 2¼", V2p98–6, $18.00.

Rosevelt Brand, Ginger, 3¾ x 2¼ x 1¼", V2p159–7, $60.00.

Rosevelt Simax, Type Ribbon, ¾ x 2½ x 2½", no photo, $12.00.

Ross Betsy, Tan Shoe Paste, ⅞ x 1¾", no photo, $15.00.

Roundtrees sample, Cocoa, no photo, $80.00.

Roussin's, Green Pain Capsules, ¼ x 1⅝ x 1⅝", V2p98–8, $18.00.

Rowles sample, Mentho-Sulphur, ¼ x 1¼", V1p147–11, $22.00.

Rowles sample, Red Pepper Rub, ¼ x 1½", V1p147–12, $22.00.

Rowntree sample, Cocoa, ¾ x 1¾ x 2½", V1p222–7, $180.00.

Rowntree's sample, Cocoa, 1 x 1⅜ x 1⅝", V2p122–5, $65.00.

Roworth's, London-Hospital Lozenges, ½ x 1¾ x 3", no photo, $75.00.

Royal, Cosmetic, no photo, $20.00.

Royal, Type Ribbon, ¾ x 2½ x 2½", V2p188–5, $20.00.

Royal 200, Needles Phono, ⅜ x 1⅛ x 2⅜", V1p210–4, $25.00.

Royal Blue, Turmeric, 3 x 2¼ x 1¼", V2p160–1, $20.00.

Royal Crown sample, Hair Dressing, ¼ x 1½", V1p39–10, $25.00.

Royal Crown sample, Men's Pomade, ½ x 2⅜", V1p39–12, $15.00.

Royal Crown sample, Men's Pomade, ¼ x 1½", V1p39–11, $15.00.

Royal King, Red Pepper, 1½ x 2¼ x 3¼", V2p160–3, $65.00.

Royal sample, Brass Polish, ½ x 1½", V1p219–2, $30.00.

Royal sample, Coffee, no photo, $90.00.

Royal Saxon, Metal Polish, ⅜ x 1", V1p219–3, $30.00.

Royal Scarlet, Cloves, 2⅛ x 2⅛ x 1¼", V2p160–5, $20.00.

Royal Tiger, Cinnamon, 1¾ x 2½ x 3¾", V2p160–6, $70.00.

Royal Vinolia sample, Talcum Powder, ¾ x 1⅜ x 2⅛", V2p130–5, $125.00.

Royal-Tex, Condoms, ¼ x 1½ x 2", V2p20–2, $85.00.

Royaline, Liver Regulator, 1½ x 1½ x 2¼", V1p148–1, $55.00.

Royce's, Ready Mustard, ¾ x 2⅜", V1p148–2, $30.00.

Roytype, Type Ribbon, ¾ x 2½", V1p322–8, $18.00.

Roytype, Type Ribbon, ¾ x 2½ x 2½", V1p322–9, $18.00.

Ruby Moca Java sample, Coffee, 2½ x 3", V1p236–1, $190.00.

Rubyfluid, Solder Paste, ⅞ x 2⅜", no photo, 4.00.

Rundle's $.25, Laxative, ¼ x 1½ x 1⅞", V2p99–1, $12.00.

Rundle's $.35, Liniment Salve, 1 x 3⅜", V2p99–4, $12.00.

Runkel's sample, Cocoa, 1¼ x 1¼ x 2", V2p122–7, $125.00.

Runkel's sample, Cocoa, 1¼ x 1¾ x 2½", V1p222–8, $140.00.

Runkel's sample, Cocoa, 1¼ x 1¾ x 2½", V1p222–9, $120.00.

Runkel's sample, Cocoa, 1⅛ x 1⅛ x 1⅝", V1p222–10, $130.00.

Runkel's sample, Cocoa, ¾ x 1⅛ x 1½", V1p222–11, $115.00.

Runkel's sample, Cocoa #5, ⅞ x 1⅛ x 1½", V1p223–1, $125.00.

Runkel's sample, Cocoa Pure, 1¼ x 1¼ x 2", V2p122–7, $125.00.

Rupaner, Laxative Tablets, ¼ x 1¼ x 1¾", V1p148–3, $22.00.

Rutter's, Salve, ½ x 1¼", V1p148–4, $10.00.

Rx (18 tablets), Aspirin, ¼ x 1¼ x 2", V1p148–5, $12.00.

Rydale Remedy, Cre-mo-la Salve, 1⅛ x 2½", V1p148–6, $45.00.

Rydale's, Headache Tablets, ¼ x 1¼ x 1¾", V1p148–7, $25.00.

Rydale's $.25, Liver Tablets, ⅜ x 2⅛", V2p99–6, $40.00.

S & F, Ginger, 3¼ x 2¼ x 1¼", V2p160–2, $15.00.

S & M (Skillin), Watch Main Spring, ¾ x 3 x 3⅜", V1p339–11, $35.00.

S & S $.05, Cough Drops, ½ x 2", no photo, $60.00.

S.D & G. Little Wonder, Tire Repair Kit, ½ x 1½ x 2¾", V1p15–6, $75.00.

S.E.L., Condom, ¼ x 1⅝ x 2", V1p24–8, $50.00.

S.S.S. Fursten, Needles, ⅜ x 1¼ x 1¾", V2p114–8, $45.00.

S.W.C., Saffron, 1¼ x 1¾ x 1¼", V2p203–5, $8.00.

Saf-t-way, Condom, ¼ x 1⅝ x 2⅛", V2p20–4, $70.00.

Safe O, Watch Parts, ¼ x ¾ x 1¼", V1p339–12, $5.00.

Safe Owl, Mace, 3 x 1⅞ x 1", V2p160–4, $30.00.

Safety First, Shoe Preservation, ¾ x 2", V1p281–6, $15.00.

Safto Jewel Point, Needles, no photo, $35.00.

Sagamore, Salve, no photo, $30.00.

Sage's Violet, Pepsin Gum, no photo, $115.00.

Sahara, Shoe Polish, ⅝ x 1¾", V1p281–7, $45.00.

Sal-ethyl sample, Carbonate w\Amid., ¼ x 1½ x 1¾", V1p148–8, $15.00.

Sal-Fayne, Pain Pills, ¼ x ¾ x 1⅞", V1p148–9, $5.00.

Salem's $.25, Green Tablets, ⅞ x ⅞ x 2⅝", V1p148–10, $20.00.

Sale's $.60, Salve, ¾ x 2½", V1p148–11, $15.00.

Saleto, Aspirin, ¼ x 1¼ x 1¾", V1p148–12, $8.00.

Salo-Sedatus sample, Fever\Pain Tablets, ¼ x 1¼ x 1¾", V2p99–2, $25.00.

Salon Tanz Nadlin, Needles, no photo, $30.00.

Salter's, Aseptic Dental Floss, 1 x 1⅜", V1p56–3, $50.00.

Salter's, Dental Floss, ¼ x 1⅛", V1p56–4, $20.00.

Salter's, Dental Floss Wax, 1⅛ x 1⅜", V1p56–5, $50.00.

Salutine, Headache Tablets, 1¼ x 1¾ x 2½", V1p149–1, $25.00.

Salva-cea, Ointment, ¾ x 2", V2p99–3, $12.00.

Salvador $1.00, Cure for Liquor, ½ x 2 x 3¼", no photo, $70.00.

Samoline, Cleaner Paint, ⅞ x 2¾", V1p22–8, $35.00.

Samoline sample, Cleaner, ¼ x 1⅛", V2p39–1, $12.00.

Samovar, Tea Tablets, no photo, $18.00.

Samuel sample, Indigestion Tablets, ⅜ x 1¼ x 1¾", no photo, $30.00.

Samuel's, Liver & Bowel Pills, ¼ x 1¼ x 1¾", no photo, $20.00.

Samurai Corylopsis sample, Talcum Powder, ¾ x 1⅛ x 2", no photo, $95.00.

Samurai sample, Talcum Powder, 1 x 2⅛", V1p261–2, $75.00.

Samurai Wisteria sample, Talcum Powder, ¾ x 1⅛ x 2", no photo, $85.00.

San-it, Hygenic Tablets, ¼ x 1½ x 2", no photo, $6.00.

Sanafrio $.10, Headache, ¼ x ⅞", V1p149–2, $20.00.

Sanette, Adhesive Tape, 1 x 1", V1p347–11, $8.00.

Sanette, Condom, no photo, $45.00.

Sanford's Ink, Indelible Ink, 1¼ x 1⅜ x 1½", V1p179–12, $20.00.

Sanisalva $.25, Salve, ⅞ x 2¾", V2p99–5, $18.00.

Sanitary, Tooth Soap, no photo, $65.00.

Sanitary Health, Condom (Sponge), ¾ x 1¾", V1p27–10, $125.00.

Sanitary Health, Condom (Sponge), ¾ x 1¾", V1p27–2, $65.00.

Sanitary Health Sponge, Condom, ¾ x 1¾", no photo, $60.00.

Sanitary Netted, Condom (Sponge), ¾ x 1¾", V1p27–7, $75.00.
Sanitary Sponge, Condom, ¾ x 1¾", V1p27–5, $60.00.
Sanitary Sponge, Condom, ¾ x 1¾", V1p27–6, $55.00.
Sanitary Sponge, Condom, ⅞ x 1¾", V1p27–8, $120.00.
Sanitary Sponge, Sponge, 1 x 1¾", no photo, $40.00.
Sanitary Sponge, Sponge, ¾ x 1¾", no photo, $30.00.
Sanitol, Tooth Powder, 1 x 1¾", V1p58–10, $90.00.
Sanitol, Tooth Powder, 1 x 2⅛", V1p58–11, $85.00.
Sanitol, Vanity-box Face Powder, ½ x 2½", no photo, $60.00.
Sanitol sample, Violet-Elite Talcum, ¾ x 1¼ x 2⅛", V1p261–3, $100.00.
Sanka ¼ lb., Coffee, 2¾ x 3½", V1p236–3, $60.00.
Sanka sample, Coffee, 1½ x 1¼ x 3", V1p236–2, $50.00.
Sante Fe Brand, Red Pepper, 3¼ x 2¼ x 1¼", V2p160–7, $40.00.
Sapo sample, Hand Soap, ¾ x 1¾", V2p34–4, $50.00.
Sapolin, Varnish, 1⅝ x 1⅞", V1p182–4, $15.00.
Sarah's, Thread Holder, no photo, $20.00.
Saraka, Laxative, 1 x 1⅝ x 2¼", V1p149–4, $20.00.
Saraka sample, Laxative, 1 x 1⅝ x 2¼", V1p149–3, $35.00.
Saraka sample, Laxative, 1 x 1⅝ x 2¼", V1p149–5, $25.00.
Saratoga sample, Ointment, ¼ x 1¼", V2p99–7, $20.00.
Saratoga sample, Ointment, ¼ x 1⅝, no photo, $8.00.
Satin, Rose Tint, ¼ x ⅞", V1p31–11, $8.00.
Satin sample, Skin Cream, ¼ x ⅞", V1p31–8, $10.00.
Satin Skin sample, Cream, ¼ x ⅞", V1p31–10, $10.00.
Satin Skin sample, Cream, ¼ x ⅞", V1p31–9, $12.00.
Sauer's, Aspirin, ¼ x 1¼ x 1½", V2p100–1, $10.00.
Sauer's, Ginger, no photo, $20.00.
Savana 200 Loud, Needles, no photo, $30.00.
Savarin sample, Coffee, 2¾ x 3⅜", no photo, $45.00.
Save the Horse sample, Ointment, ½ x 1¾", V1p333–3, $75.00.
Savita, Bouillon Cubes, ½ x 1½ x 3", V1p20–5, $15.00.
Savita sample, Yeast Extract, 2 x 2½", V1p246–1, $25.00.
Savoie Hollow, Tire Patch Kit, no photo, $65.00.
Savoy, Cloves, 4 x 2¼ x 1¼", V2p161–1, $30.00.
Savoy, Sage, 3½ x 2¼ x 1¼", V2p161–4, $40.00.
Saxon, Aspirin 24, ¼ x 1¾ x 2⅝", V1p149–6, $10.00.
Saxon, Sweetlax, ⅜ x 2¼ x 3⅝", V2p100–3, $15.00.
Saxon, Sweetlax Chocolate Lax, ¼ x 1¼ x 1¾", V2p100–5, $8.00.
Saxon, Sweetlax Laxative, ⅜ x 1¼ x 1⅝", V2p100–7, $15.00.
Saxon 25, Laxative Cold Tablets, ½ x 1⅝ x 2⅝", V2p100–2, $18.00.
Sayman, see Dr. Sayman.
Sayman, Hair Trainer, ⅞ x 2¾", V1p40–1, $18.00.
Sayman sample, Salve, ¼ x 1¼", V2p100–4, $10.00.
Sayman sample, Salve, ⅜ x 1", V1p149–8, $15.00.
Sayman's, Healing Salve, ⅞ x 2¼", V1p149–7, $35.00.
Sayman's, Salve ¼ oz, ¼ x 1¼", V1p149–9, $15.00.
Sayman's $.25, Healing Salve, ⅞ x 2¼", no photo, $25.00.
Sayman's sample, Salve, ¼ x 1¼", no photo, $15.00.
Sayman's sample, Salve, ¼ x 1¼", V1p149–11, $12.00.
Sayman's sample, Salve ⅛ oz., ¼ x 1⅛", V1p149–10, $20.00.
Scarless $.30, Gall Remedy, 1 x 2¾", V1p333–4, $25.00*.
Schaum-Vaugham Corp., Type Ribbon, ¾ x 2½ x 2½", V2p188–2, $15.00.
Schell H.A., Polish (Oxblood), ⅞ x 2¼", V1p281–8, $25.00.
Schenck's, Liver Pills, ½ x ⅞ x 1⅞", V1p150–1, $15.00.
Schenck's, Liver Pills, ¾ x 1¾ x ½", V1p150–2, $15.00.
Schenck's, Mandrake Pills, ½ x ⅞ x 1¾", V1p150–3, $18.00.
Schepp's sample, Cocoanut, 2 x 3½ x 2½", V1p246–2, $80.00.
Schering & Glatz, see Peralga Tablets, V1p133–5, $12.00.
Scherzer's $.25, Old Reliable Salve, ¾ x 2", V1p150–4, $15.00.
Schick, Razor Blades, ½ x 1¾", V1p269–5, $15.00.
Schieffelin, Gum Violet, ⅜ x 1½ x 2⅜", V2p173–3, $30.00.
Schilling sample, Coffee, 1⅞ x 2½", V2p124–6, $50.00.
Schlctt A.A., Liliput-Harmonica, ⅜ x ½ x 1¾", V2p213–5, $40.00.
Schneider Wm., Jewelers, ¾ x 1½", V1p180–4, $8.00.

Scholars Companion $.05, Pencil Holder, ⅜ x 1 x 6", no photo, $55.00.
Scholars Companion $.05, Ruler & Eraser, ⅜ x 1 x 6", V1p199–6, $55.00.
Scholars Companion $.05, Ruler and Eraser, ⅜ x 1 x 6", V1p199–7, $55.00.
Schrader, Valve Cores, ¼ x 1⅛ x 1½", V1p17–7, $6.00.
Schrader, Valve Insiders, ¼ x 1⅛ x 1½", V1p17–9, $8.00.
Schrader, Valve Insiders, ⅛ x 1 x 1½", V1p17–8, $8.00.
Schrader N.4000, Valve Insiders, ⅛ x 1 x 1½", V1p17–10, $12.00.
Schrader Universal, Valve Caps 880, ½ x 1 x 1½", V1p16–5, $12.00.
Schrader Universal, Valve Insides, ⅛ x 1 x 1½", V1p17–11, $8.00.
Schulman's $.01, Violet Chicle Beans, ⅜ x 1 x 1⅝", no photo, $30.00.
Schulman's Blood Org., Chicle Beans, ¼ x 1 x 1½", V1p298–4, $30.00.
Schulman's Violet, Chicle Beans, ½ x 1 x 1¼", V1p298–5, $30.00.
Schwartz, Fruit Waffers, no photo, $25.00.
Schwarz's, Lime Waffers, 1 x 2⅞ x 3", V1p289–4, $35.00.
Scotch, Gall Remedy, no photo, $45.00.
Scotch $.10, Gift Wrap Tape, ¼ x 1½", V1p199–8, $3.00.
Scott $.25, Vegatable Tablets, ½ x 1⅜ x 2½", V2p100–6, $50.00.
Scott's, Vitamin A & D, ¼ x 1½ x 2¼", V2p100–8, $30.00.
Scott's $1.00, Blood Tablets, ½ x 2 x 3⅛", V1p150–5, $80.00.
Scott's $1.00, Santal Pepsin, ½ x 2 x 3⅛", V1p150–6, $70.00.
Scotts Java sample, Coffee, 2 x 2¼", V1p236–4, $90.00.
Scott's Marvel $.50, Salve, ¾ x 2⅜", V2p101–1, $15.00.
Scott's Sure-eez $.25, Corn Remedy, ½ x 1¼", V1p150–8, $8.00.
Scout Brand, Type Ribbon, ⅞ x 2½", V2p188–4, $10.00.
Scowcroft's, Cayenne, 3½ x 2¼ x 1¼", V2p161–6, $30.00.
Seabury, Pharmacal Lab., ½ x 1⅜", V2p101–3, $45.00.
Seabury & Johnson, Billiard Cloth Mend, ¾ x 2¾", V1p199–9, $18.00.
Seabury & Johnson, Gold Cross Adhesive Plaster, 1¼ x 1¾", no photo, $25.00.
Seabury & Johnson, Oxide Zinc Plaster, 1 x 1", V1p348–1, $25.00.
Seabury & Johnson, Ready-Aid, ½ x 3¼ x 3½", V1p150–8, $15.00.
Seabury & Johnson, Silk Isenglass Plaster, 1 x 7⅝", V1p347–12, $40.00.
Seabury's, Bunion Plaster, ½ x 1¾ x 3⅛", V2p101–5, $70.00.
Seabury's, Corn Plaster, ½ x 1¾ x 3⅛", V1p150–10, $70.00.
Seabury's, Toilet Soap, 2 x 3 x 1⅞", V1p53–1, $50.00.
Seabury's 1 Doz., Pastilles, 1⅜ x 2¼ x 3½", V1p150–9, $65.00.
Seal Brand, Type Ribbon, 1¾ x 1¾ x 2", V1p322–10, $45.00.
Seal-Tite, Condom, ¼ x 1½ x 2", no photo, $50.00.
Sealect, Valve Cores, ¼ x 1 x 1⅜", V1p18–1, $15.00.
Seargent's, Rheumatic Pills, ½ x 1½ x 2⅜", no photo, $25.00.
Sears Roebuck, Needle Mill, ½ x 2⅜", V1p186–6, $45.00.
Sears Roebuck, Needle Mills, ¾ x 2¼", V1p186–5, $45.00.
Sears Roebuck, Needles Sewing 50, ⅝ x 2¼", V1p186–7, $45.00.
Sears Roebuck Co., Dry Ink, ¼ x 1⅛ x 2⅜", V2p213–7, $40.00.
Seccotine, Medicine, ½ x 1 x 2¼", V2p101–7, $8.00.
Security Brand, Cloves, 3¾ x 2¼ x 1¼", V2p161–2, $50.00.
Security Brand sample, Coffee, no photo, $80.00.
Sedafen $.25, Tablets 16, ¼ x 1¾ x 1⅞", V1p150–11, $15.00.
Sedarex, Tablets, ¼ x 1¼ x 1¾", V1p150–12, $12.00.
Sedarex, Tablets, ¼ x 1¼ x 1¾", V1p151–1, $12.00.
Sedarex, Tablets, ¼ x 1¼ x 1¾", V1p151–2, $12.00.
Sedets, Pain Tablets, ¼ x 1¼ x 1¾", V1p151–3, $6.00.
Sekurity, Condom, ¼ x 1⅝ x 2", V1p24–7, $65.00.
Selaw sample, Cleanser, ¾ x 2", V2p39–3, $25.00.
Select sample, Talcum Powder, ¾ x 1¼ x 2⅛", V1p261–4, $35.00.
Selected Imported, Paprika, 2 x 4½", no photo, $25.00.
Selmer, Joint Grease, ½ x 1½", V1p11–3, $20.00.
Sem, Needles, no photo, $35.00.
Sem FS 12, Needles Phono, 1¼ x 1¼ x 1¾", V1p210–6, $35.00.

Sem Gold, Needles, ¼ x 1¼ x 1⅝", V1p210–5, $30.00.
Semets, Throat Troches, ⅜ x 2¾ x 3¼", V1p294–6, $8.00.
Seminole, Indian Salve, ¾ x 3⅝", no photo, $55.00.
Sen-Sen $.10, Breath Mints, ¼ x 1½ x 2", V1p289–5, $22.00.
Sen-Sen $.10, Breath Mints, ¼ x 1½ x 2", V1p289–6, $22.00.
Sen-Sen $.10, Breath Mints, ¼ x 1½ x 2", V1p289–7, $22.00.
Senate (bank), Coffee, 3 x 2¼ x 2¼", V1p236–5, $120.00.
Sendol, Cold and Pain Tablets, ⅜ x 2½ x 1¾", V2p101–2, $6.00.
Sendol, Cold Tablets, ¼ x 1¾ x 2½", V1p151–5, $10.00.
Sendol, Pain Tablets, ¼ x 1¼ x 1¾", V1p151–4, $12.00.
Sendol, Vitamin Tablets, no photo, $15.00.
Seneca, Curry Powder, 3¼ x 2¼ x ¾", V2p161–3, $35.00.
Sent-a-nel $.25, Laxative, ¼ x 1⅞ x 2½", V2p101–4, $22.00.
Sentinel, Adhesive Tape, ¾ x 2¼", no photo, $5.00.
Sentinel, Bandaids, 1¼ x 3½", V1p152–6, $8.00.
Sentinel, Dental Floss, ¼ x 1⅛", V1p56–6, $25.00.
Sentinel, First Aid Kit, ¾ x 2¼ x 3¾", V1p152–8, $35.00.
Sentinel, Handy Bandages, 1¼ x 3¾", V1p151–7, $10.00.
Sentinel, Vitamin Tablets 25, ½ x 1¾ x 3¼", V1p152–10, $10.00.
Sentinel A&D, Vitamin Tablets 30, ⅜ x 1¾ x 2½", V1p152–9, $10.00.
Septorin, Antiseptic Laxative, ⅜ x 1½ x 2½", no photo, $20.00.
Septorin $.10, Laxative Tablets, ¼ x ⅞ x 1¾", V1p151–11, $18.00.
Septorin $.25, Laxative, ⅜ x 1¼ x 2½", no photo, $15.00.
Sergeant's $.50, Sure Shot Capsules, 1¾ x 1¾ x 1½", V1p333–5, $40.00.
Sergeant's sample, Pine Oil Disinfectant, 1¼ x 2¼ x 2", V1p199–10, $20.00.
Seroco Chemical, Dr. McBain's Pills, V1p94–3, $45.00.
Seroco Chemical, see Dr. Wordens Female Pills.
Seroco Chemical, see English Pile Remedy.
Seroco Chemical, see Wonder Heart Cure", V1p168–2, $60.00.
Seroco Chemical $1.00, see Dr. Hammonds Nerve\Brain.
Seroco Cure $.50, Tobacco Habit, ½ x 2 x 2⅝", V1p151–12, $65.00.
Serts, Rectal Suppository, ⅝ x 1 x 2", V1p152–1, $5.00.
Service, Type Ribbon, ¾ x 2½ x 2½", no photo, $95.00.
Severa's, Cold Tablets, ½ x 1⅝ x 2½", V2p101–6, $8.00.
Severa's, Esko Itch Ointment, no photo, $12.00.
Sewell's, Catarrh Jelly, no photo, $35.00.
Sewickly $.15, Corn\Wart Exterminator, ⅜ x ⅞", V2p101–8, $20.00.
Shac, Headache Tablets, ¼ x 1¼ x 1¾", V1p152–2, $15.00.
Shadows, Condom, ¼ x 1⅝ x 2⅛", V2p20–5, $35.00.
Shadows $1.00, Condom, ½ x 1½ x 1½", V1p24–9, $40.00.
Shakespear, Flexolyn, ¾ x 2¾", V1p177–4, $5.00.
Sharp & Dohme, Acetidine Tablets, ¼ x 1¼ x 1¾", V1p152–3, $6.00.
Sharp & Dohme sample, Spirets, ¼ x 1¼ x 1¾", V2p102–1, $12.00.
Sharp-O No.3 $.10, Strop Dressing, ½ x 1¼", V2p136–3, $25.00.
Shawmut, Auto Fuses, ¼ x 1¼ x 1¾", V1p10–3, $25.00.
Sheafer's, Fineline Lead, ⅜ x ¼ x 3", no photo, $4.00.
Sheafer's $.15, Fineline Erasers, ⅜ x ¼ x 1⅝", no photo, $4.00.
Sheafer's $.15, Fineline Erasers, ⅜ x ⅜ x 2¾", no photo, $4.00.
Sheaffer's Fineline, Pencil Lead, ¼ x ½ x 1¾", V1p182–10, $3.00.
Sheaffer's Skrip, Pencil Refill, ¼ x ⅜ x 1½", V1p182–11, $5.00.
Shebry sample, Deodorant Crm., ¼ x 1", V1p31–12, $18.00.
Sheik, Condom, ¼ x 1½ x 2", V1p24–11, $50.00.
Sheik, Condom, ¼ x 1½ x 2⅛", V1p25–3, $40.00.
Sheik, Condom, ¼ x 1½ x 2", V1p24–12, $55.00.
Sheik, Condoms, ¼ x 1½ x 2", V1p25–1, $55.00.
Sheik, Condom, ⅜ x 1½ x 1½", V1p25–2, $80.00.
Sheik $.50, Condom, ¼ x 1⅝ x 2⅛", V2p20–7, $45.00.
Sheik $.50, Condom, ¼ x 1⅝ x 2⅛", V2p21–1, $55.00.
Sheik $.60, Condoms, ¼ x 1½ x 2", V1p25–3, $40.00.
Shell 200 #16, Phono Needles, ⅜ x 1¼ x 1¾", V2p115–1, $35.00.
Shell 200 #3, Extra Loud Needles, ⅜ x 1¼ x 1¾", V2p115–3, $35.00.
Shield, Condom, ½ x 1½", V1p25–4, $65.00.
Shinola sample, Black Shoe Polish, 1 x 2", V2p120–6, $18.00.
Shoes Wont Leak, Shoe Grease, 1 x 3", V1p281–9, $20.00.
Shores, Black Pepper, 1¼ x 2⅛ x 3¼", V2p161–5, $65.00.
Shores, Jamaica Ginger, 2 x 3 x 4 ¾", V2p161–7, $60.00.
Shot Gun, Sights, no photo, $40.00.
Shu-Sno, Shoe Cleaner Wht., ⅝ x 2¼", V1p281–10, $12.00.
Shurfire Brand, Nutmeg, 3¼ x 2¼ x 1¼", V2p162–1, $15.00.
Shurlite, Lighter Flints, ⅜ x 1 x 1¼", $4.00.
ShurSong $.30, Bird Food, 1½ x 2⅜ x 3⅝", V1p199–11, $18.00.
Shuttle Looper, Sewing Attachment, ½ x ⅞ x 2¾", V1p186–8, $6.00.
Sila, Headache Pills, ½ x 1½ x 2", no photo, $18.00.
Silbert, Watch Parts, ½ x 1⅛", V1p340–1, $4.00.
Silhouette, Type Ribbon, ¾ x 2¼", no photo, $12.00.
Silhouette, Type Ribbon, ¾ x 2¼", V1p322–11, $8.00.
Silk Fibre, Type Ribbon, ¾ x 2½ x 2½", V1p322–12, $18.00.
Silk Gauze, Type Ribbon, ¾ x 2½ x 2½", V1p323–1, $8.00.
Silk Gauze, Type Ribbon, ¾ x 2¼", no photo, $10.00.
Silk Gauze, Type Ribbon, ¾ x 2¼ x 2¼", V1p323–2, $18.00.
Silk Gauze (Dragon), Type Ribbon, ¾ x 2¼", V1p323–3, $12.00.
Silk Hat, Hankerchief, no photo, $115.00.
Silk 'Y' Fiber, Type Ribbon, ¾ x 2½ x 2½", V1p323–4, $18.00.
Sills $.25, Corn\Callous Ointment, ½ x 1⅜", V1p152–4, $12.00.
Siltex Egyptian, Type Ribbon, ¾ x 2½ x 2½", V2p188–6, $15.00.
Silver, Needle Phono, ½ x 1¼ x 1½", V1p210–7, $25.00.
Silver Gem, Gum, ¼ x 1¼", V1p298–6, $25.00.
Silver Gem, Gum, ¼ x 1¼", V1p298–7, $25.00.
Silver Knight, Condom, no photo, $70.00.
Silver Line, Aspirin, ¼ x 1¾ x 2⅝", V1p152–5, $15.00.
Silver Sea, Whole Allspice, 2 x 4", V2p162–3, $60.00.
Silver Tex De Luxe, Condom, ¼ x 1⅝ x 2⅛", V2p21–3, $60.00.
Silver-Tex, Disease Prevent., ¼ x 1⅝ x 2⅛", V2p21–5, $50.00.
Silver-Tex ¼ doz., Condom, ¼ x 1⅝ x 2⅛", V2p21–6, $50.00.
Silverine $.25, Metal Polish, 2 x 3 x 1½", V2p39–5, $50.00.
Silverod, Type Ribbon, ¾ x 2½ x 2½", V1p323–5, $8.00.
Silvertex, Condom, no photo, $50.00.
Silvertone (Sears), Needles, ½ x 1½ x 2½", V1p210–9, $35.00.
Silvertone 500, Full-Tone Needles, ⅝ x 1⅞", V1p210–8, $65.00.
Silvertone Loud, 200 Needles, ⅜ x 1¼ x 1¾", V2p115–5, $60.00.
Silvertone Soft, 200 Needles, ¼ x 1¼ x 1½", V2p115–7, $60.00.
Sim-Trex, Corn Remedy, ¼ x 1⅝", V1p152–6, $10.00.
Simmons, Liver Purifier, 1¼ x 1⅝ x 2⅜", V1p152–7, $50.00.
Simmon's A.C., Laxative Powder, 1½ x 2¼ x 2⅝", V2p102–3, $35.00.
Simmons M.A., Laxative, 1¾ x 1¾ x 2⅛", V1p152–8, $40.00.
Simplex, Needles, ⅜ x 1¼ x 1¾", V1p210–10, $25.00.
Sims 12, Laxative Asprin, ¼ x 1¼ x 1¾", V2p102–5, $6.00.
Sinapex, Mustard Plaster, ⅜ x 1¾", V1p152–9, $10.00.
Sing a Song Six Pence, Candy Pail, 3¾ x 6 x 3", $225.00.
Sisto, Deodorant Powder, 1¾ x 4", V1p45–9, $60.00.
Skat, Hand soap, no photo, $20.00.
Skin Tight, Condom, no photo, $50.00.
Skoda's $.35, Little Tablets, ¼ x 1⅜ x 2½", V1p152–11, $75.00.
Skookum, Syrum, no photo, $25.00.
Skowhegan, Waterproof Paste, ¾ x 1¾", V1p281–11, $18.00.
Slades', Oxford Mustard, 3¾ x 2¼ x 1", V2p162–5, $20.00.
Slades', Tumeric, 1¼ x 1¾ x 2¾", V2p162–6, $25.00.
Sleep-Eze, Sleep Pills, 1 x 1¾", V1p152–11, $10.00.
Slothowers $.30, Healing Salve, 1 x 2⅜", V1p152–12, $22.00.
Smile's Prid, Healing Ointment, ⅝ x 1⅞", no photo, $8.00.
Smith Bros. $.10, Cough Drops, ½ x 2¼ x 3¾", V1p294–7, $250.00.
Smith Co., Imported Saffron, ⅝ x 2¼", no photo, $20.00.
Smith James P. Co., Curry Powder, 1¾ x 1⅜ x 4", V2p162–2, $30.00.

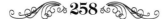

Smith L.C., Type Ribbon, ¾ x 2¼ x 2¼", V1p323-6, $18.00.
Smith L.C., Type Ribbon, ¾ x 2⅛ x 2⅛, no photo, $18.00.
Smith L.C. Bros., Type Ribbon, 1¾ x 1¾ x 2⅛", V1p323-7, $55.00.
Smith Premier, Type Ribbon, 1¾ x 2 x 1¾", V1p323-8, $45.00.
Smith Sandy, Knitting Needles, ⅝ x 9", V1p187-3, $65.00.
Smith, Kline & French, Aceto-Sal Cold Tablets, ¼ x 1¼ x 1¾", V1p153-1, $25.00.
Smith, Kline & French sample, Benzedrine Sulfate Tabs, ¼ x 1¼ x 1¾", no photo, $8.00.
Smith, Kline & French, Casca-Phen Laxative Tonic, ¼ x 1¾ x 2⅝", V1p153-3, $25.00.
Smith, Kline & French sample, Indigestion Tablets, ¼ x 1½ x 2", V1p153-2, $30.00.
Smither's sample, Witch Hazel Balm, ¼ x 1½ x 1½", no photo, $15.00.
Smithies, Condom, ¼ x 1⅝ x 2⅛", V2p21-2, $65.00.
Smith's, Foot Ointment, ⅝ x 1¾", no photo, $10.00.
Smith's, Rose Bud Salve, ⅞ x 2⅛", V1p153-9, $12.00.
Smiths $.25, Rose Bud Balsam, ¾ x 2⅛", V1p153-5, $55.00.
Smith's $.25, Rose Bud Salve, ½ x 1¾", V1p153-8, $15.00.
Smith's $.25, Rose Bud Salve, ¾ x 2", no photo, $15.00.
Smith's $.25, Rose Bud Salve, ⅞ x 2⅛", V1p153-6, $25.00.
Smith's $.25, Rose Bud Salve, ⅞ x 2⅛", V1p153-7, $18.00.
Smith's sample, Balsam Rose Buds, ¼ x ⅞", V2p102-6, $15.00*.
Smith's sample, Rose Bud Balsam, ⅜ x ⅞", V1p153-4, $60.00.
Smith's Tip Top, Type Ribbon, ¾ x 2¼ x 2¼", no photo, $15.00.
Smith's W.F., Dyspepsia Tablets, no photo, $35.00.
Smith's W.F., Pills, ¼ x 2 x 2⅞", no photo, $65.00.
Smith's W.F. $.17, Triple Cure Catarrh Cream, no photo, $55.00.
Smith's W.F. $.50, Triple Cure Pills, ½ x 1⅝ x 2⅞", V2p102-2, $65.00.
Smith's W.F. $.50, Triple Cure Tablets, ½ x 1⅝ x 2⅞", V2p102-4, $70.00.
Smith's W.F.Buchu $.25, Lithia Pills, ½ x 2 x 2⅞", V1p153-10, $70.00.
Smooth, Powder for Men, 1 x 3 x 4", V1p199-12, $5.00.
Smooth-On #1, Stop Leaks, 1¼ x 1¾", V1p281-12, $8.00.
Smut-less, Type Ribbon, ¾ x 2¼ x 2¼", no photo, $12.00.
Snow King sample, Baking Powder, 2 x 3¼", V2p126-5, $60.00.
Snow White, Bleaching Cream, ¾ x 2¾", V2p30-4, $22.00.
Snow White, Bleaching Cream, ⅞ x 2½", V1p28-12, $22.00.
Snow-proof sample, Waterproofing, ⅞ x 2⅛", V1p282-1, $15.00.
Snuffene $.25, Cold Remedy, ⅝ x 1⅝ x 2¾", V1p153-11, $55.00.
Soam $.50, Rheumatic Cure, ⅝ x 2¼ x 3½", V2p102-6, $145.00.
Society Brand sample, Coffee, 2½ x 2", no photo, $200.00.
Society Brand sample, Coffee, 2 x 2½", V1p236-6, $160.00.
Sodascorbate, Medicine, no photo, $18.00.
Sol-fa, Troches, no photo, $35.00.
Solarine, Metal Polish, 1 x 1¾", V1p219-4, $65.00.
Solitaire sample, Coffee, 2½ x 1⅝", V1p237-1, $70.00.
Solo, Saffron, ¾ x 2", V1p188-2, $5.00.
Solo Radiogram, Needles, no photo, $35.00.
Solo X Loud, Needles, ¼ x 1¼ x 1¾", no photo, $25.00.
Solox Compound, Pennyroyal Pills, no photo, $35.00.
Solrite, Type Ribbon, ¾ x 2½ x 2½", V2p189-1, $18.00.
Somers Bros., Pill Box, ⅝ x 2¼ x 3½", V1p153-12, $125.00.
Somerville, Chewing Gum Vanilla, ½ x 1 x 3", no photo, $125.00.
Somerville's, Chewing Gum, no photo, $120.00.
Sommerset Club sample, Coffee, no photo, $120.00.
Songster 100, Golden Needles, ⅜ x 1¼ x 1¾", V1p211-5, $35.00.
Songster 100, Trailer Needles, ⅜ x 1¼ x 1¾", V2p115-9, $40.00.
Songster 100 Bronze, Pick Up Needles, ⅜ x 1¼ x 1¾", V1p210-11, $35.00.
Songster 100 Loud, Needles, ¼ x 1¼ x 1¾", V2p115-2, $35.00.
Songster 200, Loud Needles, ⅜ x 1¼ x 1¾", V1p211-3, $35.00.
Songster 200, Medium Tone, ⅜ x 1¼ x 1½", V2p115-4, $35.00.
Songster 200, Medium Tone Needle, ¼ x 1¼ x 1¾", V1p211-1, $35.00.
Songster 200, Needles, no photo, $35.00.
Songster 200, Soft Tone Needles, ⅜ x 1¼ x 1¾", no photo, $35.00.
Songster 200, Spear Point Needles, ⅜ x 1¼ x 1¾", V1p210-12, $35.00.
Songster 200, XLoud Needles, ¼ x 1¼ x 1¾", V1p211-2, $35.00.
Songster 200, XSoft Needles, ¼ x 1¼ x 1¾", V1p211-4, $35.00.
Songster 200 Soft, Needles, ⅜ x 1¼ x 1¾", V2p115-6, $35.00.
Sonora 300, Needles, ⅜ x 1¼ x 1½", V1p211-6, $30.00.
Sonorets $.25, Familex Licorice, ⅜ x 1½ x 2½", V2p171-2, $12.00.
Soothene, Ointment, 1¾ x 1¾ x 1¾", V1p154-1, $22.00.
Soovain, Tablets, ¼ x 1¼ x 1¾", V1p154-2, $8.00*.
Soule's $.25, Corn Remover, ⅜ x 1⅜", V1p154-3, $18.00.
Southern Girl sample, Rouge, ¼ x 1⅜", V1p48-10, $15.00.
Southern I A Brand, Type Ribbon, ¾ x 2½ x 2½", V1p323-9, $12.00.
Southwell Chas.Co., Unknown, 1 x 2⅝ x 3¾", no photo, $30.00.
Soverign, Condom, no photo, $50.00.
Sozodont Powder, Tooth Powder, 1 x 2 x 2¾", V1p58-12, $65.00.
Sozodont sample, Teeth Powder, ⅝ x 2", V1p59-2, $140.00.
Sozodont sample, Tooth Powder, ½ x 1⅝ x 2¼", no photo, $80.00.
Spartan $.10, Aspirin, ⅜ x 1¼ x 1¾", V2p102-8, $12.00.
Spayd's $1.00, Type Ribbon, 1½ x 1½ x 2", no photo, $65.00.
Spearmint, Tooth Powder, no photo, $40.00.
Speedo, Aspirin, ¼ x 1¼ x 1½", no photo, $10.00.
Speedwell, Corn Caps, ½ x 1¼ x 2½", V1p154-4, $15.00.
Spencerian, Steel Pens, ¼ x ¾ x 2", V2p213-2, $40.00.
Spencerian, Steel Pens, ⅜ x ¾ x 2⅛", no photo, $30.00.
Spencer's $.10, Cough Lozenge, ⅝ x 1½ x 2¾", V1p294-8, $45.00*.
Sperry's Allwrite, Type Ribbon, ¾ x 2¼ x 2¼", no photo, $15.00.
Sphinx, Condom, no photo, $75.00.
Sphnix (Lindsay), Needles Phono, ½ x 1¼ x 1½", V1p211-7, $35.00.
Sphnix Brand, Needles, ⅜ x 1¼ x 1½", V1p211-8, $35.00.
Spice House, Spice, no photo, $22.00.
Spiehler's sample, Talcum Powder, no photo, $70.00.
Splendid, Watch Main Spring, ¾ x 3 x 3⅜", V1p340-2, $45.00.
Sponge, Condom, 1 x 1⅞", V1p27-9, $45.00.
Sponge, Condom (Sponge), 1¼ x 2", V1p27-11, $35.00.
Spratt's, Flea Powder, 1 x 1¾ x 4½", V1p200-1, $25.00.
Spratt's, Sing Song, ¾ x 1¼ x 2", V2p193-4, $20.00.
Spratt's, Sing Song Birds, ¾ x 1¼ x 2", V1p200-2, $5.00.
Spring Blossoms, Cosmetic, no photo, $25.00.
Sproule's Germicide, Ointment, ⅝ x 1½", V1p154-5, $12.00.
Spurlock-Neal $.50, Carboil, ¾ x 2⅛", no photo, $40.00.
Square Circle, Monogram, no photo, $20.00.
Squibb, Aspirin, ¼ x 1¼ x 1¾", V1p154-6, $10.00.
Squibb, Aspirin, ¼ x 1¼ x 1¾", V1p154-7, $12.00.
Squibb 30, Milk of Magnesia, ¼ x 2⅜ x 2¾", V1p154-8, $8.00.
Squibb Bouquet sample, Talcum Powder, ¾ x 1¼ x 2⅛", V1p261-5, $35.00.
Squibb's sample, Carnation talcum, 1 x 2⅛", V2p130-2, $45.00.
Squibb's Violet sample, Talcum Powder, 1 x 2¼", V1p261-6, $45.00.
SR, Adhesive Plaster, 1 x 1¼", V1p348-2, $20.00.
SR, Zinc Oxide, 1 x 1", no photo, $15.00.
St. John's, Skin Tonic, ⅝ x 1⅝", V1p53-2, $50.00.
St. Joseph $.10, Pure Aspirin, ¼ x 1¼ x 1¾", V1p154-11, $10.00.
St. Joseph $.10, Pure Aspirin, ¼ x 1¼ x 1¾", V2p103-1, $10.00.
St. Joseph $.25, Laxative Tablets, ¼ x 1¼ x 1¾", V2p103-3, $7.00.
St. Joseph $.25, Liver Pills, ¼ x 1¼ x 1¾", V2p103-5, $8.00.
St. Joseph 2223, Liver Pills, ¼ x 1¼ x 1¾", V1p155-4, $15.00.
St. Joseph's, Anti-Histamine Tablets, ¼ x 1¼ x 1¾", V1p154-9, $8.00.

St. Joseph's $.10, Pure Aspirin, ¼ x 1¼ x 1¾", V1p154–12, $8.00.

St. Joseph's $.10, Pure Aspirin, ¼ x 1⅝ x 1¾", V1p154–11, $12.00.

St. Joseph's $.12, Aspirin, ¼ x 1¼ x 1¾", V1p155–1, $10.00.

St. Joseph's $.25, Aspirin, ¼ x 1¼ x 1¾", V1p155–2, $6.00.

St. Joseph's $.25, Aspirin, ¼ x 2⅝ x 2⅝", V1p155–3, $15.00.

St. Joseph's 223 $.25, Laxative Pills, ¼ x 1¼ x 1¾", V1p255–5, $15.00.

St. Joseph's Penetro, Mutton Suet Salve, ¼ x 1¼ x 1¾", V1p255–6, $25.00.

St. Mary's $.05, Aspirin, ¼ x 1 x 1¼", V1p155–7, $15.00.

St. Mary's $.10, Aspirin, ¼ x 1¼ x 1¾", V1p155–8, $12.00.

St. Mary's $.10, Aspirin, ¼ x 1¼ x 1¾", V1p155–9, $10.00.

St. Mary's $.10, Laxative Cold Tablets, ¼ x 1¼ x 1¾", V2p103–6, $12.00.

St. Mary's $.10, Timely-Lax, ¼ x 1⅝ x 1⅝", V1p155–11, $18.00.

Sta-so sample, Hair Pomade, ⅜ x 1½", V1p40–2, $35.00.

Stacomb, Hair, ¾ x 1¾", V1p40–3, $15.00.

Stafford's, Type Ribbon, ¾ x 2¼ x 2¼", V1p323–10, $15.00.

Stafford's, Type Ribbon, ⅞ x 2½ x 2½", V1p323–11, $12.00.

Stafford's Immaculate, Type Ribbon, ⅞ x 2½", V1p323–12, $8.00.

Stafford's Superfine, Type Ribbon, ¾ x 2½ x 2½", V2p189–4, $18.00.

Staffords Superfine, Type Ribbon, ¾ x 2¼", V1p324–1, $20.00.

Staffords Superfine, Type Ribbon, ⅞ x 2½ x 2½", no photo, $12.00.

Stag Brand 200, Gramophone Needles, ⅜ x 1¼ x 1¾", V2p115–8, $40.00.

Stahlnadeln Feinste 200, Victrolia Needles, ¼ x 1¼ x 1¾", V1p211–9, $35.00.

Stamco, Type Ribbon, ¾ x 2½ x 2½", V2p189–6, $12.00.

Stanback, Headache Tablets, ⅜ x 1¼ x 1¾", V1p155–12, $6.00.

Stanback $.25, Aspirin, ¼ x 1¼ x 1¾", no photo, $5.00.

Stanback $.25, Aspirin, ¼ x 1¼ x 1¾", V1p155–11, $5.00.

Stanco $.15, Aspirin, ¼ x 1¼ x 1¾", V1p156–1, $8.00.

Standard, Gall Salve, no photo, $25.00.

Standard, Radio Crystal, ¾ x 1", V1p200–3, $15.00.

Standard, Type Ribbon, ¾ x 2½ x 2½", V1p324–2, $10.00.

Standard Drug, Seidlitz Powders, 1¾ x 3 x 4½", $10.00.

Standard Laboratories, Bell's Salve, ⅞ x 2⅜", V2p103–2, $10.00.

Standard Motor, Auto Fuses, ¼ x 1¼ x 1¾", V1p10–2, $12.00.

Stanley's, Complexion Powder, 1 x 2¾", V1p45–10, $45.00.

Stanvar, Varnish, no photo, $20.00.

Staples sample, Prepared Wax, ⅝ x 2", V1p343–6, $30.00.

Star, Bouillon Cubes, ¾ x 1¾ x 2⅝, no photo, $10.00.

Star, Hack Saw Blades, ½ x 2¼ x 8 ½", V1p190–7, $30.00.

Star, Razor Case, ¼ x 1½ x 2¼", V1p271–9, $60.00.

Star, Safety Blades, ¼ x 1⅛ x 2¼", V1p269–6, $70.00.

Star, Safety Razor, 1¼ x 2⅛", V2p136–5, $185.00.

Star, Safety Razor Blade, ¼ x 1 x 2", no photo, $60.00.

Star, Safety Razor Blades, ¼ x 1⅛ x 1¾", V2p136–2, $60.00.

Star, Type Cleaner, ¾ x 1¾ x 2½", V1p324–3, $15.00.

Star $2.00, Safety Razor, 1¼ x 2¼", V1p271–10, $75.00.

Star $.50, Type Cleaner, ¾ x 1¾ x 2½", V1p324–4, $15.00.

Star $1.50, Safety Razor, no photo, $145.00.

Star $1.50, Safety Razor\Blades, 1⅜ x 2¼ x 1¾", no photo, $75.00.

Star $2.00, Safety Razor, no photo, $95.00.

Star $2.00, Safety Razor, 1¼ x 2¼", V1p271–11, $115.00.

Star $2.00, Safety Razor, 1¼ x 2¼", V1p272–1, $150.00.

Star $2.00, Safety Razor, 1¼ x 2¼ x 1½", V1p271–8, $90.00.

Star $2.00, Safety Razor, 1⅜ x 2¼", no photo, $145.00.

Star $2.00, Safety Razor, 1⅜ x 2¼", V1p271–12, $150.00.

Star $2.00, Safety Razor, 1⅜ x 2¼", V1p272–3, $95.00.

Star $2.00, Safety Razor, 1⅜ x 2¼ x 1¾", no photo, $65.00.

Star $2.00, Safety Razor\Blades, 1¼ x 2¼ x 1⅝", no photo, $80.00.

Star Brand $1.00, Condoms, ⅝ x 1⅝", no photo, $30.00.

Star Bright, Auto Fuses, no photo, $15.00.

Star No. 1226, Type Cleaner, ¾ x 2¼ x 2¼", V1p324–5, $20.00.

Star Safety Razor, Razor Blades, ¼ x 1¼ x 2¼", V1p269–9, $55.00.

Star-O-Hair sample, Dressing, ¼ x 1⅛", no photo, $20.00.

Starless $.30, Gall Salve, 1 x 2⅝", V1p333–6, $25.00*.

Staso, Dry Cleaner, 1 x 3⅓", V1p22–9, $6.00.

Stearate of Zinc sample, Powder, ¾ x 1¼ x 2⅛", V1p266–9, $50.00.

Stearns, Aspirin, ⅜ x 1¼ x 1¾", V1p156–2, $15.00.

Stearn's, Cascara Tablets, 1 x 1⅞", V1p156–3, $22.00.

Stearns, Esterin, ¼ x 1¼ x 1¾", V2p103–4, $12.00.

Stearn's, Esterin, ¼ x 1¼ x 1¾", V2p103–7, $12.00.

Stearn's E.C., DeLyon's Hair Grower, ½ x 1¼", V1p40–4, $6.00.

Stearns Frederick, Aromatic Tooth Soap, ½ x 2 x 3⅛", V2p43–2, $75.00.

Stearns Frederick, Shac Headache Tablets, V1p152–2, $15.00.

Steel Needles 200, Needles Phono, ¼ x 1¼ x 1¾", V1p211–10, $30.00.

Steero, Bouillon Cubes, ¾ x 1¾ x 2¾", V1p20–7, $8.00.

Steero, Bouillon Cubes, ⅝ x 1⅜ x 1⅜", V1p20–6, $5.00.

Steero, Boullion Cubes, ⅞ x 1¾ x 2⅞", V1p20–8, $6.00.

Steero, Boullion Cubes, ⅞ x ¾ x 3¼", V1p20–9, $5.00.

Stein Cosmetic, Grease Paints, 1 x 2⅝ x 4½", V1p53–3, $18.00.

Stein Cosmetic, Theatrical Make Up, 1¼ x 4¼", V1p53–4, $25.00.

Stein Cosmetic, Theatrical Make Up, 1¼ x 4¼", V1p53–5, $25.00.

Steinite $.50, Crystals, ½ x 1¼", V1p200–4, $5.00.

Stein's, Black Wax, ¾ x 2", V1p53–6, $15.00.

Stein's, Black Wax, ⅝ x 1½", V2p34–6, $12.00.

Stein's, Black Wax, ⅝ x 1⅝", V1p40–5, $15.00.

Stein's, Hair Color, ⅝ x 1¼ x 2¾", V1p40–6, $20.00.

Stein's, Lining Color, ½ x 1½", V1p53–7, $15.00.

Stein's, Mexicola Rouge, no photo, $15.00.

Stein's, Toupee Wax, 1 x 2½", no photo, $12.00.

Stein's #18, Rouge, no photo, $15.00.

Stein's $.25, Nose Putty, ⅝ x 1⅝", V1p53–8, $25.00.

Stein's $.50, Face Powder, ⅝ x 2½", V1p45–11, $20.00.

Stenotype, Type Ribbon, ¾ x 1¾", V1p324–6, $22.00.

Stenotype, Type Ribbon, ¾ x 1¾ x 1¾", V1p324–7, $8.00.

Stenotype $.25, Type Ribbon, ¾ x 2¼ x 2¼", no photo, $15.00.

Sterling Remedy Co., see Cascarets Laxative.

Sterling Remedy Co., see Hobbs'.

Sterling Remedy Co., see No-To-Bac.

Sterling's sample, Vapor-Eze-Salve, ⅜ x 1¼", V2p104–1, $20.00.

Sterno 200, Needles, no photo, $30.00.

Steven's Fancy 4oz., Boneless Herring, ⅞ x 1¾ x 6", V2p213–4, $40.00.

Stevenson sample, Split Shot, ⅜ x 1⅜", V1p177–5, $20.00.

Stewart, Bottom Plate, ⅜ x 2⅛ x 3", V1p200–5, $12.00.

Stewart, Clipper Plate, ⅞ x 1⅜ x 2⅞", V1p200–6, $12.00.

Stewart, Plate for Shears, ¼ x 1½ x 2⅞", V1p200–7, $8.00.

Stewart, Plate for Shears, ⅜ x 2⅛ x 3⅛", V1p200–8, $12.00.

Stewart (Sunbeam), Clipper Blade, ¼ x 1½ x 2⅞", V1p200–9, $5.00.

Stick-um, Candle Adhesive, ⅝ x 2⅛", V1p200–10, $8.00.

Sticktape Aerial, Tape, ⅜ x 4", V1p200–11, $25.00.

Sticktite, Adhesive Plaster, no photo, $20.00.

Stock, Type Ribbon, ¾ x 2½", no photo, $8.00.

Stock, Type Ribbon, ⅞ x 2½", V2p189–2, $8.00.

Stoeger, Blasting Caps, no photo, $40.00.

Stollwerck's, Antoinette Bonbons, ½ x 2 x 3¾", V1p289–8, $120.00.

Stollwerck's, Candy Cachous, ¼ x 1¾", V1p289–9, $40.00.

Stollwerk, Cocoa, 1¼ x 3½ x 3⅞", V1p223–2, $55.00.

Stollwerk Royal, Cocoa Butter, 1 x 3½", V1p246–3, $15.00.

Stollwerk's, Indian Pearls, no photo, $60.00.

Stollwerk's Adler sample, Cocoa, no photo, $50.00.

Ston-lax $.25, Laxative, ¼ x 1¼ x 1¾", V1p156–4, $15.00.

Storm's Triangle, Type Ribbon, 1¾ x 1¾ x 2", no photo, $35.00.

Stormtex, Type Ribbon, ¾ x 2½ x 2½", V2p189–3, $15.00.
Stothert's, Foot Paste, ½ x 1¼", V1p156–5, $15.00.
Stuart's, Calcium Wafer Compound, ¼ x 1¼ x 1¾", V1p156–7, $20.00.
Stuart's, Mentha-Rub, ⅝ x 1⅞", V1p156–6, $12.00.
Stuart's, Tablets, ½ x 1⅞ x 3⅛", V1p156–8, $15.00.
Stuart's, Tablets Stomach, ½ x 2 x 3⅛", no photo, $18.00.
Stuart's, Worm Tablets, x 1¾ x 3", no photo, $25.00.
Stuart's $.25, Dyspepsia Tablets, ½ x 2 x 3⅛", V1p156–9, $20.00.
Stuart's $.25, Dyspepsia Tablets, ½ x 2 x 3⅛", V2p104–4, $22.00.
Stuart's Handy, Ginger, 3¾ x 2¾ x 1¼", V2p162–4, $60.00.
Sub Rosa, Deodorant Cream, no photo, $20.00.
Submarine, Needles, no photo, $40.00.
Sucrets, Throat Loz., ¾ x 2⅜ x 3⅛", V1p294–9, $5.00.
Sulphur, Ointment, ⅝ x 2⅛", V1p156–10, $6.00.
Sultan, Condom, no photo, $70.00.
Sun, Stove Polish, 1 x 3½", V1p219–5, $30.00.
Sun & Moon, Sacred Ointment, ⅝ x 1½", V1p156–11, $25.00.
Sun Flower, Peanut Butter, 2⅞ x 3", $70.00.
Sun Red, Saffron, ¼ x 1¼ x 1¾", V1p188–3, $20.00.
Sun-Ray sample, Metal Polish, ⅜ x 1⅛", V2p39–6, $10.00.
Sunbeam, Comb & Cutter, 1¼ x 2¼", V1p200–12, 4.00.
Sunbeam, Ginger, ⅞ x 2½ x 4", V1p189–8, $35.00.
Sunbeam sample, Coffee, 2½ x 3½", V1p237–2, $85.00.
Sunder, Phono Needles, ⅜ x 1¼ x 1¾", V2p115–10, $25.00.
Sundown Cof-e-log sample, Coffee, 3 x 2¼", V1p237–3, $95.00.
Sundstrand, Ribbon, ¾ x 1⅝", V2p189–5, $25.00.
Sundstrand, Type Speed Ribbon, ¾ x 1⅝", V1p324–11, $10.00.
Sunray $.15, Salve for Burns, ½ x 1⅜", V1p156–12, $45.00.
Sunred, Spanish Saffron, ⅜ x 1⅝ x 1⅝", V2p203–7, $8.00.
Sunset Club sample, Coffee, 2½ x 3", V1p237–4, $150.00.
Sunshyne, Type Ribbon, ¾ x 2½ x 2½", V1p324–10, $15.00.
Super Pure, Tea Herb, 1¼ x 1¾ x 2½", V1p268–5, $18.00.
Super Shell, Type Ribbon, ¾ x 2½ x 2½", no photo, $10.00.
Super Superb, Type Ribbon, ¾ x 2½ x 2½", V1p324–12, $25.00.
Super-O-Phone, Needles, no photo, $25.00.
Super-Seal, Assembly, 1⅜ x 1⅛", V1p201–1, $10.00.
Superb, Rubber Type, ½ x 2¼ x 3½", V2p213–6, $8.00.
Superb, Type Ribbon, ⅞ x 2½ x 2½", V1p325–1, $30.00.
Superb Size A, Stamp Pad, ½ x 1⅝ x 2¾", V2p200–8, $12.00.
Superior, Cold Cream, ¾ x 1½", V2p30–6, $20.00.
Superior, Cough Drops, no photo, $65.00.
Superior, Mainsprings, ¾ x 2¾ x 2¾", V1p340–3, $60.00.
Superior, Type Ribbon, ¾ x 2½ x 2½", no photo, $10.00.
Superior, Type Ribbon, ⅞ x 2½", V2p189–7, $10.00.
Superior, Violin Strings, 1¼ x 2⅝", V1p181–6, $15.00.
Superior $.40, Aspirin Tablets, ¼ x 1¾ x 2½", V2p103–6, $8.00.
Superior 200, Recoton Needles, no photo, $25.00.
Supertone 200, Medium Tone Needles, ⅜ x 1¼ x 1¾", V2p116–1, $35.00.
Suprema (Stearns), Face Powder, ½ x 1¾ x 2⅜", V1p254–2, $90.00.
Supreme, Aspirin, no photo, $12.00.
Supreme, Zinc Oxide Adhesive, 1 x 1¼", V2p197–2, $30.00.
Supreme 30, Milk of Magnesia Tablets, ¼ x 2⅜ x 2¾", V1p157–1, $8.00.
Supreme Brand, Aspirin, ¼ x 1¼ x 1½", V2p104–2, $10.00.
Sure Grip, Glue, 1⅜ x 2", V1p201–2, $15.00.
Sure-Rite, Type Ribbon, ⅞ x 2½", V2p190–1, $15.00.
Surety, Aspirin, ¼ x 1¼ x 1¾", V1p157–2, $12.00.
Surety, Cold Tablets, ¼ x 1¼ x 1¾", V1p157–3, $12.00.
Surety, Laxative, ¼ x 1⅝ x 1⅝", V1p157–4, $15.00.
Surety, Milk of Magnesia, ¼ x 1¼ x 1¾", V1p157–5, $15.00.
Surety, Milk of Magnesia, ⅜ x 1¼ x 1¾", V2p104–3, $15.00.
Surety-Lax, Chocolate Laxative, ⅜ x 1⅝ x 1⅝", V2p104–5, $20.00.
Surgeon's, Rubber Adhesive Plaster, ⅝ x 2", V2p197–3, $35.00.
Surrey, Type Ribbon, ¾ x 2½ x 2½", V1p325–2, $22.00.
Susie Q sample, Hair Dressing, ⅝ x 1¼ x 1¾", V1p40–7, $15.00.
Swain,Earle sample, Coffee, 2½ x 2¼", V1p237–5, $165.00.
Swallow Brand, Type Ribbon, ¾ x 2¼ x 2¼", V1p325–3, $40.00.
Swallow Brand, Type Ribbon, ¾ x 2¼ x 2¼", V2p190–3, $25.00.
Swan Meyer, Benzedo Compound, ¼ x 1¼ x 1½", no photo, $15.00.
Swanson's, see 5 Drop Salve.
Swartchild, Mainsprings, ⅝ x 2¾ x 5⅛", V1p340–4, $50.00.
Swartchild, Watch Material, ⅝ x 1¾", V1p340–5, $3.00*.
Swartchild, Watch Parts, ½ x 1", V1p340–6, $4.00.
Swartchild, Watch Parts, ½ x 1¼", V1p340–8, $3.00*.
Swartchild, Watch Parts, ½ x 2", no photo, $15.00.
Swartchild, Watch Parts, ¼ x 1⅜", no photo, $5.00.
Swartchild, Watch Parts, ¼ x ¾ x 1¼", V1p340–7, $8.00.
SWC, Saffron, no photo, $12.00.
Sweden House sample, Coffee, 3½ x 2½", V1p237–6, $55.00.
Sweet Georgia Brown, Hair Dressing, ¼ x 1", V1p40–8, $8.00*.
Sweet Life, Spices, 5¼ x 2¼ x 1¼", V2p162–7, $45.00.
Sweet Pea sample, Talcum Powder, ¾ x 1⅛ x 2", no photo, $60.00.
Sweetheart, Allspice, 1¼ x 2¼ x 3¼", V2p163–1, $25.00.
Sweetlax, see Saxon.
Swift's, Bouillon Cubes, ¾ x 1¾ x 2⅝", V1p20–10, $25.00.
Swigart Co., Watch Parts, ⅜ x 1⅛", V1p340–9, $2.00.
Swigart E. & J., Watch Parts, ½ x 1¼", V1p340–10, $2.00.
Swigart E. & J., Watch Parts, ½ x 1¼", V1p340–11, $4.00.
Swigart E. & J., Watch Parts, ½ x 1½", V1p340,#12, 2.00.
Sy-Lac sample, Tooth Powder, 1 x 2⅛", V1p59–3, $20.00.
Sylvan Orris Myrrh, Tooth Soap, no photo, $65.00.
Sylvan Violet sample, Talcum Powder, ¾ x 1¼ x 2", V1p261–7, $70.00.
Sylvatone 20 Loud, Needles, ½ x 2", no photo, $30.00.
Symns, Red Pepper, 3¼ x 2¼ x 1¼", V2p163–3, $35.00.
Symonds Inn Brand, Bouillon Cubes, ¾ x 1¾ x 2⅞", V1p20–11, $15.00.
Syntrogel, Roche, ¼ x 1¼ x 1¾", V1p157–6, $8.00.
Syntrogel sample, Antacid, ¼ x 1¼ x 1¾", V1p157–7, $12.00.
T.M., Smokers Tooth Powder, ⅞ x 2¾", $8.00.
Tabcin, Cold Tablets, ¼ x 1½ x 2", V1p157–8, $8.00.
Tabloid, Tea Tablets, ⅞ x 2 x 3", V1p268–6, $35.00.
Tac-Cut sample, Coffee, 2½ x 3¼", V1p238–1, $140.00.
Tagger, Type Ribbon, 1⅝ x 1⅝ x 2", V2p190–5, $45.00.
Tagger, Type Ribbon, ¾ x 2¼ x 2¼", no photo, $10.00.
Tagger, Type Ribbon, ¾ x 2 x 2", V1p325–4, $12.00.
Tahapone, Needles, no photo, $30.00.
Taj Mahal 200, Needles, ½ x 1¼ x 1¾", V2p116–3, $35.00.
Tak-A-Lax, Chocolate Laxative, ⅜ x 1¼ x 2¼", V2p104–7, $45.00.
Tak-A-Lax, Laxative, ⅜ x 1¼ x 2¼", V1p157–9, $45.00.
Tak-A-Lax, Laxative, ⅜ x 2¼ x 3⅝", V1p157–10, $35.00.
Taka-Diastase, Parke,Davis sample, ¼ x 1 x 2⅛", V1p157–11, $20.00.
Takalon sample, Talcum Powder, no photo, $25.00.
Takara, Hygienic Powder, 1¼ x 1¾ x 1¾", V1p45–12, $20.00.
Takoff, Weight Loss, ¼ x 3⅛ x 3½", V1p157–12, $35.00.
Talking Machine, Needles, ¾ x 2½", V1p211–11, $45.00.
Tally-Ho, Condon, ¼ x 1⅝ x 2", V2p21–4, $200.00.
Tamco, Allspice, 1⅛ x 2¼ x 1¼", V2p163–5, $45.00.
Tangee, Rouge, ¼ x 1⅛", V1p48–12, $5.00.
Tangee, Rouge, ⅜ x 1⅛", V1p49–1, $5.00.
Tangee $.15, Dry Rouge, ⅜ x 1½", V1p49–2, $10.00.
Tangee sample, Cream Rouge, ⅜ x 1", V1p48–11, $15.00.
Tangee sample, Face Powder, ¼ x 1⅝", V1p254–4, $10.00.
Tangee sample, Face Powder, ¼ x 1⅝", V2p25–4, $12.00.
Tangee sample, Rouge Compact, ¼ x 1¼", V1p49–3, $25.00.
Tansen, Phono Needles, ⅜ x 1¼ x 1¾", V2p116–5, $30.00.
Tansy Pennyroyal, Pills, ¾ x 1¾ x 2⅞", V2p105–1, $45.00.
Taps $.10, Laxative, ¼ x 1 x 1½", V1p158–1, $18.00.
Tar-oid $.50, Salve, ¾ x 2⅛", V2p105–4, $30.00.
Tar-Oid sample, Ointment, ½ x 1⅛", V2p105–6, $40.00.

Tara Thoroughbread, Type Ribbon, ¾ x 2½ x 2½", no photo, $15.00.
Tasty-Lax, Laxative, ⅜ x 1⅝ x 1⅝", V1p158–2, $12.00.
Taurocal sample, Laxative, ¼ x 1¼ x 1¾", V1p158–3, $15.00.
Taxol sample, Tablets, ¼ x 1¼ x 1½", V1p158–4, $12.00.
Taylor, Cherry Extract, 2½ x 4", no photo, $35.00.
Taylor D.F., Toilet Pins, no photo, $10.00.
Taylor Geo. H., Watch Main Spring, ¾ x 3 x 3⅜", V1p341–1, $40.00.
Taylor's J.A. sample, Quick Act Ointment, ¼ x 1¼", V1p158–5, $22.00.
Taylor's Matchless, Type Ribbon, ¾ x 2½ x 2½", no photo, $20.00.
Taylor's sample, Blue Bird Talcum, ½ x 1¼ x 2⅛", V2p130–4, $195.00.
Taylor's sample, Infant Talcum Powder, ¾ x 1¼ x 2⅛", V2p130–6, $125.00.
Taylor's sample, Valley Violet Talcum Powder, ¾ x 1¼ x 2⅛", V2p131–1, $115.00.
Teateana $.50, Tablets, ⅝ x 2 x 3¾", no photo, $20.00.
Tech, Pure Spices, 3½ x 2¼ x 1¼", V2p163–6, $15.00.
Tecumseh, Type Ribbon, ¾ x 2½ x 2½", V1p325–5, $5.00.
Ted-Lax, Laxative, ¼ x 1⅝ x 1⅝", V1p158–6, $15.00.
Teddy Bear, Sweets, no photo, $85.00.
Tee-Lax $.10, Laxative, ¼ x 1½ x 1⅞", V2p105–2, $18.00.
Tee-Tone, Aspirin, ¼ x 1¼ x 1¾", no photo, $12.00.
Teenie Weenie, Pencil Box, ¾ x 3 x 4", no photo, $40.00.
Telraphon, Needles, no photo, $25.00.
Tempel Garden, Spices, no photo, $18.00.
Temple of Heaven, Balm (salve), ¾ x 1½", V1p158–7, $8.00.
Terpinol, Cure Tablets, ½ x 1⅜ x 2⅝", V1p158–8, $55.00.
Tetley's sample, Tea, ¾ x 1¾ x 2⅜", V1p268–7, $25.00.
Tetley's sample, Tea India & Ceylon, ½ x 2 x 3", V1p268–8, $40.00.
Tetterine, Salve, ¾ x 2⅛", V1p158–9, $8.00.
Tex Ret $.25, Liver Tablets, ⅜ x 1¼ x 1¾", V1p158–10, $18.00.
Texas Brand, Type Ribbon, ¾ x 2½", V1p325–6, $18.00.
Texas Pride, Type Ribbon, ¾ x 2½", V1p325–7, $18.00.
Texcel, Tape Cellophane, ½ x 2½", V1p201–3, $5.00.
Texide, Condom, ¼ x 1¾ x 2", V1p25–5, $70.00.
Thacher, Aspirin, ¼ x 1¼ x 1¾", V1p158–11, $12.00.
Thacher, Aspirin, ¼ x 1¼ x 1¾", V1p158–12, $12.00.
Thayer's sample, Rem-ola, ¼ x 1⅝", no photo, $8.00.
The Boys Delight, Needles, no photo, $40.00.
The Ladys Own, Pill, no photo, $35.00.
The Twin, Phonograph Needles, ¼ x 1¼ x 1½", V2p116–7, $35.00.
Theatrical, Cold cream, no photo, $20.00.
Theo-Medicone sample, Rect Suppository, ⅜ x 1¼ x 1¾", V1p159–1, $10.00.
Theyer Henry & Co., see Cascara-Elm, V1p81–4, $40.00.
Tholene $.25, Salve, ⅞ x 2⅛", V1p159–2, $35.00.
Tholene $.25, Salve, ⅞ x 2⅛", V2p105–3, $20.00.
Tholene $.50, Ointment, ¾ x 2", V1p159–3, $20.00.
Thomas G.B., Type Ribbon, ⅞ x 2½ x 2½", V1p325–8, $4.00.
Thompson Slotted, Rivet (Stimpson), ⅝ x 1⅞ x 3", V1p63–4, $25.00.
Thompson's sample, Malted Milk, 1⅝ x 2½", V1p246–4, $70.00.
Thomson Judson L., Rivets, ⅝ x 1¾ x 2⅞", V1p63–5, $25.00.
Thornton Minor sample, Rectal Cones, ⅜ x 1¼ x 1½", V1p159–4, $15.00.
Thornward (MW), Gall Cure, ¾ x 1¾ x 2⅞", V1p333–7, $120.00.
Thoroughbread, Saddle Soap, 3", no photo, $15.00.
Thorsen "Indiana," Tire Repair Tool, ½ x 1½ x 2½", V2p16–2, $70.00.
Thorsen Sure Shot, Tire Repair Tool, ½ x 2 x 3", V1p15–7, $80.00.
Three Arch Brand, Needles (phono), ⅜ x 1¼ x 1¾", V1p211–12, $45.00.
Three Crow, Allspice, 3 x 2¼ x 1", V2p163–2, $40.00.
Three Crow, Ginger, 1 x 1⅜ x 3⅜", V2p163–4, $30.00.
Three Crow Brand, Mustard, 4 ⅝ x 3¼ x 2⅛", V2p163–7, $70.00.
Three Flowers, Face Powder, ¼ x 1⅝", V1p254–6, $22.00.
Three Flowers RH, Face Powder, ¼ x 1⅝", V1p254–5, $15.00.
Three Flowers sample, Face Powder, ¼ x 1⅝", V1p254–7, $22.00.
Three Flowers sample, Face Powder, ⅜ x 1¼", V1p254–8, $10.00.
Three Graces, Condom, no photo, $150.00.
Three Knights, Condom, ¼ x 1¼ x 2", V1p25–6, $100.00.
Three Pirates, Condom, no photo, $175.00.
Three Springs Fisheries, Fish Food, ⅞ x 2½", V1p201–4, $18.00.
Three Swan, Needles, no photo, $45.00.
Thrift, Type Ribbon, ¾ x 2½ x 2½", V1p325–9, $15.00.
Throat Ease, Lozenges, ⅞ x 1¾ x 3", V1p294–10, $95.00.
Throat Joys, Cough Drops, ½ x 2 x 3¼", no photo, $40.00.
Tidd's, Antiseptic Healing, ½ x 2", no photo, $20.00.
Tidewater, Tobacco, 2¼ x 2¼ x 2½", V2p213–8, $30.00.
Tiger, Boot Polish Blk, ⅝ x 2", V1p282–2, $20.00.
Tiger 200, Needles, ⅜ x 1 x 2¼", no photo, $20.00.
Tiger Brand, Red Shoe Polish, ¾ x 1¾", V2p121–1, $30.00.
Tiger Brand, Russet Shoe Polish, ¾ x 1¾", V2p121–3, $30.00.
Tilleys, Suede Powder, 1⅜ x 2½ x 3¾", V2p121–2, $18.00.
Time O'Day, Sage, 3 x 2¼ x 1¼", V2p164–1, $18.00.
Time O'Day sample, Coffee, 3¼ x 2¼", V1p238–2, $70.00.
Tintograph, Color Box, ¼ x 1⅝", V1p201–5, $10.00.
Tintograph, Color Box, ¼ x 1⅝", V2p214–1, $10.00.
Tip Top #10, Stamp Pad, ⅜ x 1¼ x 2½", V1p180–1, $15.00.
Tip Top Three, Condom, L. (2 women), no photo, 170.00.
Tiz-Dry $.25, Glass & Leather, ⅝ x 1½", no photo, $5.00.
To-Mo-Lo, Foot Ointment, ¾ x 2", V2p105–5, $12.00.
Toba-Cure, Cure, ½ x 2¼ x 3⅜", no photo, $65.00.
Tobacco to the Dogs, Cure, ½ x 2¼ x 3¾", no photo, $75.00.
Tobaceen, Smokers Tonic, ¼ x 1⅛ x 2⅛", V1p159–5, $65.00.
Tod Co, Dental Floss, ¼ x 1¼", V2p43–4, $25.00.
Toddy sample, Malt Drink, 1⅝ x 1¾", V1p246–5, $90.00.
Toketa, Face Powder, no photo, $25.00.
Tolysin, Aspirin, ¼ x 1⅝ x 2⅛", V1p159–6, $15.00.
Tolysin, Tablets 48, ½ x 1½ x 2½", V1p159–7, $12.00.
Tongaline, Tablets, 1¼ x 1⅝ x 2⅜, no photo, $40.00.
Tongaline 100, Tablets, 1¼ x 1⅝ x 2¼", V1p159–8, $35.00.
Tonique, Tablets, ⅜ x 1¾ x 2¾", V2p105–7, $35.00.
Toof E.J., Needle\Thread Pack, ¼ x 1⅛ x 2⅛", V1p186–9, $80.00.
Topaz sample, Coffee, 2 x 2½", V1p238–3, $75.00.
Tops, Sweet Snuff, 1¾ x 2¼", V2p214–3, $20.00.
Tord Caesar A., Medicine, ½ x 1¼", V1p201–6, $6.00.
Torrey, Safety Blades, ¼ x 1 x 2⅛", V1p269–10, $140.00.
Torrey, Safety Razor, V1p272–4, $250.00.
Torrey, Strop Dressing, 2", no photo, $35.00.
Torrey #B, Safety Razor, 1 x 2¼ x 3½", V1p272–5, $285.00.
Torrey Commet, Safety Razor, 1 x 2¼ x 3½", no photo, 290.00.
Torrey J.R. No. 2., Sharpening Dressing, ⅞ x 1¾ x ½", V2p136–4, $60.00.
Torrey Razor Edge, Paste Stropping, ⅝ x ⅞ x 1¾", no photo, $40.00.
Torrey's, Strop Dressing, 1⅛ x 2", V1p275–3, $30.00.
Torrey's, Strop Dressing, ½ x 1½", V2p136–6, $40.00.
Tower Marvello, Type Ribbon, 1 x 2½", V1p325–7, $6.00.
Tower No. 6, Tacks, 1⅜ x 2", V1p201–7, $20.00.
Towles Log Cabin sample, Syrup, 1¼ x 1⅞ x 2½", V2p126–2, $275.00.
Towle's Maple sample, Log Cabin Syrup, 1¼ x 1⅞ x 2½", V1p246–6, $350.00.
Town and Country sample, Coffee, 1¾ x 2¼ x 2⅝", V1p238–4, $75.00.
Toxaway, Coffee, 3 x 2½ x 2½", V1p238–5, $200.00.
Trader O. James, Watch Material, ½ x 1½", V1p341–2, $4.00.
Trailing Arbutus, Face Powder, no photo, $40.00.
Trailing Arbutus sample, Talcum Powder, no photo, $80.00.
Train Scene, Unknown, 1 x 3 x 5", V1p201–8, $600.00.

Trek 100, Needles Deluxe, ⅜ x 1 x 2⅛", V1p212–1, $25.00.

Trey-Pak, Condom, ¼ x 1¼ x 1¾", no photo, $55.00.

TriTabs, Piles\Constipation Tablets, ⅝ x 1⅞ x 2⅝", V1p159–9, $20.00.

Triumph, Eyelets, ⅞ x 2", V1p186–10, $4.00.

Trix $.10, Breath Perfume, ⅜ x 1⅛", V2p171–4, $12.00.

Trojan, Condom, ¼ x 1½ x 2", V1p25–7, $50.00.

Trojan, Condom, ¼ x 1¾ x 2", V1p25–8, $60.00.

Trojan, Improved, 1¼ x 1⅝ x 2", no photo, $115.00.

Trojan $.50, Improved Condom, ¼ x 1⅝ x 2⅛", V2p21–7, $55.00.

Trojan Gold, Condom, ¼ x 1⅝ x 2⅛", V1p25–9, $55.00.

Trojan Gold, Condoms, ⅜ x 1⅝ x 2⅛", no photo, $40.00.

Trompito 200, Needles, no photo, $45.00.

Tropical Brand, Ginger, ⅞ x 2 x 4", V1p189–9, $50.00.

Tru, Aspirin, ¼ x 1¼ x 1¾", V1p159–10, $15.00.

Tru-Lax, Aspirin, ¼ x 1¼ x 1¾", V2p106–1, $10.00.

Tru-Lax, Choc Mint Lax, ¼ x 2⅜ x 3", V1p159–11, $12.00.

Tru-Lax $.10, Laxative, ¼ x 1⅛ x 1⅛", V2p106–3, $15.00.

Tru-Lax $.10, Laxative, ⅜ x 1⅝ x 1⅝", no photo, $12.00.

Tru-Lax $.15, Cold Tablets, ¼ x 1¼ x 1¾", V1p159–12, $12.00.

Tru-Lax $.50, Laxative, ⅜ x 2¾ x 3⅛", no photo, $15.00.

Tru-Pak, Aspirin, ¼ x 1¼ x 1¾", V1p160–1, $15.00.

Tru-Test, Auto Fuses, no photo, $10.00.

Tru-Test, Auto Glass Fuses, no photo, $10.00.

Tru-Test $.10, Aspirin, ¼ x 1¼ x 1¾", V1p160–2, $20.00.

True Mark Brand, Type Ribbon, ¾ x 2½", V1p325–8, $15.00.

True-Rite, Type Ribbon, ¾ x 2½ x 2½", no photo, $12.00.

Truetone, Disc Record Needles, ½ x 1 x 1⅝", V1p212–2, $35.00.

Trutone $1.00, Health Tonic, 1⅜ x 2", V1p160–3, $15.00.

Tryalax, Chocolate Laxative, ¼ x 1⅝ x 1⅝", V1p160–4, $18.00.

Tryme, Aspirin, ¼ x 1¼ x 1¾", V1p160–5, $8.00.

Tubbs, Ski Wax, no photo, $15.00.

Tube Rose, Scotch Snuff, 1⅜ x 1¾", V1p191–12, $30.00.

Tuberose, Ointment, ¾ x 2⅜", V2p106–5, $18.00.

Tubular Rivet & Stud, Rivets No. 1, ¾ x 1⅝ x 3⅛", V1p63–6, $25.00.

Tulipe D'or, Face Powder, no photo, $30.00.

Tums, Ant acid, ¾ x 2¼", V1p160–6, $4.00*.

Tung-Sol, Auto Fuses, ¼ x 1¼ x 1¾", V1p10–4, $12.00.

Tung-Sol, Auto Fuses, ¼ x 1¼ x 1¾", V1p10–5, $15.00.

Tungsten, Spark Plugs, 1⅛ x 1¼ x 3⅞", V1p12–6, $55.00.

Tungsten, Spark Plugs, 1⅛ x 1¼ x 4½", V1p12–5, $55.00.

Tungstyle sample, Needles Phono, ¼ x 1 x 2", V1p212–3, $45.00.

Turf-Stahlstecknadeln, Needles, no photo, $25.00.

Turkey Brand, Red Pepper, 3 x 2⅛ x 1¼", V2p164–3, $45.00.

Turkey Red, Spice, no photo, $30.00.

Turkish, Dyspepsia Tablets, ⅝ x 2 x 3", no photo, $35.00.

Turner's $.30, Salve, ¾ x 1⅞", V1p160–8, $15.00.

Turner's $.60, Salve, 1 x 2⅜", V1p160–9, $15.00.

Turner's sample, Inflammacine, 4 x ⅞", V1p160–7, $45.00.

Turpo sample, Ointment, ½ x 1", V1p160–10, $15.00.

Turpo sample, Turpentine Ointment, ⅜ x 1¼ x 1¾", V1p160–12, $15.00.

Turpo sample, Turpentine Ointment, ⅜ x 1⅜", V1p160–11, $20.00.

Tuskeege Belle $.25, Hair Dressing, 1⅜ x 2½ x 3", V1p40–9, $45.00.

Tuxedo Club, Pomade, 1¼ x 2", V1p40–10, $18.00.

Tuxedo Club sample, Pomade Hair Tonic, ⅝ x 1¾", V1p40–11, $25.00.

Twenty Grand, Aspirin, ¼ x 1¼ x 1¾", V1p161–1, $12.00.

Twenty Grand, Razor Blade Drier, ⅝ x 2", V1p275–4, $15.00.

Twin Brothers, Axel Grease, no photo, $35.00.

Twin City, Watch Supply, ½ x 1½", no photo, $6.00.

Twin City Superior, Type Ribbon, ¾ x 2½ x 2½", no photo, $18.00.

TwinTex, Type Ribbon, ¾ x 2½", V1p325–12, $15.00.

Two in One, Shoe Polish, 1⅛ x 2¾", V1p282–3, $10.00.

Two in One, Suede Stick, 1 x 3⅞", V1p282–4, $12.00.

Two n One, Shoe Polish, 1 x 3", V1p282–5, $15.00.

TWR, Auto Fuses, no photo, $10.00.

Tybon's Domitor, Type Ribbon, ¾ x 2½", no photo, $15.00.

Tylers, Thyme, 1¼ x 2¼ x 3¼", V2p164–5, $15.00.

Typal, Type Ribbon, ¾ x 2½ x 2½", V2p190–2, $15.00.

Type Bar, Type Ribbon, ¾ x 1¾ x 1¾", V1p326–1, $8.00.

Type Bar, Type Ribbon, ¾ x 2½ x 2½", V1p326–2, $12.00.

Type-Bar, Type Ribbon, ¾ x 1¾ x 1¾", V1p326–3, $6.00.

Typecraft, Type Ribbon, no photo, $8.00.

Tyrrell's, Rectal Soap, 1¾ x 3⅜", V2p106–2, $75.00.

U C A, Salve Skin, ¾ x 2⅜", V1p161–2, $8.00.

U C A $.25, Mentho Salve, ¾ x 2⅜", V1p161–3, $15.00.

U C A $.25, Vapor Balm, ¾ x 2⅜", V2p106–4, $8.00.

U S Varsity Line, Type Ribbon, ¾ x 2½", V1p326–10, $10.00.

U-All-No, Breath Mints, ¼ x 1½ x 2¼", V1p289–10, $18.00.

U-All-No, Campus Mints, 1½ x 1½ x 2", V2p168–8, $30.00.

U-All-No, Mint (after dinner), 1⅛ x 3 x 3", V1p289–11, $12.00.

U-Must-Have-A $.25, Corn Remover, ⅝ x 1½", V1p161–4, $18.00.

U-Re-Ka, Silver Polish Powder, 3 x 1¾", no photo, $35.00.

U.S., Line Dressing, ¾ x 2¾", no photo, $12.00.

U.S. Brand, Type Ribbon, 1⅝ x 1⅝ x 1¾", V1p326–9, $45.00.

U.S. Brand, Type Ribbon, ¾ x 2½", V1p326–6, $18.00.

U.S. Brand, Type Ribbon, ¾ x 2¼", no photo, $18.00.

U.S. Brand, Type Ribbon, ¾ x 2¼ x 2¼", V1p326–8, $20.00.

U.S. Gauge Co. $1.25, Tire Pressure Gauge, ¾ x 2 x 2½", no photo, $30.00.

U.S. Musket, Remington Caps, ¾ x 2", V1p65–3, $55.00.

U.S. Musket (UMC), Blasting Caps, ¾ x 2", V1p65–4, $40.00.

U.S. Steel, Type Ribbon, ¾ x 2½ x 2½", V1p326–7, $18.00.

U.S. Tire Co., Tire Repair Kit, ⅜ x 1¾ x 2⅞", V1p15–8, $35.00.

U.S.P., Blue Ointment, ½ x 1⅜", V1p185–6, $40.00.

U.S.P., Zinc Ointment, ¾ x 2", V1p161–5, $25.00.

Ulceroid $.50, Ulcer Medicine, 1 x 1¾ x 2⅞", V1p161–7, $20.00.

Ulceroid sample, Ulcer Medicine, ¼ x 1 x 1⅝", V1p161–6, $25.00.

Ultimo, Type Ribbon, ¾ x 2½ x 2½", V2p190–4, $25.00.

Ultra Copia, Type Ribbon, ¾ x 2½ x 2½", no photo, $5.00.

Ultrex Platinum, Condoms, ¼ x 1⅝ x 2⅛", V1p25–10, $25.00*.

Umatilla $.50, Indian Catarrh Cure, ⅝ x 1½ x 2⅝", V2p106–6, $150.00.

UMC, Primers 8½, 1 x 1½", V1p66–4, $30.00.

UMC No. 2, Primers 250, ⅞ x 1½", V1p66–5, $40.00.

Uncle Sam, Shoe Polish, ¾ x 1⅝", V1p282–7, $45.00.

Uncle Sam, Shoe Polish, ⅝ x 1¼", V1p282–6, $40.00.

Uncle Sam, Shoe Polish, ⅝ x 2⅛", V1p282–8, $50.00.

Underwood, Type Ribbon, 1⅝ x 1⅝ x 1⅞, no photo, $20.00.

Underwood, Type Ribbon, 1⅝ x 1⅝ x 1⅞", V2p190–6, $35.00.

Underwood, Type Ribbon, 1 x 1⅝, no photo, $7.00.

Underwood, Type Ribbon, ¾ x 2½ x 2½", no photo, $5.00.

Underwood (Noiseless), Type Ribbon, ¾ x 2½ x 2½", V2p191–1, $8.00.

Underwood (stock), Type Ribbon, ¾ x 2½ x 2½", V1p326–4, $4.00.

Underwood Remington, Type Ribbon, ⅞ x 2½ x 2½", V2p191–4, $10.00.

Underwood Royal, Type Ribbon, ¾ x 2½ x 2½", V2p191–6, $6.00.

Underwood Sundstrand, Type Ribbon, ⅞ x 1⅝", V1p326–5, $8.00.

Ung. Hyd., Eye Ointment, ½ x 1¼", V2p107–1, $25.00.

Ung. Hydrophen sample, Oint. Skin Infect., ¼ x 1¾", V1p161–8, $10.00.

Ungt Compound, Aseptinol Salve, ⅜ x 1½", V1p161–9, $40.00.

Ungt sample, Aseptinol Comp., ¼ x 1⅛", V2p107–3, $30.00.

Unguentine, Burn Ointment, ½ x 2", V1p161–10, $8.00.

Unguentine, Burn Ointnent, ⅝ x 1⅞", V1p161–11, $6.00.

Unguentine, Surgical Dressing, ½ x 2", V1p161–12, $8.00.

Uni-Sun, Type Ribbon, ¾ x 2½ x 2½", no photo, $10.00.

Uniformity Brand, Type Ribbon, ¾ x 2½ x 2½", no photo, $15.00.

Union 20 amp., Auto Fuses, ¼ x 1¼ x 1¾", no photo, $12.00.

Union 3 AG, Auto Fuses 15 AMP, ¼ x 1¼ x 1¾", V1p10–6, $15.00.

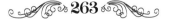

Union 5-AG 15 Amp., Auto Fuses, ½ x 1¾ x 2⅝", V1p10–7, $15.00.

Union Drug, Aspirin, ¼ x 1¼ x 1¾", V1p162–1, $8.00.

Union Metalic Cartg., Percussion Caps, ⅝ x 1½", V1p65–5, $40.00.

Union Metalic Cartridge, Blasting Caps, ¾ x 1½", V1p65–6, $75.00.

Union Metallic Cart., Percussion Caps, ½ x 1½", V1p65–8, $40.00.

Union Metallic Cart., Percussion Caps, ¾ x 1½", V1p65–7, $40.00.

United, Curry Powder, 3¼ x 2¼ x 1¼", V2p164–6, $40.00.

United, Tire Valve Cores, ¼ x 1 x 1½", V1p18–2, $15.00.

United Drug, Aspirin 901, ¼ x 1¼ x 1¾", no photo, $6.00.

United Drug Co, see Puretest Aspirin.

United Drug Co., see Firstaid Bandaids.

United Drug Co., see Rexall.

United Machine & Sup., Matches (Knapsack), ½ x 1¼ x 1¾", V1p180–9, $20.00.

United States, Army Caps 100, ¾ x 2", V1p65–9, $70.00.

Unitex, Thread, no photo, $15.00.

Universal, Type Ribbon, ¾ x 2½ x 2½", no photo, $10.00.

Universal, Watch Springs, ¾ x 2½ x 2½", V1p341–3, $50.00.

Universal Sales Co., Type Ribbon, ¾ x 2½ x 2½", no photo, $12.00.

University, Patent Leather Paste, ¾ x 2⅛", V1p282–9, $100.00.

Univex #1000, Safety Film, ½ x 1⅞", V2p213–5, $5.00.

Unknown, 1 x 2", no photo, $15.00.

Unknown, ⅝ x 1¾", no photo, $10.00.

Unknown, Candy, 1⅛ x 1⅜ x 2¼", V1p289–12, $30.00.

Unknown, Marie Antoinette, ¾ x 2", V1p201–6, $55.00.

Unolla, Needles Phono, ½ x 1¼ x 1½", V1p212–4, $35.00.

Upjohn's, Quinine Pills, ¼ x ¾ x 2", V1p162–3, $35.00.

US Sapolio, Monogram Stamp, ½ x 1", no photo, $20.00.

Usola, Camphor Ice, ¾ x 1¾ x 2¾", V1p162–4, $12.00.

USP, Cocoa Butter, 1 x 3½", V1p246–7, $10.00.

Utah Elders, Damiana Wafers, no photo, $90.00.

Utility, Type Ribbon, ¾ x 2½ x 2½", V1p191–2, $15.00.

V.V.V., Tablets, ¾ x 1⅞", V1p162–5, $5.00.

Valentine Labs., Aspirin, ¼ x 1¼ x 1¾", no photo, $8.00.

Valvlox, Tire Air Valves, ⅜ x 1¼ x 1¾", V1p18–3, $12.00.

Vamos, Lung Tablets, ½ x 2 x 3", no photo, $35.00.

Van Cleef Bros., Valve Grinding Compound, ¾ x 2½", V2p16–3, $18.00.

Van Curler, Ginger, 3½ x 2¼ x 1¼", V2p164–2, $40.00.

Van Dyck's $.25, Gall V Cure, ⅞ x 2⅝", V1p333–8, $30.00.

Van Roy, Mustard, 5¼ x 2⅜ x 1⅜", V2p164–4, $25.00.

Van-L-N, Cubes, ⅜ x 1⅝ x 2⅜", V1p20–12, $15.00.

Vanco, Paste Soap, ⅝ x 2", V1p53–10, $10.00.

Vanderslice, Tire Repair Outfit, ½ x 1⅜ x 2", V2p16–4, $45.00.

Vantine Kutch sample, Sandalwood Talcum, ¾ x 1⅛ x 1⅞", V1p261–8, $40.00.

Vantine's, Incense, ¼ x 1¼ x 1⅛", V2p199–3, $10.00.

Vantine's, Incense, ¼ x 1⅛ x 1¼", V1p178–7, $10.00.

Vantine's, Incense Apple Blossom, ½ x 2½ x 3⅛", V1p178–3, $20.00.

Vantine's, Incense Pine, ¼ x 2 x 4", V1p178–4, $20.00.

Vantine's, Incense Sandalwood, ¼ x 2 x 4", V1p178–5, $20.00.

Vantine's, Rose Insense, ¼ x 1⅜ x 4", V2p199–4, $15.00.

Vantine's, Sandalwood Insense, ¼ x 1⅜ x 4", V2p199–2, $15.00.

Vantine's, Sandalwood Incense, ¼ x 1⅞ x 3⅞", V1p178–6, $22.00.

Vantine's, Wisteria Incense, 1⅛ x 1¾ x 2", V1p178–8, $25.00.

Vantine's Demo, Incense Temple, ⅜ x 2 x 4", V1p178–9, $30.00.

Vantine's Kutch sample, Sandalwood Talcum, ¾ x 1⅛ x 1⅞", V1p261–9, $50.00.

Vantines sample, Cones, ¼ x 1⅛ x 2", V2p199–5, $12.00.

Vantines sample, San Dermal Talcum Powder, 1 x 2⅛", V2p131–3, $450.00.

Vapex, Pomade, no photo, $15.00.

Vaporole, Aromatic Ammonia, ½ x 1⅝ x 2¼", V1p162–6, $4.00.

Varcon DeLuxe, Auto Fuses, ¼ x 1¼ x 1¾", no photo, $12.00.

Vari-Tone, Type Ribbon, ¾ x 2½", no photo, $15.00.

Varsity Brand (Stfrd), Type Ribbon, ¾ x 2½ x 2½", V1p326–11, $18.00.

Vaseline, Camphor Ice, 1 x 3½", no photo, $6.00.

Vaseline, Camphor Ice, 1 x 3½", V1p162–7, $15.00.

Vaseline, Camphor Ice, 1 x 3½", V1p162–8, $8.00.

Vaseline, Camphor Ice, ¾ x 1¾ x 2⅞", V1p162–9, $6.00.

Vaseline, Camphor Ice, ¾ x 1¾ x 2⅞", V2p107–6, $5.00.

Vaseline, Petroleum Jelly, ⅝ x 2½, 4.00.

Vaseline sample, Cold Cream, ½ x 1½", V2p31–1, $18.00.

Vaseline sample, Cold Cream, ½ x 1⅜", V1p32–1, $25.00.

Vege-Lene, Face Powder, 1¼ x 2¾", V1p46–1, $50.00.

Vegetable $.10, Liver Pills, ⅜ x 1¼", no photo, $65.00.

Vegex Almonds $.10, Vitamin Food, ⅜ x 2 x 2¾", V1p162–10, $10.00.

Velaxo $.25, Laxative, ½ x 1⅜ x 2½", V1p162–11, $20.00.

Velcrest $.30, Laxative Cold Tablets, ⅜ x 1½ x 2½", V1p162–12, $10.00.

Velcrest $.60, Laxative Cold Tablets, ⅜ x 2¾ x 3½", V1p163–1, $10.00.

Velpaus, Female Regulative Pills, ⅞ x 2⅞ x 3", V1p163–2, $20.00.

Veltex Juniper, Tar Hair, no photo, $15.00.

Veltore, Pomade, ⅞ x 3½", V1p40–12, $15.00.

Velvet, Face Powder, 1⅛ x 2⅞", V1p46–2, $35.00.

Velvetina $.25, Face Powder, 1½ x 2½ x 3½", V1p46–3, $55.00.

Vemo (J&J), Deodorant Powder, ¾ x 1¼x 2¼", V2p202–3, $50.00.

Vendol $.25, Laxative Tablets, ⅜ x 1¼ x 1¾", V2p107–2, $12.00.

Venetian, Mints, ¼ x 1¼ x 1¾", V1p290–1, $18.00.

Venus, Car Finish, no photo, $40.00.

Vera Perles sample, Sandalwood Compound, ¼ x 1¼ x 1¾", V1p163–3, $18.00.

Veragreen, Ointment, ¾ x 2½ x 2½", V2p107–4, $15.00.

Veritables, French Laxative, ¼ x 1¼ x 1½", V1p163–4, $15.00.

Vernal Iron\Nerve, Food Tablets, no photo, $50.00.

Verona, Needles, ⅜ x 1½ x 1½", V2p116–2, $40.00.

Verona, Needles, ⅜ x 1⅝ x 1⅝", V1p212–5, $40.00.

Vesuvius, Spark Plugs, 1⅜ x 3⅝", V1p12–7, $70.00.

Veteran Brand, Mustard, 1¼ x 2½ x 3½", no photo, $60.00.

Vi-G-Or, Catarrh Cream, ¾ x 1⅞", V1p163–5, $4.00.

Vici Herbs, Blood Purifier, 1 x 2¼ x 3⅜", no photo, $20.00.

Vick, Vaporub, ½ x 1⅝", V2p107–7, $3.00.

Vick's, Inhaler, ⅝ x 2½", V1p163–6, $5.00.

Vick's, Salve, ¼ x 1½", V1p163–7, $18.00.

Vick's, Vapor Rub, ½ x 1½", V1p163–12, $6.00.

Vicks Prof. sample, Vapor Rub, ½ x 1¾", V1p163–11, $7.00.

Vick's sample, Salve, ¼ x 1½", V1p163–8, $12.00*.

Vicks sample, Salve, ¼ x 1½", V2p108–1, $12.00.

Vicks sample, Vapor Rub, ½ x 1½", V1p163–9, $8.00.

Vick's sample, Vapor Rub, ⅜ x 1¼", no photo, $10.00.

Vick's sample, Vapor Rub Salve, ⅜ x 1¼", no photo, $15.00.

Vicks test sample, Salve, ¼ x 1¾", no photo, $12.00.

Vicks test sample, Vapor Rub, ¼ x 1⅝", V2p108–3, $18.00.

Victor, Auto Fuses, no photo, $12.00.

Victor, Auto Fuses, ¼ x 1¼ x 1¾", no photo, $10.00.

Victor, Needles, no photo, $75.00.

Victor, Needles, ½ x 1¼ x 1½", V1p212–11, $55.00.

Victor, Needles, ½ x 1¼ x 1½", V1p212–9, $60.00.

Victor, Needles, ½ x 1¼ x 1½", V1p213–7, $60.00.

Victor, Needles, ½ x 1¼ x 1½", V2p116–4, $55.00.

Victor, Needles, ⅜ x 1¼ x 1¾", V1p212–8, $40.00.

Victor, Needles, ⅝ x 1¼ x 1½", V1p212–12, $55.00.

Victor, Needles, ⅝ x 1⅞ x 2⅜", V1p212–6, $75.00.

Victor, Needles 200, ½ x 1¼ x 1½", V2p116–6, $60.00.

Victor, Ointment, ¾ x 1⅞", V2p108–5, $40.00.

Victor, Tire Valve Cores, ¼ x 1 x ¼", V1p18–4, $10.00.

Victor (Extra Loud), Needles, ½ x 1½ x 2½", V1p213–1, $55.00.

Victor (Full Tone), Needles, ½ x 1½ x 2½", V1p213–2, $60.00.

Victor (Half Tone), Needles, ½ x 1½ x 2½", V1p213–3, $55.00.

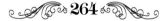

Victor (Half Tone), Needles, ½ x 1½ x 2½", V1p213–4, $60.00.

Victor (Half Tone), Needles, ½ x 1¼ x 1½", V1p213–6, $55.00.

Victor (Soft Tone), Needles, ½ x 1¼ x 1½", V1p213–5, $55.00.

Victor 200, Loud Tone Needles, ¼ x 1¼ x 1¾", V1p213–8, $40.00.

Victor 200, Needles, ½ x 1¼ x 1½", V1p213–7, $45.00.

Victor 300, Needles, ½ x 1¼ x 1¾", V1p213–9, $50.00.

Victor 300, Needles, ½ x 1¼ x 1¾", V2p116–8, $50.00.

Victor Extra Loud, Needles, ½ x 1¼ x 1½", V2p117–1, $45.00.

Victor Half Tone, Needles, ½ x 1½ x 2½", no photo, $55.00.

Victor Half Tone, Needles, ½ x 1½ x 2½", V2p117–3, $55.00.

Victor Half Tone, Needles, ½ x 1¼ x 1½", V1p213–10, $55.00.

Victor Loud Tone, Needles, ½ x 1¼ x 1¾", V1p213–11, $60.00.

Victor Loud Tone, Needles Gramaphone, ½ x 1¼ x 1½", V1p212–10, $50.00.

Victor Quick Repair, Tire Repair Kit, ½ x 1¾ x 2⅞", V1p15–9, $60.00.

Victor sample, Tungs-Tone Stylus, ¼ x ⅞ x 2", V2p117–5, $55.00.

Victor Soft Tone, Needles, ½ x 1¼ x 1¾", V2p117–7, $45.00.

Victor Soft Tone, Tungs Tone Needles, ¼ x 1 x 2", V2p117–2, $40.00.

Victor X Loud Tone, Needles, ½ x 1½ x 2½", V2p117–4, $45.00.

Victoria, Complexion Cream, 1 x 2", no photo, $20.00.

Victoria, Complexion Cream, ¾ x 2", V2p31–3, $20.00.

Victoria & Albert, Needles, no photo, $35.00.

Victoria Washington, Type Ribbon, ⅞ x 2¼ x 2¼", no photo, $18.00.

Victrola, Needles (Full Tone), ¼ x ⅞ x 2", V1p213–12, $35.00.

Victrola, Needles (X Loud Tone), ¼ x 1 x 2", V1p214–1, $50.00.

Victrola, Needles Tone Styles, ¼ x ⅞ x 2⅛", V1p214–2, $40.00.

Victrola, Needles Tungs Tone, ¼ x 1 x 2", V1p214–3, $35.00.

Victrola Soft Tone, Needles, ¼ x 1 x 2", V1p214–4, $35.00.

Videx, Menstral Dist., ¼ x 1¼ x 1¾", V1p164–1, $15.00.

Viegay Woodworth sample, Face Powder, ¼ x 1⅝", V1p254–9, $20.00.

Vienna sample, Coffee, 3 x 2¾", V1p238–6, $50.00.

Viking Line, Type Ribbon, ¾ x 2½ x 2½", V1p326–12, $25.00.

Viking Line, Type Ribbon, ¾ x 2½ x 2½", V2p191–3, $25.00.

Viking sample, Coffee Bank, 1¾ x 2¼ x 4", V2p124–2, $25.00.

Village Lip Lickers, Lip Gloss (Rootbeer), ⅜ x 1 x 2", V1p53–11, $5.00.

Vince sample, Mouth Wash Powder, 1¼ x 1⅝ x 2", no photo, $18.00.

Vinlax $.10, Laxative, ⅜ x 1¼ x 1⅝", V1p164–3, $15.00.

Vinlax $.25, Laxative Tablet, V1p164–2, $15.00.

Violet Brutum sample, Talcum Powder, no photo, $55.00.

Violet Dulce sample, Talcum Powder, ¾ x 1¼ x 2", V1p261–10, $30.00.

Violet Dulce sample, Talcum Powder, ¾ x 1¼ x 2", V1p261–11, $30.00.

Violet Sec sample, Talcum Powder, ¾ x 1¼ x 2⅛", V2p131–5, $80.00.

Violox, Breath Mints, ⅜ x 1⅜ x 2", V1p290–2, $65.00.

VIP, Medicine, ⅜ x 1⅜ x 2½", V1p164–4, $60.00.

Virginia Plug, Tobacco, ¾ x 1¾ x 2¼", V2p214–6, $18.00.

Vis-Quin, Type Ribbon, 1¾ x 1¾ x 2", V2p191–5, $40.00.

Vivaudou, Astringent Cream, ½ x 1⅛", V2p31–5, $120.00.

Vivaudou, Tissue Cream, 12 x ⅝", V1p53–9, $95.00.

Vivid, Type Ribbon, ¾ x 2½ x 2½", no photo, $8.00.

Vogue, Type Ribbon, ¾ x 2½", V1p327–1, $8.00.

Von Kennen, Salve, ¾ x 1⅞", V2p108–7, $12.00.

Vulcan, Ink Tablets, ½ x 1¼ x 1½", V1p201–10, $10.00.

Vulcanol No.5, Stove Polish, ⅞ x 3¼", V1p219–6, $20.00.

W B, Oxide Zinc Plaster, 1 x 1¼", V1p348–3, $20.00.

W H S, Watch Parts, no photo, $30.00.

W-B, Auto Fuses, no photo, $12.00.

W.C.E.(Enck Co.), Cough Drops, 1¼ x 1⅝ x 2½", V1p294–11, $115.00.

Wag's, Aspirin, ¼ x 1¼ x 1¾", V1p164–5, $40.00.

Wahoo $.25, Wonder Workers, ⅜ x 1⅝ x 1⅝", V1p201–11, $18.00.

Wait's Green Mountain, Tablets, ¼ x 1⅜ x 2⅛", V1p105–7, $10.00.

Walgreen, Adhesive Plaster, 1⅛ x 1¼", V2p197–5, $18.00.

Walgreen's, Aspirin, ¼ x 1¼ x 1¾", V1p164–6, $12.00.

Walgreen's, Aspirin Pure, ¼ x 1¼ x 1¾", V1p164–7, $12.00.

Walgreen's, Milk of Magnesia, ¼ x 2⅜ x 2⅝", V1p164–8, $10.00.

Walk Over, Shoe Polish, ¾ x 1¾", V1p282–10, $22.00.

Walker, Aspirin Tablets, 1 x 3", V1p164–10, $18.00.

Walker's, Chilie Powder, 1½ x 3⅝", V2p164–7, $15.00.

Walker's Madam, Glossine, no photo, $40.00.

Walker's Madam, Hair Grease, no photo, $35.00.

Walker's Madam, Temple Grower, ¾ x 2", V1p36–5, $45.00.

Walker's Madam, Wonder Hair Grow, ¾ x 2½", V2p36–4, $50.00.

Walker's Madam $.50, Scalp Ointment, ¾ x 2¾", V1p36–6, $65.00.

Walker's Madam $.50, Tetter Salve, ¾ x 2¾", V1p36–7, $65.00.

Walker's Madam sample, Tan-Off, ⅜ x 1⅞", V2p31–2, $30.00.

Walker's sample, Analga Cream, ¼ x 1½", V1p164–9, $25.00.

Wallace, Pencil Holder, no photo, $35.00.

Wallis Loud, Needles, no photo, $45.00.

Wallis Loud Tone, Needles, ½ x 2", no photo, $45.00.

Waltham, Watch Main Springs, ½ x 2¼ x 4⅝", V1p341–4, $30.00.

Waltham, Watch Screws, ¼ x ⅝ x 1⅛", V1p341–5, $1.00.

Waltham #16, Watch Mainsprings, ½ x 2⅞ x 5¼", V1p341–6, $30.00.

Waltham #18, Watch Mainsprings, ⅝ x 2¾ x 5⅛", V1p341–7, $35.00.

Waltham Horo. School, Watch Main Spring, ¾ x 3 x 3¾", V1p341–8, $40.00.

Waltz 200, Needles, ½ x 1¼ x 1⅝", V1p214–5, $35.00.

Wampole's, Throat Lozenges, ⅜ x 1¼ x 1¼", V2p171–6, $15.00.

Wang $.25, Hair Tonic, 1 x 3", V1p41–1, $15.00.

Wang sample, Olive\Coconut Oil, ¼ x 1⅝", V1p41–2, $20.00.

Wapello, Spice, 1⅜ x 2⅜ x 3¼", no photo, $45.00.

Wapello Chief, Spice, no photo, $60.00.

Wards, Needles Phono, ¼ x 1¼ x 1¾", V1p214–6, $25.00.

Wards, Valve Cores, ¼x 1 x 1½", V1p18–5, $12.00.

Ward's &.25, Tooth Soap, ½ x 2 x 3", V2p43–6, $90.00.

Wards sample, Mentho-campho, ⅜ x 1¼", V1p164–11, $10.00.

Ware Brothers, Auto Fuses, ⅜ x 1¼ x 1¾", no photo, $10.00.

Warner's sample, Safe Pills, ¼ x ⅞", V1p164–12, $35.00.

Warren, Chain Compound, 1 x 4", V1p174–7, $45.00.

Warren-Ohara, Enamels, 1 x 1", V1p182–5, $6.00.

Wasco, Billiard Mender, ¾ x ¾ x 3", V1p201–12, $6.00.

Washburnes O K, Paper Fasteners, ¾ x ⅜", V1p63–8, $15.00.

Washburn's OK 2.B, Paper Fasteners, 1¼ x 1⅞", V1p63–9, $15.00.

Washington Belle, Hair Victoria, no photo, $30.00.

Washington George sample, Coffee, 1½ x 2", V1p239–3, $45.00.

Washington George sample, Coffee, 2½ x 3⅜", V1p239–1, $30.00.

Washington George sample, Coffee, 2½ x 3⅜", V1p239–2, $30.00.

Washington George sample, Coffee, ⅜ x 2 x 3", V1p239–6, $30.00.

Washington George sample, Coffee 2½ oz., 2¾ x 3", V1p239–4, $60.00.

Washington George sample, Coffee Instant, 1¾ x 2⅜", V1p239–5, $45.00.

Washington Martha, Knitting Needles, 1 x 9", V1p187–4, $70.00.

Waterbury Mfg., Harness Leather, ⅜ x 1⅜ x 2½", V1p202–1, $150.00.

Watkins, Acotin Tablets 24, ⅜ x 1¾ x 2⅝", V1p165–1, $15.00.

Watkins, Allspice, 1¾ x 1¾ x 3½", V1p189–10, $30.00.

Watkins, Aspirin 24, ¼ x 1¾ x 2½", V1p165–2, $12.00.

Watkins, Headache Tablets, ½ x 1½ x 2½", V1p165–6, $50.00.

Watkins', Headache Tablets, ½ x 1½ x 2½", V2p108–2, $45.00.

Watkins, Laxative Cold & Grip, ½ x 2⅞ x 3½", V1p165–12, $10.00.

Watkins, Laxative Cold Grip Tab, ½ x 2⅝ x 3½", V1p166–1, $12.00.

Watkins, Laxative Cold Tablets, ½ x 2¾ x 3⅜, no photo, $12.00.
Watkins, Laxative Cold Tablets, ⅝ x 2¾ x 3¼", V1p166–3, $8.00.
Watkins, Laxative Wafers, ⅜ x 3¼ x 3½", V1p166–2, $15.00.
Watkins, Menthol Camphor, ½ x 1½", V1p165–7, $6.00.
Watkins, Menthol Camphor, ⅝ x 2⅜", V1p165–8, $6.00.
Watkins, Mustard, 1¾ x 1¾ x 3½", V1p189–11, $30.00.
Watkins, Petro-Carbo Salve, 1¼ x 2½", V1p165–9, $6.00.
Watkins $.15, Corn Salve, ½ x 1½", V1p165–3, $15.00.
Watkins $.50, Laxative Wafers, ½ x 3¼ x 3¾", V1p165–10, $15.00.
Watkins $.50, Laxative Wafers, ½ x 3¼ x 3¾", V1p165–11, $15.00.
Watkins ⅜ oz., Corn Cure, ½ x 1½", no photo, $12.00.
Watkins ⅜ oz., Corn Salve, ½ x 1½", V1p165–4, $10.00.
Watkins ⅜ oz., Corn Salve, ½ x 1½", V2p108–4, $10.00.
Watkins ⅜ oz., Vapor Balm, ¾ x 1½", V1p166–4, $6.00.
Watkins sample, Baking Powder, 1⅞ x 2½", V1p246–8, $70.00.
Watkins sample, Deodarant Powder, ⅞ x 1½ x 2½", V1p249–5, $20.00.
Watkins sample, Deodorant Powder, ⅞ x 1½ x 2¾", V1p249–6, $22.00.
Watkins sample, Menthol Camphor, ¾ x 2⅜", V2p108–6, $8.00.
Watkins sample, Menthol Camphor Oint., ¾ x 2½", no photo, $10.00.
Watkins sample, Menthol Camphor Ointment, ⅝ x 2⅜, no photo, $8.00.
Watkins sample, Talcum Powder, 1 x 3", no photo, $15.00.
Watkins sample, Talcum Powder, ¼ x 1⅛", V1p262–1, $25.00.
Watkins sample, Talcum Powder, ⅝ x ⅞ x 1⅞", V1p261–12, $25.00.
Watkins trial size, Malted Milk, 1¾ x 2½", V1p246–9, $75.00.
Watkin's trial size, Malted Milk, 1¾ x 2½", V2p126–4, $75.00.
Watlow 3 AG, Auto Fuses, ¼ x 1¼ x 1¾", V1p10–8, $10.00.
Watson 30 AMP, Auto Fuses, ⅜ x 1¼ x 1¾", no photo, $10.00.
Waverite $.25, Hair Dressing, ⅞ x 2¾", V1p41–3, $18.00.
Wavine, Skin Whitner Oint., ¾ x 1⅞", V1p32–2, $25.00.
Wavolena, Antiseptic Ointment, ¾ x 2⅜", V1p166–5, $12.00.
Wawil, Fish Food, 1⅜ x 2⅜", V1p202–2, $15.00.
Way's, Ointments, ¾ x 1¾", V2p108–8, $40.00.
Wear-Ever, Type Ribbon, ¾ x 2½ x 2½", V1p327–2, $10.00.
Webber's $.10, Stamping Material, ⅜ x 1¾", V1p202–3, $10.00.
Webber's Walter P. $.25, Stamping Material, ½ x 3¼", V1p202–4, $60.00.
Weber, Floataline, ¾ x 2⅝", V1p177–6, $5.00.
Webley 500, Rifle Pellets, ¾ x 2⅜ x 4", V2p214–2, $30.00.
Webley Special, Pellets, no photo, $15.00.
Webster, Type Ribbon, ¾ x 2½ x 2½", V1p327–6, $25.00.
Webster, Type Ribbon, ¾ x 2 x 2", V1p327–3, $12.00.
Webster, Type Ribbon, ¾ x 2 x 2", V1p327–4, $15.00.
Webster, Type Ribbon, ⅝ x 2 x 2", V1p327–7, $15.00.
Webster, Type Ribbon, ⅞ x 2⅛ x 2⅛, no photo, $12.00.
Webster's, Type Ribbon, 1½ x 1⅝ x 1⅝", V1p327–5, $45.00.
Webster's Hemlock, Tooth Soap, ½ x 2 x 3⅛", no photo, $80.00.
Weck's Ideal, Composition, no photo, $60.00.
Weck's Ideal Comp., Razor Strap Dress., 1¼ x 1⅞", V1p275–5, $45.00.
Wei De Meyer's, Catarrh Cure, ½ x 2 x 3¼", V1p166–6, $35.00.
Weikel's, Allspice, 3¾ x 2⅜ x 1⅝", V2p165–1, $35.00.
Welch's Bathasweet, Bath Powder, ¾ x 1½ x 3⅞", V1p264–11, $25.00.
Welco, Troches, ½ x 2 x 3⅛", V2p171–8, $45.00.
Welcome Brand, Type Ribbon, ⅞ x 2½ x 2½", V1p327–8, $18.00.
Welke's, Fish Food, 1⅜ x 2⅜", V1p202–5, $12.00.
Wellman, Allspice, 1¼ x 2¼ x 3¼", V2p165–3, $25.00.
Wellman sample, Coffee, 2 x 2½", V1p240–1, $90.00.
Wells', Tablets 100, ⅝ x 2 x 3", V2p109–1, $25.00.
Wells' $1.00, Tablets 200, ¾ x 2¾ x 3⅝", no photo, $20.00.
Wells Richardson, Lactated Food, 1½ x 1½ x 2", no photo, $25.00.
Wells' Tablets, Nux Vomica, ⅝ x 2 x 3⅛", V1p166–7, $25.00.
Wells Tablets $.50, Family Medicine, ½ x 2 x 3", V2p109–3, $22.00.
Wernet's sample, Denture Powder, ¾ x 1¼ x 2¼", V2p43–8, $30.00.
West Point, Cloves, 3 x 2 x 1¼", V2p165–5, $40.00.
Westbrook Garanteed, Type Ribbon, ¾ x 2½ x 2½", no photo, $15.00.
Western Clock Co., Keys (meter time), ¾ x 1¾ x 3", V1p341–9, $25.00.
Western Electric, Type Ribbon, ¾ x 2½ x 2½", no photo, $15.00.
Western Wire Prod., Cotter Pins, 1½ x 2", V1p202–6, $15.00.
Wetmore, Anti-Dyspeptic, 1¼ x 2⅛ x 3", V1p166–8, $35.00.
Weyenberg sample, Grease (shoes), ¾ x 1⅞", V1p282–11, $10.00.
Whale Amber, Leather Dressing, ¾ x 3", V1p282–12, $75.00.
Whalene $.10, Lubricant Bearings, ½ x 1¾", V1p11–4, $50.00.
Wheel of Fortune, Game, no photo, $120.00.
Wheel of Fortune, Game, ⅝ x 2 x 3⅛", V1p175–2, $120.00.
Wheelock's $.25, Veterinary Healing Salve, 1 x 2⅝", V2p193–6, $40.00.
Whelco, Aspirin, ¼ x 1¾ x 2½", V1p166–9, $8.00.
Whitaker, Auto Fuses, ¼ x 1½ x 1¾", V1p10–9, $10.00.
Whitch Hazel, Tooth Soap, ½ x 2 x 3¼", V1p60–5, $70.00.
White, Cloverine Salve, ⅜ x 1¼", V1p166–10, $5.00*.
White $.25, Cloverine Salve, ¾ x 2⅝", V1p166–11, $4.00.
White $.25, Ma-Le-Na Salve, 1 x 2⅜", V1p166–12, $5.00.
White (Landford), Adhesive Tape, 1 x 1⅜", no photo, $15.00.
White 100 A F\H, Fastners, 1⅛ x 1½", V2p214–5, $10.00.
White Bear Brand, Nutmeg, 3¼ x 1¾ x 1½", V2p165–7, $40.00.
White Chicle Co., Pepsin Qubits, ⅜ x 1⅜ x 2", V1p298–8, $30.00.
White Cross, Adhesive Plaster, 1 x 2", V1p348–4, $8.00.
White Cross, Surgical Adhesive, 1 x 1¼", V1p348–9, $30.00.
White Cross sample, Foot Powder, ⅞ x 1½ x 2⅜", V2p202–5, $35.00.
White Goose Brand, Cinnamon, 3¼ x 2¼ x 1½", V2p165–2, $30.00.
White House, Coffee, 2½ x 3½", V1p240–2, $75.00.
White House, Tea, ⅞ x 2⅜", V1p268–9, $75.00.
White House 4oz, Coffee, 3 x 3", V1p240–3, $45.00.
White House sample, Moca Java Coffee, 1¾ x 3¼", V1p240–4, $75.00.
White Lions sample, Cocoa, no photo, $75.00.
White Rose sample, Coffee, 2 x 2½", V1p240–5, $50.00.
White S.S. sample, Violet Talcum Powder, no photo, $60.00.
White Star Line, Match Safe, ⅜ x 1⅝ x 2½", V1p180–10, $100.00.
White Swan, Cinnamon, 2¾ x 2¼ x 1¼", V2p165–4, $35.00.
White Villa, Allspice 2oz, 1¼ x 2¼ x 3¾", V1p189–12, $45.00.
White Villa, Cream Tartar, 1¼ x 1⅝ x 3⅜", V1p190–1, $55.00.
White Villa, Sage 2oz, 2 x 3¾", V1p190–2, $45.00.
White Villa 2 oz., Whole Cinnamon, 2 x 3¾", V1p190–3, $45.00.
White Witch sample, Talcum Powder, ¾ x 1¼ x 2⅛", V1p262–2, $95.00.
White Wonder sample, Cold\Flu Salve, ⅛ x ⅞", V2p109–5, $25.00.
White's, Face Cream, ⅝ x 1⅞", V1p32–3, $8.00.
White's, Face Cream Bleach, ⅝ x 2", V1p32–4, $10.00.
White's, Specific Face Cream, ½ x 1⅞", V1p32–5, $8.00.
White's $.10, Pink Tablets, ¼ x 1¼ x 1¾", V2p109–7, $15.00.
White's 1 oz., Pomade, 1⅛ x 1⅞", V1p41–4, $18.00.
White's sample, Specific Face Cream, ¼ x 1⅛", V1p32–6, $15.00.
White's sample, Specific Face Cream, ¼ x 1⅛", V2p31–4, $12.00.
White's Specific, Face Cream, ½ x 2", V2p31–6, $15.00.
White's Specific, Face Cream, ¾ x 1⅞", V1p32–7, $10.00.
Whitley William, Needles, no photo, $35.00.
Whitman Stephrn F., Marshmallows, 1⅛ x 4⅛ x 6⅛", V1p177–8, $75.00.
Whitman's 4¼ oz., Chocolate Syrup, 2⅛ x 2⅞", V2p126–6, $25.00.
Whitmer's, Aspirin, ½ x 2 x 2⅝", V1p167–2, $18.00.
Whitmer's, Aspirin Tablets, ⅝ x 1⅝ x 2½", V2p109–2, $22.00.
Whitmer's, Quinine Cold Tablets, ½ x 1⅝ x 2⅝", V2p109–4, $15.00.

Whitmer's, Quinine Cold Tabs, ½ x 2 x 2⅝", V1p167–3, $22.00.
Whitmers sample, Corn Salve, ½ x 1⅛", V1p167–1, $15.00.
Whitmore Bros., Shoe Polish Star Russet, ⅝ x 1¾", V1p283–1, $12.00.
Whitney, Watch Jewelry, ⅝ x 2¾ x 5 ¼", V1p341–10, $45.00.
Whitney E.A. Co., Watch Main Spring, ½ x 3½ x 4¾", V1p341–11, $60.00.
Whittemore Bro's, Patent Leather Polish, ⅞ x 1⅞", V1p283–2, $18.00.
Whittemore Bros., Baby Elite Polish, ⅝ x 1¾", V1p283–3, $25.00.
Whittemore Bros., Star Polish Russet, ⅞ x 1¾", V1p283–4, $18.00.
Whittemore Bros., Suededene Powder, 1⅜ x 2½ x 3⅝", V1p283–5, $30.00.
Whittemore's, Black Oil Paste, 1 x 2⅞", V2p121–4, $12.00.
Whittemore's, Polish New Era, 1 x 3½", V1p283–6, $20.00.
Whittemore's, Polish New Era, 1 x 3½", V1p283–7, $18.00.
Whittemore's, White cake, 1 x 3", V1p283–8, $10.00.
Whittenmore, Baby Elite Polish, ⅞ x 1⅞", no photo, $18.00.
Whiz, Brake Waffers, 1¼ x 2¼", no photo, $60.00.
Whiz Bang, Medicine, ¼ x 1 x 2", no photo, $25.00.
Whiz sample, Soap, 1¼ x 1½", V1p18–10, $35.00.
Whiz Speedry, Car Wash Powder, 2 x 3", V1p18–11, $70.00.
Who, Cough Drops sample, no photo, $70.00.
Widlar's, Tumeric, 3⅝ x 2¼ x 1", V2p165–6, $25.00.
Wiel $.10, Garlic Tablets, ¼ x 1¼ x 1¾", V2p109–6, $15.00.
Wiggins, Wigg's Cleanser, 2 x 1½", V2p39–2, $12.00.
Wigg's $1.00, Cleanser, 1¼ x 2", no photo, $6.00.
Wigwam, Ginger, 2½ x 2¼ x 1¼", V2p165–8, $60.00.
Wilbert, Safety Razor, 1½ x 1¾ x 2½", V1p272–6, $180.00.
Wilbert, Safety Razor, 1½ x 1¾ x 2½", V1p272–7, $190.00.
Wilbert's, Bem-Tof, ⅞ x 2½", V1p167–4, $30.00.
Wilbur's sample, Cocoa, 1 x 1 x 1", no photo, $140.00.
Willard's, Adhesive Plaster, 1 x 1¼", V2p197–7, $18.00.
Willard's, Tablets, ¼ x 1⅝", V1p167–5, $6.00.
Williams, Shaving Stick, 1⅛ x 2½", no photo, $15.00.
Williams & Clark, Bone\Meat Fertilizers, ½ x 2 x 3⅛", V1p333–9, $145.00.
William's Carnation sample, Talcum Powder, ¾ x 1¼ x 2¼", no photo, $65.00.
Williams' Karsi sample, Talcum Powder, no photo, $75.00.
Williams Lab. $2.50, Improved Special, ½ x 2⅜ x 3¼", V1p167–6, $10.00.
Williams sample, Anti-Pain Ointment, ⅜ x 1¼", V1p167–7, $18.00*.
William's sample, Anti-Pain Ointment, ⅜ x 1⅛", V1p167–8, $22.00.
William's sample, Baby Talcum, ¾ x 1¼ x 2¼", V2p131–2, $75.00.
William's sample, Carnation Talcum, ¾ x 1¼ x 2¼", V2p131–4, $60.00.
William's sample, Carnation Talcum Powder, ¾ x 1¼ x 2¼", V1p262–3, $60.00.
William's sample, Carnation Talcum Powder, ¾ x 1¼ x 2¼", V2p131–6, $55.00.
William's sample, English Lilac Talcum, ¾ x 1¼ x 2¼", V1p262–6, $50.00.
William's sample, English Lilac Talcum Powder, ¾ x 1⅜ x 2¼", V2p132–1, $65.00.
William's sample, La Tosca Rose Talcum, ¾ x 1¼ x 2¼", V1p262–7, $75.00.
William's sample, LaTosca Rose Talcum, ¾ x 1¼ x 2¼", V1p262–8, $75.00.
William's sample, LaTosca Rose Talcum, ¾ x 1¼ x 2⅛", V2p132–3, $75.00.
William's sample, LaTosca Rose Talcum, ¾ x 1⅜ x 2¼", V2p132–5, $55.00.
William's sample, Mustard Cream, ¼ x 1¼", V1p167–9, $18.00.
William's sample, Mustard Cream, ¼ x 1⅝", V1p167–10, $15.00.
William's sample, Shaving Powder, 1 x 2", V1p275–6, $65.00.
William's sample, Violet Talcum Powder, no photo, $60.00.
William's sample, Violet Talcum Powder, 1 x 1⅞", V2p132–4, $80.00.
Williams sample, Violet Talcum Powder, ¾ x 1¼ x 2¼", V1p262–5, $65.00.
William's sample, Violet Talcum Powder, ¾ x 1¼ x 2¼", V1p262–9, $65.00.
William's sample, Violet Talcum Powder, ¾ x 1⅜ x 2¼", V2p132–2, $75.00.
Willis "Star," Tabacco Domino, ¼ x 1 x 2", V2p214–7, $25.00.
Wills $.25, English Formula Pills, ⅜ x 1⅜ x 2½", V1p167–11, $50.00.
Will's $.25, English Pills, ½ x 1¼ x 2½", V1p167–12, $55.00.
Wills Bulwark sample, Cut Plug Tabacco, ¼ x 1 x 1⅞", no photo, $20.00.
Will's Pills $.25, English Pills, ⅜ x 1⅝ x 2½", V2p109–8, $50.00.
Will's Star, Cigarettes, ¼ x 1 x 1⅞", no photo, $15.00.
Willson, Goggles, ½ x 2⅛ x 5 ½", V1p177–10, $15.00.
Willson T.A., Steel Spectacles, 1⅜ x 3 x 5 ½", V1p177–11, $75.00.
Willson's, Cathartic Laxative, ½ x 2⅝ x 4", V1p168–1, $25.00.
Willson's Monarch, Cloves, 3¾ x 2¼ x 1⅜", V2p166–1, $70.00.
Willson's Monarch, Nutmeg, 3¾ x 2¼ x 1⅜", V2p166–4, $70.00.
Wilson's Corega, Dental Powder, ¾ x 1¼ x 2", V1p59–5, $30.00.
Wilson's Corega, Denture Adhesive, ¾ x 1¼ x 2", V1p59–6, $55.00.
Wilson's Corega, Denture Adhesive, ¾ x 1¼ x 2", V1p59–7, $40.00.
Wilson's Corega, Tooth Powder, ¾ x 1¼ x 2", V1p59–9, $45.00.
Wilson's Corega $.35, Denture Adhesive, ⅞ x 1¾ x 3⅜", V1p59–10, $40.00.
Wilson's Corega $.35, Denture Powder, ⅞ x 1½ x 3¼", V1p59–11, $45.00.
Wilson's Corega sample, Denture Powder, ⅞ x 1½ x 2⅜", V1p59–12, 80.00.
Winchester, Safety Razor, 1⅜ x 2⅝", V1p272–8, $240.00.
Windsor sample, Coffee, 1¼ x 2½", no photo, $65.00.
Winner, Type Ribbon, ¾ x 2½ x 2½", no photo, $18.00.
Winner $.75, Safety Razor, 1⅜ x 2⅜", V1p272–9, $175.00.
Winner 200 Loud, Needles, ½ x 1¼ x 1½", V2p117–6, $40.00.
Winns $.05, Breath Mints, ¼ x 1¼ x 1½", V1p290–3, $25.00.
Winsor's sample, Coffee Cereal, 1½ x 2½", V1p240–6, $75.00.
Winterton's, Satsuma Wafers, ¾ x 1½", no photo, $30.00.
Winthrop Chemical Co., see Creamalin, V1p84–9, $8.00.
Winx (Ross Co.), Eye Lash Black, ½ x ½ x 1⅞", V1p54–1, $8.00.
Wise Old Indian, Salve, 1 x 2½", no photo, $35.00.
Wisteria sample, Talcum Powder, ¾ x 1⅛ x 1⅞", V1p262–10, $85.00.
Witch Hazel, Tooth Soap, ⅝ x 2⅛ x 3¼", no photo, $60.00.
Wixom Spice Co., Paprika, 2 x 4¼", V2p166–6, $35.00.
Wixon Brand, Ginger, 3⅞ x 2½ x 1⅞", V2p166–2, $25.00.
Wizard, Dental Rubber, no photo, $65.00.
Wizard, Mainsprings, ⅝ x 3 x 3⅜", V2p194–7, $60.00.
Wolverine, Tire Repair Outfit, no photo, $60.00.
Wolverine, Washers, ¾ x 2¾ x 3¾", V1p202–7, $18.00.
Wonder, Perfume Stone, no photo, $30.00.
Wonder, Scratch Filler, no photo, $15.00.
Wonder, Type Ribbon, ¾ x 2½ x 2½", no photo, $10.00.
Wonder Heart Cure, Pills, ⅞ x 1¾ x 2⅞", V1p168–2, $60.00.
Wonder Salve $.50, Salve, ¾ x 2", V1p168–3, $25.00.
Wonderful Dream $.30, Salve, ⅝ x 2½", V1p168–4, $40.00.
Wonderful Dream 1.2oz., Salve, ¾ x 2¼", V1p168–5, $10.00.
Wood Albert F., Rosetint Cream, ¼ x ⅞", V1p31–11, $12.00.
Wood J.R.& Son, unknown, ½ x 1⅛", V1p202–8, $4.00.
Woodbury's, Facial Powder, ½ x 2⅛", V2p25–6, $55.00.
Woodheads, Tea, ¾ x 2 x 3", V1p268–10, $15.00.
Wood's, Lollacapop, ¾ x 1¾ x 3¼", V1p168–6, $50.00.
Wood's sample, Gilt Edge Coffee, 1½ x 2½", V1p241–1, $55.00.

Wood's sample, Gilt Edge Coffee, 1½ x 2½", V1p241–1, $55.00.
Wood's sample, Gilt Edge Coffee, 1½ x 2½", V1p241–2, $60.00.
Wood's Thomas sample, Java Cassin Coffee, ⅜ x 1½ x 2½", V2p124–4, $175.00.
Woodside Samuel Co., Tea, Sample 3 x 3 x 2", V1p268–11, $45.00.
Woodstock, Type Ribbon, ¾ x 2½ x 2½", no photo, $30.00.
Woodstock (Manchester), Type Ribbon, ⅞ x 2½", V1p327–10, $12.00.
Woodstock (Stanford), Type Ribbon, ⅞ x 2½", V1p327–9, $12.00.
Woodworth's sample, Trailing Arbutus Talcum, ¾ x 1¼ x 2¼", V1p262–11, $110.00.
Woodworths sample, Violets of Sicily, ⅞ x 1¼ x 1½", V1p264–12, $40.00.
Woodworth's sample, Violets Sicily Talcum, ⅞ x 1¼ x 2½", no photo, $70.00.
World, Valve Cores, ¼ x 1¼ x 1½", V1p18–6, $12.00.
World Superior Qual., Auto Fuses, no photo, $8.00.
Wrang-Tang $.25, Ointment, ⅞ x 2⅝", V1p168–7, $40.00.
Wren, Boot Polish, no photo, $18.00.
Wren's, Dubbin, ⅝ x 2¾", V1p202–9, $8.00.
Wright Myrrh, Tooth Soap, ½ x 2 x 3⅛", V1p60–6, $110.00.
Wright-Ditson, Sport Tape, ¼ x 1¼ x 2⅜", V1p202–10, $22.00.
Wright's, Indian Vegetable Pills, ⅝ x 1 x 2", V1p168–8, $18.00.
Wrisley's sample, San Toy Talcum, ⅞ x 1⅛ x 2", V1p262–12, $85.00.
Write, Type Ribbon, ¾ x 2½ x 2½", V1p327–11, $15.00.
Write Right, Type Ribbon, ¾ x 2½ x 2½", no photo, $12.00.
Wyalin, Choc Laxative, ¼ x 1¼ x 1¾", V1p168–9, $10.00.
Wyandoids, Rectal Suppository, ½ x 1⅛ x 1½", V1p168–10, $5.00.
Wyeth, A.M.T. 30 Tablets, ¼ x 2⅜ x 2¾", V1p168–11, $8.00.
Wyeth, Amphojel Tablets, ¼ x 1¼ x 1¾", V2p110–1, $8.00.
Wyeth, Amphojel Tablets, ⅜ x 2¼ x 2¾", V1p168–12, $8.00.
Wyeth AMT, Tablets, ¼ x 1¼ x 1¾", V1p69–7, $8.00.
Wyeth John, Lozenges (charcoal), ¾ x 2½ x 4", V1p294–12, 80.00.
Wyeth sample, Sopronol Powder, 1¼ x 2", V2p110–5, $15.00.
Wyeth Wyanoids sample, Hemroid Suppository, ½ x 1⅝ x 1⅝", V2p110–3, $8.00.
Wyeth's Wyanoids sample, Hemorrhoidal Suppository, ½ x 1½ x 1½", V1p169–1, $12.00.
Wylon sample, Pressing Oil, ½ x 1¾", V2p36–6, $18.00.
Wynne's sample, Rising Mist, ¼ x 1⅝", V1p169–2, $18.00.
X-Cel #5 sample, Stove Polish Powder, 2⅛ x 2⅛", V2p39–4, $50.00.
X-Ray sample, Ointment, ¼ x 1⅛", V1p169–3, $30.00.
X-Ray sample, Ointment, ⅜ x ⅞", V1p169–4, $25.00.
Xcello's, Condom, ¼ x 1½ x 2", V1p25–11, $50.00.
Xlent, Ointment, ⅝ x 1¾", V1p169–5, $12.00.
XLNT Brand, Type Ribbon, ¾ x 2½", V2p191–7, $12.00.
Xylopin, Wood Needles, ¼ x 1¼ x 1¾", V2p117–8, $30.00.
Y & S, Licoric (cough drops), ⅝ x 1¼ x 2", V1p295–1, $15.00.
Y & S, Licorice Wafers, ¼ x 1¾ x 2⅛", V1p295–3, $15.00.
Y & S, Licorice Wafers, ¾ x 1¼ x 2", V1p295–4, $12.00.
Y & S, Licorice Wafers, ⅜ x 1¾ x 2⅛", V1p295–4, $12.00.
Y & S, Licorice Wafers, ⅝ x 1⅜ x 2⅛", V1p295–2, $15.00.
Yale sample, Coffee, 2½ x 2¼", V1p241–3, $100.00.
Yale sample, Moca & Java Coffee, 2½ x 2¼", V1p241–4, $115.00.
Yankee, Razor Blade, ¼ x 1 x 2", V1p269–11, $195.00.
Yankee, Razor Blade, ¼ x 1 x 2⅛", V1p269–12, $150.00.
Yankee, Safety Razor, no photo, $180.00.
Yankee, Safety Razor, 1⅜ x 1¾ x 2½", V1p272–11, $280.00.
Yankee, Safety Razor, 1⅜ x 2¼", V1p272–10, $215.00.
Yankee, Type Ribbon, no photo, $30.00.
Yankee Girl, Spice, no photo, $40.00.
Yankee sample, Nickel Polish, ⅜ x 1⅜", V2p39–7, $25.00.
Yellow Bonnet sample, Coffee, 3 x 2½", V1p241–5, $450.00.
Yerkes, Pure Nutmeg, 1¼ x 2¼ x 3¼", V2p166–3, $25.00.
Yewabit, Metal Polish, no photo, $20.00.
Yodora sample, Deodor Creme, ¼ x 1¼", V1p32–8, $12.00.
Young E.F. Jr., Hair Dressing, ⅞ x 3½", V1p41–5, $12.00.
Young E.F. Jr., Pressing Oil, ⅞ x 3½", V1p41–6, $12.00.
Young Lucille, Lash Darkner, ⅜ x 1½", V1p54–2, $20.00.
Young Otto, Watch Main Spring, ⅝ x 2¾ x 5⅛", V1p341–12, $45.00.
Young's $.25, Carbolic Ointment, 1⅛ x 2½", V2p193–8, $25.00.
Young's Victoria, Cream, no photo, $18.00.
Yuban sample, Coffee 4oz., 3⅜ x 2½", V2p124–7, $20.00.
Yueta, Gum, no photo, $125.00.
Z.B.T. sample, Baby Powder, 1 x 2⅛", V1p265–1, $18.00.
Z.B.T. sample, Baby Talcum, 1 x 2⅛", V2p132–6, $25.00.
Zaegel's, Essence Pills, ¼ x 1⅛", V1p169–6, $10.00.
Zaegel's sample, Essence Pills, ¼ x ⅞", V2p110–7, $10.00.
Zahnol, Tooth Soap, no photo, $95.00.
Zalva sample, Ointment, ⅜ x 1¼", V2p110–2, $15.00.
Zam-Buk, Healing Ointment, ¾ x 1⅞", V2p110–4, $8.00.
Zam-Buk, Healing Ointment, ¾ x 1⅞", V2p110–6, $8.00.
ZamBuk sample, Herbal Balm, ¼ x ⅞", V1p169–7, $15.00.
Zane Products, Aspirin, ¼ x 1¼ x 1¾", V2p110–8, $6.00.
Zanol, Allspice, 4 x 2¼ x 1¼", V2p166–5, $40.00.
Zanol, Family Salve, ¾ x 2¾", V1p169–8, $8.00.
Zanol, Paprika, 1¾ x 3¼", V2p166–7, $35.00.
Zanol M-32, Laxative Quinine Cold, ⅜ x 1¾ x 2½", no photo, $4.00.
Zanolax, Candy Laxative, ½ x 2 x 2½", V1p169–9, $15.00.
Zell's, Nerve Tablets, no photo, $40.00.
Zemo $.25, Laxative Pepsin Tablets, ⅜ x 1½ x 1⅞", V1p169–10, $15.00.
Zemo $.60, Ointment, ⅞ x 2⅜", V1p169–11, $8.00.
Zenith, Needles Extra Loud, ¼ x 1¼ x 1¾", V1p214–7, $25.00.
Zeno, Pepsin Gum, ⅝ x 1 x 3¼", V1p298–9, $225.00.
Zeno Bicycle, Chewing Gum, no photo, $260.00.
Zeno Bicycle, Wild Cherry Gum, no photo, $285.00.
Zeno Forbidden, Peppermint Fruit Gum, ⅝ x 1 x 3⅛", V2p173–5, $225.00.
Zig Zag, Gum, 1¼ x 2", V1p298–10, $100.00.
Zig Zag, Gum, 1¼ x 2", V1p298–11, $100.00.
Zig Zag, Gum, 1 x 2½", V1p299–10, $120.00.
Zig Zag, Gum, 1 x 2½", V1p299–12, $120.00.
Zig Zag, Gum, 1 x 2½", V2p173–7, $130.00.
Zig Zag, Gum, 1 x 2⅜", V1p299–6, $120.00.
Zig Zag, Gum, 1 x 2⅜", V2p173–2, $140.00.
Zig Zag, Gum, 1 x 2⅝", V1p299–7, $120.00.
Zig Zag, Gum, 1 x 2⅝", V1p299–8, $120.00.
Zig Zag, Gum, 1 x 2⅝", V1p299–9, $120.00.
Zig Zag, Gum, 1 x 2⅝", V2p173–4, $120.00.
Zig Zag, Gum, ¾ x 1⅜", V1p299–4, $60.00.
Zig Zag, Gum, ¾ x 1⅝", V1p299–1, $75.00.
Zig Zag, Gum, ¾ x 1⅝", V1p299–2, $75.00.
Zig Zag, Gum, ¾ x 1⅝", V1p299–3, $60.00.
Zig Zag, Gum, ¾ x 1⅝", V1p299–5, $60.00.
Zig Zag, Gum, ¾ x 1⅝", V2p173–6, $60.00.
Zig Zag, Gum, ⅜ x 1¼ x 1¾", V1p300–1, $130.00.
Zig Zag, Gum, ⅜ x 1¼ x 1⅞", V1p300–2, $125.00.
Zig Zag, Gum, ⅞ x 2⅜", V2p173–8, $120.00.
Zinc Oxide, Adhesive Plaster, 1 x ¾", V1p348–7, $15.00.
Zinc Oxide, Adhesive Plaster, 1x 1¼", V1p348–6, $18.00.
Zincora, Tooth Powder, no photo, $60.00.
Zion Brand, Type Ribbon, no photo, $10.00.
ZIP sample, Grinding Compound, ⅝ x 1¾", V2p16–5, $18.00.
Zo, Adhesive, ¼ x 1¼ x 2¼", V1p348–8, $25.00.
Zo-No, Ointment, ⅞ x 2", no photo, $5.00.
Zonophone, Needles, ½ x 1¼ x 1⅝", V1p214–8, $35.00.
Zonweiss, Cream for teeth, ¾ x 2", V1p61–5, $130.00.
Zum, Aspirin, ¼ x 1⅜ x 1¾", no photo, $7.00.
Zylax, Laxative, ¼ x 1¼ x 1¾, V1p169–12, $6.00*.

The Encyclopedia of
Advertising Tins
Smalls & Samples
Volume I

David Zimmerman's first Volume of Advertising Tins, containing 3,500 different photos, is an excellent resource to accompany Volume II.

The index of Volume II also includes references to Volume I.

8½ x 11" • 348 pages • #4821 • $29.95

COLLECTOR BOOKS
A Division of Schroeder Publishing Co., Inc.

COLLECTOR BOOKS

Informing Today's Collector

For over two decades we have been keeping collectors informed on trends and values in all fields of antiques and collectibles.

DOLLS, FIGURES & TEDDY BEARS

4707	A Decade of **Barbie** Dolls & Collectibles, 1981–1991, Summers	$19.95
4631	**Barbie** Doll Boom, 1986–1995, Augustyniak	$18.95
2079	**Barbie** Doll Fashion, Volume I, Eames	$24.95
4846	**Barbie** Doll Fashion, Volume II, Eames	$24.95
3957	**Barbie** Exclusives, Rana	$18.95
4632	**Barbie** Exclusives, Book II, Rana	$18.95
4557	**Barbie**, The First 30 Years, Deutsch	$24.95
4847	**Barbie** Years, 1959–1995, 2nd Ed., Olds	$17.95
3310	**Black Dolls**, 1820–1991, Perkins	$17.95
3873	**Black Dolls**, Book II, Perkins	$17.95
3810	**Chatty Cathy Dolls**, Lewis	$15.95
1529	Collector's Encyclopedia of **Barbie** Dolls, DeWein	$19.95
4882	Collector's Encyclopedia of **Barbie** Doll Exclusives and More, Augustyniak	$19.95
2211	Collector's Encyclopedia of **Madame Alexander Dolls**, Smith	$24.95
4863	Collector's Encyclopedia of **Vogue Dolls**, Izen/Stover	$29.95
3967	Collector's Guide to **Trolls**, Peterson	$19.95
4571	**Liddle Kiddles**, Identification & Value Guide, Langford	$18.95
1513	**Teddy Bears & Steiff** Animals, Mandel	$9.95
1817	**Teddy Bears & Steiff** Animals, 2nd Series, Mandel	$19.95
2084	**Teddy Bears, Annalee's & Steiff** Animals, 3rd Series, Mandel	$19.95
1808	Wonder of **Barbie**, Manos	$9.95
1430	World of **Barbie** Dolls, Manos	$9.95
4880	World of **Raggedy Ann** Collectibles, Avery	$24.95

Note: Story of Barbie, Westenhouser, 3826, $19.95 appears in this section.

TOYS, MARBLES & CHRISTMAS COLLECTIBLES

3427	**Advertising Character** Collectibles, Dotz	$17.95
2333	Antique & Collector's **Marbles**, 3rd Ed., Grist	$9.95
3827	Antique & Collector's **Toys**, 1870–1950, Longest	$24.95
3956	Baby Boomer **Games**, Identification & Value Guide, Polizzi	$24.95
4934	**Breyer Animal** Collector's Guide, Identification and Values, Browell	$19.95
3717	**Christmas** Collectibles, 2nd Edition, Whitmyer	$24.95
4976	**Christmas** Ornaments, Lights & Decorations, Johnson	$24.95
4737	**Christmas** Ornaments, Lights & Decorations, Vol. II, Johnson	$24.95
4739	**Christmas** Ornaments, Lights & Decorations, Vol. III, Johnson	$24.95
4649	Classic Plastic **Model Kits**, Polizzi	$24.95
4559	Collectible **Action Figures**, 2nd Ed., Manos	$17.95
3874	Collectible Coca-Cola Toy **Trucks**, deCourtivron	$24.95
2338	Collector's Encyclopedia of **Disneyana**, Longest, Stern	$24.95
4958	Collector's Guide to **Battery Toys**, Hultzman	$19.95
4639	Collector's Guide to **Diecast Toys & Scale Models**, Johnson	$19.95
4651	Collector's Guide to **Tinker Toys**, Strange	$18.95
4566	Collector's Guide to **Tootsietoys**, 2nd Ed., Richter	$19.95
4720	The Golden Age of **Automotive Toys**, 1925–1941, Hutchison/Johnson	$24.95
3436	Grist's Big Book of **Marbles**	$19.95
3970	Grist's Machine-Made & Contemporary **Marbles**, 2nd Ed.	$9.95
4723	**Matchbox** Toys, 1947 to 1996, 2nd Ed., Johnson	$18.95
4871	**McDonald's Collectibles**, Henriques/DuVall	$19.95
1540	**Modern Toys** 1930–1980, Baker	$19.95
3888	**Motorcycle** Toys, Antique & Contemporary, Gentry/Downs	$18.95
4953	Schroeder's Collectible **Toys**, Antique to Modern Price Guide, 4th Ed.	$17.95
1886	Stern's Guide to **Disney** Collectibles	$14.95
2139	Stern's Guide to **Disney** Collectibles, 2nd Series	$14.95
3975	Stern's Guide to **Disney** Collectibles, 3rd Series	$18.95
2028	**Toys**, Antique & Collectible, Longest	$14.95
3979	**Zany Characters** of the Ad World, Lamphier	$16.95

FURNITURE

1457	American **Oak** Furniture, McNerney	$9.95
3716	American **Oak** Furniture, Book II, McNerney	$12.95
1118	Antique **Oak** Furniture, Hill	$7.95
2271	Collector's Encyclopedia of **American** Furniture, Vol. II, Swedberg	$24.95
3720	Collector's Encyclopedia of **American** Furniture, Vol. III, Swedberg	$24.95
3878	Collector's Guide to **Oak** Furniture, George	$12.95
1755	Furniture of the **Depression** Era, Swedberg	$19.95
3906	**Heywood-Wakefield** Modern Furniture, Rouland	$18.95

1885	**Victorian** Furniture, Our American Heritage, McNerney	$9.95
3829	**Victorian** Furniture, Our American Heritage, Book II, McNerney	$9.95

JEWELRY, HATPINS, WATCHES & PURSES

1712	Antique & Collector's **Thimbles** & Accessories, Mathis	$19.95
1748	Antique **Purses**, Revised Second Ed., Holiner	$19.95
1278	Art Nouveau & Art Deco **Jewelry**, Baker	$9.95
4850	Collectible **Costume Jewelry**, Simonds	$24.95
3875	Collecting Antique **Stickpins**, Kerins	$16.95
3722	Collector's Ency. of **Compacts, Carryalls & Face Powder Boxes**, Mueller	$24.95
4854	Collector's Ency. of **Compacts, Carryalls & Face Powder Boxes**, Vol. II	$24.95
4940	**Costume Jewelry**, A Practical Handbook & Value Guide, Rezazadeh	$24.95
1716	Fifty Years of Collectible **Fashion Jewelry**, 1925–1975, Baker	$19.95
1424	**Hatpins** & Hatpin Holders, Baker	$9.95
4570	Ladies' **Compacts**, Gerson	$24.95
1181	100 Years of Collectible **Jewelry**, 1850–1950, Baker	$9.95
4729	**Sewing Tools** & Trinkets, Thompson	$24.95
2348	20th Century Fashionable Plastic **Jewelry**, Baker	$19.95
4878	Vintage & Contemporary **Purse Accessories**, Gerson	$24.95
3830	Vintage **Vanity Bags & Purses**, Gerson	$24.95

INDIANS, GUNS, KNIVES, TOOLS, PRIMITIVES

1868	Antique **Tools**, Our American Heritage, McNerney	$9.95
1426	**Arrowheads** & Projectile Points, Hothem	$7.95
4943	Field Guide to **Flint Arrowheads & Knives** of the North American Indian	$9.95
2279	**Indian Artifacts** of the Midwest, Hothem	$14.95
3885	**Indian Artifacts** of the Midwest, Book II, Hothem	$16.95
4870	**Indian Artifacts** of the Midwest, Book III, Hothem	$18.95
1964	**Indian Axes** & Related Stone Artifacts, Hothem	$14.95
2023	**Keen Kutter** Collectibles, Heuring	$14.95
4724	Modern **Guns**, Identification & Values, 11th Ed., Quertermous	$12.95
2164	**Primitives**, Our American Heritage, McNerney	$9.95
1759	**Primitives**, Our American Heritage, 2nd Series, McNerney	$14.95
4730	Standard **Knife** Collector's Guide, 3rd Ed., Ritchie & Stewart	$12.95

PAPER COLLECTIBLES & BOOKS

4633	**Big Little Books**, Jacobs	$18.95
4710	Collector's Guide to **Children's Books**, Jones	$18.95
1441	Collector's Guide to **Post Cards**, Wood	$9.95
2081	Guide to Collecting **Cookbooks**, Allen	$14.95
2080	Price Guide to **Cookbooks & Recipe Leaflets**, Dickinson	$9.95
3973	**Sheet Music** Reference & Price Guide, 2nd Ed., Pafik & Guiheen	$19.95
4654	**Victorian Trade Cards**, Historical Reference & Value Guide, Cheadle	$19.95
4733	**Whitman Juvenile Books**, Brown	$17.95

GLASSWARE

4561	Collectible **Drinking Glasses**, Chase & Kelly	$17.95
4642	Collectible **Glass Shoes**, Wheatley	$19.95
4937	Coll. **Glassware** from the 40s, 50s & 60s, 4th Ed., Florence	$19.95
1810	Collector's Encyclopedia of **American Art Glass**, Shuman	$29.95
4938	Collector's Encyclopedia of **Depression Glass**, 13th Ed., Florence	$19.95
1961	Collector's Encyclopedia of **Fry Glassware**, Fry Glass Society	$24.95
1664	Collector's Encyclopedia of **Heisey Glass**, 1925–1938, Bredehoft	$24.95
3905	Collector's Encyclopedia of **Milk Glass**, Newbound	$24.95
4936	Collector's Guide to **Candy Containers**, Dezso/Poirier	$19.95
4564	**Crackle Glass**, Weitman	$19.95
4941	**Crackle Glass**, Book II, Weitman	$19.95
2275	**Czechoslovakian Glass** and Collectibles, Barta/Rose	$16.95
4714	**Czechoslovakian Glass** and Collectibles, Book II, Barta/Rose	$16.95
4716	**Elegant Glassware** of the Depression Era, 7th Ed., Florence	$19.95
1380	Encyclopedia of **Pattern Glass**, McClain	$12.95
3981	Ever's Standard **Cut Glass** Value Guide	$12.95
4659	**Fenton Art Glass**, 1907–1939, Whitmyer	$24.95
3725	**Fostoria**, Pressed, Blown & Hand Molded Shapes, Kerr	$24.95
4719	**Fostoria**, Etched, Carved & Cut Designs, Vol. II, Kerr	$24.95
3883	**Fostoria Stemware**, The Crystal for America, Long & Seate	$24.95
4644	**Imperial Carnival Glass**, Burns	$18.95
3886	**Kitchen Glassware** of the Depression Years, 5th Ed., Florence	$19.95

4725	Pocket Guide to **Depression Glass**, 10th Ed., Florence	$9.95
5035	Standard Encyclopedia of **Carnival Glass**, 6th Ed., Edwards/Carwile	$24.95
5036	Standard **Carnival Glass** Price Guide, 11th Ed., Edwards/Carwile	$9.95
4875	Standard Encyclopedia of **Opalescent Glass**, 2nd ed., Edwards	$19.95
4731	**Stemware Identification**, Featuring Cordials with Values, Florence	$24.95
3326	**Very Rare Glassware** of the Depression Years, 3rd Series, Florence	$24.95
4732	**Very Rare Glassware** of the Depression Years, 5th Series, Florence	$24.95
4656	**Westmoreland Glass**, Wilson	$24.95

POTTERY

4927	**ABC Plates & Mugs**, Lindsay	$24.95
4929	**American Art Pottery**, Sigafoose	$24.95
4630	**American Limoges**, Limoges	$24.95
1312	**Blue & White Stoneware**, McNerney	$9.95
1958	So. Potteries **Blue Ridge Dinnerware**, 3rd Ed., Newbound	$14.95
1959	**Blue Willow**, 2nd Ed., Gaston	$14.95
4848	Ceramic **Coin Banks**, Stoddard	$19.95
4851	Collectible **Cups & Saucers**, Harran	$18.95
4709	Collectible **Kay Finch**, Biography, Identification & Values, Martinez/Frick	$18.95
1373	Collector's Encyclopedia of **American Dinnerware**, Cunningham	$24.95
4931	Collector's Encyclopedia of **Bauer Pottery**, Chipman	$24.95
3815	Collector's Encyclopedia of **Blue Ridge Dinnerware**, Newbound	$19.95
4932	Collector's Encyclopedia of **Blue Ridge Dinnerware**, Vol. II, Newbound	$24.95
4658	Collector's Encyclopedia of **Brush-McCoy Pottery**, Huxford	$24.95
2272	Collector's Encyclopedia of **California Pottery**, Chipman	$24.95
3811	Collector's Encyclopedia of **Colorado Pottery**, Carlton	$24.95
2133	Collector's Encyclopedia of **Cookie Jars**, Roerig	$24.95
3723	Collector's Encyclopedia of **Cookie Jars**, Book II, Roerig	$24.95
4939	Collector's Encyclopedia of **Cookie Jars**, Book III, Roerig	$24.95
4638	Collector's Encyclopedia of **Dakota Potteries**, Dommel	$24.95
5040	Collector's Encyclopedia of **Fiesta**, 8th Ed., Huxford	$19.95
4718	Collector's Encyclopedia of **Figural Planters & Vases**, Newbound	$19.95
3961	Collector's Encyclopedia of **Early Noritake**, Alden	$24.95
1439	Collector's Encyclopedia of **Flow Blue China**, Gaston	$19.95
3812	Collector's Encyclopedia of **Flow Blue China**, 2nd Ed., Gaston	$24.95
3813	Collector's Encyclopedia of **Hall China**, 2nd Ed., Whitmyer	$24.95
3431	Collector's Encyclopedia of **Homer Laughlin China**, Jasper	$24.95
1276	Collector's Encyclopedia of **Hull Pottery**, Roberts	$19.95
3962	Collector's Encyclopedia of **Lefton China**, DeLozier	$19.95
4855	Collector's Encyclopedia of **Lefton China**, Book II, DeLozier	$19.95
2210	Collector's Encyclopedia of **Limoges Porcelain**, 2nd Ed., Gaston	$24.95
2334	Collector's Encyclopedia of **Majolica Pottery**, Katz-Marks	$19.95
1358	Collector's Encyclopedia of **McCoy Pottery**, Huxford	$19.95
3963	Collector's Encyclopedia of **Metlox Potteries**, Gibbs Jr.	$24.95
3837	Collector's Encyclopedia of **Nippon Porcelain**, Van Patten	$24.95
2089	Collector's Ency. of **Nippon Porcelain**, 2nd Series, Van Patten	$24.95
1665	Collector's Ency. of **Nippon Porcelain**, 3rd Series, Van Patten	$24.95
4712	Collector's Ency. of **Nippon Porcelain**, 4th Series, Van Patten	$24.95
1447	Collector's Encyclopedia of **Noritake**, Van Patten	$19.95
3432	Collector's Encyclopedia of **Noritake**, 2nd Series, Van Patten	$24.95
1037	Collector's Encyclopedia of **Occupied Japan**, 1st Series, Florence	$14.95
1038	Collector's Encyclopedia of **Occupied Japan**, 2nd Series, Florence	$14.95
2088	Collector's Encyclopedia of **Occupied Japan**, 3rd Series, Florence	$14.95
2019	Collector's Encyclopedia of **Occupied Japan**, 4th Series, Florence	$14.95
2335	Collector's Encyclopedia of **Occupied Japan**, 5th Series, Florence	$14.95
4951	Collector's Encyclopedia of **Old Ivory China**, Hillman	$24.95
3964	Collector's Encyclopedia of **Pickard China**, Reed	$24.95
3877	Collector's Encyclopedia of **R.S. Prussia**, 4th Series, Gaston	$24.95
1034	Collector's Encyclopedia of **Roseville Pottery**, Huxford	$19.95
1035	Collector's Encyclopedia of **Roseville Pottery**, 2nd Ed., Huxford	$19.95
4856	Collector's Encylopeida of **Russel Wright**, 2nd Ed., Kerr	$24.95
4713	Collector's Encyclopedia of **Salt Glaze Stoneware**, Taylor/Lowrance	$24.95
3314	Collector's Encyclopedia of **Van Briggle** Art Pottery, Sasicki	$24.95
4563	Collector's Encyclopedia of **Wall Pockets**, Newbound	$19.95
2111	Collector's Encyclopedia of **Weller Pottery**, Huxford	$29.95
3876	Collector's Guide to **Lu-Ray Pastels**, Meehan	$18.95
3814	Collector's Guide to **Made in Japan** Ceramics, White	$18.95
4646	Collector's Guide to **Made in Japan** Ceramics, Book II, White	$18.95
4565	Collector's Guide to **Rockingham**, The Enduring Ware, Brewer	$14.95
2339	Collector's Guide to **Shawnee Pottery**, Vanderbilt	$19.95
1425	**Cookie Jars**, Westfall	$9.95

3440	**Cookie Jars**, Book II, Westfall	$19.95
4924	Figural & Novelty **Salt & Pepper Shakers**, 2nd Series, Davern	$24.95
2379	Lehner's Ency. of **U.S. Marks** on Pottery, Porcelain & China	$24.95
4722	**McCoy Pottery**, Collector's Reference & Value Guide, Hanson/Nissen	$19.95
3825	**Purinton Pottery**, Morris	$24.95
4726	**Red Wing Art Pottery**, 1920s–1960s, Dollen	$19.95
1670	**Red Wing Collectibles**, DePasquale	$9.95
1440	**Red Wing Stoneware**, DePasquale	$9.95
1632	**Salt & Pepper Shakers**, Guarnaccia	$9.95
5091	**Salt & Pepper Shakers** II, Guarnaccia	$18.95
2220	**Salt & Pepper Shakers** III, Guarnaccia	$14.95
3443	**Salt & Pepper Shakers** IV, Guarnaccia	$18.95
3738	**Shawnee Pottery**, Mangus	$24.95
4629	Turn of the Century **American Dinnerware**, 1880s–1920s, Jasper	$24.95
4572	**Wall Pockets** of the Past, Perkins	$17.95
3327	**Watt Pottery** – Identification & Value Guide, Morris	$19.95

OTHER COLLECTIBLES

4704	Antique & Collectible **Buttons**, Wisniewski	$19.95
2269	Antique **Brass & Copper** Collectibles, Gaston	$16.95
1880	Antique **Iron**, McNerney	$9.95
3872	Antique **Tins**, Dodge	$24.95
4845	Antique **Typewriters & Office Collectibles**, Rehr	$19.95
1714	**Black** Collectibles, Gibbs	$19.95
1128	**Bottle** Pricing Guide, 3rd Ed., Cleveland	$7.95
4636	**Celluloid Collectibles**, Dunn	$14.95
3718	Collectible **Aluminum**, Grist	$16.95
3445	Collectible **Cats**, An Identification & Value Guide, Fyke	$18.95
4560	Collectible **Cats**, An Identification & Value Guide, Book II, Fyke	$19.95
4852	Collectible **Compact Disc** Price Guide 2, Cooper	$17.95
2018	Collector's Encyclopedia of **Granite Ware**, Greguire	$24.95
3430	Collector's Encyclopedia of **Granite Ware**, Book 2, Greguire	$24.95
4705	Collector's Guide to **Antique Radios**, 4th Ed., Bunis	$18.95
3880	Collector's Guide to **Cigarette Lighters**, Flanagan	$17.95
4637	Collector's Guide to **Cigarette Lighers**, Book II, Flanagan	$17.95
4942	Collector's Guide to **Don Winton Designs**, Ellis	$19.95
3966	Collector's Guide to **Inkwells**, Identification & Values, Badders	$18.95
4947	Collector's Guide to **Inkwells**, Book II, Badders	$19.95
4948	Collector's Guide to **Letter Openers**, Grist	$19.95
4862	Collector's Guide to **Toasters** & Accessories, Greguire	$19.95
4652	Collector's Guide to **Transistor Radios**, 2nd Ed., Bunis	$16.95
4653	Collector's Guide to **TV Memorabilia**, 1960s–1970s, Davis/Morgan	$24.95
4864	Collector's Guide to **Wallace Nutting Pictures**, Ivankovich	$18.95
1629	**Doorstops**, Identification & Values, Bertoia	$9.95
4567	Figural **Napkin Rings**, Gottschalk & Whitson	$18.95
4717	Figural **Nodders**, Includes Bobbin' Heads and Swayers, Irtz	$19.95
3968	**Fishing Lure** Collectibles, Murphy/Edmisten	$24.95
4867	**Flea Market Trader**, 11th Ed., Huxford	$9.95
4944	**Flue Covers**, Collector's Value Guide, Meckley	$12.95
4945	**G-Men and FBI Toys** and Collectibles, Whitworth	$18.95
5043	**Garage Sale & Flea Market Annual**, 6th Ed.	$19.95
3819	**General Store Collectibles**, Wilson	$24.95
4643	**Great American West** Collectibles, Wilson	$24.95
2215	Goldstein's **Coca-Cola** Collectibles	$16.95
3884	Huxford's Collectible **Advertising**, 2nd Ed.	$24.95
2216	**Kitchen Antiques**, 1790–1940, McNerney	$14.95
4950	The **Lone Ranger**, Collector's Reference & Value Guide, Felbinger	$18.95
2026	**Railroad** Collectibles, 4th Ed., Baker	$14.95
4949	**Schroeder's Antiques Price Guide**, 16th Ed., Huxford	$12.95
5007	**Silverplated Flatware**, Revised 4th Edition, Hagan	$18.95
1922	Standard **Old Bottle** Price Guide, Sellari	$14.95
4708	Summers' Guide to **Coca-Cola**	$19.95
4952	Summers' Pocket Guide to **Coca-Cola** Identifications	$9.95
3892	**Toy & Miniature Sewing Machines**, Thomas	$18.95
4876	**Toy & Miniature Sewing Machines**, Book II, Thomas	$24.95
3828	Value Guide to **Advertising Memorabilia**, Summers	$18.95
3977	Value Guide to **Gas Station** Memorabilia, Summers & Priddy	$24.95
4877	Vintage **Bar Ware**, Visakay	$24.95
4935	The **W.F. Cody Buffalo Bill** Collector's Guide with Values	$24.95
4879	**Wanted to Buy**, 6th Edition	$9.95

This is only a partial listing of the books on antiques that are available from Collector Books. All books are well illustrated and contain current values. Most of these books are available from your local bookseller, antique dealer, or public library. If you are unable to locate certain titles in your area, you may order by mail from COLLECTOR BOOKS, P.O. Box 3009, Paducah, KY 42002-3009. Customers with Visa, Discover or MasterCard may phone in orders from 7:00–5:00 CST, Monday–Friday, Toll Free 1-800-626-5420. Add $2.00 for postage for the first book ordered and $0.30 for each additional book. Include item number, title, and price when ordering. Allow 14 to 21 days for delivery.

Schroeder's
ANTIQUES
Price Guide

. . . is the #1 best-selling antiques & collectibles value guide on the market today, and here's why . . .

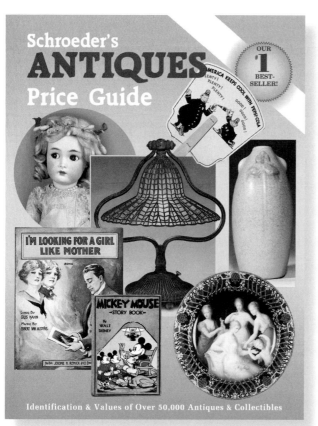

8½ x 11, 612 Pages, $12.95

• More than 450 advisors, well-known dealers, and top-notch collectors work together with our editors to bring you accurate information regarding pricing and identification.

• More than 45,000 items in almost 550 categories are listed along with hundreds of sharp original photos that illustrate not only the rare and unusual, but the common, popular collectibles as well.

• Each large close-up shot shows important details clearly. Every subject is represented with histories and background information, a feature not found in any of our competitors' publications.

• Our editors keep abreast of newly developing trends, often adding several new categories a year as the need arises.

If it merits the interest of today's collector, you'll find it in *Schroeder's*. And you can feel confident that the information we publish is up to date and accurate. Our advisors thoroughly check each category to spot inconsistencies, listings that may not be entirely reflective of market dealings, and lines too vague to be of merit. Only the best of the lot remains for publication.

Without doubt, you'll find
SCHROEDER'S ANTIQUES PRICE GUIDE
the only one to buy for
reliable information and values.

COLLECTOR BOOKS
A Division of Schroeder Publishing Co., Inc.